The Art of Jewelry

The Art of Jewelry

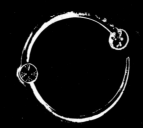

The Art of Jewelry

A Survey of Craft and Creation

Graham Hughes

Studio Vista London

© Graham Hughes 1972
All rights reserved
Published by Studio Vista Publishers,
Blue Star House, Highgate Hill,
London N19

ISBN 0 289 70287 9

Designed and produced by
George Rainbird Ltd,
Marble Arch House,
44 Edgware Road, London W2

House Editor: Penelope Miller
Designer: Michael Mendelsohn

Set by Westerham Press Ltd,
Westerham, Kent.
Printed by
The Senefelder Printing Co. Ltd,
Purmerend, Holland.
Bound by Van Rijmenam NV,
The Hague, Holland

To Serena

Acknowledgments

Quotations in the text have been taken from the following copyright works, and acknowledgment is made to: Thames and Hudson Limited and McGraw-Hill Book Company for the quotations from *Gold* by C. H. V. Sutherland, and from *Cities of Destiny* edited by Arnold Toynbee; the Executors of the Literary Estate of Sir Malcolm Darling and The Hogarth Press Limited for the quotations from *Apprentice to Power* by Sir Malcolm Darling; The Phaidon Press Limited for the quotation from *The Engraved Gems of the Greeks, Etruscans and Romans* by Gisela M. A. Richter; Hutchinson and Company Limited and Simon & Schuster Inc. for the quotation from *Pantaraxia* by Nubar Gulbenkian; The Society of Authors, on behalf of the Bernard Shaw Estate, for the quotation from *The Intelligent Woman's Guide to Socialism and Capitalism* by George Bernard Shaw; William Heinemann Limited and Harper & Row Inc. for the quotations from *The Glitter and the Gold* by Consuelo Vanderbilt Balsan; George Weidenfeld and Nicolson Limited for the quotations from *Daily Life of the Aztecs* by Jacques Soustelle, translated from the French by Patrick O'Brian;

Hamish Hamilton Limited and Harper & Brothers for the quotation from *Saint-Simon at Versailles* by M le duc de Saint-Simon, translated from the French by Lucy Norton; Chatto and Windus Limited and Mrs Nancy West for the quotation from *Hindoo Holiday* by J. R. Ackerley; BBC Publications, John Murray (Publishers) Limited and Harper & Row Inc. for the quotations from *Civilisation* by Kenneth Clark; The Hamlyn Publishing Group Limited and G. P. Putnam's Sons for the quotation from *The New Larousse Encyclopedia of Mythology*; the Executors of the Estate of Rosita Forbes for the quotations from her *India of the Princes*; A. D. Peters and Company for the quotations from *The Sun King* and *Madame de Pompadour*, both by Nancy Mitford; the Trustees of The British Museum and The Museum of the University of Pennsylvania for the quotation from *Ur Excavations*, Vol. II, by Sir Leonard Woolley; Fratelli Fabbri Editori for the quotations from *Greek and Roman Jewellery* by Filippo Coarelli, translated from the Italian by Dr D. Strong; and The University Museum, Philadelphia, for the quotation from an article in *Expedition* – 'Digging in Iran: Hasanlu 1958' by Robert H. Dyson, Jr.

Contents

List of Colour Plates

Introduction

Jewelry may be the oldest art. It has always meant something important to almost all the human race: sometimes it has been money, sometimes a prayer to the gods, sometimes a status boast or an invitation to seduction, almost always a reflection of character and a contribution to beauty. Jewelry style is poised between the requirements of dress on the one hand, and of airing one's importance and personality on the other, even of expressing one's religion and enlisting the magical help of one's gods; it has the background, too, that artists in every medium, at any period, speak to some extent with a common language.

Jewels take their name from the Italian 'joy'—they are instinctive fun. They tend rightly to be enjoyed more than studied. Even so, it is surprising how few books and how little academic thought they have generated. I hope this survey of the nature of jewelry will attract more scholarly attention to the subject.

Jewels are thrilling partly because they are so elusive. Jewelry is continually being lost, stolen or reset, exchanged for later models, pawned in the face of disaster. A jewel, like a butterfly, looks better flashing about on the move than it does pinned in a showcase. It is essentially mobile in its impact, it requires changing light and silhouette, changing colour and setting, to be its best. It is almost like music, a performing art: the jewel is the instrument, the woman and the lighting are the players. Ornament and wearer are not much good unless they are in harmony—if the jewel is uncomfortable, then the wearer may look grumpy and awful. It is easy to describe a violin in its case, but very difficult to catch the full effect once it is being played. Similarly one can write about every physical feature of a jewel lying in its box, and still miss its true essence.

Jewelers have always had to ply their craft with discretion, conducting their business in private, like doctors or lawyers, rather than in public, like a car manufacturer. It is indeed the one secret art today, when other arts are being dis-

sected so thoroughly: the owners of jewelry may be ashamed of having spent their money in such an indulgent way, they may be frightened of having their treasures stolen, they may be subject to the common pressures of the age of the common man. We all want to look alike: it makes us uncomfortable to feel that we are too much the subject of other people's envy. So, if we have any jewelry, we tend to keep quiet about it.

Jewels are an inaccessible, difficult subject. To some extent they are the reverse of history. When there was 'history', dramatic events causing lavish written records, there was usually also destruction and looting as we know from many vivid descriptions. It was at such moments that treasures vanished, usually without a trace. We have the records and inventories, but we have lost the objects themselves. Conversely, when there was peace and routine, as in Hellenistic and Roman imperial times, or as in nineteenth-century England, then wealth and jewels simply accumulated with no excitement and no written sagas, so we now have the jewels without the records. Nevertheless I have tried throughout the book to give some contemporary literary colour to my illustrations.

In my chapter 'Style—The Evolution of Design', I try to hint at the range of ideas which the human race has miraculously packed into tiny bits of gold, though of course I cannot illustrate more than a few pieces from each epoch. I look round the world today, my own special scene, in 'The Artist-Jeweler', interviewing some of the leading characters. In 'Technique' I have tried to illustrate the incredible skill of the human hand. It is inspiring that human beings have achieved so much beauty with so little material equipment. In no field has necessity been less the mother of invention than in jewels, because craftsmen did everything with almost nothing, and still do today, in the ancient manner inherited from their predecessors. There was, and is even now, no need for sophisticated machinery: skilled brain and hands with a small workbench still

The Lady of Elche. Stone statue, life-size. To our eyes she seems to be wearing too much jewelry for comfort and convenience; perhaps she was a ritual goddess for whom an abnormal amount of gold emphasized her supernatural quality. Iberian, perhaps 700 BC. Archaeological Museum, Madrid

produce the best jewelry. This is an art almost without technology.

I touch in 'Discovery' on what is hidden under the sand or turf, how it is dug up, whether the motive is the eternal search for truth or whether it is something more powerful, the lust for booty. Then in 'Collections' I go on tour, spying out what is most worth seeing, tracing jewels' transition from earning private, individual glory for their original wearers to lying sadly in dead museum vaults today. Finally I try what I know is impossible, a definition of the idea 'Value'. I examine the worth of the mineral freaks which have affected us all so deeply—above all, that universal panacea, gold; then diamonds and emeralds, rubies and precious stones; the way in which some people wear jewels instead of using banks (if not wearing their heart on their sleeve, then carrying their wealth on their bosom). But jewels are part of the magic of beauty and that one can only acknowledge, not define.

There are fine books upon which I have drawn liberally, and to which I make my acknowledgments in the right place in the text, especially Joan Evans's writings, culminating in her *History of Jewellery*, and Erich Steingräber's *Antique Jewellery*.

I am grateful to those scholars who have generously guided me on this exciting journey. Sir Stanley Robinson, my father-in-law, inspired me with ancient Greek coins; Dr Joan Evans—without whose books on jewels and magnificent gifts to the Ashmolean Museum in Oxford and the Victoria and Albert in London, jewelry scholarship might still not even have started—with her special knowledge of the Middle Ages; Mr John Hayward of Sotheby's with his pioneering work on the international high Renaissance in metalwork; and Dr W. F. Grimes, Director of the Institute of Archaeology, who lifted some of the treasures from the mud at the Sutton Hoo ship burial in Suffolk. Each of these has very kindly read a few of my pages in proof, though of course any mistakes remain my own.

For help in various ways I have to thank my colleagues at Goldsmiths' Hall —especially Mr John Houston and Miss Jane Lister—Mr Greg Cooper, Dr Joseph Raftery, Dr Reynold Higgins, Mrs K. R.

Maxwell-Hyslop, Mr Peter Dickinson, Mrs Phyllis Phillips, Mr and Mrs Roger King, Mrs John Hayward, Mr and Mrs Stefan Buzas, Mr and Mrs Alan Irvine, Dr Pozzi, Dr Joachim Menzhausen, Lord Harris, Mr Richard Norton, Miss Jill Clark, Mr John Jesse and Mrs Nevin Holmes. I am grateful to them all.

Many private owners, who have for security reasons preferred to remain anonymous, have let me examine, borrow and photograph their jewels. Mr and Mrs Afzal Khan and Miss Zarrin Bokhari in Karachi helped me to meet many distinguished jewel owners in Pakistan. Mr Afzal Ahmad in the National Museum at Karachi allowed me to examine some of the Taxila hoard there. Mr I. D. Mathur similarly gave me access to some of the Moghul treasures in the Delhi National Museum, as did Mr Rashid, Director of the Iraqi Museum, Baghdad, to some of his unparalleled span of Mesopotamian jewels from five or six millennia.

The book started when my employers, the Worshipful Company of Goldsmiths, the London medieval guild of goldsmiths, silversmiths and jewelers, gave me sabbatical leave for nine months in 1969. I hope, now they can see the fruits of their generosity, that they feel it was beneficial. De Beers have kindly allowed me to use for the chapter 'The Artist-Jeweler' much of the material which they commissioned for their house magazine *Optima* in 1970. Studio Vista have allowed me to use from my books *Modern Jewelry* and *Modern Silver* some thoughts relating to value and others on Art Nouveau. I owe much to Mr John Hadfield, Mrs Penelope Miller and Mr Michael Mendelsohn of George Rainbird Ltd.

The pictures in this book are nearly all dramatically enlarged: this is the best way to help everyone to look carefully at jewels. I have tried to choose pieces which have never been reproduced before, and unless otherwise stated these are in private collections.

I must warn my readers that as with music so with jewelry: the obsession tends to grow steadily in power. Jewelry is an ancient and delightful cult. Collectors, once charmed by it, are seldom converted back into a state of logical detachment.

G.H. London 1972

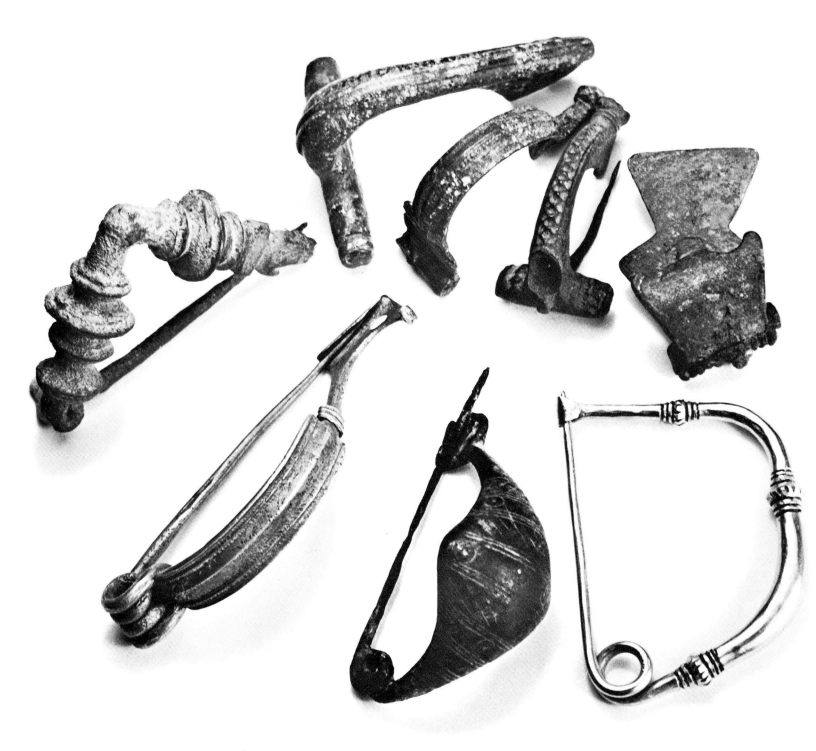

Style – The Evolution of Design

The idea of the safety pin or fibula evolved from a bent pin, which became a normal device about the thirteenth century BC in Minoan Crete. In archaic Greece, it was often given a flat socket with decorations, and the Etruscans at the same time fattened and lengthened the back, covering it with tiny animals and birds modelled in the round (see illustration on p. 25). The present pieces are, from bottom right, clockwise: the double-arched type, gold, popular in Cyprus, perhaps 3rd century BC; the remainder are in bronze—the swollen 'leech' form, discovered in the forum at Rome, Etruscan, 4th century BC; Roman, perhaps 1st century AD; (with a hand as clasp) perhaps Persian from Hasanlu, 4th century BC; four pieces influenced by the La Tène Celtic tribes, who developed the bilateral spring: first, found at Hadrian's Wall; second, in Kent, 1st or 2nd century AD; third, found at Brough, Westmorland, showing the Roman early empire fashion for a hinge rather than a spring; fourth, found in Kent. In the Dark Ages the back of the pin swelled to become a ring brooch (see illustrations on p. 71).

Jewelry is a hybrid. It is partly fashion: in the thirteenth century, for instance, clothes were heavy and covered everything, and jewels functioned as fasteners and clasps and buttons, to hold the cloaks and gowns together. By the fifteenth century, clothes were light and elegant, there was plenty of naked skin to decorate with pendants, and people showed off not so much by winning wars as by living graciously. The early medieval jewel was a sort of glorified safety pin. Two centuries later, fashion had transformed it into a golden flower.

Partly jewelry is bullion: for most of history, and even today in surprisingly large areas of the world, people cannot bank their wealth. Instead, they wear it. In the west before 1914 it was normal to do both: to be a success you not only needed a big family fortune but you needed to impress your friends with its size, and the way you did it was not much inhibited by our present ideas of discretion and good taste. In the evenings you wore ornaments on the neck, hands, ears, and bosom all together, not, as today, just one at a time for fear of exciting unpleasant envy. Consuelo Vanderbilt Balsan, one of the great American heiresses, who married the Duke of Marlborough in 1895, records with a childhood memory how usual it was in New York for wealthy people to want to wear their wealth:

Occasionally Willie and I were permitted to join my mother in her handsome bedroom and watch her evening toilet. There was one memorable evening when the safe in which her jewels were kept could not be opened. My mother was going to a big dinner at which it would almost have been considered an offence to wear no jewels. Something of the prevailing feeling of panic must have reached me, for I ran to my room and prayed fervently that a miracle would open the safe.

Partly jewelry is a lovely confidence trick: a big parade of jewels may be to advertise the wearer's real status, but it may also hide his secret instability. One of the most flamboyant medieval courts, Burgundy, was also one of the least secure. It is especially well documented because the last duke, Charles the Bold, lost his treasures in battle in 1476, and the Swiss victors catalogued them with characteristic care. At that time Charles was considered the richest sovereign alive. The reason he and his court travelled with their treasury, their chancellery, and their sacristy, was partly to imitate great rulers of antiquity, mainly to dazzle his negotiating partner and his opponents.

A fourth aspect of jewelry is, of course, architectural style: the passionate Renaissance interest in the human figure showed through in high Renaissance jewels around 1550, the late Gothic soaring perpendicular lines and pointed cusps frame innumerable delicate fifteenth-century pictorial brooches. But the connection between architecture and jewelry is tenuous. The classical orders of architecture do not impinge on the fantasy of Greek and Roman jewels, even if Minoan pieces from Crete do show an occasional reminiscence of the shapely girls in the frescoes there. In Georgian England the acanthus moulding and the Palladian pediment, which meant so much to the aristocratic patrons of buildings and furniture, have no echo in the elegant stone-set flower sprays and the abstract patterns of their jewels. Art connoisseurs who could easily date to within a hundred years, for instance, two buildings as similar as the ancient Greek temple of Segesta in Sicily and the nineteenth-century National Monument on Edinburgh's Calton Hill, who could differentiate between the robust *chinoiserie* of English Tudor silver, and the elegant rococo fantasies of the same idiom when it recurred two centuries later, who know the difference in silver between Lamerie and Storr, or in furniture between Chippendale and Vile, will flounder miserably in an antique jewelers, because architectural detail, the easy key to dating, is so seldom to be seen there.

Of all artists, jewelers have been and usually still are the most obscure, the least famous and respected. And of all artefacts, jewels are among the most complicated to explain. So it is small wonder if jewelers themselves have hardly ever emerged into the limelight, if historians have declined to illuminate the subject as a whole. It is today in much the same unexplored state as Greek and Roman antiquities were when Winckelmann first came to study them in Rome in 1755.

Jewelry often helps to show what we are like and what we admire. During the Stone Age coloured beads were all that was possible; the primitive achievement of being able to make shapes was sufficient to justify the stone-bead necklaces. Next, in the Bronze Age, technique was everything: the fabulous virtuosity of Mycenaean gold seal-rings, of Greek filigree pins, of Scythian chiselled gold, and of Etruscan granulation, surprise us not so much for their marvellous designs as for their execution. Up to Roman times, jewelers were intoxicated with their own skill, carried away with the pleasures of complexity, much as, in the Renaissance, Paolo Uccello was with the new science of perspective. This ancient jewelry, so minute that nobody can perceive its full glory with the naked eye, shows a fascinating confidence. These craftsmen, like the societies in which they lived, felt they could do anything they tried.

Dark Age jewelry is simply barbaric. No preoccupation here with intricacy: Carolingian or Lombard work is heavy, simple, massive. Ideas such as the talisman for good luck, the reliquary for salvation, the badge of office rather than the expression of individual character, all these may be called tribal, not rational; instinctive, not logical; expressions of hope rather than of fact.

In the Middle Ages we see the evolution from barbarism and splendour to fastidiousness: from the massive and magnificent to the delicate; from strife to enjoyment; from the tremendous to the sophisticated. Jewels were still available only for the very rich, just as presumably all through history hitherto, for bishops, princes and kings. Whereas the few surviving crowns from the Dark Ages have a harsh and rather crude appearance, accurately symbolizing the blatant power which was necessary to rulers in those times, the many fourteenth- and fifteenth-century royal pieces hint at a different conception of order: perfection, grace, delicacy, stability, the ideal static balance between church and state.

The Khmer civilization in Cambodia left magnificent evidence of its jewelry on the temple carvings round Angkor— like this 12th century AD crowned head in stone (height: 5·5 inches) above—but almost no actual jewels have survived.

Although very little Assyrian jewelry has survived, their carved friezes show people wearing elaborate jewels even when, as so often, hunting or fighting. Right Soldier's head with necklace, bracelets, earring and arm-band, from Nimrud, c. 800 BC. British Museum, London

Money has always been of vital importance, even during the Middle Ages. It is not absurd to claim that the arrival of precious stones in jewelry towards the end of the sixteenth century might not have happened but for the success of the great banking families like the Medici or Strozzi of Florence, and the Fuggers or Welsers of Augsburg. For the first time, it became easy for money to change the nature of life quickly: a poor man could expect to die rich much more easily than, for instance, the Pastons in fifteenth-century agricultural England, who were extremely successful yet probably multiplied their fortune only twice or three times.

If Dark Age jewelry meant worldly power, and medieval jewelry spiritual uplift, Renaissance jewelry meant wealth. The old court treasuries in Dresden and Florence, in Moscow and Stockholm and many other cities, survive to tell the tale.

Today, the latest great phase, artists are leading us into a jewelry modern movement just as in painting and in architecture. They think that big stones lead to barren art, that women should wear jewels simply to enhance their personality. But the modern revolution is due not only to designers liking what is personal, and fearing what is precious. There is also the huge social revolution: for the first time in history jewels are worn by almost everyone, while, conversely, almost nobody cares obviously to outshine. Jewelry is becoming a discreet addendum to individual character, and all the better for that.

MESOPOTAMIA, TURKEY AND SUMERIA

It was once supposed that the world had a finite beginning and the oldest cultures were as described in the Old Testament. But modern archaeology has been uncovering layer upon layer of evidence, each one enlarging the span of prehistory; recently remains at Jericho were discovered dating back to an amazing 8000 years ago. Current excavations at Çatal Hüyük and Hacilar in Turkey have led to a new 'oldest' culture there perhaps going back as early as 7000 BC. In the Baghdad Museum there are groups of fine marble figurines dated to the sixth millennium BC. The young science of archaeology is always making us older. It has evolved from the nineteenth-century treasure hunt into a high pre-

cision instrument of knowledge, using X-rays, underground periscopes, radiography, geology, and, of course, the art historian's primary tool—dating by the artistic style of the object found, which can often be related to other comparable objects, or to carvings, or to pictures.

The earliest jewelry so far known may be from Sumeria, where metal was first used in the fourth millennium BC. Its gold work is of simple aspect, but of great charm and variety. As befits the precious metal, it was beaten very thin, many of the pieces made from this foil being inspired by leaf motifs, either dangling in a fringe, or, more surprisingly, contrived into a sort of mesh hair-net or breast ornament.

Perhaps the best Sumerian jewels were actually made for the dead, not the living. The idea of perpetual life for rulers is quite normal, not only in Sumeria but, for instance, in Egypt where the pyramids helped the pharaohs' souls to a smooth passage into after-life, or in Cambodia where the Khmer kings were similarly perpetuated with huge temples; even such comparatively recent figures as Alexander the Great or Frederick II ('Stupor Mundi') have given birth to legends that they were still alive centuries after their death. So we can consider Sumerians more normal than horrible if they thought death as important as life, and hastened to reach it enriched with their finest possessions.

The most charming Sumerian pieces were the carved stone animal and bird weights and charms, often pierced for wearing as pendants, often with seals carved beneath: these are the first and some of the most delightful magic jewels. Some of the most marvellous work from Ur, according to our present ideas, was simply beads of lapis lazuli, carnelian, semi-precious stones and glass. It used to be thought that glass was first made in Egypt. In fact, it originated in western Asia in the third millennium BC, being by 2000 BC available in several parts of Mesopotamia and the Caucasus. Probably glass started its service to the human race not for utensils, but for jewelry beads; only by about 1600 BC were the first small glass bottles becoming common.

Almost contemporary with Sumeria were the cultures of Asia Minor, probably beginning at the citadel of Hissarlik, the legendary Troy. Schliemann wrongly identified much of the gold he discovered there with Homer's *Iliad* and *Odyssey*. Whatever their exact date may be, some of the several cities superimposed one upon another at Troy disclosed quite extraordinary wealth. Of heavier construction than Sumerian work, the Trojan pieces are more abrupt in feeling, stubby and direct, with borders often ornamented by a simple loop design which might almost have come from the Bauhaus in the 1920s. Sumerian gold is whimsical and elegant, Trojan, hard and vigorous.

After great conflagrations at Troy at the end of the third millennium, the Hittite kingdom emerged, extending its power beyond the Euphrates into Syria, even conquering Babylon about 1595 BC. From its capital at Bogazköy, the little-known Hittite kingdom developed into a great empire from about 1500–1100 BC, eventually collapsing with the rise of the Urartians, round Lake Van, and with the opposition from Babylon and Nineveh. Hittite jewels there must have been, but survivals are so scarce as to make an assessment impossible. Perhaps indeed the discoveries at Troy were not representative of the area: the later and earlier cities' remains, deposited above and below those found by Schliemann, contain very few jewels. The most likely explanation is the dominance of the Mediterranean in the second millennium by Crete and Mycenae, the great imperial powers who have left us in no doubt as to their love of luxurious ornament.

Further south, the great Mesopotamian powers of Babylon and Assyria arose, clashed and succeeded one another throughout the second and the first half of the first millennium BC. Their most famous kings were Nebuchadnezzar (604–562 BC) of Babylon and, in Assyria in the north, with their capitals at Nimrud, Khorsabad and Nineveh, the Ashurnasirpals, Ashurbanipals, the Sargons and Sennacherib himself. These are great names and their seals suggest great power. Almost their only surviving jewels are seals cut in steatite, carnelian, agate and other hard stones, usually exquisitely engraved on cylinders whose impression was rolled onto clay. The Babylonian fashion was hieratical—priests and kings in full regalia and official gowns, paying tribute to each other, usually standing up with sometimes one seated on a throne seemingly of sparse openwork scaffolding. Assyrian seals tend to show more movement—their version of hunts, of proces-

sions of men and animals, of people chasing each other, may all stem from Assyria's being a warrior state.

EGYPT

The Egyptians had a small vocabulary of ornament, all of it closely related to their hieroglyphic writing and their conception of immortality. The amazing Egyptian achievement was colour, its medium was lapis lazuli or glass with gold, its form was most often the scarab. From the Middle Kingdom they used *cloisonné* and milling: perhaps their coloured glass and faience and enamels are the finest chromatic displays in the history of the craft. Under the New Kingdom, *c.* 1500 BC, coloured glass paste took the place of stones, the decoration becoming softer in surface and more supple in line, with filigree in goldsmiths' work and *millefiori*—infinite little dashes of colour —in glass making.

The Egyptians started by using cylinder seals, the idea for which presumably came from their neighbours in Mesopotamia. The hieroglyph word for seal shows a cylinder threaded for wearing horizontally as a pendant, thus proving both that cylinders were normal in early times, and that they were worn as jewels, a sort of aristocratic identity card before writing with letters had been invented. In later Assyria and neo-Babylonian times in Mesopotamia, around the sixth century BC, the cylinder seal for rolling an endless frieze slowly became less popular than the flat-bottomed stamp seal for making one small, neat impression, till under the Parthians and Sassanians stamp seals are the distinctive survival. Similarly in Egypt, the stamp displaced the cylinder, probably earlier on, because the Egyptians invented paper and the stamp type of seal is ideal for paper. The stamp did for Egyptian paper what the cylinder had done for Assyrian clay: it made it personal.

In Egypt the stamp seal became so distinctive and shapely that its form— the scarab—is almost a national emblem. The scarab was mounted as a spindle on a ring, fixed on a pendant gold jewel, or simply suspended round the neck on a silken thread passed long-wise through its body. This was the classic universal charm or amulet, popular for burial as well as in life, so popular indeed that it was imitated both by the Greeks and the Etruscans.

This tiny beetle turns up everywhere. He became one of the symbols of the sun god Ra. Between his legs, just to make his meaning clear, he dragged the sun-disk. He acquired magical significance, apparently because of his habit of blowing before him a little ball of excretion, which was thought by observers to be moving because of a spontaneous otherworldly impulse. Further evidence of the beetle's special nature came from the capacity of other almost microscopic balls (in fact, they were eggs) to give forth life.

Much, perhaps most of early Egyptian jewelry was intended for the dead, not the living. Many of the best artists and craftsmen were exiled permanently in the Valley of the Dead, working as slaves, preparing a tomb for the pharaoh and, when he died, starting on the next. If, like Tutankhamen, he died young, there would have been time to build only two or three small rooms with their accompanying treasure, carvings and paintings. Longer reigns might allow as many as fifteen or twenty of these underground sepulchres. It is from them that Egyptian jewels come, at least until the New Kingdom.

These jewels, like all the tomb decorations, no doubt idealized the real life in the Valley of the Living, outside across the Nile. The pictures show the pharaohs as gods, with divine tokens, not as human beings with equipment for life. Much of the incredibly gorgeous early jewelry was thus probably never worn, only laid round the dead mummies.

There is one field in which the Egyptians showed a true fantasy, not at all the sort of static paralysis for which they are usually known: that is, in their crowns. Nobody knows what these imaginative conceits were made of; they can be seen only in carvings and flat reliefs and pictures. Solid gold would have been almost unbearably heavy to wear, and would surely have survived till today. Some fragments suggest that gilt leather may have been the basis. If so, this is another example of the technical wizardry of very early times: the Egyptians were indeed masters of their limited world.

For Egyptians, jewelry was easily related to divinity: often by the scarab; often by showing pictorially the symbol of a god; often by bearing the name of a ruler or priest. By contrast, jewels for the Ptolemaic Romans, who came to govern Egypt, were very much harnes-

Gold pendant jewel (a large ring behind each of the figures is the attachment). The centre of the three statues, cast in solid gold, represents Osiris; with him King Osorkon II is identified, squatting on a shrine carved from lapis lazuli inscribed with the king's names. He is protected on one side by his wife, Isis, and on the other by his son, falcon-headed Horus wearing the double crown. Isis wears a tight-fitting fashionable dress and a long wig with lappets which were probably originally blue. The pendant is a superb example of casting, chasing and carving in solid gold. Egyptian, XXIInd Dynasty. Mid-2nd millennium BC. Louvre, Paris

sed to this present life. They were large and gross to advertise the owner's wealth, and often, to make sure there was no misunderstanding, they actually bore the owner's name or badge carved into them. These were the first worldly status jewels which, in the fifteenth century AD, led to the badges of the orders of chivalry, and, today, to the presidents' badges of the chambers of commerce. In Egypt one can trace the development from religious symbolism during the hieratic, unchanging third and second millennia through to worldly pleasures under the Roman Ptolemies. For the non-Egyptologist, it is impossible to read adequately the message of Egyptian jewelry. One can only follow the cycle from the heavy, barbaric Nubian work with its mysterious second burst of vitality in early Christian times far south of, and quite different from, the Coptic peoples. The incredibly sophisti-

cated dynastic culture farther north in Egypt gave birth to the delicate, complicated, static Egyptian style, and then one can see the craftsmanship becoming softer and less crisp as glass came to displace stone, and as outside influences dissipated the original Egyptian dynastic rigidity, first under the New Kingdom, then under the pleasure-loving Romans.

CRETE AND MYCENAE

It is almost impertinent to try to analyse achievement which sounds so wonderful in ancient myth. Achilles and Odysseus, Paris and Helen, Menelaus, Aegisthus and Electra—these people have contributed as much to fantasy as to history. But, in fact, archaeologists have been usefully inspired by such romantic stories as the *Iliad* and *Odyssey*. Discoveries have made the legends more,

not less, obsessive. Schliemann was fired by these great epics to unearth not only the treasures of Troy but also the amazing riches of the palaces of Mycenae and its dependent Tiryns. The jewelry found by him, Sir Arthur Evans and many others is no less than fabulous, heroic in design, bewildering in intricacy, absolutely distinctive.

Just as human and animal forms assume a special shape in Minoan stone carvings and frescoes, so in Minoan gold jewelry we see the same tight-waisted girls with large, uncovered breasts, the same bulls with magnificent curling horns. This imagery is peculiar to Minoan work—it is mostly representational in contrast to the more abstract patterns of Mycenae.

The deciphering of Minoan linear B script by Michael Ventris in 1953 indicates that the Cretans were indeed Greek; but the Mycenaean jewels are

The most imaginative Egyptian jewels may have been their crowns, none of which has survived intact. Under the early dynasties of the third millennium BC, the simple tapered conical crown represented Upper Egypt, while a more elaborate 'chair' shape, somewhat like the doges' cap in Venice, stood for the Nile delta—Lower Egypt. Later, symbolism and decoration became much more fantastic. The crowns were probably made of gilt

and coloured leather. Left to right: the tomb of Sennedjem showing Osiris with flail and sceptre; the tomb of Ramesses III showing the Pharaoh with the Goddess Isis; the back rest of the throne of Tutankhamen showing him and his wife Ankhesenamun, who seems to be helping with the king's toilet, c. 1350 BC. Cairo Museum (other three at Thebes); the tomb of Queen Nefertari in the Valley of Queens

Lombards and other tribes, who got their inspiration from the Romans. The break between Knossos and Mycenae is surprisingly clear.

Mycenaean jewels are among the most mysterious of all—they are so large, so fine, and yet we know so little about the wearers. The seventh-century Homeric 'Hymn to Aphrodite' describes the goddess, showing how desirable gold was:

> She wore a dress brighter than the
>   flames of fire,
> Spiral bracelets, gleaming flower-
>   earrings and
> Beautiful necklaces on her delicate neck,
> All of gold, superbly wrought.

Even as late as the early fifth century BC, Pindar wrote: 'Water is best of all things, but gold shines like a fire in the night, above all great riches' and 'gold is Zeus' child'.

Mycenaean jewels of about the thirteenth century are commoner than those of classical Greece of the fifth century and later, perhaps because early Mycenae was a domestic civilization, based on the home and family, whereas by Periclean times, the mid-fifth century BC, it was the *agora* or market-place and its public life and the city state that counted. The home had become little more than a bed to sleep on, and the family just an instrument for procreation. So jewels were no longer needed for outside show—it was the simple masculine virtues that were admired to the exclusion of ornament.

The National Museum in Athens shows marvellous rings, each engraved with extremely elaborate battle or hunting scenes of minute scale. They must have been used as seals, as signatures and identity cards, as locks and keys: in Aeschylus' *Agamemnon* the great king is comforted by his wife Clytemnestra when he returns to Mycenae from Troy

Women seem to have been prominent and sophisticated in the Minoan civilization. These jewelled girls, above, *whose fashion sense appears entirely modern, are part of a fresco from the Knossos Palace, 17th century* BC. *Now in the Heraklion Museum, Crete.*

nevertheless distinct from Minoan, presumably made at a later date by a people who did not want to copy their former lords. This is quite the reverse, for instance, of the way the Romans, when they became dominant, derived their jewel ideas from the earlier Etruscans, Greeks and Egyptians whom they succeeded; and, later again, the Goths and

—he need not worry about his treasure, she says, because all the seals are intact. These enormous rings were evidently important symbols for very grand people. Even so, it is surprising that they are cut in such deep relief, that the superlative compositions are so crowded, that the rings are often too large for convenient wearing. Perhaps the scenes chosen are more like stories than like family crests or insignia, because they suggest the owner's career. Anyway, these rings are one of the miracles of the goldsmiths' craft, fine, strong, and desirable from every point of view, the first mystery of ancient gold.

The second surprise of this period is the range of abstract ornament like the myriad large buttons, presumably sewn as ornaments on clothes, sometimes ten or twenty of the same pattern but nevertheless with a seemingly endless fertility of invention. Schliemann found over 700 of them at Mycenae alone. Rather soft and fleshy lobes impinge one upon another with extreme confidence. Why is Mycenaean work so different from Minoan? How did this dominant race achieve such amazing vitality in its jewels, inspired as they are with so

many different shapes and details? Political domination, such as the Mycenaeans seem to have enjoyed, normally leads to artistic quietude as with the Egyptian, Persian or Roman empires: perhaps the reason for the continual agitations in Mycenaean jewels is simply that the empire, when it was destroyed around 1200 BC, had itself still not achieved stability.

The gold funeral masks are the third wonder dug up at Mycenae: unlike anything else in art, they confound our modern definitions of craft. Superb chasing indeed they are, so they must have been the product of what we now call craftsmen. But why are they so random in their finish round the edge? Was it too difficult to centre the composition? How was the thin metal kept from breaking, without the modern facility of heat softening? Recent excavations at Pylos imply that the craftsmen of Mycenae enjoyed quite a grand position in the community. Certainly the variety of the idiom chosen by their jewelers and the confidence of their design are without parallel. If one word were needed to summarize the impact of these extraordinary objects, it would be strength.

PERSIA, PHRYGIA AND LYDIA

From now on, western jewelry always derives from one country to another. The craftsmen themselves probably travelled extensively because they had no anchor, unlike, for instance, sculptors who had to be near the source of stone and marble; and the jewels themselves were standard booty of war, transferred from one treasury to another with each successive victory. The Phrygians, whose kings were called Midas, may have caused the downfall of the Hittite kingdom around 1100 BC; anyway they acquired an enviable reputation for wealth. This may be substantiated by the current American excavations at Gordion, the Phrygian capital, where one of the tombs is no less than 170 feet high. But if, as legend says, all that Midas touched turned to gold, it is disappointing that none capable of attribution now survives—indeed, rather the reverse: only silver has so far been found in Phrygia, and that was made in neighbouring Lydia.

Following the raids which destroyed Phrygia and caused the suicide of the last king Midas around 680 BC, Lydia became the leading power. She was the chief source of electrum, the natural alloy of part gold, part silver, and the world's first producer of coins. The invention of coins was important for jewelry because coins eroded some of the banking function of jewels, and must also have diverted some of the best jewelers into coin making, filling people's pockets instead of adorning their persons. The world's earliest coins, according to Stanley Robinson, seem to be Lydian of the late seventh century BC, discovered beneath the temple of Artemis at Ephesus. Herodotus vaguely credited King Croesus (560–546 BC) with the invention of coins but it was under Croesus that Lydia may have found surface gold supplies or discovered how to separate the two elements, gold and silver. Certainly she must have been very rich: Croesus' benefaction to the Delphic oracle included thousands of pounds' weight of gold, together with a golden statue of a woman almost life size. But little good it did him! His advice from the seers was that if he invaded Persia he would destroy a great army, which, unforeseen by him, turned out to be his own. Cyrus the Persian sacked Croesus' capital at Sardis and so Croesus vanishes from history.

The finest display of Persian jewels, or indeed of any other ancient wares, is carved in stone on the walls of Darius' ceremonial ways at Persepolis. Nobody knows how much these jewels are the product of Darius' fifth-century court, how much they are of Medes or of the northern powers including Urartu, Babylonia and Assyria, or even of the Scythian tribes of Asia, or of contemporary Greece. Greek craftsmen are known to have been hired by the all-pervading, uninventive Persians, and Greek colonists anyway travelled far and wide in search of trade. Admirers of the splendid virility of ancient Athens see no more than its echo in Achaemenid gold.

The main inspiration for Persian jewels, wherever it came from, is nature: fronds of leaves, heads of deer and sheep and lions, horns of rams, all formalized into a stiff pattern, lifeless and immortal. The ibex, the royal animal of the Achaemenids, was understandably popular. Persian work is usually chased from thin sheet, sometimes with appliqué ornament too.

Apart from these seemingly endless and often identical friezes, the vast wealth in gold has left surprisingly little trace either in literature or in fact. A graphic American reconstruction suggests one reason why: wealth caused conquest, conquest caused destruction.

A gold bowl was excavated with such care by Robert H. Dyson, in Iran in 1958, that he was able to reconstruct the dramatic circumstances under which it was buried almost three thousand years ago, in the course of the destruction of the citadel of Hasanlu. The bowl was being carried out of the flaming building by one of three men who were on the second floor at the moment it gave way. The leader of the group fell sprawled forward on his face, his arms spread out before him to break the fall, his iron sword with its handle of gold foil caught beneath his chest. The second man, carrying the gold bowl, fell forward on his right shoulder, his left arm with its gauntlet of bronze buttons flung against the wall; his right arm and the bowl dropped in front of him, his skull crushed in its cap of copper. As he fell, his companion following on his left also fell, tripping across the bowl carrier's feet and plunging into the debris.

Herodotus recorded a gigantic loss of Persian treasure after the great Greek victory at Plataea:

Then Pausanias made a proclamation that no one should touch the booty, but that the Helots should collect it and bring it to one place. So the Helots went and spread themselves through the camp, wherein they found many tents richly adorned with furniture of gold and silver, many couches covered with plates of the same, and many golden cauldrons; and the bodies of the slain furnished bracelets and chains, and scimitars with golden ornaments—not to mention embroidered apparel, of which no one made any account. The Helots at this time stole many things of much value, which they sold in after times.

The Ziwiye treasure, discovered in 1949 in a great citadel some 1800 metres high in Kurdistan, and now in the Teheran Museum, is of such varied and mostly moderate quality that it is probably not ancient Persian at all, but the personal accumulation of a Scythian tribal chief on the move.

The Oxus treasure at the British Museum, much more consistent and beautiful, includes at least one gold arm-band represented in stone on the *apadana* of Darius' palace at Persepolis; to be precise, it is probably not an arm-band, though it is usually incorrectly so called, but a covenant ring. It was held out in one's own sword hand towards the person with whom one was in treaty, partly to show one was not

Opposite *One of the most famous jewels of all antiquity: the golden bee or hornet pendant from Khrysolakkos near Mallia. Minoan, 17th century BC. Height: 1.8 inches. Now in the Heraklion Museum, Crete*

Below *Archer's ring. Widely used in the east and in India to sheathe the archer's thumb from chafing by the cord when the bow is released. Bronze, Achaemenid Persian, 6th century BC*

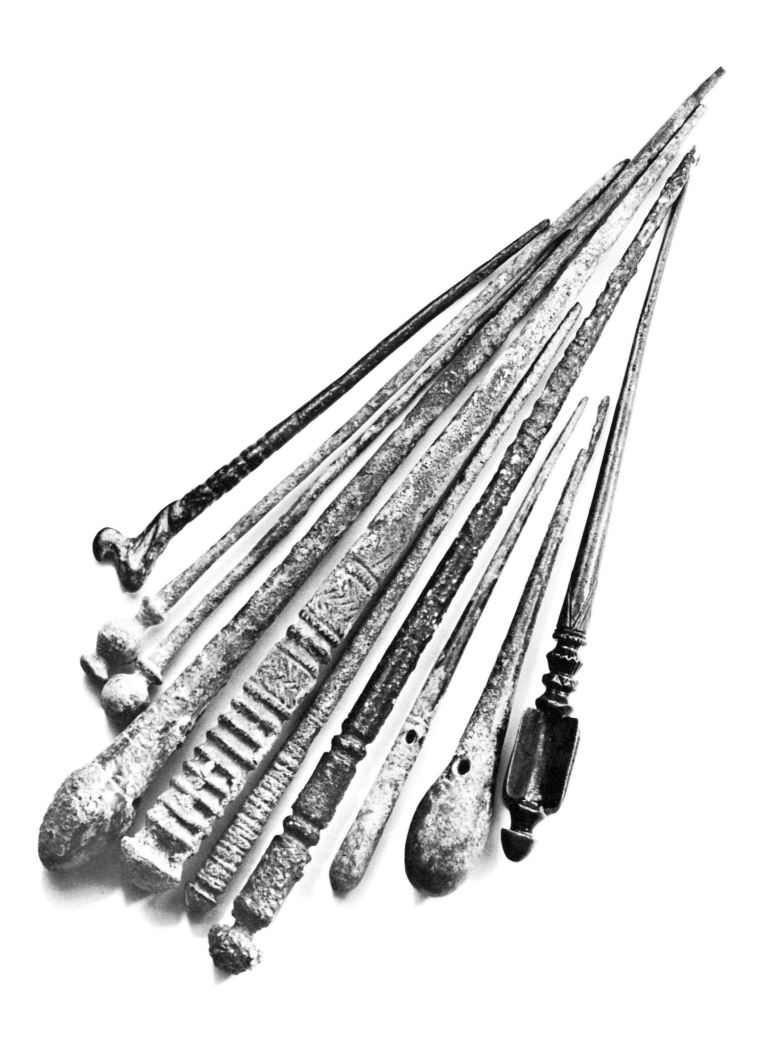

carrying a weapon, partly to give one's companion something to grasp as a token of friendship—it was in fact the original handshake.

But Persian survivals are disappointing in the context of what we know Alexander the Great found when he finally vanquished the Persians in 330 BC. The plunder from Darius' capital at Susa and the other Persian treasuries was vast: much of the gold was turned into coins of the new Attic type, much was squandered, perhaps to bring new vigour to the static Persian economy. But it did not vanish without a trace; much of it must have reached Greece and the rest of Alexander's Mediterranean empire, providing the most exciting outburst of vitality in the history of jewelry.

GREECE AND ETRURIA

The Greeks gave a rather special place to their god of metal, Hephaestus, the Roman Vulcan. Born of Hera and probably of Zeus, almost alone among the gods who were otherwise notable for their grace and symmetry, he looked ridiculous, being lame and twisted. Known mostly as a blacksmith, he worked on Lemnos, the Lipari Islands and Mount Etna in Sicily. What Hephaestus lacked in romance, he more than made up for by his hard work, showing amazing energy and skill. According to Robert Graves, he was ceaselessly active:

As well as the palaces on Olympus with their bronze trimmings, he fashioned Zeus' golden throne, sceptre and thunderbolts, the fearful aegis, the winged chariot of Helios, the arrows of Apollo and Artemis, Demeter's sickle, Hercules' cuirass, the arms of Peleus, the armour of Achilles, the necklace which Harmonia, wife of Cadmus, wore for her nuptials, Ariadne's diadem, Agamemnon's sceptre, the hypogeum or underground chamber of Oenopion. Nor should one forget the golden goblet which Zeus offered to Aphrodite, a vase given by Dionysus to Ariadne, the harp of Perseus, and Adonis'

hunting equipment. To Hephaestus were also attributed such works of wonder as the tripods with golden wheels which rolled of their own accord into the assembly of the gods, the bronze bulls whose nostrils spurted forth flame, the golden and silver dogs of Alcinous' palace, and even the giant Talos, 'that man of bronze' whose duty it was to guard the Cretan tree and prevent its being approached.

Nothing was impossible to him. When he moulded Pandora, the first woman, to perfect his work he encircled her brow with a golden crown which he himself had engraved.

Perhaps we can read into this magnificent legend a feeling that craftsmen in Greece were not as much respected as we might today suppose. Very few of them appear on the vase paintings, an otherwise thorough documentation of Greek life; many were certainly slaves. Coin makers, for instance, who were probably goldsmiths too, sometimes had no name other than their country of origin—like 'The Lydian'—indicating that they were immigrant slaves with the lowest possible social status. Craftsmen and to some extent artists were at the bottom because they taught themselves. Poets, because inspired by the gods, were at the very top. Plato admired the skill of craftsmen but ranked it among the lowest of human gifts. Surprisingly, the same rather insulting estimation is given not only to craftsmen but artists, too, by Plutarch in his life of Pericles: 'No youth of proper character, from seeing the Zeus at Olympia or the Hera at Argos, longs to be Phidias or Polyclitus. . . . For it does not necessarily follow that, if the work delights you with its grace, the one who wrought it is worthy of your esteem.'

Another aspect of the same situation is that craftsmen worked for money, and that, as an incentive, was dishonourable. They were *banausic* or money-earning. Crafts (including many which we would call arts) were mostly hereditary: teach-

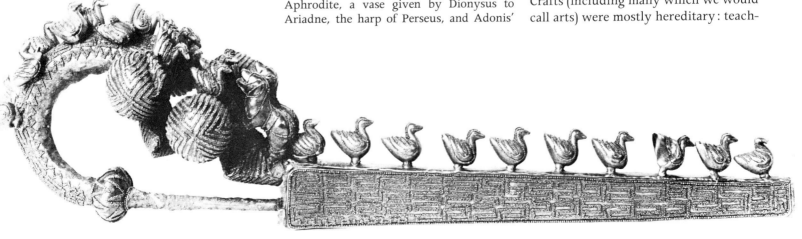

Above *Head of the goddess Athene wearing the close-fitting Athenian helmet with garlands perhaps of olive leaves, possibly gold: some solid gold ears of corn, dedicated to Demeter, have survived. Athenian silver tetradrachm, c. 480 BC*

Right *While gold has always been the jeweler's favourite metal, bronze came next, particularly in early times when gold was very scarce. Three bracelets with snake heads (the snake, dragon or crocodile head is the oldest and most constant theme throughout jewelry). Persia, probably Luristan, c. 900 BC*

Overleaf *Ancient Greeks, like the Renaissance Italians two thousand years later, gloried in the human figure. They loved to decorate it in the most complicated and delicate way, especially with tiny dots of gold granulation. Here are three from a set of five gold plaques forming a pectoral ornament. One plaque may have two or three thousand grains of gold defining its decoration. The winged goddess, Artemis, with lions is in the Daedalic style, related to the earlier Minoan Crete and to contemporary Egypt. From Camirus. Rhodes, 7th century BC. Height of plaque: 1.6 inches. British Museum, London*

ing and skills were developed and passed on from father to son (Socrates was a sculptor by profession, and the son of a sculptor).

One cannot melt stone and one can only break pots into potsherds, but jewels, unless they are buried with the dead as they were in Sumeria, Egypt and Etruria, are almost always changed or lost. The Mycenaeans buried their grandest dead—hence their fabulous surviving jewels. For the Greeks six hundred years later, by contrast, burning, not burying, was the highest end. Life to them was more important than death.

Archaic Greek jewelry is therefore so scarce compared with sculpture or pots as to make criticism almost impossible. Survivals show a distressing thinness, a poverty of invention quite opposite to the dignity of contemporary sculpture. Though the Greeks sometimes made pins and clasps or fibulae fairly long or wide to fasten their simple clothes, the gold is always extremely thin. Perhaps the true explanation is, as often, the most obvious. First, women had a subsidiary role compared, for instance, with politicians or soldiers; therefore precious metals may have been used mostly for public ornaments in public places, on sculpture, on armour and at the shrines, where almost none has survived, though we know from records that it once existed. Secondly, there simply was not much gold or silver, as the economics of the time show very clearly. The gold mines in Macedonia, at Mount Pangaios, were not developed until the time of Philip II's and Alexander's empires which they helped to make possible; the old mines at Siphnos and Thasos did not last. Gold was very scarce and therefore valuable. There are no old Athenian gold coins: gold coins, even when they did appear, continued to be a sign of great emergency even as late as the second century BC, when gold became commoner. Gold from the pagan temples later came into circulation with the rise of Christianity.

Silver was more normal, perhaps even as common to the Greeks as copper and bronze to the Romans. Even so, the silver mines on Cape Sunium were a continual worry to the Athenians. New veins might not be discovered to replace those worked out. One important new find was between the time of the battles of Marathon and Salamis: Themistocles sensibly used it to bolster the national economy with new silver coins rather than distributing it immediately.

The route of Alexander the Great's conquests covered every big gold source in the east. He was keenly interested in economics. Greece, after the battle of Issus, was flooded with gold, much as Spain in the sixteenth century, and the effect on Greek jewelry was similarly dramatic. Large stocks in the Persian royal treasuries had been built up over the decades as tribute from the outlying parts of the huge Persian empire. Herodotus lists the places in about 425 BC— he mentions little gold but it must have been brought regularly. The emissaries carrying it can be seen today carved on the stone friezes of Darius' palace at Persepolis. Added to this great windfall for the Hellenistic Greeks at the end of the fourth century BC was the steady production of the mines round the eastern Mediterranean. All these brought a new richness and internationalism to jewels in the third century BC and after.

If ancient Greeks are identified with achievement, then Etruscans signify pleasure: women are prominent in their surviving sculptures and frescoes, and there was little shortage of raw materials —the many tombs opened near the great cities, for instance Tarquinia and Caere, have yielded up dazzling hoards. The Etruscan conception of death and what follows it may have been more like the Egyptian; we do not know because we cannot read Etruscan writing. Anyway the tombs were equipped with the most lavish art and furniture.

Etruscan manners are well known, and their surviving jewels numerous. But the influence upon them by archaic Greece remains obscure. Probably because Greece herself offered poor opportunity, immigrant Greek goldsmiths certainly gave a fillip to Etruscan work in the sixth century. The great Etruscan achievement was granulation: tiny, almost microscopic balls of gold were soldered to the main surface, to give it a delicacy of feel hitherto unknown. Often, as in their tomb sculpture, Etruscans were portrayed in their gold earrings and pendants, mysterious miniature human faces, detached and ethereal; there are lions' heads, too, but these became commoner in later Hellenistic and Roman work—it is the full face view of the human head asleep or contemplating, idealized and perhaps preparing for death, which is so characteristic.

If the types of ornament were limited, the jewels themselves were endlessly

varied: the Etruscans seem to have made everything that we wear today, using jewelry to give the same uninhibited panoply as we do now. They wore bracelets, fibulae or clasps, earrings of great splendour—in Italy called *bauli* because they resembled a suitcase or Gladstone bag—necklaces and pendants, equipped with chains of modern intricacy and complete flexibility, nearly always decorated with patterns picked out by granulation or filigree, often by inlay or enamelling too. In their jewels the Etruscans seem to have achieved a better weight and feel than the early Greeks, an unerring perfection both of form and technique.

GREEK EMPIRE (HELLENISTIC)

The united empires first of Alexander, then of his successors the Seleucids, then of the early Romans, brought widespread prosperity and with it an international character, so that jewels began to look much the same all over the Mediterranean.

Jewels in the great old centres like Rome and Athens were probably dug up and dispersed centuries ago, like the contents of most Egyptian tombs, which were melted by robbers as bullion when the past was considered unimportant compared with present needs. It is recent excavations round the fringes of the empire in the Aegean islands, Anatolia, Syria and the Near East, southern Italy and northern Greece, that have yielded us our evidence. Nobody knows to what extent work in the fashionable cities may have been better than in these provinces; but with communications rapidly improving, style anyway became more universal.

With the new political stability, gold was distributed and found much more widely than ever before; in river beds, in rock on the surface of the land, sometimes as picturesquely as Herodotus records:

In India the ants, which were larger than foxes (though smaller than dogs), built hills filled with gold nuggets which they kicked from their tunnels. The Indians raided the ant-hills during the heat of the day when the ants were napping. They were careful not to arouse the ferocious creatures who would pursue and destroy any thieves they could catch.

This tale is not entirely fanciful. Even in modern times ant-hills and animal burrows have led to rich gold veins by re-

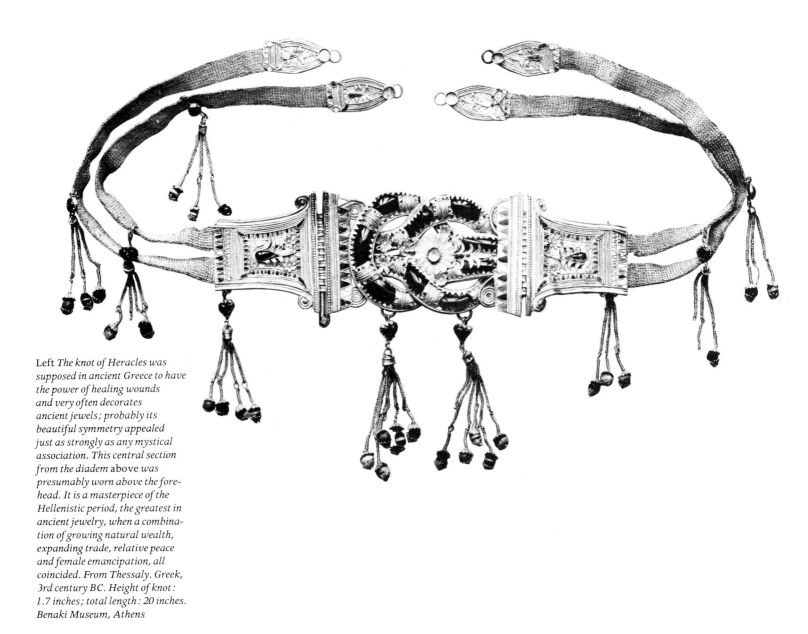

Left *The knot of Heracles was supposed in ancient Greece to have the power of healing wounds and very often decorates ancient jewels; probably its beautiful symmetry appealed just as strongly as any mystical association. This central section from the diadem above was presumably worn above the forehead. It is a masterpiece of the Hellenistic period, the greatest in ancient jewelry, when a combination of growing natural wealth, expanding trade, relative peace and female emancipation, all coincided. From Thessaly. Greek, 3rd century BC. Height of knot: 1.7 inches; total length: 20 inches. Benaki Museum, Athens*

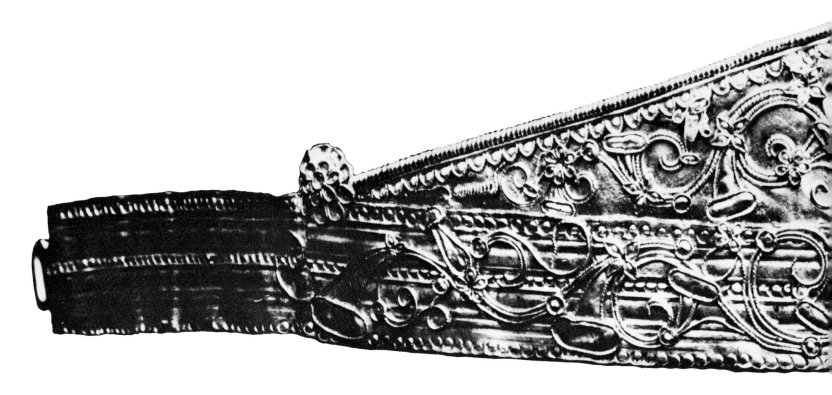

vealing on the surface a sample of the treasure beneath.

When the surface deposits were exhausted, the underground search was agonizing, as described by Diodorus in the first century BC in Egypt:

Those who have been consigned to the mines, being many in number and all bound with fetters, toil at their tasks continuously both by day and all night long, getting no rest and jealously kept from all escape. . . . The hardest of the earth which contains the gold, they burn with a good deal of fire, and make soft, and work it with their hands; but the soft rock and that which can easily yield to stone chisels or iron is broken down by thousands of unfortunate souls. A man who is expert in distinguishing the stone supervises the whole process and gives instructions to the labourers. . . . Those who are specially strong cut the glittering rock with iron pickaxes, not by bringing skill to bear on their tasks but by sheer brute force, and they hew out galleries, not following a straight line but according to the vein of the glittering rock. Living in darkness, because of the bends and twists in the galleries, they carry lamps fitted on their foreheads. They contort their bodies this way and that to match the behaviour of the rock. What they hew out they throw down on the floor—all this without pause, and under the severe lash of an overseer. . . . There is absolutely no consideration nor relaxation for sick or maimed, for aged man or weak woman; all are forced to labour at their tasks until they die, worn out by misery, amid their toil.

Wealth must have been more evenly spread among the new merchant classes,

jewels worn further down the social scale. For these reasons, the fertility of invention became spectacular—new pieces worn in new places, new ornamental schemes. This was the age of the diadem or *stephanos*, often built round a Heracles' knot in gold or garnets, what we call the reef knot. It came from Egypt, where it seems to have been no more than enrichment, but by Pliny's time it had the power of healing wounds, one of the first recorded expectations that specific types of jewels would bring specific benefaction. Perhaps the knot was more effective than we imagine: it appears on necklaces, thigh-bands (the seductive forerunner of the Edwardian Gaiety girls' black elastic garter), even on finger rings.

There were earrings shaped like Eros, bigger models of Aphrodite on pins and brooches; and, perhaps of the least immediate significance and representing no obvious deity, the lion. The commonness of the lion and its graceful cousins the lynx and the cat, indeed, suggests what common sense also suggests: that Hellenistic jewels were not primarily magic or devotional—perhaps for the first time in history, they were meant to enhance the wearer's personality.

Necklaces were worn not only round the neck, but pinned shoulder to shoulder, hanging presumably as breast ornaments, often with rows of fascinating miniature pendants like wine-jars (amphorae), spears, animal or human

Diadems of varied shape were a feature of Hellenistic jewelry: unlike most other contemporary jewelry they were not robust enough for frequent wear. Above *Gold diadem or* stephanos *with head of Helios, from Santa Eufemia del Golfo near Monteleone, Italy. Height: 1.6 inches. 3rd century BC. British Museum, London*

The winged erote *or cupid was a favourite in classical jewelry.* Below *Greek gold earrings, 3rd century BC. Benaki Museum, Athens*

Exceptionally rich jewels have survived at the colony started by the Spartan Greeks at Tarentum in southern Italy: its jewels, like its pots, showed a spirit of exuberance. Earrings, gold, 4th century BC, from Crispiano. National Museum, Taranto

heads, crescents coming no doubt from the east and related to the moon, or the Isis crown from Egypt. Most characteristic and delightful, however, are the naturalistic heads of lions and lynxes, of snakes and horses and dolphins, which so often formed the ends of bracelets and earrings in lovely abstract patterns and heavy granulation.

It may be that the source of this imaginative outburst from the fourth century BC until Roman times was Greece rather than Persia or Italy, because it can, to some extent, be related to ancient Greek coins. Under the Athenean and Spartan empires precious metals were so scarce that they were probably concentrated by decree into the coinage; it was most likely goldsmiths who made these coins, and it is on the sixth- and fifth-century coins that many of the symbols first occur which later appear so delightfully in jewels. Hellenistic jewels inherited some of their marvellous imagery from classical Greek coins and the coins found theirs sometimes in the surrounding country. The bull, for instance, was often shown on coins of colonies associated with rivers which made a similar roaring noise, and caused a rush of destruction, like the mountain torrents in Greece. The bull looks especially fine on the coins from rich Sybaris with its seasonal, threatening torrent. The boy on a dolphin is Taras with, on the other side, the joint founder of Tarentum, Philanthos—another vivid image in-

spired no doubt by dolphins in the great harbour from which the Greeks earned their wealth; this colony, unlike Sybaris (which was extinguished as early as 510 BC by neighbouring Croton), lived on to become one of the richest of all, and is still today, as Taranto, the main maritime buttress of southern Italy.

Art on the fringes of empires was often delightfully uninhibited: the British in India and Australia and America, for instance, developed a special brand of colonial architecture for each place in the eighteenth and nineteenth centuries, often more amusing and personal than the hard Palladian style at home. The Romans had the only other empire of comparable size, and there again the outskirts were more fun than the centre: Leptis Magna and Sabratha, the great cities near Tripoli, were built by their native Emperor Septimius Severus in an abandoned style that is almost baroque; perhaps if the Roman empire had lasted longer, the true baroque style would have emerged then, rather than in the seventeenth century.

The Hellenistic empire, which developed from the self-governing classical Greek colonies, was much less centralized, so one would expect more individuality anyway from its component parts. But in one city so much gold jewelry has been found that it earns a special niche of its own in the hall of fame. Tarentum was one of the last Greek colonies to become Romanized

Roman women may have been the first whose wealth and social standing allowed them to wear jewelry freely where and how they wished, as in this 1st century AD fresco at Pompeii, in which gold noticeably predominates over clothing.

Probably the largest known carved antique cameo: the Grande Camée de la Sainte Chapelle, the Apotheosis of Germanicus, carved in sardonyx in the manner especially enjoyed by the Romans. Height: 12 inches. 1st century AD. Cabinet des Médailles, Bibliothèque Nationale, Paris

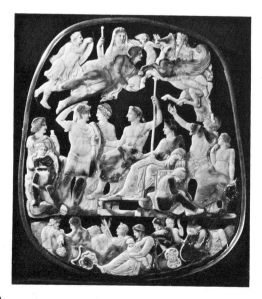

(Naples was probably the last of all). Finally under Rome it again showed its independent spirit: its citadel always held out against the new conquerors of the area, Hannibal and the Carthaginians. Because of its great harbour, it was always very rich, and, perhaps because it was not on a main trunk route for invaders, its surviving relics are very numerous. Its jaunty pots, often with large, relaxed, cheerful human faces on the side, are well known; its jewels less so. But they are well represented in private collections, and in the Taranto National Museum. In the Bari Museum is a typically fantastic silver dish with gold inlay, a garnet beneath, and reliefs of a youth, girl, dog, and a frieze of masks. It dates from the fourth century BC but is nevertheless very free and easy. It is not surprising to learn that Tarentine women had a reputation for wantonness. Here, as in Alexandria, they liked to wear diadems and garlands when alive, not only after death. Indeed, later on, Juvenal called it 'crowned Tarentum'. It was a favourite holiday place for the Romans, like Horace, who went there to escape from everyday worries. Although federated to Rome after the Pyrrhic wars about 270 BC, it maintained some independence. Its final decline came when it ceased to be the starting point for the journey from Rome to Greece—when the main road from Rome was extended in the second century BC beyond Tarentum to Otranto and Brindisi.

Superbly made, still using the full technical armoury from the Etruscans and the classical Greeks, Tarentine work has a bigness and sense of spontaneity which one can only describe with the word genius: these jewels are some of the most original of all time. They give the impression, like for instance Picasso or Michelangelo drawings, that their makers worked quickly, and that the work gave them enormous pleasure. Certainly they are an inspiration today, a relief from the sometimes over-finickety details of the older Greeks.

Probably the easier supply of gold enabled goldsmiths everywhere to express in jewels what their predecessors had confined to coins. It is fascinating to contemplate the correspondence between richness in trade and quality in design; most of the richest places under Greek influence did, in fact, achieve the best coins and art, like Messina and Reggio with their grip on trade between

Sicily and Italy, or Syracuse and Tarentum with their harbours so necessary in a storm. Given money, the Greeks could not help but produce beauty. How sad that the same did not apply to contemporary Carthage, nor indeed to most of the subsequent great empires of the world.

ROME

Etruscan fragility evolved into Hellenistic fantasy; then Rome brought order and solidity to jewelry just as it did to politics. A surprising quantity of Roman jewels suggest the function of the signature and identity card. Seals, for instance, were engraved not, as under Mycenae, with epic scenes of drama in solid gold, not, as in archaic Greece in the sixth and fifth centuries, with a single man or animal drilled or cut into carnelian or hard semi-precious stone, depicted in a state of tension with muscles straining, representing the sinewy essence of health. For Romans, seals had everyday scenes like a cupid or *erote* carrying an athlete's oil-bag and playing music on his pipes, or a seated woman, maybe the wearer's wife. These seals showed that the wearer was somebody, an individual with status, not just an ordinary anonymous part of the human mass. Romans liked to be rich and substantial citizens and earn respect as such by wearing jewels as an obvious token of rank.

One may guess, too, that the Romans liked size and weight more than intricacy: some Roman jewels are constructed of disks and spheres. They are reflections in gold of the breathtaking Roman engineering of the aqueducts at Segovia, outside Tunis or at Pont du Gard; arcades and straight channels in gold, geometrical rectitude contrasting with the Greek love of animals and people. For the first time architecture shows through into jewelry.

The Romans loved simple shapes, which make some modern jewels, and even ancient Greek ones, look shoddy. And they loved plain stones—one rounded carnelian or lapis, for instance, in the middle of a disk earring, an emerald crystal pendant beneath, with its unfussy hexagon or pentagon shape; these are the sort of unaffected colour schemes especially admired round the Anatolian coast. Roman jewels have had a hard deal from scholars whose snobbish verdict has too often been 'technically inferior imitation of Hellenistic prototype'. This unperceptive view is not only unjust aesthetically, but factually wrong too, as proved by many recent dated finds from excavations round the fringes of the Roman Empire: the Romans evolved a sensible style to suit their own way of life.

Gold became steadily more plentiful with the capture of Spain and what is now Rumania, so could be worn more freely. It was normal for women to be buried wearing their earrings, but most Roman jewels are of sensible design suitable for everyone, everywhere, alive not dead. Throughout most of history jewelry, like fashion, has been a matter of delicate insinuation; but for the Romans gold may have been almost too accessible for health. Pliny, the unadventurous, lamented that instead of being satisfied with our surroundings, gold enabled us to challenge nature. Such philosophy may not have worried the normal Roman house too much, to judge from the comfortable remains at Pompeii or Herculaneum. The various sumptuary laws restricting the use of jewels were ineffective; Lucian deplored the extravagance of women, also without effect:

What can one say of their other fancies which cost more still? On their earrings are stones worth many talents; on their wrists and arms gold snakes which ought to be real live ones! On their heads, crowns enriched with all the jewels of India; precious necklaces round their necks. The gold goes right down to their feet and there are bangles around their ankles. Oh, would that it were an iron chain round their legs.

An amusing domestic record is the *nouveau riche* dinner party in Petronius' rather coarse *Satyricon*—domestic life, and with it women's jewels, have become very important to Trimalchio and his wife Fortunata:

Fortunata came with her skirt tucked up under a yellow sash to show her cerise petticoat underneath, as well as her twisted anklets and gold-embroidered slippers.

Soon Fortunata took the bracelets from her great fat arms and showed them to the admiring Scintilla. Then she even undid her anklets and her gold hair net, which she said was pure gold. Trimalchio had it all brought to him, and said, 'A woman's chains, you see. This is the way us poor fools get robbed. She must have six and a half pounds on her. Still, I've got a bracelet myself, made up from the one-tenth per cent offered to Mercury—and it weighs not an ounce less than ten pounds.'

To prove it, he had some scales brought in and had them passed round to test the weight. Scintilla took a little gold locket, which she called her lucky box, from round her neck, and from it showed to Fortunata two 'crotalia'-earrings with jingling beads.

'A present from my good husband,' she said, 'and no one had a finer set.'

'Hey!' said Habinnas, 'you cleaned me out to buy you a glass bean. Honestly, if I had a daughter, I'd cut her little ears off. If there weren't any women, everything would be dirt cheap.'

Tacitus shows how popular gold was; he lists among the trophies carried in the triumph of Pompey after his victory over Mithridates, 'three gold dining couches; enough gold vessels inlaid with gems to fill nine display stands; three gold figures of Minerva, Mars and Apollo respectively; thirty-three pearl crowns; a square mountain of gold with deer, lions and every variety of fruit on it, and a golden vine entwined around it; and a grotto of pearls, on the top of which there was a sundial. There was also a portrait of Pompey rendered in pearls.'

Palmyra, the great desert staging post on the road to the east, may, to judge from its gorgeous women in portrait sculpture, have used bigger and more boastful jewels than anywhere else. Pollio, the diarist, visited Queen Zenobia there and, like all her other visitors, succumbed to her. She wore a helmet 'girt with a purple fillet, which had gems hanging from the lower edge, while its centre was fastened with the jewel called cochlis, used instead of the brooch worn by women, and her arms were frequently bare'. This cochlis that Zenobia wore was probably a gold jewel in the shape of a snail's shell. Pliny, who was interested in precious stones, explains in his *Natural History* that eastern kings often attached these massive snail-shaped jewels to the frontlets on their horses' heads. Perhaps Zenobia decorated her white Nubian horse in the same way. Her Roman conqueror Aurellan rated her jewels high: 'I bid you surrender, promising that your lives shall be spared. . . . Your jewels, your gold, your silver, your silks, your horses, your camels, you shall . . . hand over to the Roman treasury.' After her final defeat by Aurelian in AD 272 she was paraded in triumph in Rome. Vopiscus described the procession: 'And there came Zenobia too, decked with jewels and in golden chains, the weight

Centre links of gold bracelets, repeated gold hemispheres: similar pieces are in the Louvre and at Pompeii. Roman, 1st century AD

Panther, gold and stones, perhaps the centrepiece of a shield, found in 1903 at Kelermes. Maybe 6th century BC. Hermitage Museum, Leningrad. 14.4 × 6.3 inches

of which was borne by others.' The jewels of the queen helped her to be a true woman; though captive, it was still she who looked beautiful, others who bore her burdens.

Almost all the gold of Rome was lost with the barbarian invasions. Alaric, King of the Visigoths was typical: he plundered Rome, tried and failed to get to Sicily, and died at Cosenza in AD 410. His vast treasure and coffin vanished for ever, buried according to legend by the Ponte Alerico on the River Busento in the remotest southern countryside.

STEPPES AND TRIBES

Outside the great empires gold was a substitute for home; you lived on your horse, you stole what you could, often after killing the owner, you went hundreds and often thousands of miles searching for more, and whatever you took, you either consumed, destroyed or converted into portable treasure. The most devoted goldsmiths in history were the Scythians, who from about the sixth to the fourth century BC dominated central Asia, whose tomb mounds have disgorged amazing riches over thousands of miles from Siberia to Turkey, from the Crimea in the south as far north as Moscow. Some of their work they bought in exchange for the produce of the interior, from Greek goldsmiths along the Black Sea coast; much of it they made themselves.

If the best symbol for ancient Greece may be sculpture, for Rome engineering, for modern America the car, then for the Scythians it must be gold jewels. Tribal jewels were the one lasting factor in a changing life, so it is natural that design would remain static as an expression of the tribe's character which nobody wanted to change. Scythian work cannot be dated by its appearance; it continued throughout the history of these ferocious horsemen, a dramatic denial of the equation of great art with high civilization values.

Most jewels are too small to call 'great'. Scythian work is large, unlike anything before or since. It was inspired by animal life not, as with the Greeks, idealized into noble static forms. Often brilliantly contrived from thin sheets of metal, Scythian animals are all pulsing with life, the most organic jewelry ever made, the most active beasts ever translated into metal. Mostly carved from solid lumps, sometimes inlaid with garnet or turquoise or coloured glass, as was common with many wandering tribes, what distinguishes Scythian work is simply its nobility of form and the eerie way in which it suggests life and movement.

The Scythians, like many barbarian tribes, had weird burial rites. The king would go under his tumulus mound fully clothed and jewelled, his golden animals often having smaller and smaller gold models within them, interwoven in corners and curves, suggesting endless life and reproduction, hoping no doubt to perpetuate the king's influence. With the king, as Herodotus records, would be buried one of his concubines killed by strangling, his other servants, and 'some golden cups for they use neither silver nor brass'. Outside the tomb, the chief warriors would sit on their horses facing inwards, killed by a great stake driven through the middle of each so that they could remain the king's helpers. Hardly a savoury introduction to some of the world's most sensitive gold work, superb craftsmanship expressing an unrivalled sense of wonder at the marvels of nature!

After the Scythians, most other tribal jewels round the north and east of the Roman empire showed similar themes: coloured inlay either of big rounded stones, or of smaller square and triangular chips, usually of dark-coloured garnets or glass; rough surfaces—the gold is used more to glow than to glitter, lots of wild life, especially bulls presumably derived from Greece, and eagles perhaps from Rome. But the main feature of these wanderers' ornaments was its weight. This can hardly have been because of technical incompetence; beating gold thin is not difficult and this workmanship seems generally to rise to the demands of the design; this heavy, thick use of gold must reflect the chieftain's own attitude, that size is power, and delicacy, weakness.

From perhaps the fourth century BC till the fourth AD, the Sarmatians, who had been the Scythians' eastern neighbours, succeeded them. According to Herodotus they were the fruit of union between unmarried Scythian men and Amazons. The animal style slowly vanished, perhaps because the tribes became residential and therefore less dependent on beasts, perhaps because of changes in the magic cult whereby the power of animals slain was incorporated in their gold representations.

In their architecture, and sometimes also in their jewels, the Byzantines liked to avoid flat surfaces and straight lines, preferring the mystery of endless arches and perforations. Right *Silver ring, 12th century AD. Height: 1.5 inches. National Museum of Antiquities, Bucharest*

Below *The Empress Theodora and the Emperor Justinian. Details from the mosaic portraits of about AD 547 on the wall of the Church of San Vitale, Ravenna. The Byzantine court used great quantities of gold and jewels, partly because it inherited the enormous richness of the eastern Mediterranean with centres of production at Alexandria, Antioch and Constantinople itself; partly because the elaborate court hierarchy required ceremonial dress.*

It was probably Rumania's richness in gold which made its first great kingdom, Dacia, such a lure to the Romans, who under Trajan had a hard struggle to overcome the native king Decebalus in AD 106. Gold mines were developed by the Romans at Cetatile Ponorului in the second and third centuries AD. Just as the earlier Scythians achieved the apotheosis of animals in gold, so these later Dacians gave compelling rhythm to their spotted inlay work.

This, then, is the powerful, compulsive jewelry of the migration period, part Persian, mostly tribal from the shores of the Black Sea. Perhaps it was the wanderers' only art; it expresses feelings of majesty and awe, of barbaric force. The Goths carried the style across Europe to distant Spain, the Alemanni to Switzerland where it adorns the museums of Berne and Basle, the Franks to Germany where it formed the basis of medieval art.

BYZANTIUM

The main classical tradition is, of course, not what radiated out beyond the Roman boundaries with such thrilling consequences; it is what remained intact within the empire's eastern half, Byzantium. This was the rich and static culture where the ceremonial may have been more important than ever before or since. Humphrey Sutherland gives us impressive statistics: after Heraclius (AD 610–41) took much of the Persian royal treasure, the Iconoclasts in the eighth and ninth centuries took for the state the contents of many churches. The emperors themselves built up great stocks: Anastasius at his death in 518 left a personal treasure of 320,000 lb of gold. Theodora, when she handed over power to Michael III in 856, possessed 109,000 lb. Steven Runciman sets an evocative scene for the great Christian capital in the tenth century:

The palace area was surrounded by a strong wall and carefully guarded. For whoever held the palace held Constantinople and the empire. . . . The treasure of the empire was kept in its vaults, from which was extracted the salary of every imperial official. Down on the eastern slopes was the factory where women operatives wove the famous imperial brocades destined for the ceremonial wear of the court and occasionally as gifts to specially favoured foreign potentates. The visitor passed first through the vestibule of the Chalce, built by Justinian. Long arcades permitted him to go on under shelter to the

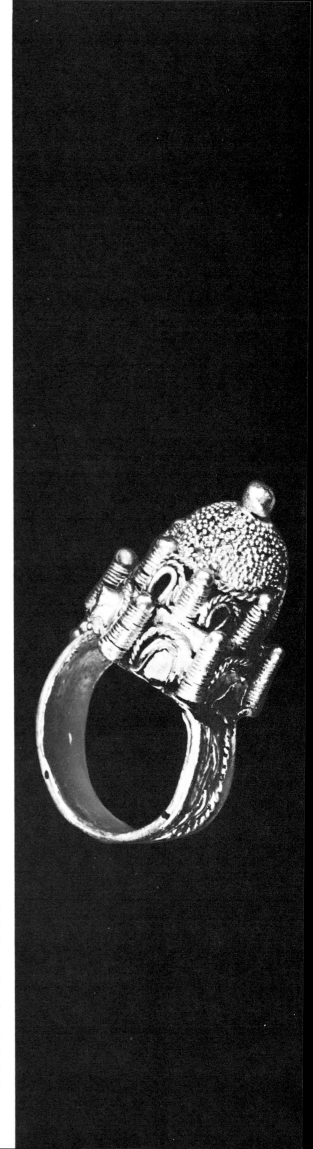

other ceremonial halls. There was the Chrysotriclinium, a throne-room lined with gold mosaic, built by the Emperor Justin II. There was the later throne-room of the Triconchus, built in the ninth century by Theophilus and modelled on the fashionable architecture of Baghdad. It was here, now, that foreign envoys were received in audience, with all the fantastic accompaniments that Byzantine ingenuity could devise. While the ambassador bowed down before the Presence, his forehead touching the ground, the throne would slowly rise, and he would lift his eyes again to find the emperor seated high above him; and at the same moment the golden lions that flanked the throne would roar and wave their tails, and the jewelled birds that sat on the gold and silver trees round the chamber would open their beaks and sing.

In neighbouring shrines were the holiest relics of Christendom—the Crown of Thorns, the Lance, the Seamless Coat, part of the wood from the Cross, a phial of the Holy Blood, and the Virgin Mary's girdle—some of which later came to the west.

Grouped together, nearest of all the crafts to the palace, were the goldsmiths and silversmiths. The Byzantines loved gold to ornament their lives, as witness their surviving mosaics. In Ravenna there is the famous contemporary sixth-century portrait of the Emperor Justinian's wife, Theodora, in the church of San Vitale, which shows her festooned with gold embroidery and chain, huge earrings and crown. In Sicily, at Cefalù and Monreale, the twelfth-century Byzantine Norman mosaics show God in a heaven made of solid gold. For the Byzantines, gold represented heaven and perfection. In contrast, for the early Renaissance painters heaven had usually become blue, and later on for Signorelli or Michelangelo, what counted was not colour but people: heaven and hell at Orvieto Cathedral and in the Sistine Chapel, Rome, were jammed with people of all shapes and sizes, but in rather muted colours. The Byzantine period golden altars at St Mark's, Venice, and at Sant' Ambrogio, Milan, though not jewels themselves, illustrate in their enamelled panels lots of jewelry being worn. The altars were made by actual jewelers, so the pieces represented are presumably authentic. We can trace there the same qualities as in the architecture and mosaics: elaborate ornament, uncertainty as to where each shape or plane gives way to the next, luminous colours, the richest and most varied that have yet appeared in jewelry. It is indeed this colour which is the dis-tinctive Byzantine achievement, and the main medium for it was enamel.

Byzantine craftsmen specialized in *cloisonné*. Whereas the contemporary barbarian tribes filled their *cloisons* or compartments with whatever stone was easily accessible, often garnets, in Constantinople enamels were used instead, perhaps an inheritance from the late Roman passion for glasswork in Syria and Egypt. Almost all Byzantine jewels are distinguished by this dignified, opaque, dark colour scheme, no doubt more faded by time than are their mosaics. There was quite a sudden outburst of *cloisonné* enamelling about the ninth century, probably because of a discovery enabling craftsmen to use more varied colours more closely together, so that enamelling began to displace figurative painting as the medium for religious imagery.

While the craft of enamelling developed to a strength and variety during the thousand years of the Byzantine empire which it has hardly known before or since, the subject matter, as in other branches of Byzantine art, remained strangely unenterprising. Perhaps if opaque *cloisonné* enamelling is the Byzantine hall-mark, the human figure is its signature: a very large number of surviving jewels carry the outline of a man, often to be identified as a saint; sometimes there is an animal or bird instead, always with the timeless hieratic quality which makes them stand not as individuals but as symbols of the divine order. A popular device was to mount coins, usually showing an emperor's head surrounded with all the finery of the times: coarse filigree, carved semi-precious stones, malachite, onyx, alabaster, serpentine. Icons, effigies and jewels are all similar: they all express man's nearness to the divine.

One aspect of Byzantine architecture is its mystery and deliberate lack of definition. The Istanbul churches, like Karye Djami, and Justinian's cathedral, Santa Sophia, all show this feeling for endless space; the walls are not so much enclosures as a series of perforations; the carved capitals on the columns are often similarly full of holes; the outsides, with their numerous domes and minarets, are continually leading the eye through and round, rather than inviting it to rest. In the same way Byzantine gold jewels are often constructed in high relief, using arcades and galleries round the bottom of earrings, for instance, rather than the

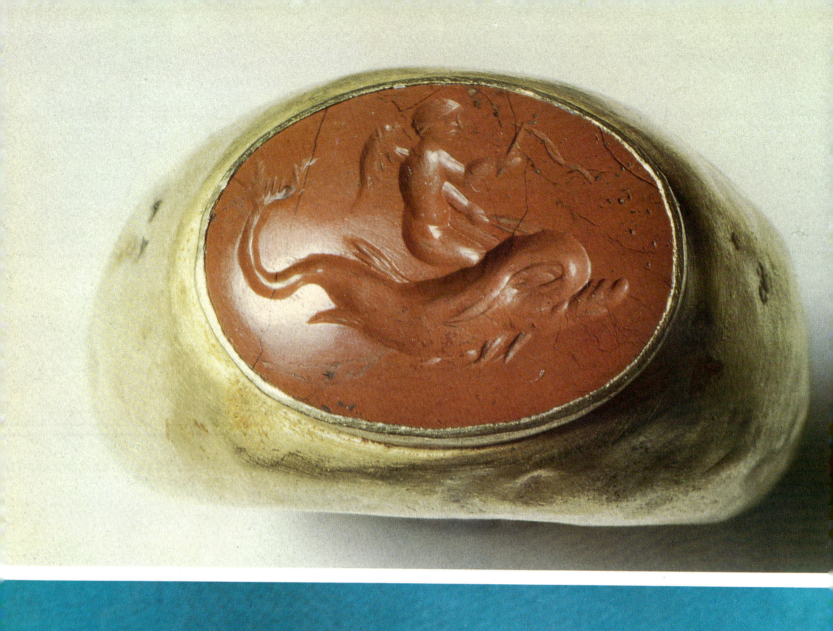

simple Roman solid knobs. Coloured enamel is no doubt the most distinctive aspect of Byzantine work, but there is one word which applies equally to their architecture and theology, their constitution and their goldsmithing: it is complicated.

INDIA

The Indus valley civilization of five thousand years ago at Mohenjo Daro and Harappa (in what is now Pakistan), the Buddhist masterpieces perhaps two thousand five hundred years old from Taxila, and the very rare relics of Alexander the Great's Indian invasion in 327 BC are a far cry from self-perpetuating Byzantium. The cultures did not become interdependent until the Indian subcontinent attracted, in 1532, the Mongol invaders, later called Moghuls. They came from the same area as the Turks who took Constantinople in 1453. From then on, Indian stones and gold became increasingly important to Europe.

Only beautiful beads have so far been found from the Indus Valley: gold seems not to have become common until the first millennium BC. Then it was flavoured with ancient Persia and its geometrical sun symbols like the swastika, with elaborate, square, geometrical designs probably stamped, sometimes enamelled, and later with Greek granulation and delicate birds and cherubs; eventually it was dominated by the stylized curves of Buddhist sculpture. Surviving pieces are too rare to trace any continuity. All they prove is that, here as everywhere, jewels were part of ordinary life from the beginning, and the jewelers' skill showed no inhibitions for lack of equipment.

There are startling records: the Ajanta cave paintings show Buddhist women of the eighth century AD wearing colossal gold crowns and many necklaces. The masterly temple nude sculptures of twelfth century date and before, for instance at Khaju Raho, are greatly embellished by their dangling pearls and gems, all deeply cut in black stone.

But Indian jewelry really came into its own with the Moghul emperors; descendants of Tamberlaine who ruled central Asia from his capital at Samarkand, the Moghuls moved south by stages from Afghanistan. The first, Babur, remained a hill countryman; the second, Humayun, being exiled to Per-

Tippoo Sultan, ruler of Mysore in southern India, was supposed to be the richest man of his day. He was killed at the battle of Seringapatam in 1799 and the British commander, Lord Harris, took some of his jewels as the customary spoils of victory: this necklace, right, used his rubies, mounted with gold and diamonds in London c. 1800.

Left Ancient jewelers used almost as big a variety of stones as we do today, though less precious. The Romans developed a taste for easily wearable rings, robust and magnificent, evolved from the earlier Greek seal rings which were much more intricately engraved, and of a shape more awkward to wear.
Top Massive man's ring, 1.4 inches in diameter, gold and carved red jasper, intaglio (incuse or recessed). 2nd century AD. The boy on a dolphin was a favourite Greek and Roman fantasy, as on the coinage of the sixth-century BC Greek colony, Tarentum, nearby Balethas, Brundisium, Lesbos and Iasus in Asia Minor. Dolphins may in fact have been tamed and ridden by children in the shallow Mediterranean bays. A stone carving from the River Sele at Paestum shows Odysseus riding a sea-turtle.
Bottom Massive man's ring, 1.5 inches in diameter. Cameo (carved in relief), striped onyx and gold. Horse and chariot scenes must have reminded the wearer of the pleasures of the amphi-theatres and hippodromes which the Romans built throughout their empire. Roman, with the extra vigour which was often found in the provinces, from Dacia; 1st or 2nd century AD. National Museum of Antiquities, Bucharest

sia, brought back with him to Delhi a nucleus of Persian miniature painters and probably of goldsmiths too. From then on, the succeeding emperors lived in ever greater luxury, using their marvellous furnishings as trappings of power. Being always wanderers at heart and often travelling on campaign as well, the emperors, like nomad tribes, especially cherished their jewels, to represent permanence with so much threatening change around.

Moghul jewelry, like their architecture and art, is a highly sophisticated amalgam of Moslem Persia with Hindu India, both leavened by European ideas introduced by the numerous foreign embassies. The Moslems did not invent new patterns; they refined existing forms, many of which are mentioned in the ancient Hindu *Ramayana* and are

those so farre remote easterne princes', continually complained that presents from the English Government were not big enough or good enough to impress in India. He wrote of Jehangir's leaving Ajmer:

On his head he wore a rich turban with a plume of heron tops (aigrette) not many, but long; on one side hung a ruby unset, as big as a walnut; on the other side a diamond as great; in the middle an emerald like a hart, much bigger. His sash was wreathed about with a chain of great pearls, rubies and diamonds drilled; about his neck he carried a chain of most excellent pearls, three double, so great I never saw; at his elbows armlets set with diamonds; on his wrist three rows of several sorts. His hands bare, but almost on every finger a ring.

When Rowe saw the imperial ladies peering through a window, he could

jewelry, Shah Jehan must have shown a special love for stone carving: several of his cups survive, of distinctive soft shape. The Venetian lapidary, Hortensio Bronzoni, worked for Shah Jehan and for his successor, Aurangzeb, till his death in 1677, only one of many European adventurers, artists and craftsmen who introduced natural forms, perhaps inspired from the court menageries.

Malucci, another Venetian at Aurangzeb's court half a century later, told of the harem. The princesses wore necklaces of jewels on both shoulders like scarves, often three or five rows of pearls hanging from neck to lower stomach; on top of the head bunches of pearls hung to the forehead with a gold gem-set ornament above the nose often shaped as sun, moon or flowers. In their ears were valuable stones, on their arms,

still in use today: like the Nauratan, the pendant with nine stones supposed by some to counteract evil influences, a superstition from earliest times, later adapted to stand for the nine courtiers of Akbar.

Captain Hawkins, at Agra from 1609 to 1611, wrote of the artistic emperor Jehangir (1569–1627) who 'inherited the wealth of his nobles and took a present from every one who came before him . . . and had eight chains of beads, every one of which contains four hundred; they are of pearls, diamonds, rubies, emeralds, lignum, aloes and coral.'

Sir Thomas Rowe, ambassador to Emperor Jehangir, 'the first that ever was imployed in his hie nature to any of

not see much but wrote that if he had had 'no other light, their diamonds and pearls had sufficed to show them'. In 1617 he was at Jehangir's weighing ceremony: 'His head, neck, breast, arms above the elbows, at the wrists, his fingers every one with at least two or three rings, fettered with chains of drilled diamonds, rubies as great as walnuts (some greater) and pearls such as mine eyes were amazed at.'

Jehangir's successor, Shah Jehan, was India's greatest builder. He built the Taj Mahal; the French diamond dealer Tavernier claimed to have seen the beginning and the end, with twenty thousand craftsmen working at Agra for twenty-two years, using only the finest materials. If Jehangir stimulated gold

armlets two inches wide with bunches of pearls hanging, on their wrists bracelets or many strings of pearls so thick that one could not feel the pulse beneath; on the fingers, rings; on the thumb, a ring set with a mirror in which they looked at themselves; a gold waist-band two fingers wide covered in stones, trouser strings with bunches of pearls at the end, and metal leg ornaments finished the primary scheme for winning imperial favour.

Even in eighteenth-century Delhi, when the Moghuls were in decline, goldsmiths' work seems as fine as ever. Aurangzeb, like his father and grandfather, probably weighed himself against gold coins or precious stones, and still kept an amazing ceremonial routine,

Indian princes wore, and sometimes still wear today, fine costumes, each with its own local or family character. This group of portraits from Rajasthan, perhaps the area with the fiercest family loyalties, shows how some typical Indian jewels were worn, like the jiqa or turban ornament in front, usually including some very big stones to emphasize the family's wealth and prominence. Left to right the builder of Jaipur (Man Singh), and princes of Bundi, Jaipur, Jodhpur, Udaipur and Jodhpur, all 18th century

punctuating the courtiers' pleasures of kite-flying and quail-fighting.

Jewels in India were a sort of barometer: you could tell how big a ruler was by how much gold he wore. Although the direct patronage of the Moghul emperors created much the finest craftsmanship, bigger, coarser work was normal everywhere, some of the biggest pieces being made for Hindu temples like Tirupati (the huge Kohinur diamond is supposed to have been the eyeball from an image in another).

In Bengal during the wars of Robert Clive, one of his junior officers, John Corneille, described a typical ruler of that time who, when defeated by Clive in 1757, naturally tried to save his jewels as well as his women.

In the south, the ruler of Mysore was Tippoo Sultan, reputed then to be the richest man in the world. He was killed when the British armies under Lord Harris overwhelmed Seringapatam in 1799. He had a superstitious reverence for tigers, as may be seen from his extraordinary relics in the Wallace Collection, London, from his tiger-mouthed cannon at Powis Castle in Wales, and above all from an extraordinary representation in the Victoria and Albert Museum. It is an almost life-size 'royal tiger' devouring a prostrate European, incorporating an organ whose noise resembles the 'cries of a person in distress intermixed with the roar of a tiger'. This 'Tippoo's Tiger' was captured by the British at Seringapatam.

Tippoo's royal throne made in 1786 was, of course, of gold. His love for jewels may have helped to bring him to his doom: his turban jewel was seen by a soldier, causing him to be noticed when he might otherwise have been overlooked during the confused fighting at the last battle of Seringapatam.

Afterwards there was a terrible breakdown of discipline:

On the fall of Seringapatam on May 4th 1799, the town itself was given over to looting. Soldiers, both British and Indian, as well as the city's riff-raff, ransacked houses and shops. It was said that for a bottle of spirits fabulous pearls and diamond bracelets worth a fortune could be bought in the camp. On the morning of the 5th, Col. Arthur Wellesley [later the Duke of Wellington] took over as Commandant of Seringapatam, while General Baird left to make his report in person to the Commander-in-Chief [Lord Harris]. Wellesley then became responsible for the town and its property and on May 8th despatched a report relating the events of the 4th night. 'Scarcely a house in the town was left unplundered, and I understand that in camp jewels of the greatest value, bars of gold, etc., have been offered for sale in the bazaars of the army by our soldiers, sepoys and foreigners. I came in to take command on the 5th and by the greatest exertion, by hanging, flogging, etc., in the course of that day, I restored order among the troops, and I hope I have gained the confidence of the people. They are returning to their houses, and beginning again to follow their occupations, but the property of everyone is gone.

Eventually official presents reached King George III in London, including the gold tiger's head from the throne, made of wood and covered with plates of the purest gold about a tenth of an inch thick.

The British, eventually in undisputed control, made individual treaties with many local princes and used them as their political representatives, enabling these princes to amass vast fortunes. Most of the surviving Indian jewels are no doubt from this period—the earliest Moghul pieces having been lost.

Sir Malcolm Darling, a sort of prime minister in the state of Dewas, visited his Raja's grandmother about 1900. He recorded:

The Maharani was a remarkable woman. On the one hand, during her Regency she had hanged seven men, one for attacking a noble with a sword without hurting him, so it was said. On the other hand, she had sold her jewels to build a hospital, and in those days a normal Indian lady would almost sooner have parted with her eyes than with her jewels. And for her to build a hospital was in itself almost an eccentricity.

Darling wrote to E. M. Forster, his successor, 'Dewas is the oddest corner of the world outside *Alice in Wonderland*'. Odd it may have been, but undoubtedly rich.

'One morning we drove to the Treasury to see the "Crown Jewels",' Darling recalled;

the state's annual revenue was no more than £50,000 but the jewelry was worth, it was said, £60,000. A tray 'large enough to hold tea for six' was set before us laden with bracelets and bangles, necklaces, anklets and rings for nose and ear. We fingered them gingerly, eyed by a Committee of six who had to be present when they were viewed. Five more trays appeared with ropes of pearls, each about four feet long. At Curzon's Delhi Durbar one of them got caught in the Raja's diamond-studded sword and broke. After the Durbar pearls were shaken out of his dress, but a number were lost, for the Durbar was hardly the moment to hunt for them. As tray followed tray, I 'sickened' at the sight of so much barbaric pearl and gold. The pearls too had lost their lustre and the diamonds looked like glass. 'Give me rather,' I wrote, 'a flight of pelicans over the Indus or the stars as they are tonight' . . .

On tour in Jaipur, by then probably the state with the richest jewels of all, Darling saw Diwali, the Hindu festival in honour of Lakshmi the goddess of wealth. 'That night I found H. H. had just finished worshipping his jewelry. At Diwali, he said, all Hindus worship their wealth that they may have more.'

In 1919 Prince Hari Singh, heir presumptive to the realm of Jammu and Kashmir, the mountainous land in the western Himalayas, visited London for for the first time. His uncle had given him six hundred thousand pounds for his current bank account: nothing unusual for a rich young Indian out to enjoy the pleasures of peace-crazy England. But there was a scandal when the prince returned to Kashmir having been swindled out of no less than one hundred and fifty thousand pounds, partly in jewels, by a confidence trickster. The young prince wrote his loss off against experience: a true story which recalls Robert Louis Stevenson's jolly fantasy *The Rajah's Diamond*. In those days legendary riches were still openly enjoyed, not, as often today, furtively concealed.

Rosita Forbes, traveller and lover of the Indian princes, gives a last colourful record in 1939 of their extraordinary and now vanished hoards; many of the treasures were made by the old European crown jewelers like Garrard of London or Chaumet of Paris. Some of them were of no artistic value, simply being piles of stones like those in Hyderabad; some like those of the northern Sikh state in Patiala, 'the House of Diamonds', were not far different from the stock of a 1930s Paris shop. Miss Forbes wrote:

In Jodhpur the present Maharajah, shy and quiet, devoted to sport, interested only in the most practical politics, dresses and lives with the utmost simplicity. He does not care for the ancient splendours to which he is entitled. I have never seen him wear jewels.

Yet in his armoury there are children's toys made of solid gold and nursery balls set with rubies. I saw rose-water basins and dishes, jugs, perfume bottles and censers, betelnut sets and palm-leaf boxes all made of gold. There were writing-table sets encrusted with precious stones, swords whose scabbards and hilts were a solid pattern of emeralds, diamonds and pearls. The furniture was plated with silver and gold, or with small squares of looking-glass.

There were pairs of women's shoes, pathetically small and amusingly down-trodden at the heel, so thickly sewn with diamonds that I could not see the stuff of which they were made. There were eyebrows of diamonds – thin, curved streaks of light with hooks to hold them over the ears, which the princesses of olden days used to wear across their foreheads. And there were rows and rows of exquisitely enamelled crutches, those tall, slender sticks with gem-studded handles on which the Thakurs (great nobles) of Rajputana leaned during the long ceremonies when, owing to the presence of their sovereign, they might not sit.

In olden days, when a queen or a princess died, her jewels were packed away and stored among the family treasure. Her successor was dowered with a completely new outfit of precious stones. Thus from generation to generation the royal treasure accumulated. Nowadays some of the jewels are handed down to daughters and daughters-in-law. . . .

In the armoury of Jodhpur, handling now a snakeheaded anklet encrusted with emeralds and now an earring like an inverted pagoda, each storey built of rubies and hung with infinitesimal bells, I remember telling, while we looked at a jewelled bridle that must have been very uncomfortable to handle, how, in a southern Indian palace, I saw the ruling Maharani in full dress. The weight of her jewels was so great that she could not stand without the support of two attendants. Her anklets of gold, studded with emeralds weighed 100 oz. each and were valued at £1,400. Over her slender feet she wore flat strips of gold attached by chains to jewelled toe rings. The same precious metal covered the backs of her hands and was held in place by diamond links attached to her rings and bracelets. She could not bend her elbows because her arms were covered solidly from wrist to shoulder with wide bracelets of precious stones. Diamonds blazed upon her breast and hung in a multitude of chains far below her waist. Her throat was stiffened by collars of emeralds and rubies.

Down the full length of her plaited hair, from the crown of her head to her knees, hung a sort of fishtail of gold set with jewels. It was about three inches wide at the top and it tapered to the point where a pear-shaped diamond hung. I calculated that the eighteen-year-old queen was wearing more than her own slight weight in treasure and the value of at least a quarter of a million sterling.

Byzantine jewels are closely related to Ptolemaic Egypt. They combined the massive quality of Roman work with the fantastic intricacy of Greek. Byzantium looked back to Greece and Rome, just as these had looked to ancient Egypt, using its scarabs and some of its gods. In this gold necklace, the head from a coin of Domitian is presumably used as a form of flattery to someone powerful. The decorative roundels are of typical eastern Mediterranean style. Very few jewelers today can make by hand such a chain. Ptolemaic Egyptian, 1st century AD. British Museum, London

The young Maharajah of Jaipur, India's most popular sportsman, possesses a necklace of spinel rubies, each as large as a bantam hen's egg. There are three rows of these fabulous stones and their market value must be enormous, for there are no other such spinels in the world. They were collected by Babur, the great Moghul conqueror of India, and the necklace was added to by his son Akbar.

Among the State jewels which are occasionally shown to His Highness's friends are three great emeralds and two pearls strung together to form a sort of fringe worn across the front of a turban. The largest stone is of 490 carats and such emeralds are worth anything up to £200 sterling a carat. In Jaipur the statues of the Hindu goddesses in one of the temples wear tiaras set with pear-shaped diamonds of 70 carats each....

In Patiala . . . I was shown the famous . . . emeralds, each as large as a dessert spoon, and a necklace which when I tried it on, covered half my person and contained pink, yellow-greenish and what I should call pale brown diamonds all as large as my thumbnails....

The Maharajah of Gwalior has 'tons of pearls', so many that he cannot even count the strings. His great friend and neighbour the Maharaj-Rana of Dholpur, a philosopher who devotes his whole time to the care of his State, sometimes wears the most famous pearls in India, nine rows, perfectly matched, each as large as a thrush's egg.

The Sovereign of Baroda possesses a carpet made solely of jewels. The groundwork is of pearls and the design of turquoises, rubies, emeralds and diamonds.

Kapurthala is justly famous because its Maharajah is one of the best and most popular hosts in India. But it should also rank among the legendary States because its generous and accomplished ruler, to whom —as in the case of his fellow princes—half the land owes employment, possesses a fabulous crown which he wears on top of his turban. It is made of three thousand carefully selected diamonds and pearls. Another exquisite possession of this distinguished prince is a topaz belt buckle. I believe it is the biggest topaz in the world. It must be nearly four inches long and it is of an indescribably burning amber-yellow colour. Such jewels represent the iron ration of the State, a treasure that would serve in moments of national emergency.

Nobody will ever know the true extent to which India realized her lust for gold, her distrust of paper currency. But it is established that India is the leading gold importer in the twentieth century, though of all the great countries she is the one which needs the least for her official banks. The Indian princes undoubtedly still possess today many of their family heirlooms. But since the partittion in 1947 a fear of the new wealth tax, together with the new fear of criticism for showing one's wealth, and universal considerations of security, have led to a new discretion and even secrecy. Only the great occasions, like the 1971 marriage at Dholpur, uniting the houses of Bharatpur and Dholpur and Naba, still call out a show of finery probably unparalleled elsewhere in the world.

It may be that the idea of exhibitionism is incompatible with the best art. It is arguable, for example, that Louis XIV, the greatest megalomaniac in French history, overstrained the inherent subtlety and distinction in French art, simply by overproduction; coarse patrons get what they deserve. It is no chance if the buildings of Madame de Pompadour, Louis XV's mistress, commissioned by her around 1750, because she loved them, are overwhelmingly beautiful, whereas Versailles, built for Louis XIV, is just overwhelming. In the same way, much Indian jewelry was commissioned by princes simply to outdo their neighbours, or at least to keep up with them— it can be coarse and badly made, more than that of almost any other country. But the best is marvellous.

Deposits of diamonds in the Deccan near Golconda, rubies in Burma, sapphires in Siam and many other stones in Ceylon and elsewhere, have given India a natural advantage. The largest stones have always been used, and with the greatest abandon, with irregular cuts, often with bright-coloured metal-foil backing, to improve the stone's brilliance and colour. But stone-cutting has never been as popular in India as in Europe: the smooth depths of rounded cabochon surfaces had a peculiar glamour for Indian men.

Some of the old ruling families still talk today in a competitive way of their famous necklaces, like the emeralds of Faridcot, the pearls of Dholpur, and the long emerald necklace of Bhawalpur which reaches down below the navel. There the gold and diamond crown is bigger than a rugby football; its big stones are of irregular shape, rubbed smooth and pierced to hold a thread. Most families had at least one great stone worn hanging from the prince's neck, or from his turban frontal ornament, which curves over on top, something like a glittering question mark.

The use of glass, jargoons or zircons instead of diamonds, for instance, is indeed a common deception throughout India.

Small pendant gold cross with garnet. This may be dated to early Byzantium because it is accurately made and cast solid with an even collet. A similar cross was found in Syria at Gebel. Later work tended to be rougher and hollow, by the tenth century using claw settings. The decorative gold balls are relics of the microscopic granulation of the ancient Greeks and Etruscans. Byzantine, probably from Syria where the Roman style lingered. 5th or 6th century AD. Length: 1.7 inches

It is no more unattractive than the false façades of European baroque churches: offensive to Ruskin, because dishonest, but generally liked today. The further from the Moghul court centres round Delhi, the less refined the jewelry becomes: Bikaner is known, for instance, for the large frontal expanse of its jewels compared with the thinness front to back. Often Bikaner enamels, rather big and of simple colour, suggest a great weight; but the reverse side is not even enamelled, simply coated with resin to stabilize the front.

The finest Indian jewels were probably made in the reign of Jehangir in response to his known love of the decorative arts and that of his wife Nur Jahan. Surviving pieces suggest that the art of enamelling then reached its peak with delicate lace patterns inlaid at Jaipur, still the centre of the craft today, still obsessed with delicacy and an amazing blend of different colours. Red is the most difficult colour to enamel and the red of Jaipur is its special glory. At Lucknow, colours tended to be deeper and richer, less varied but more dramatic, often with a whole aspect of a piece such as the cheek or chin of a dragon in one colour instead of, as at Jaipur, with many shades together. At Benares pale pink and white were preferred, often blending softly one into the other instead of, as in the other two centres, being clearly contrasted: Benares enamels are a little reminiscent of English eighteenth-century Battersea enamels, with the subtlety of porcelain allied to the hardness of metal.

Delhi, being the heart of the empire, seems not to have developed a strong local school of enamels, concentrating more on carved stone and jade, certainly the favoured materials of Shah Jehan. Delhi enamels may have been like those of Jaipur but with a wider range of colours, and with less use of white opaque enamel surrounds to pick out central patterns. The stone carvings, however, developed a very distinct idiom: grooves were cut into the jade or gold background, a different metal being hammered into the grooves, stones being set in that different metal. With cheap work, and even with expensive work, in order to facilitate the exchange of stones which was so normal, lead would sometimes be melted into the gold setting, the stones being set in the soft lead: not the best way to make stones glitter, but Moghul inlaid stones nevertheless often seem to achieve the richest colours in all jewelry.

Just as southern Indian architecture and sculpture have a less sinuous, more fleshy character than in the north, so with the old jewels: they tended to be goldwork, less sophisticated and heavier. To European eyes the finest Indian jewels are Moghul work from the north. They are close to Turkish and Persian, to Afghan and to Russian prototypes. Yet they have their own quite distinct charm, if only because so many types of jewels like the turban ornament, or, for women, the arm-band or the forehead pendant, became popular there and nowhere else.

AFRICA

It is absurd to try to contain gigantic Africa in one small chapter. Although tribal jewels have obviously been of fundamental importance throughout the continent they are really a whole separate story on their own. They were mostly not metal at all, but beads of local wood and seed and beans, even of imported glass from nineteenth-century Venice or Birmingham, which hardly qualifies as creative art.

One of the salutary lessons from the history of these vast areas is the leavening influence they all enjoyed from trading one with another. Even as early as the eighteenth century and before, Chinese jewelers were working in Bombay; the Memon community there adopted a distinctive trinkety oriental style, made up of small linked geometrical units, squares and triangles which scintillate as they jiggle about in the bright tropical light, a flashing metallic mesh. The surfaces are flat, often chiselled, faceted almost like modern stones. From Bombay the Indians in the nineteenth century brought this sort of metalwork to South and East Africa, where many of the best craftsmen still today are Indian, not European or African, showing how the beauty of gold helps to bring the different races together.

The perpetual surprise of jewelry is the extraordinary technical accomplishment possible without modern equipment. A dazzling example is Ashanti, the kingdom now in Ghana, formerly and more significantly called the Gold Coast. This, alone among the African tribes, seems to have enjoyed almost endless gold, long after supplies in ancient Egypt were exhausted, long

In Africa, gold was important to the early pre-Christian Egyptians and Ethiopians, then perhaps in Mashonaland round Zimbabwe, then south of the Sahara in the Manding empire of the Mali peoples from the twelfth to the fifteenth century. From the sixteenth to the nineteenth the only known supplies seem to have been south of Mali, in the area conquered by the vigorous Ashanti tribes for whom gold became one of the main national trades and acquired a mystic significance. Right Cast bronze Ashanti gold weights were used by the gold traders to weigh gold dust. Less famous but equally beautiful are these dress ornaments of extraordinary vitality and imagination. Ashanti, from the Gold Coast, perhaps 19th century. Diameter: c. 2.8 inches. British Museum, London

Distinctive features of Indian jewelry are very large stones, often of impure and charming appearance, usually rubbed smooth or rounded; the irregular cuts on the small stones, often called 'plate cut'; and the superb enamelling, never surpassed in its rich colour and technical perfection. Left Necklace in gold, gold braid, emeralds, rubies, pearls and enamel, probably Jaipur, 18th century

49

before the discoveries around 1870 in South Africa on the Rand. Nobody knows how far back the Ashanti kingdom stretched: one clue is in the British Museum, London—a huge English bronze ewer bearing King Richard II's badges of about 1400, found on one of the shrines of the Asantehene, or King of Kings, in the palace at Kumasi, the capital. 'The golden trade of the Moors' evidently existed from the early Middle Ages at least. But the Ashanti kingdom in its present home, and therefore its numerous surviving jewels, may be no older than three hundred years. However old they are, Ashanti jewels had a very strong decorative power. They shared this with the bronze weights with which goldsmiths weighed local gold dust, apparently the main Ashanti industry, forming the basis of national trade. Presumably cast, these are usually dull on the surface, often decorated with curled wires of uniform thickness, sometimes abstract, sometimes formed as animals or human beings with clearly accented features, eyebrows, hair or tail. The trappings of royalty—handles to the thrones, crests to the crowns—were all of solid gold.

The ancestral gold throne or golden stool was the symbol of the kingdom: from it came the people's life force. Slaves and prisoners were sacrificed before it and their blood poured over it. The Ashanti people believed that the nation would sicken and die if harm came to this glittering totem, and so indeed it turned out when the stool was hidden and lost from 1900 until 1920: never has gold been more potent.

It was not until after the 1873 Ashanti war that thinner sheet beaten over wood began to act as substitute for the solid metal. The mystical identity between the divine king and the glorious metal began to yield to a modern European idea of making the greatest show for the smallest price. Already by the second British Ashanti war in 1896, the thin sheet had often been superseded by paper-thin foil; the splendid native modelling, fertilized as it was by contact with Portuguese traders in the sixteenth and seventeenth centuries, could no longer withstand the pervasive European influence.

Gold was used elsewhere, too, in West Africa, although beads, being much more common, were much more characteristic. The magnificent bronze portrait heads and animal sculpture of Nigeria,

especially those from Benin, have long been the marvel of art historians: perfect waste-wax casting was achieved in deepest jungle, in a cannibal society. The Oba of Benin had a monopoly of coral beads, giving some to his chieftaïns, but keeping most for himself; there was an annual ceremony when a man was sacrificed above them. The Benin legend is that this coral grows at the Niger Delta where the great Oba Esigue wrestled with the god of the sea and of wealth, in about 1500, and won his beads from him. In fact the coral must have come from the western Mediterranean because it grows only there, and must have been bought from the Portuguese because they were the only regular voyagers: some wrestling!

Another picturesque legend explains the 'Bird of Disaster'. The same Oba Esigue, going to war about 1515, heard this bird squawking overhead; soothsayers interpreted this as advice not to proceed. But the king was determined, ordered the bird to be killed, won a great victory and thereafter ordained that bronze birds should be cast, and beaten in the king's presence. For the Oba, weight equalled importance. His bead crowns are extremely heavy; his flywhisk weighs as much as two and a half kilograms and needs a special elbow rest. There are several hundred chiefs at Benin to participate in royal ceremonies and there are, of course, similar tribal customs throughout Africa. Here is a field for endless research. Sir Hans Sloane, founder of the British Muscum, noted one typical adornment which he discovered two centuries ago 'a flapp made of grasse worn to cover the pudenda': the difference between clothes and jewels in tribal Africa does not exist.

AMERICA

Whether or not Thor Heyerdahl is absolutely correct, this distinguished Norwegian has already proved his main case: the Egyptians under Rameses III may easily have emigrated to Mexico three thousand years ago, taking with them some of their mythology and burial habits, and the idea of pyramids, burial chambers (the first in Mexico has been found at Palenque), and mummies. The resemblance of the habits of ancient Egypt and of Olmec Mexico—the similarity of face shapes and eyes, even the same use of the word *Ra* for sun—are extraordinary. Exactly how the early

Right Gold funeral mask; emerald eyes and red paint. These were often laid on top of the corpses' folded clothes in Peruvian tombs. As the ground is very dry, they are well preserved. Chimu, 12th–13th century AD. Height: 16.9 inches. Mujica Gallo Museum, Lima, Peru

Overleaf Celtic gold ornament, perhaps a collar, with an ingenious sliding catch in the front. This is the largest surviving piece of Irish Celtic gold. The Celts did not achieve a great all-round civilization but their goldwork is some of the most beautiful ever made. In Ireland it linked in time the Bronze Age gold necklets to the early Christian masterpieces of the eighth and ninth centuries. 1st century BC. Diameter: 7.2 inches. National Museum of Ireland, Dublin, from Broighter, Co. Derry

cultures like the Maya in North America, and the apparently later ones south of the Isthmus came into being, we may never know. But their effect on jewelry was immense, first because they loved jewels themselves, and secondly because they provided Europe with gold in the sixteenth and seventeenth centuries. But their main gift to the world is stimulation of modern artists everywhere with a new vision. What was for the Spanish conquistadors just money, seems to us now to be superb art. The more primitive a civilization, the less distinction it makes between art and craft, the more mystical its jewels often are, and therefore the more impact they have in our present materialistic age.

To Columbus it was a question not of beauty but of survival. At Hispaniola in in 1494 he decreed that every adult must bring a hawk's bell full of gold and every chief a full calabash, each quarter; for receipt, Columbus gave a small brass medal to wear round the neck. There was so little gold on the island that many of the natives committed suicide rather than appear empty handed before their brutal conquerors, after working many hours washing and panning in the mountain streams. For the Indians, gold was of little interest but they quickly learned the horror it could cause: one contemporary print shows them pouring molten gold down a Spaniard's throat.

It is, of course, the famous cultures, the Aztecs and the Mixtecs and the Mayas whose cities and customs we know today. Jacques Soustelle records some of the fifteenth-century Mexican background. One group of craftsmen specially honoured were the goldsmith, the jeweler and the maker of feather-mosaics.

They were known by the name of *tolteca*, 'the Toltecs', for the origin of their crafts was assigned by tradition to the ancient Toltec civilisation, the civilisation of the god-king Quetzalcoatl and the marvellous city of Tula . . . 'They knew a great deal; nothing was difficult for them. They cut the green stone (*chalchiuitl*), they melted the gold (*teocuitlapitzaia*) . . . and all these crafts and sciences came from Quetzalcoatl.'

Clothes were very rich; the sandals of the emperor, Motecuhzoma (Montezuma), for instance, were heavily ornamented with gold. Soustelle elaborates:

The women wore earrings, necklaces and bracelets on their arms and ankles. The men had the same ornaments, but in addition they pierced the septum of their nose to hold gem or metal jewels; they also made holes in the skin beneath their lower lip so as to wear chin-ornaments of crystal, shell, amber, turquoise or gold; and they placed huge and splendid structures of feathers upon their heads or their backs.

In this display of rank and luxury everything was strictly regulated in conformity with the hierarchic order. Only the emperor might wear the turquoise nose-ornament— the division between his nostrils was perforated with great ceremony after his election —and only warriors of a certain kind had the right to wear such and such a jewel, whose kind and shape was exactly laid down. The 'emblems' or feather ornaments, dazzlingly coloured head-dresses, bronze-green plumes of *quetzal* feathers, immense butterflies, cones made of feathers or gold, cloth or feather-mosaic banners to be fixed to the shoulders of chiefs, decorated shields—all these were reserved for those who had won the right to them by their exploits, and death was the punishment for any man who should presume to attribute to himself one of these marks of honour.

The Indians of Mexico and Central America have, since the remotest antiquity (as may be seen in the Mayan frescoes of Bonampak) literally worshipped feathers—the long, splendid green plumes of the *quetzal*, the red and yellow of the parrots. They formed one of the most important articles to be delivered up to the tax-collectors under the Aztec empire. The huge feather-ornaments, together with the jewels of gold and turquoise, raised the warrior, the dignitary and the emperor high above ordinary humanity.

Soustelle imagines a memorable scene, explaining how a man became

something greater than a man, almost a divine being, hieratic and filled with splendour. When, to the hollow scream of conchs, the beat of gongs and the harsh cry of trumpets, there suddenly appeared to the people crowded on the central square, the emperor, rigid beneath the gold and turquoise diadem, amidst the brilliance of green plumes, while the armour, the emblems and the banners of the great men formed a mosaic of a thousand colours around him, who would not have thought that here was the chosen of Tezcatlipoca, 'the ruler of the world', 'the father and mother of the people'? In that society, with its very marked graduations, ornaments and jewels, gold and feathers, were the symbols of power and of the ability to govern.

When the Spaniards landed near Vera Cruz they were given several excellently worked, very rich golden objects, and made the natives bring them ten loads of beautiful white cloth made of cotton and feathers. According to native sources, Motecuhzoma sent Cortes

a costume of Tlaloc, with a crown of green plumes and jade earrings . . . a golden disk, a turquoise sceptre and golden bracelets and

Gold lunulae. Of unknown use, they were perhaps neck ornaments. The contrast between the plain shape and the engraved ornament is very effective. All found near Shannon, they are the oldest type of Irish gold to survive; Bronze Age, c. 1800 BC. National Museum of Ireland, Dublin

anklets. The list goes on with a mitre of jaguar-skin adorned with plumes and gems, turquoise and gold earrings, a jade and gold breastplate, a shield made of gold and *quetzal* plumes, a golden mitre with parrot-feathers and a mitre made of thin sheets of gold.

Among the treasures that Cortes received from Motecuhzoma II and which he sent to Charles V in July 1519 were

a golden necklace of eight sections with 183 small emeralds and 232 garnets set in it and 27 little golden bells hanging from it; a wooden helmet covered over with gold; a gold sceptre studded with pearls; 24 shields made of gold, feathers and mother of pearl; 5 fishes, 2 swans and other birds of cast and moulded gold; 2 large gold shells and 1 gold crocodile with filigree decorations; several head-dresses, mitres, plumes, fans and fly-whisks, all made of gold and feathers.

The menagerie of Montezuma had birds, animals, reptiles and snakes which were brought to him from every province; and those which could not be found, he had made in gold and precious stones.

Even Cortes was overwhelmed, and, quite rightly, feared the envy of the emperor back in Madrid; to allay this, he sent back a present of an unusually large proportion of the treasures.

Alas, very nearly all the Aztec treasure was melted down to pay for Charles V's Roman Catholic missionary wars. At least one shrewd observer who saw and recorded them, however, was Albrecht Dürer, during his Low Countries journey in 1520–1. He wrote:

I also saw the things that were brought to the king from the new land of gold: a sun entirely of gold, a whole fathom wide, and a moon entirely of silver, of equal size, likewise two rooms of rare accoutrements, of all manner of their weapons, armour, bows and arrows, wonderful arms, strange garments, bed hangings and all manner of wonderful things for many uses, all much fairer to behold than any marvel. These things are all so precious that they are valued at one hundred thousand guilders. And in all the days of my life I have seen nothing that has so rejoiced my heart as these things. For I saw among them strange and exquisitely worked objects and marvelled at the subtle genius of the men in distant lands. The things I saw there I have no words to express.

This marvellous craftsmanship with its imagery of skulls and horror expresses the ferocity of Aztec religion, the death wish of the people; and with its use of local material, gold, rock crystal, tur-

quoise, and obsidian, it shows not only the superstitions of its time, but the geological quality of Mexico too.

Central and South America were, like Mexico, the scene of shattering Spanish conquests in the sixteenth century. They have left us poorer literary evidence, but an enormous bulk of solid gold to remind us of the Incas and their neighbouring empires. In the Inca city, Cuzco, the reverence for gold was obvious: it was called 'sweat of the sun' while silver was 'tears of the moon'. The main temple was covered with plaques of gold and a golden sun, with rooms dedicated to the moon, bride of the sun, and others to the different stars, all decorated with precious metal.

The modern Spanish poet Lorca summed it up: 'O Peru! Land of metal and of melancholy!'

The terrible story is well known of the imprisonment of the great Atahualpa by Pizarro, the payment by the Incas of the agreed ransom of a room filled with gold, and then the murder of Atahualpa by Pizarro, one of the most awful betrayals in all history and certainly the one with the biggest consequences on jewelry. W. H. Prescott describes Pizarro's decision to divide some of the gold before the room was filled:

It was necessary to reduce the whole to ingots of a uniform standard for the spoil was composed of an infinite variety of articles, in which the gold was of very different degrees of purity. These articles consisted of goblets, ewers, salvers, vases of every shape and size . . . curious imitations of different plants and animals. Among the plants the most beautiful was the Indian corn, in which the golden ear was sheathed in its broad leaves of silver . . . A fountain was also much admired, which sent up a sparkling jet of gold . . . The business of melting down the plate was entrusted to the Indian goldsmiths, who were thus required to undo the work of their own hands. They toiled day and night, but such was the quantity to be recast that it consumed a full month.

From the beginning the Spaniards valued the gold, and, later, the emeralds which they discovered further inland, simply as money—*pesos*—and used it to bolster the Spanish empire. By 1540 it is estimated that some seventy-nine ships left Spain for America and forty-seven returned; by 1564 a regular convoy system was operating: gold from the new world allowed Spain to dominate the old.

Fortunately for us, burial rites throughout the present Panama, Colombia and

The simple but inspired symbolism of pre-Columbian gold is often stronger and more abstract than so-called modern abstract sculpture today. Gold eagle or condor pendant. Peruvian, c. AD 1200

Peru were extremely complicated, and because the earth, especially down the west of Peru, is very dry, thousands of tombs have survived intact. In them was found what is probably the biggest range of old gold work in the world: thin sheet gold beaten into funeral masks with attached noses and pendants; heavy-cast animals inspired by local life; pumas, iguanas, frogs, snakes and so on, usually solid. The Incas may have produced more gold than their predecessors, but the Spaniards discovered and melted it almost all; it is the earlier peoples whose gold we are now discovering, like the early Chavin, then the Mochica in the north, the Nasca in the south, the Chibcha, and finally the Chimu conquered by the Incas. These different cultures produced great metalworkers perhaps from the fourth right through to the sixteenth century. South American gold work may have been less colourful than the north American because it did not use many stones; but it was certainly, it seems, more widespread, more preoccupied in its imagery with present-day surroundings than with the imaginary hereafter; with nature more than with gods.

It is interesting that this pre-Columbian gold was hardly ever burnished bright; as with West African gold of similar date and indeed with European Dark Age gold, and early medieval church work, a dull lustre was preferred. One could almost claim that such soft glowing surfaces imply a spiritual, superstitious view of life, while a liking for bright polish is a sign of a materialist civilization. If so, the bright chrome plate plastered over our American cars, the excessive importance attached to the 'mirror finish' bright polish in the modern silver factories of Sheffield, or in the jewelry workshops of Hatton Garden, London, and 47th Street, New York, condemn us as a worldly lot. But there is a little more to it than that: ancient American natural gold alloys were very impure, containing a high proportion of copper, just as ancient European alloys contained silver; both were more difficult to polish than our modern pure metals. And modern polishing tools are better. The Incas, for instance, because they did not have the wheel, had to burnish entirely by manual rubbing, and hard burnishing metals and stones like agate must have been laborious to produce and always in short supply.

South American gold, despite its rela-

tive commonness, was always beaten rather thin, a tribute to the skill of the craftsmen. They must have understood from the beginning the need for annealing, that is for softening under heat metal hardened under the hammer. All their cast gold, like the charming votive llamas, tended to be very thick and often solid right through, always beautifully modelled; their fabricated pieces on the other hand, like their mugs and jugs with effigy heads and faces and figures on the side, though surprisingly thin and well raised from the flat sheet, often made do without solder. Joins were made simply by sewing with gold straps, the only time in the history of the craft anywhere that the noble metal has been so ignobly fitted: perhaps there was enough heat for annealing but not for solder. The cylindrical crowns in gold and the local copper alloy *tumbaga*, the human masks laid in tombs on top of the corpse's piled clothes, the thin bracelets and armbands embossed with wild-life patterns, were all often assembled in this rather tawdry way. One can actually date and place Peruvian work to some extent by the construction methods: the paper-thin gold, for instance, became almost transparently thin by the twelfth-century Mochica period, and solder by then was normal.

Always famous because of its galvanic effect on Pizarro and the Spaniards, this gold is only just being recognized as art. Even in this century, the British Museum, as Adrian Digby, one of its keepers, recalls, used to buy it for only ten per cent over melt value to stop its actually being melted, and the Bank of England did in the nineteenth century, in fact, melt great quantities from Costa Rica. The Peruvian *huaqueros* or treasure hunters used to probe the desert sand with long thin rods hoping that a hard bump beneath the surface would indicate a hidden grave; they would dig up whatever they found, without any records or research, often selling valuable old pots and jewels just as curios to passers-by. Now, with antique dealers thirsting the world over, forgers help by casting animals and pendants almost indistinguishable from the old, to satisfy the sudden demand. The great collections in the underground rooms in the garden of Señor Mujico Gallo's home at Lima, and in the superb modern building of the Bogota gold museum, have grown up to testify to the extraordinary vision of long ago.

In Panama and western South America, gold jewels and ornaments had the same degree of passionate expression as some western Dark Age tribal jewelry, probably for the same reason: there were very few buildings and fixed homes, so that jewels were the most permanent and grandest human aspiration; in America there was an additional overtone —gold represented the sun.
Left *Ceremonial knife from Lambayeque, 12th century AD. John Wise Collection, New York*

Right *Sections of four necklaces, gold, diamonds and enamel. The Moghul love of patterns, so evident in the pavings and inlaid stonework of their buildings, gave unique distinction to their jewels. Indian, the top probably from Jaipur, the penultimate probably Deccan. 18th century*

IRISH GOLD AND INTERNATIONAL INFLUENCES

Ireland is rather a special case: it has no really early history except its gold, almost no old stones or buildings or pots or bones. In this respect one can bracket it with, for instance, Colombia in South America, about which almost nothing is known until Pizarro arrived in 1539: the history of Colombia, like the history of Ireland, is hidden in its magnificent gold, and both countries are therefore almost unique.

The impact of old Irish gold is tremendous: it strikes the observer almost like electric current or thunder. This is partly because of its size—the pieces are enormous; partly because they are very rare and now almost all stored together in one overpowering room at Dublin's National Museum; partly because the ideas are so irrational, yet obviously must have been quite normal to their primitive society. Mainly, though, its power lies in its confident, imaginative design.

The earliest group, of the early Bronze Age from about 2000 to 1600 BC, are the *lunulae*, so called because of their crescent shape. Half a dozen examples have been found outside Ireland in England, France, Germany, Luxemburg and Denmark; it is just possible that they are made not from local Irish gold, but from imported metal. More likely Ireland herself had rich surface deposits of gold now altogether vanished.

Of the same date, and similarly bearing most original patterns—embossed whereas the *lunulae* were engraved—are the 'sun disks', perhaps used as clothes ornaments like those found by Schliemann in such numbers, often round the legs of the skeletons at Mycenae. Then there are the 'basket' earrings, again of most confident form, only found elsewhere in Cyprus and Israel, evidence of far-flung early trade.

About 1500 BC came the great spiral Bronze Age torcs, some of a good size to go round the human neck, others much too big, others too small. Sometimes two gold ribbons were each bent into a 'v' section, being soldered together along the point; sometimes a single ribbon was twisted. Contemporary with these were the plain necklets, simple and dignified cones and circles joined by an unpretentious curved bar. The largest early Bronze Age find in western Europe was a multitude of these clasps and orna-ments, revealed in 1854 when a railway was being cut through a hillside—the great find of Clare. By the late Bronze Age—800–700 BC—a marriage may be observed between the earlier spiral torcs and this plain Clare-type necklet, the 'gorget'. A mixture of the two, it was a ribbed horseshoe shape with a circle at each end, found only round the lower Shannon River, and possibly used as a chest ornament. The evolution of these two rather dissimilar conceptions into one compromise, over perhaps a thousand-year span, is a fascinating example of unselfconscious design.

Forms were simple but technique was dazzling. One sort of circular earring, for example, was unadorned but made of the thinnest wire wound round to form a continuous spiral web. Already waste-wax casting was common for bronze.

All these noble objects (and they are numerous) show the swing in taste which one finds throughout history—elaborate to plain, and then, in the next age, back to elaborate. But these Irish pieces are mysterious as well as beautiful: nobody knows what they were used for, where the metal came from, or who made them. They are one of the strangest and strongest of all the messages which gold brings us from the past.

The endless interlacing of the Celts began before the Romans, continued beside them round their north and western borders, and survived after them, especially in Ireland where the bogs have yielded work of magnificent weight and delicacy.

The Celts are almost part of recorded history. Strabo found that 'to the frankness and high-spiritedness of their temperament must be added the traits of childish boastfulness and love of decoration. They wear ornaments of gold, torcs on their necks, and bracelets on their arms and wrists, while people of high rank wear dyed garments besprinkled with gold.' Their special contribution to gold was the sinuous line later re-expressed around 1895 by Art Nouveau. Celtic work is often thin and holey—gold was no doubt scarce so the Celts used silver and bronze, and often made it heavier than gold. Their interwoven ornaments, famous from the early Christian manu-scripts and stone carvings, in Ireland and Northumberland, were often picked out by piercing, usually chased not en-graved, giving a soft curve of extra-ordinary grace.

Top Stone carving and inlay were a special characteristic of Moghul jewelry. The Emperor Shah Jehan stimulated this specialized craft by giving it his personal patronage in the early seventeenth century. Hairpin, carved jade, gold, enamel and stones; probably from Delhi, 18th century. Salar Jung Museum, Hyderabad, India.
Bottom Gold and enamel bracelet with dragons' heads; the eyes are diamond, the tongues, which move, ruby. A common Moghul type. Probably Lucknow, 18th century. Diameter: 3.1 inches

By Celtic times gold had become so scarce that part of what is probably a great crown—the 'Petrie crown'—is of sheet bronze; but Celtic gold shows the organic forms one would expect from the Iron Age wandering tribes. The earliest pieces contain copper, the smiths apparently changing the content to get the effect they wanted; some of the latest Iron Age pieces contain platinum, a hint that they may have obtained their metal from the upper Rhine where this alloy was found. The source of metal, like the source of ideas and the use to which these splendid objects were put, remains unknown; only one of the pieces came from a grave, the others being found quite alone. All that can be deduced from this is that Ireland did have active contacts overseas from earliest times.

The later Celts of the sixth to the eighth century AD became in Ireland the western world's last Christian outpost. They made a suitable monument in their ornament: they were masters of incredibly intricate pattern. While their predecessors' torcs now appear in much coarser form in Denmark, as gold necklets around AD 400 to 600, the contemporary Celts in Ireland had developed another goldsmiths' triumph. The Tara brooch, for instance, and the Ardagh chalice, both partly of silver, used almost every known technique including granulation, filigree, enamels, inlay and solder and a splendid system of laying perforated silver onto copper, to make a tracery pattern of one colour on another, rather like niello which itself did not reach Ireland till the twelfth century. They are glories of craftsmanship; but as convincing designs, with their balance between smooth surfaces and restless ornament, they are still more impressive.

THE VIKINGS AND SCANDINAVIA

At the end of the migrations, the Vikings of the ninth and tenth centuries came to dominate the coasts of Europe, first physically, then artistically too.

It is a short step stylistically from Ireland to the Vikings of northern Denmark, Norway, Sweden, and the tiny but commanding Baltic island, Gotland. But whereas the later Celts in Ireland and central Europe express harmony, for the Vikings all is savage war. The endless Celtic line, like Art Nouveau, which it helped to inspire in the next millennium, is smooth and curved; the Viking more sharp and angular. Late Celtic beasts are static, the Vikings' look ready to eat you. The Celts liked soft *repoussé* work. Vikings liked modelling and casting finished with carving of the hardest precision: they brought agitated

The Vikings' ornament, like their life, was adventurous, restless and often ferocious; in its strength and variety it shows the same fantastic enterprise as their feats of navigation in small boats. The Vikings were essentially seafarers, probably having very little home life. Their work seldom showed human beings. It evolved from the Germanic and Nordic invaders. Some of their most beautiful goldwork and stone carving was on the small Baltic island of Gotland, including this large 6th-century gold pendant, left, nearly 4 inches in diameter, with two small pendants and a neck ring. The decoration may owe something to Roman coins and medallions but the vigour is due much more to the astonishing confidence of the tribes. National Museum of Antiquities, Stockholm

Right Snake head rings or bracelets, gold, Viking, from the Parish of Gardslösa, in Öland, Sweden. All 9th century AD. Diameter: 2.5 inches. National Museum of Antiquities, Stockholm

movement to jewelry such as it has never known before or since.

As one might expect, it was in the outlying places that style was at its most original. Nearer the centre were the Anglo-Saxons, masters of the garnet and of the minute mosaic effect called *mille-fiori*: tiny red stones seem to vibrate in geometrical formation, brightly polished, unlike Celtic and Viking work, with perfection of finish unlike the central Europeans. Here is the fascination of the patchwork quilt made immortal.

If Celtic work suggests peaceful achievement, and Viking, the excitement of war, the Saxon royal burial treasure at Sutton Hoo in Suffolk or the Alfred jewel at Oxford, or the Kingston brooch at Liverpool, mean kingship and sumptuous magnificence.

Some of the most historic pagan jewelry is the 'Treasure of Childeric' (the first king of France and a founder of the Merovingian dynasty in the fifth century AD) which was forgotten and found by accident at Tournai by a labourer in 1653. Childeric was surrounded by badges and buckles, his sword and bracelet, some thirty golden pieces, his robe of state, his signet ring and other miscellaneous valuables. No wonder Louis XIV was excited by this array, and used it as part of his proof that France was really old and great. Some of Childeric's pieces were stolen in 1831, but others are still near where Louis XIV placed them in his palace at the Louvre, in the Cabinet des Médailles at the Bibliothèque Nationale. A century later, Napoleon Bonaparte, proclaimed emperor of the French and even a reborn Charlemagne, used on the design for his imperial robe ideas from this fifth century regalia, again to emphasize the ancient glory of France.

As Christian influence grew stronger so burials became poorer: the dead were buried near a church without gifts because the passage to Heaven might, according to the Gospel message, be easier unencumbered. It was during this period that, as Christian influence spread, graves began to loose their glitter. By the early Middle Ages, graves usually contained no more than, for instance, one episcopal ring for one bishop.

For the pharaohs of Egypt or the chieftains of Scythia, jewels had stayed with the owner after his death as well as throughout his life, a sort of personal passport to immortality. During the Dark Ages and early Middle Ages, jewels were often talismans, intended to bring supernatural benefits to the wearer. Of course, for centuries to come, kings and chieftains were still respected for their magic power, but jewels had begun their long evolution from tokens of superstition to tools of state. They became more like badges of office, first symbols of spiritual grace delegated to the wearer, then, later, just symbols of the wearer's seniority. Jewels ceased to do a portmanteau job. The growing medieval division between church and state showed in jewels too: specifically Christian jewels, on the one hand, and specifically secular, on the other, became distinct.

DARK AGE MIGRATIONS
Merovingian, Carolingian, Lombard, Anglo-Saxon, Kentish, Celtic

Whatever the 'Dark Ages' may have meant in terms of human chaos, their jewels are probably their brightest testimony. It is possible to study the period from the sixth to the eleventh century as a steady coalescence of several very distinct streams: nothing could be more different than the jiggly high-relief interlacings of Viking gold, inspired with animal shapes and physical action, and the noble band of gold decorated with abstract crosses and flowers, made for Theodelinda, the Lombard queen at Monza in the sixth century. Yet by the end of these six centuries of migrations of tribes from central Asia and the north, of the virtual expulsion from western Europe of Christianity, and its rekindling from the outposts of Ireland, Iona and Northumberland, after all this general turmoil, gold work reached the international idiom of Romanesque throughout Europe, so that one country's work became surprisingly like another's.

One way of looking at it is to trace the survival and evolution of the Roman Mediterranean tradition through all its vagaries. There is direct descent from Rome through Byzantium for all the decorative arts; but this is really not very relevant because so much Byzantine jewelry uses Christian imagery such as saints and their symbols, who hardly had impinged on Roman work before the fall of the Roman Empire. Another big difference between Rome and Byzantium is that the Byzantines loved enamel, as we can prove not only from their few surviving jewels but also from the many mosaics. Colour intoxicated the Byzantines just as mass did the Romans.

The back of an arm jewel (Taviz or Bazuband) which sometimes contained a secret drawer. The varied colours—especially the glowing red and the white background—and the delight in nature are all typical of Jaipur which became the great centre for Moghul enamelling. Jaipur, 18th century. Length: 2.9 inches. The front of the jewel is shown on p. 237.

The Graeco-Roman styles certainly survived into the various invasions—the Lombard kingdom in northern Italy, the Ptolemies and Fatimids in Egypt, the Visigoths in Spain, the Allemanni in Switzerland, the Franks in Germany, the Ostrogoths to the east, the Anglo-Saxons and Jutes in England, all produced jewels rather like each other, each influenced by native survivals; but each was more different from Roman that it was alike. There was much more continuity in classical building than there was in jewelry: architecturally, the stream flowed on to Byzantium with occasional conscious revivals in the west as under Charlemagne. Roman jewelry was not better, nor better made, than that of the tribes outside the empire—all one can say is that the Mediterranean characteristics, filigree and fastidious gold work, survived to fertilize the rougher, tougher inspiration of the marauding tribes with their animal styles.

To the Mediterranean delicacy was joined the glorious vigour of the 'barbarians'. For them jewels were probably the only substitute for home; because they had no home they were constantly on the move. Innovations were firstly size: the Romans of Palmyra may have worn the biggest jewels of ancient times, but their normal wear was never so big as, for instance, the Viking or Jutish round brooches, or the Celtic solid gold neck torcs. Secondly, there was a new richness from the use of smooth rounded coloured stones, often garnets, set in gold *cloisons*; perhaps while Romans got most of their colour from beautiful homes, and fabrics, the barbarians looked to jewels for theirs. Thirdly, the barbarians used animals and birds: being fundamental to the hunting nomad life it was natural to use them in jewels, as symbols of the wearer's strength and of his prowess.

Kenneth Clark has shrewdly observed what a poor figure man is made to cut in art at this time: humble and diminutive, he is everywhere overwhelmed by the ornament around him. Perhaps man had proved inadequate and felt himself unable to cope.

One apparent universal love, almost a fetish, is introduced by Lord Clark in his *Civilisation*:

Apart from this small, enclosed society of scholars, what kept that wandering culture alive? Not books. Not building. . . . What did they have? The answer comes out in the poems: gold. Whenever an Anglo-Saxon poet wants to put into words his ideal of a good society, he speaks of gold.

There once many a man
Mood-glad, gold bright, of gleams
   garnished
Flushed with wine-pride, flashing
   war-gear,
Gazed on wrought gemstones, on gold,
   on silver,
On wealth held and hoarded, on
   light-filled amber.

The wanderers had never been without craftsmen; and all their pent-up need to give some permanent shape to the flux of experience, to make something perfect in their singularly imperfect existence, was concentrated in these marvellous objects. They achieved, even in the chasing of a torque, an extraordinary intensity. But nothing shows more clearly how the new Atlantic world was cut off from the Graeco-Roman civilisation of the Mediterranean. The subject of Mediterranean art was man, and had been ever since early Egypt. But the wanderers, struggling through the forests, battling with the waves, conscious chiefly of the birds and animals that hung in the tangled branches, were not interested in the human body.

Lord Clark concludes:

This love of gold and wrought gemstones, this feeling that they reflected an ideal world and had some kind of enduring magic, went on right up to the time when the dark struggles for survival were over. It is arguable that western civilisation was saved by its craftsmen. The wanderers could take their craftsmen with them. Since the smiths made princely weapons as well as ornaments, they were as necessary to a chieftain's status as were the bards whose calypsos celebrated his courage.

Important secular pieces like the Molsheim brooch become less common and Christian imagery begins to dominate metal work. Portable reliquaries become more popular—purses or boxes containing part of a saint, a tooth or bone, for instance, or, more often, something hallowed by touching a saint's tomb. This is perhaps not what is normally meant by jewelry, but it evolved into the wearable reliquary jewels of the later Middle Ages. In the huge monastery at Centula, consecrated in 798, Angilbert was especially proud of the relics he had acquired from popes, kings and emperors everywhere. St Stephen's purse, now at Vienna, stayed in Charlemagne's capital, Aachen, right up till 1798 when it was moved to Paderborn to escape Napoleon.

The flat or low-relief ornament of the Frankish and Alemannic and Saxon

Gold ear, nose and throat jewels worn by a rich woman in Mali, West Africa. In the Middle Ages, from the thirteenth to the sixteenth century, the Manding-speaking people of the Mali Empire made fine jewels and conducted an international trade in gold, especially northwards from Timbuktu in the Sahara Desert

work, where the stones are polished to make one continuous flat surface with the gold, yields to bulging cabochon stones and the heavy filigree work originating south of the Alps. Such flat decoration as remained was often by engraving, as in the magnificent cross of Lothair at Aachen, or with black niello as on the Tassilo chalice at Kremsmünster; and there was a revival in stone engraving, a craft apparently not used by the barbarians but never lost in Italy, as used in the 'coronation jewel of Charlemagne' in Paris. The stones, at least by Ottonian times, in the ninth and tenth centuries, often had claw settings instead of the older Roman type collets or metal sockets. In a strange way, as the barbarian strife in Europe settled into the framework we know today, European jewelry became not smoother but rougher, not more but less delicate.

Very little survives; the epic stories surrounding two of the greatest pieces show how lucky we are to have any at all. The 'Talisman of Charlemagne', containing some of the Virgin's hair and the 'True Cross', perhaps originally set in crystal, is one: it is supposed to have been buried with Charlemagne when he died at Aachen in 814, and was found round his neck when his tomb was opened by Otto III in 1000; it was preserved in the cathedral treasury until Napoleon's time. Then it was given by the canons to Empress Josephine in 1804, to wear at her coronation, as a thank-offering for the return of most of the treasures from Paderborn in 1804. It was inherited by Napoleon III from his mother; and finally given by his widow, before she died, to the Archbishop of Rheims as her reparation for the 1914 bombardment of his cathedral, where it now is.

Another saga concerns Lothair's crystal. Its inscription refers to him as king of the Franks—he was Lothair II (855–69) probably. According to the abbey chronicle of Vasor near Dinant on the Meuse, it belonged in the first half of the tenth century to the wife of Eilbert, Count of Florennes, in Namur province. He pledged or pawned it with a canon of Rheims cathedral for a fine horse he bought at a fair. Later he went to Rheims to redeem the jewel, but the canon denied its existence. The count then returned with an army of his retainers but the canon evaded him by hiding in the cathedral. Eilbert surrounded it and set it on fire, smoking out the canon. The

jewel was found hidden in his clothes. The count finally repented his incendiary act and gave the pendant to Vasor Abbey which he had founded near Florennes. There it remained till the French revolution when it disappeared. A Belgian dealer found it and sold it in the mid-nineteenth century, saying it had been fished up in the Meuse. Perhaps indeed a monk had dropped it there, intending to recover it, not realizing the ferocity of the impending revolution. A French collector bought the crystal for twelve franks, then passed it to an English collector, Bernal, from whose sale in 1855 the British Museum acquired it. Its fifteenth-century mount was probably to adapt the original pendant to a morse or clasp.

These are extraordinary tales of survival. The crystal-engraved crucifixion from St Denis Abbey now at the British Museum is another marvellous reminder of ancient skill. The gold altar made by Volvinio, whose name suggests he may have been Frankish, at Sant' Ambrogio church in Milan, and the Pala d'Oro in St Mark's Cathedral in Venice, both showing the impact of Byzantium, are some of the remarkable surviving evidence we can add to the written accounts of what is lost. In 796 the Frankish armies in Italy broke into the Avars' 'ring' or camp and captured an immense treasure, a large part of which was sent with Angilbert to the Pope for him to give to the Frankish magnates. Later in the year Pippin brought more treasure from the Pannonian Avars who were still pagan. Avars' jewels, with their glass incrustations and fine granulation, found in Czechoslovakia and now in museums at Brno, Bratislava, Prague and Leningrad show the mixed styles which no doubt made up these tribal hoards, using both oriental and Christian themes, and showing Greek influence in the thinness of their granulation, Byzantine and Roman in their heaviness.

We can only imagine the riches now lost, the diversity of metal still buried underground. The Sutton Hoo royal treasure at the British Museum was discovered as recently as 1939 and is not only the richest archaeological strike ever made in Great Britain, but the outstanding example throughout Europe of metalwork during the sixth and seventh centuries. This revelation knocked sideways, in one blow, the deductions of generations of patient scholars. Further discoveries will no doubt yield a fuller

picture to modern science, aerial surveys and deep ploughing. Meanwhile the Dark Ages still remain quite mysterious. Jewelry was still a mixture of pagan and Christian, of tribal and national, of royal and of chieftains' aspirations.

Charlemagne died in 814. His end shows how jewels were becoming for a Christian king in Europe not his own personal accoutrement for the next life, as they would have been a few centuries before, not tangible prayers to God, as portable relics later became for all wealthy people, but an establishment of the validity of the king:

. . . he put on the royal garb and a crown on his head; then he entered the Palace Chapel on the altar of which he had placed a crown of gold, different from the one he wore; after Louis had promised to serve his subjects well, his father ordered him to take in his own hands the crown that lay on the altar and to put it on his head to remind him of all that his father had exhorted him to do: this he did; they heard mass together and went into the palace.

Charlemagne represents a turning point: the divine right of kings and the possession of crown jewels became interdependent.

The rise of Christianity caused this development and to some extent it was the monks themselves who made it physically possible: it was they who preserved the manual skill, established stable conditions and kept alive international communications, so that at last a united European style emerged about 1100. Wars went on as usual, but it seems to have been about this time that jewelry and gold achieved the status they kept right through the Middle Ages: they were the grand art; gold was the most precious material known, so, it was argued, it must obviously be the closest to heaven, the universal goal.

THE MIDDLE AGES

Dating jewels is never easy because they were usually made of gold. This shows an unbelievable resistance to corrosion: it may look brand new when it is thousands of years old, and usually its history is impenetrable even by modern scientific probing. Some Mesopotamian, Etruscan, Roman and Egyptian friezes and some Roman portrait sculpture heads, particularly those from Palmyra, do, it is true, show jewels; sketches of jewelled ornaments are often as flamboyant as the real object; but the treatment is usually too superficial to

Above The crystal of Lothair illustrating eight scenes in the story of Susanna from the Apocrypha; carving, Carolingian, 9th century AD; copper gilt mount, 15th century. The piece has survived dramatic losses and rediscoveries. Diameter: 4.5 inches. British Museum, London

Left Bird brooch, gold and cloisonné garnets, in the manner typical of the migrating tribes, from Cesena. Similar brooches have been found in Spain. Ostro-gothic, 5th century AD. German National Museum, Nuremberg

69

give an accurate record, and anyway the distribution of surviving remains is not thorough enough to give a fair spread. It is not until the Middle Ages that painting, both on parchment miniatures and in court pictures, assumed something like the precision of modern photography. So we do by then know what to look for, even if we cannot find it.

Early work of the twelfth and thirteenth centuries is still extremely rare. Almost none of the big treasuries now intact started before the fifteenth century. One of the few, that of the Lombards at Monza, is almost unique in being well documented, and almost unaltered. Another, the German Holy Roman Emperors' at Vienna, has lost its true beginnings in legend. There and at Aachen Cathedral and in Paris at the Louvre there are pieces identified with Charlemagne (crowned in Rome in 800) but they were probably made long after his death. Otto the Great (crowned in Rome in 962) was the first Holy Roman Emperor, and it was he who established the imperial idea through the principle of heredity rather than of personal power; but nobody knows quite what jewels he initiated. Mostly, we depend upon pieces dug from graves (and Christian graves were extremely austere) or on pieces which have simply been used down the centuries with no documentary evidence.

With the Middle Ages, several new influences came to bear on jewelry. First, the distinction begins between fine and applied art. One reason why jewels of the barbarian tribes have such power is because these nomads had no fine art at all: to express their deepest feelings they used not cathedrals or symphonies or sonnets, but jewelry.

Secondly, during the four centuries of the Middle Ages, and before, one can trace the rise of women, though not the decline of men, as jewelry wearers. Early frescoes, as in Crete or Assyria, show men more weighted down with metal than women; surviving Hellenistic and Roman jewels probably belonged more to women even if dead, than to men—earrings and diadems, for instance, were buried with their female wearers. By the Dark Ages, jewels seem to have become again the prerogative of kings and chieftains rather than their wives: the jewels were something like badges of office, and, as the wives had no official jobs, so they tended not to have jewels. Of course, there were exceptions, notably Theodelinda, Queen of the Lombards who, to judge from her surviving treasures at Monza Cathedral, must have been quite an impulse buyer. But generally until medieval times jewels seem to have been for men.

Thirdly, there is fashion. One may define this in its several senses as the design of clothes, as the wish to look one's best, and as part of the herd instinct: people want to look alike and change their dress styles in similar ways at similar times, even though individuals want to look different. As Cecil Beaton, the modern master, says, fashion is a mass phenomenon but it feeds on the individual. All these aspects of fashion probably existed in ancient Egypt, whose women have left us such lavish surviving beauty equipment; and, similarly in ancient Rome whose women, to judge from the frescoes and statuary, wore their jewels in many different places and ways. But when women were almost like slaves, as sometimes in Greece, or, as in the Dark Ages, when life can often have been no more than a fight for survival, fashion was impossible.

With fashion came chivalry: the urge men have not simply to outfight each other but to outshine each other as well in the estimation of beautiful women. Perhaps this started in the peaceful courts of the troubadours in twelfth-century Provence. A typical instance was in 1503 at Barletta in southern Italy: the war between Louis XII and Ferdinand the Catholic led to a combat not of huge forces ending in massacre, but of just thirteen of the most valiant knights of Italy and France on each side, conducted respectively by Colonna and Bayard, *sans peur et sans reproche*. The Italians won and we may be sure their womenfolk cheered them on.

Life became more secure and peaceful; so jewels became more delicate—unselfconscious evolution became conscious design. The revival of finger rings about the thirteenth century may be because manual work was no longer so general. But pendants, though often magical, are conscious fashion, using the *décolletage* of the fifteenth century, revealing lovely bare shoulders and breast; hair ornaments came a little later, to decorate the piled-up, playful new creations of the coiffeur with gemstudded gauze, and led to aigrettes with featherlike rows of stones spraying out of their combs.

Below Pair of gold fibulae: the simple form seems unusual. From Ruvo di Puglia, Greek colonial, 6th century BC. National Museum, Taranto

During the great migrations, pins slowly turned into penannular brooches (with an interrupted ring and swivel pin), then into ring brooches and then massive boss brooches. Right, top to bottom: Tribal safety pins were more elaborate than the central Roman types. From Münsingen, Alemannic bronze and enamel, 4th century BC. Length: 3.2 inches. Historical Museum, Berne. Bronze fibula, Merovingian, perhaps 7th century AD. Cluny Museum, Paris.

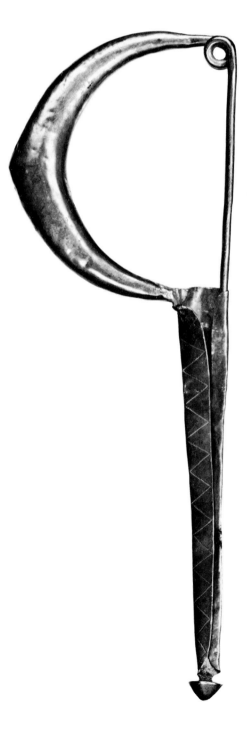

70

Bronze and enamel belt buckle, Visigothic. Perhaps 5th century AD. Archaeological Museum, Madrid.
Ring brooch or fermail, gilded silver; the ornamental surround for the pin is at last becoming more important than the pin itself. French, 13th century AD. Cluny Museum, Paris.
Brooch, gold and stones; the pin which dominated fibula design from Roman times is at last invisible; perhaps because clothes are becoming lighter and more elegant, the bulk of fabric to be fastened is less and no longer requires so big a pin. French, 14th century AD. Cluny Museum, Paris

Evidence of the increasing power of fashion during the Middle Ages is the development of the decorative brooch. Since earliest times jewelry served the need to clasp together across the chest two sides of a rough cloak. Sometimes the ancient equivalent of a safety pin was used: two parallel strips of bronze wire, with a spring one end. This type of 'fibula' was quite common in bronze, for instance, under the Greeks three millennia ago; but, with their usual ingenuity, they added a semi-circular flange for easy handling to one side of the safety pin, upon which they imposed or incised patterns. The Etruscans did much the same thing in gold at much the same time, but usually, instead of the flange, provided one flat side to the pin. Perhaps it is not too fanciful to suggest that the Persians, again at the same period, did not have quite the same wit: for them, the single pin, like a hat-pin, seems to have been standard, rather than the clever safety pin.

In the Dark Ages, a thousand years later, we see, as might be expected, a step backwards in structural efficiency: in place of the fibula, the normal fastener becomes the ring brooch, like the Tara Brooch in Dublin, with superlative decoration but of questionable engineering. The pin is held in position by material tucked through the ring and the point of the pin is no longer shielded. So it remained, with the point getting shorter, and the ring against which it engaged, more ornamental, till the thirteenth century. Then the ring brooch became rarer, and in its place appears the round brooch with a decorated central boss. By the fifteenth century, big brooches are no longer necessary because jewelry is worn with thin indoor clothes, no longer with the heavy, all-purpose, cold-weather cloak. The brooch clasp becomes an *enseigne* or hat badge and, by the beginning of the sixteenth century, the ultimate in fantasy, the Renaissance pendant. Over all these centuries the simple pin for fastening has changed slowly and naturally into a completely useless, self-conscious work of art.

It is not until the great age of medieval book illumination in the fifteenth century, for instance as painted in the 'Master of Mary of Burgundy' breviary at the Bodleian Library, Oxford, that some jewels become obviously for women rather than for men. The birth of portrait painting a century before allows

us to observe women wearing more jewels as their clothes become less austere. It is tempting to suggest that the lighter the clothing was, the more jewels were worn, but this is only partly true. In the fourteenth and fifteenth centuries clothes were certainly becoming more specialized, cooler for indoors, leaving more bare flesh, for necklaces and pendants, less need for clasps. In Italy it was not only women but men, too, whose clothes became lighter, reflecting the new open attitude of mind of the Renaissance; but in Spain and its associate empire, etiquette remained very strict, clothes stiff and thick, and jewels were increasingly popular there too—instead of being worn, they were often sewn onto the fabric of the clothes of both men and women.

If one cannot claim that through the Middle Ages clothes became uniformly lighter, it is at least true that jewels became more enormous. Perhaps a clearer explanation than the rise of fashion or the emancipation of women is simply the lessening of slaughter. Tribal wars were no longer so comprehensive, so the finer human feelings at last found an outlet again in jewelry, much as they had done in the classical world.

Fashion, then, became dominant in the Middle Ages and women began to wear as much jewelry as men. The cult of relics also promoted the jeweler. Goldsmiths devoted much energy to these, providing, for any worthwhile cathedral or church, gold or silver containers. In Germany alone, big jewelled shrines four or five feet long, made in the twelfth and thirteenth centuries, still survive today on over twenty altars, each one a gem-encrusted masterpiece. St Louis built the Sainte Chapelle in Paris in 1258, the biggest reliquary ever, to house the Crown of Thorns, which he bought at a great price from Baldwin II's sacred treasury in Constantinople.

Relics brought great profit to a church, sometimes even enough to bring a new town into being, as at Conques in France or Compostela in Spain. After the great fire at Laon Cathedral in 1112 relics paid for the huge rebuilding work: seven canons raised enough money by touring in France and England, with a display of a piece of the 'Virgin's Veil', of the 'Holy Sponge', and of the 'True Cross'. To the faithful, relics were a powerful support on every important occasion, hence the need not only to have them in church but also

hanging round one's neck. They were necessary for the consecration of a new church, for the signing of treaties, for the swearing of oaths, sometimes even built into sword hilts or carried by a merchant in the cash box. They were occasionally magical—touching them reputedly cured disease.

This adoration of inanimate matter provided a great catalyst for activity by jewelers of all sorts. At the top, crown jewels and insignia became objects of religious veneration: those of the Holy Roman Empire, for instance, were first displayed in public for this purpose in Nuremberg in 1315; by 1350 their pious contemplation could even be rewarded by ecclesiastical remission of sins. At the humblest level, a huge trade was created in pilgrims' badges. Often they were hat badges in lead, incorporating the relevant saint's symbol—for instance, a shell for Saint James the Greater of Compostela. These sentimental tourists' trivia are still common today, often found in rivers; some made of gold survive too.

The most beautiful consequence of the medieval vogue for relics was the portable reliquary, often made as a gold or enamel triptych with a small cavity behind it, in which the relic itself would be fixed. These became common from the fourteenth century. The reliquary pendant jewel, more personal and intimate than the portable reliquary, was usually embossed with a relevant religious scene. This variant of the secular pendant begins to appear in the fifteenth century, but, perhaps because of its bulk, the type never became very common.

Another feature of medieval Europe was the rise of the guilds. The British guild of goldsmiths—the Worshipful Company of Goldsmiths—in which jewelers were never considered important, grew up in the twelfth century, being incorporated in 1327. The Paris guild, too, became powerful in the thirteenth century, playing a big part in the government of the city between Philip Augustus' accession in 1180 and Louis IX's death in 1270. It was similar in all the old cities of Europe—craft guilds gave the craftsmen a corporate power which must in turn have encouraged them as independent creators.

The last new influence to affect jewels, closely related to the craft guilds, was the emergence in the fourteenth and fifteenth centuries of the various orders and fraternities, part secular, part

Boxes and altars made to contain the relics of saints were very popular in the early Middle Ages; later, holy fragments were often worn in beautiful jewels. There is a cavity beneath the gold enamelled Virgin in this gold triptych for such a relic. The enamels are Parisian in style, the piece is of an extremely delicate and sophisticated type popular in the Burgundian empire. A similar piece is in the Residenz at Munich. 1380–1400. Length, open: 2.25 inches

religious, mostly social, which brought into being some beautiful metalwork. The most famous was the order of the Golden Fleece in Burgundy, some of whose appurtenances are in the Vienna and Munich treasuries, some in Dijon, some in Berne Museum and in Brussels.

For the first time the written word now begins to give us a clear idea of what people wore. Records become quite specific—unlike those in ancient times of Herodotus and Plutarch, for instance—and sometimes exciting too. On 4 July 1194 the English army captured the French king Philip Augustus' complete baggage train at Belfogia, on the River Loir, with horses and wagons, gold coins, gold and silver tableware, archives and treasure. This seems to have been one of the greatest scoops ever made, comparable with Alexander the Great's at Granicus and at Issus.

As in most countries, medieval England possessed a state treasury and an exchequer, but the king had his own personal treasure as well; it was kept for safety in widely dispersed abbeys, but it usually travelled with the king's own baggage train. In 1216 King John was feasted at King's Lynn; his wagons could only cross the next estuary when the tide was out. The king, having taken a different route, watched the wagon loaded with treasure being trapped in quicksands and slowly engulfed. All that he valued most was lost, and he was a noted connoisseur of jewels and gems. Both personal and state property vanished, the latter being an inheritance from his grandmother, the Empress of Germany. Legendary gold and silver flagons and goblets, cups and candelabra, combs, crosses, bracelets, clasps, rings and charms, coronation robes and regalia, the gold wand and dove, the great crown and the jewelled sword of Tristan—all disappeared. Nothing has ever been recovered from this muddy tidal wave.

Another colossal loss was the treasure of the Dukes of Burgundy, captured and dispersed by the Swiss at the battles of Grandson and Murten in 1476, which caused the downfall of Burgundy, Europe's richest state. This was no less than a ducal treasury, chancery, and sacristy, all in one. Charles the Bold, the last Duke of Burgundy, took it with him on his campaign in order to impress the negotiating partners as well as to cheat the thieves at home. This ostentation made rather a sour impression on the

Fragment of a chain bearing the emblems of the Order of the Golden Fleece, the Burgundian guild which brought into being some of the most beautiful surviving late medieval goldwork. Gold and enamel, perhaps Parisian, 14th century. Museum of Fine Arts, Vienna

73

diarist Philippe de Commynes at the Treves conference with the German emperor, when Charles spread out his treasures on the tables to be admired:

The Duke of Burgundy insisted on seeing the Emperor Frederick and made a great show: the Germans despised all his talk and pomp, thinking it was just pride. The Burgundians despised the small numbers and humble clothes of the emperor's party. . . . Charles, however, was one of the very richest people —his treasures would be enough for three of the greatest palaces in Christendom.

The use of jewels here seems at last almost modern—not religious or mystical, just a fine display to enjoy and impress; and the shrewd diarist implies correctly that all this boasting by Burgundy was in fact rodomontade, put on to conceal secret insecurity.

But it was marvellous art. The breathtaking originality and delicacy of this Burgundian work inspired lesser courts throughout Europe. Most of the booty was divided among the victorious Swiss cantons, often being taken apart or cut up for easy sale so that the money thus earned could be equally distributed. Human nature does not change: a black market grew up behind the backs of the authorities, prices rocketed.

Four famous jewels, the private property of Charles the Bold, were not included with the common booty taken from the Grandson battlefield to Lucerne; they went secretly to Basle where they were hidden for twenty-eight years so that the allies should forget about them. In 1504 they were sold through three intermediaries to Jakob Fugger, the Augsburg banker. They first remained under the Fugger seal in Basle, finally being fetched by three Fugger factors in 1506, when they vanished from history. Most of the fine jewels were acquired by the emperor Maximilian, some by Henry VIII. Charles the Bold's hat was dismantled and the Fuggers sold separately the stones which had been sewn to it.

The various royal inventories help us to understand medieval jewels. As units of power got larger, assuming by the fifteenth century the shape of many modern European countries, so the concentrations of treasure became greater, and the motives behind them more complex—they were banks, keys to a secure succession of the crown, hints at the divine right of kings, and the pay-roll for armies and governments; no longer the simple barbaric delight in permanence and glitter.

One of the early finds was the Empress Gisela's treasure at Mainz from the mid-eleventh century—necklaces, filigree earrings and an eagle brooch four inches long with perhaps three other brooches; a distinguished hoard but not very much of it. Joan Evans gives us some more impressive lists: Eleanor of Provence had nine chaplets or coronets for the hair when she married Henry III in 1236, and bought eleven more. In 1301 the Countess of Artois had four crowns of jewelled gold, fourteen chaplets, and ten tressons or bandeaux. In 1272 Henry III pledged with his sister in Paris many rings, sixty-nine belts with gold or jewels, and forty-five ring brooches. Eleanor of Castile, Edward I's queen, died in 1290 leaving a gold crown with rubies, emeralds and pearls, another with pearls, another with rubies and emeralds and a great coronation crown with large balas rubies (the medieval name for spinels) and other stones. She had three ring brooches, two square brooches and two gold clasps (firmacula or tassieux) and perhaps a pair of brooches linked by a chain, two large brooches or 'ouches', one of eagle shape, probably inspired by the old barbarian pieces, and the other with a king and queen.

By the fourteenth century luxury spread from the kings to their courts, and in most places (for instance in Paris in 1331 and again in 1355, in England in 1363, and in Spain in 1380 and 1404) caused rather ineffective sumptuary laws, supposed to limit the use of jewelry in the cause of national economy. All the laws were apparently to small effect, if only because kings had to keep up with each other and, increasingly, with the Dukes of Burgundy. In 1324 Edward II of England had no less than ten crowns.

Joan Evans has catalogued the wedding presents given when Isabella of France married Richard II of England in 1396: the frontlet with spinels, sapphires and pearls from the bridegroom; the jewelled crown from the Duke of Gloucester; a fleur-de-lis fermail from her father; a circlet from the Duc d'Aumale, with brooches from other courtiers; crowns from the citizens of Dover and Canterbury; at Eltham, Richard gave her a collar of diamonds, rubies and pearls, a belt of golden feathers, a set of six jewelled gold buttons and a circlet and a chaplet of pearls; from the Earl Marshal a mirror;

Head reliquary containing the scalp of the Emperor Charlemagne (crowned in Rome, AD 800), bearing the jewelled crown of the Emperor Charles IV which he wore at his coronation in 1349, and given by him to Aachen Cathedral Treasury. Height: 34.5 inches

Reliquary once containing the head of a saint, from Basle Cathedral. Silver gilt, early 13th century. Height: 13.4 inches. British Museum, London

from the City of London, a circlet, and so on.

These early pieces are still so rare that we cannot be sure of their history. It is difficult and probably misleading, too, to be precise about dates; but there are obvious landmarks. The first is the change from the ring brooch in the early Middle Ages to the round brooch and hat badge; ring brooches were hardly made after the fourteenth century, having been the standard dress ornament for several centuries before. Then there is the revival of the finger ring about the thirteenth century which ceases to have the earlier quality of talisman, often for churchmen, and becomes a decorative appurtenance for women as well as men. The loose sleeves after 1400 encouraged a show of gold round the wrist: the bracelet was reborn.

More spectacular, and more reliable as historic evidence, were the big changes in geographical and technical development. Byzantium had transformed enamel from its original function as cheap imitation for precious stones into a thrilling art form. From the ninth to the fourteenth century Byzantine goldsmiths used a full range of colours with the greatest virtuosity. First it was *cloisonné*, with each colour separated by a metal wire, the standard method throughout history; then it was *champlevé* with enamels fused into cavities in the main metal structure; then *basse-taille*, comparable to *champlevé* but in translucent enamel, so that patterning could be carved on the metal beneath, adding a new delicacy of shading to the old silhouette idea. Ever since the marriage between Otto III and his Byzantine empress, links of trade and conquest had strengthened between central Europe and Byzantium, and probably nourished a desire for enamels there too.

The gem-set *cloisonné* tribal style of flat ornament went out of favour after the Merovingians in the eighth century, perhaps because of competition from Byzantine enamellers, even though most surviving Byzantine work is of a later age. Anyway, two great European centres of enamelling came into being from the twelfth till the fifteenth century in the area of the Rhine and Meuse, whose products were rather Byzantine in style, mostly on base metal, and mostly for large-scale altar ornaments. At Limoges the work was much simpler and sometimes on a small scale, including tiny church pyx boxes, and portable altars and pendant crosses. The simple dignity of this first Limoges period yielded to the much more sophisticated enamels in the round—*en ronde bosse*—not much made in Limoges and mostly associated with the rising power of Burgundy in the fourteenth century. Miniature sculptured scenes were decorated all over in a realistic, vivid way, the surface being shiny in contrast to the earlier opaque Limoges masterpieces. Towards the fifteenth century these shiny enamels became translucent, the ultimate in sophisticated perfection.

Precious stones and gold both became much commoner in the fourteenth century, making possible a new craft of gem cutting, in contrast to the old cameo engraving and round stone polishing. Stones henceforth were to glitter. The pyramid-shaped diamond is probably the earliest faceted stone: it is an easy progression from the natural double pyramid form in which the stone is often found. The precision of this pointed diamond shape remained popular right through to the Renaissance, with its special interest in all forms of cupola, pinnacle and tower. As early as the fourteenth century, probably in Bruges, the point was flattened to create a sort of table cut. Louis de Berquem is often but romantically credited with the invention in 1476 of modern schemes for cutting diamonds with their own powder, a claim made by a descendant in 1661.

Agnes Sorel, the renowned French courtesan, mistress of Charles VII about 1440, is, in an equally fictional way but probably with a similar basis in truth, supposed to have made diamonds fashionable at court by being the first woman to wear and talk about them. Stones satisfied the new love of luxury first of Burgundy, several of whose dukes boasted of their individual gems, then of France; but they were not yet common enough to influence design as they came to do in the seventeenth century, still less to overwhelm it as they did in the nineteenth century.

The new freedom, the quest for novel effects, became really urgent in the sixteenth century; but throughout the fifteenth century, the discipline of architectural style, as in stone work, affects jewels as a quietening influence. Architectural details appear in metal as playful whimsy. They are Gothic cusps and pointed arches framing round brooches; flower and flame finials above and around the reliquaries; enamelled screens to represent tapestries behind figures on pendants. Even the flat, four-pointed Tudor arch, so familiar in English cloisters and churches of the perpendicular period, is translated into an elegant shape for the links of neck-laces and bracelets, just as it also ap-peared in the low-cut neckline of the smartest dresses of the time.

The purpose of jewels towards the end of the fifteenth century was to give delight: no longer functional as fas-teners, mostly no longer religious, nor ceremonial, the feelings they convey are fantasy and pleasure. Joan Evans recalls birds modelled of scented clay, imported from Cyprus and placed by the Duke of Burgundy in six golden cages. Perhaps the best representative of the new thought is the golden rose, fragile, useless and charming; many were given away by the popes for services rendered. Giovanni Bartolo made eleven between 1365 and 1395; the city of Siena treasures today the one received in 1458 from Pius II. Others are in the Munich treasury and at Nuremberg. One of three orna-ments given to Henry VIII was seen by

Stowe, who described it as 'forged of fine gold and wrought with branch leaves and flowers resembling roses set in a pot of gold, which pot had three feet of an antique fashion of measure half a pint. . . . The tree was of height half an English yard, and in breadth a foot.'

THE RENAISSANCE

In most of the arts the Renaissance meant good taste. In jewelry the sixteenth-century message is less clear: nearly all the early work perished in the Reforma-tion in the 1530s and during the Thirty Years' War in the 1630s. It seems that jewels of Botticelli's time look better in his paintings than in fact; many of the great artists besides him were goldsmiths, but nothing in metal by them survives. Probably, to judge from the bejewelled women in their paintings, they expressed the new discipline of the rounded arch, of clear and careful proportion, and of restraint. Perhaps jewels were not much worn: and even then were so simple that they were easily broken up to suit

later, more vulgar fashions. Perhaps the very rich brocades and silks arriving from the orient simply left no room for jewels. It is not until the high Renaissance and Mannerist periods from about 1550 to 1630 that we really know what hap-pened.

The obvious aspects of the Renaissance begin to penetrate its jewelry after about 1530, that is after the great age of paint-ing, and these jewels, like the con-temporary paintings, are often clumsy, ill-proportioned and over-ornamented. This was the provocative Mannerist art. The feature of high Renaissance jewelry is, of course, the human figure. Portrait cameos and enamels in profile and full face used a most adventurous range of semi-precious stones—white chalce-dony for carving, for instance, or green heliotrope or red jasper; or blue lapis lazuli for framing; and pearls of all sorts and sizes, preferably big and irregular, known in later ages as 'baroque', used to represent portions of anatomy like the stomach of a person, the body of a horse, and the tail of a griffin—uncouth but fascinating. Classical legends aboun-

Later Renaissance and Mannerist jewelry was often heavy in feeling, with challenging proportions featuring the human figure, like this German mermaid pendant, above, mid-16th century : height : 5.1 inches. British Museum, London

Left Two bejewelled angels' heads by Piero della Francesca. Some of the leading Italian Renaissance painters like Verrocchio and Botticelli were trained as goldsmiths, so jewels in their paintings are presumably accurate: almost none of this simple mid-15th century early Renaissance geometric style jewelry has survived. Brera Gallery, Milan

ded, and involved nude figures, which made a sharp change from the enamelled drapery of the previous century. Men and women, both real and fictional, burst exuberantly out from Renaissance jewels.

One result of the new confidence of the Renaissance was its gorgeous pageantry, and to mount a good procession, one must look one's best. One of the tournaments which Lorenzo de' Medici organized in the square of Santa Croce at Florence has been recorded:

For the joust Lorenzo held in honour of his mistress, Lucrezia Donati, on 7 February 1469, no less an artist than Verrocchio painted his standard. Lorenzo rode into the square in a surcoat with a red and white silk cape, and a scarf embroidered with roses, some fresh and some withered, surrounding his motto, *Le Temps Revient*, picked out in pearls. A plume of gold filigree set with diamonds and rubies stood from his black velvet cap, to display a pearl of exceptional value. For the combat he wore a velvet doublet embroidered with golden lilies, and a helmet with three blue feathers replaced the jewelled cap. His shield was emblazoned with the three gold lilies of France, the privilege of bearing which had been granted to his father in 1465, and in the centre shone the great Medici diamond.

The royal courts continued to expand. Sales were offered to Henry VIII, as to every other known patron: in 1546 Vaughan, Henry's agent in Antwerp, wrote to Paget in London to tell him of a pendant formed of a large table diamond set in scrolls and masks, upheld by a satyr and a nymph, with a pendant pearl below. But the reply came back: 'This time is unmeet to pester the king with jewels, who already has more than most of the princes of Christendom.'

The world's first museums were started, and to our eyes they must have looked like a random assembly of knickknacks. They were in fact often called cabinets of curios. One of the earliest was St Mark's, 'the most glorious shrine in Venice'; the cathedral was the unimpressive San Pietro di Castello, St Mark's being almost more important as the ducal chapel. Its treasury was incidentally a collection of pious relics, and, more prominently, a collection of trophies, gifts, and booty testifying not to the city's piety, but to its conquests and prestige. The reception of a visiting ambassador or a political allegory played at the Doge's palace were typical events. In Venice, more than in most places,

the repeated sumptuary laws proved ineffective.

The astonishing surge of activity which characterized the Renaissance can possibly be explained in philosophical terms, but what mattered much more, at least for jewelry, was patronage. In Florence, where the new ideal of civilization began, bankers had a world-wide business in the fourteenth and fifteenth centuries, and the florin was a distinctly hard currency : the Bardi and the Peruzzi lost 1,365,000 florins to England in 1388 and still not only recovered, but earned immortality through Giotto's famous frescoes in their chapels in S. Croce church at Florence. Philippe de Commynes says Edward IV of England owed his crown to Florentine finance; the Strozzi brothers, builders of the famous palace, were behind much French enterprise, with branches in Lyons, Venice and Rome.

Wealth in the hands not of an old, complacent aristocracy but of the driving merchant oligarchs, foremost among them Lorenzo the Magnificent's father, Cosimo—this was what made possible more widespread luxury. In 1490 Isabella d'Este went as a bride to Mantua Castle in a triumphant carriage designed by Ercole de' Roberti who had also painted the thirteen chests that followed with her trousseau. In 1491 Beatrice d'Este was married at Pavia Castle, before which messengers from her bridegroom in Milan arrived daily at her home in Ferrara bringing gifts: for instance, a much talked-of necklace of pearls with 'flowerets' of gold, embellished with drop rubies, pearls and emeralds. The Master of Ceremonies arranged for the bride's journey, anxious that she should bring many jewelled gowns. In the event, everyone found her eighty-four new dresses excessive; they hung in a great room which seemed to her mother, Leonora, like a sacristy hung with all the canonicals.

At the Este court the duchess Leonora brought to Ferrara tapestry makers from Florence and Milan and embroiderers from Spain, and her collection (though often pawned to pay for her husband's wars) was deemed the best in Italy. Duke Ercole d'Este of Ferrara, by contrast, was so cold and reserved that he got the nickname 'The North Wind', but it came naturally in those wealthy times to use as an alternative nickname 'The Diamond'.

Later Renaissance jewelry became

fantastic and exhuberant, as we can now see in some of the finest princely treasuries. Hard stones—jasper, heliotrope, crystal and many others—became an obsession. The Holy Roman Emperor Rudolph II in Prague, the King of France in Paris and the Grand Duke of Tuscany in Florence, each set up stone-cutting and polishing workshops; others were at Milan, Augsburg and Freiburg in Bresgau. Every self-respecting principality wanted to compete: Dresden, Innsbruck, Berlin, Prague, St Petersburg, Copenhagen, Madrid and so on – each had its self-esteem, so each needed its *Kunst-und-wunderkammer*, its rarities of all sorts.

There is a kind of swashbuckling magnificence about Renaissance inventories. No reasons are offered, no religious or political overtones: it was simply natural for a Renaissance prince to live richly, to indulge himself to the utmost. In matters both spiritual and intellectual (Henry VIII for instance was a good composer) his accomplishment would probably far outclass the achievement in any of those pale ghosts called courts today. So the number and size of the jewels should not surprise—they were only one of very many expressions of gusto. Any human aspiration was considered admirable, but art and antiquity were especially so. Jewels with their newly invented designs, and their everlasting materials, represented both. The monarchs of Europe loved them.

France may have been the most lavish court for jewelry in the 1530s. When Catherine de' Medici arrived in Paris in 1533 to marry the future King Henry II her dowry included what Brantôme called the most beautiful pearls in the world; she loved jewels and used them as queen, then as regent, then as queen mother. At his coronation in 1548 Henry IV no longer wore the traditional fleur-de-lis clasp for his mantle, but a cross of nine great diamonds, five table stones for the cross and a round stone and three lance-shaped ones for the foot, set in gold with coloured enamels, that Francis I had had made.

The Electress Anna of Saxony left (on her death in 1585) five treasure-boxes, each of which had seven divisions for her bracelets, necklaces, rings and belts. One can still see today in the Munich National Museum several examples of this sort of box, a cross between a modern safe, a family shrine and a filing cabinet.

In architecture and painting one can trace the progress of the Renaissance style, beginning with the great pioneers: the goldsmith Ghiberti won the Florence baptistry doors competition in 1401, and Brunelleschi went from Florence to Rome with his sixteen-year-old friend Donatello in 1403 to study the ruins there. But jewels offer no such clear chronology. They were very international, partly because they are so easily portable and they formed such an important part of every dowry. Interdynastic marriages were in those days the chief political weapon: if you wanted to enlarge your kingdom, the best way was often for your son to marry the daughter of the neighbouring dependency, and each time this happened a load of jewels would travel across Europe, usually recorded badly, if at all. For example, nobody really knows how many of the smaller Renaissance jewels in the Medici treasury in the Pitti Palace, Florence, are actually Italian, and how many German, brought south by the Elector Palatine from Düsseldorf when he married into Florence. Jewels moved around more than paintings and, surprisingly in view of their high value, they were identified much less.

It was not only the product, but the producer too, who wandered. Most of Henry VIII's jewelers were foreign immigrants: many of Elizabeth's were English, like Hilliard; but Spilman, the chief, was German. Arnold Lulls, court jeweler to James I of England, was Dutch; and Corvinianus Saur, court jeweler to the great contemporary Christian IV of Denmark, was Bavarian. Erasmus Hornick, perhaps the most stimulating and original of these mid-sixteenth-century artists, worked in Antwerp, then Nuremberg, then Prague. The best patrons attracted to their capitals the best artist-goldsmiths available. Many of these seem in fact to have been German: perhaps their small home principalities were not such an attractive magnet as the big national patrons could provide.

The main reason for jewels being so international was, however, simply the invention of printing. Engraved pattern books containing sometimes dozens, sometimes even hundreds of designs for jewels or for details, were published during the sixteenth and seventeenth centuries in the biggest metalwork centres. Germany and the Low Countries were the main sources for designs as for craftsmen; Nuremberg and Augsburg were pre-eminent later. Later Paris and London and Holland followed, each with

Renaissance queens and princes had very large jewelry collections to judge by their inventories and their surviving jewelry caskets; here a noblewoman, sometimes called Diane de Poitiers, Henry II's mistress, is choosing her jewels. School of Fontainebleau, mid-16th century. Dijon Museum

named contributions. Through these books it became possible for the provinces to copy the capital, for the noble to ape the royal, internationally as well as in their own country. The modern idea of 'keeping up with the Joneses' had become infinitely easier to realize because these printed sheets showed, to anyone who cared to buy them, what the latest foreign fashion might be.

The designers for the first time emerge as names, even though rather humble, shadowy creatures. This obscurity remains despite fascinating recent detective work, marrying up some original drawings with their corresponding jewels often hundreds of miles away. John Hayward, Arthur Grimwade, Yvonne Hackenbroch, Charles Oman and others have given at least some identity to previously naked ciphers. The artist-goldsmiths made some progress from being simple artisans to being recognized creators: Virgil Solis of Nuremberg was one, probably designer not goldsmith.

The French court jeweler, François du Jardin, has been resurrected by Yvonne Hackenbroch: he, a Catholic, probably achieved success (he was the queen's goldsmith 1569–75) because of the expulsion of the Protestant goldsmiths. He collaborated with other court artists who must have helped in his complex creations of cameos, miniatures and scholarly allegories in enamelled gold.

The master hand at court may have been Etienne Delaune, born in 1518, Henry II's medallist from 1552, turned engraver in 1561 and being Protestant fled to Strasbourg after the massacre of Saint Bartholomew in 1572, finishing in Augsburg. His meticulous, confident ornament set the tone for French work until the 1600s. Some of his drawings are in the Ashmolean Museum, Oxford. Other collections of designs are Jakob Mores' at the Hamburg Museum and Arnold Lulls' at London's Victoria and Albert.

Probably the best documentary source, from which drawings may be compared with jewels, is in Munich. This became under Albrecht V one of the great centres of art activity. The court painter, Hans Miehlich illustrated in detail the whole of Anna's collection, much of it no doubt wedding presents; none of it now, alas, survives. But the pictures do give a unique idea of southern German taste at the time: the frontispiece shows the duke and duchess playing chess, perhaps a hint by Miehlich of the

duke's habit of settling gaming debts to his wife by giving her jewels. One jeweler whose work became prominent in Munich has been identified by Yvonne Hackenbroch as Mathias Zuendt of Nuremberg, whose engraved designs remained popular in Augsburg and Munich despite Nuremberg's Protestantism. Zuendt's heavy, solid, congested conceptions are quite distinctive: the gold backs of the jewels were a clear unit, the stones in front looking, and sometimes even actually being, separate, ready for exchange if necessary.

Another very personal style, this time of enamels, and allegorical figures at play, belonged to Jost Amman (1539–91) of Zurich who settled in Nuremberg in 1560, probably attracted by Virgil Solis's success as an illustrator. On Solis's death two years later, Amman got his job with the Frankfurt publisher Feyerabend, producing illustrations of all sorts, biblical, historical, literary and domestic. In 1577 he exchanged his citizenship of Zurich for Nuremberg.

The Wittelsbach court jeweler at Munich and Landshut after 1567, again brilliantly re-instated as an artist rather than just a name by Yvonne Hackenbroch, was the Italian, Giovanni Battista Scolari. Daniel Mignot the Huguenot, published a most fluent series of jewel designs at Augsburg 1593–6; obsessed by miniature grotesques and satyrs and his almost over-delicate ornament, his low relief is a bridge between the big gold and enamel figure jewels of the sixteenth century and the smaller, flatter stone-set pieces of the seventeenth century. It is probable that these engravers actually made nothing themselves, but their designs certainly dominated style even in such a rich centre as Dresden where from 1575 to 1595 some of the work of the Saxon court jeweler, Hieronimus Krause, seems to have come from Augsburg, as does also that of Gabriel Gipfel, his famous successor.

Some of the wider political scene was relevant, too. The terrible sack of Rome in 1527, for instance, by Charles V, and the previous French invasions of Italy, must help to explain the scarcity of early Renaissance jewels, which were probably the best; they also explain the northern awareness of southern charm—for a century or more, Italian fashions dominated France and most other northern centres too. Then in 1576 there was the brutal sack of Antwerp which had developed its own school of Mannerist paintings, and produced the finest metalwork anywhere from the time of the fifteenth-century Burgundian empire. Hornick and the other Flanders craftsmen had to move whether they liked it or not. On a vast scale, there was the import of gold and emeralds from Spanish South America, of gold and presumably jade from Mexico; raw materials from now on become more and more lavish.

Then there were the family events which, jewelry still being a court art, determined production: Mary Tudor of England, for instance, having plain habits, discouraged what Henry VIII had only begun to create, a nucleus of English genius in metal. Rudolph II of Prague, becoming Holy Roman Emperor (1576–1612), conversely created a sort of hothouse for goldsmiths in the Hradčany Castle, bringing the best people there from all over Europe and inaugurating there new standards of perfection in gold enamelling with multi-coloured arabesques, gold carved in low relief, stone and rock-crystal cutting, and, of course, the parallel and then highly aristocratic craft of the armourer and gunsmith. Ambras Castle near Innsbruck, although not a home for craftsmen, for a shorter time and on a lesser scale, became a collector's dream under the Archduke Ferdinand of Tyrol.

Finally, there were two great cataclysms. The Reformation of the 1530s led in the Protestant countries to the destruction of marvellous church treasures, and the rapid substitution for them of secular ornaments for the new rich—often badges of office to imply a legitimacy which probably was rather shaky. At Canterbury Cathedral in England, for instance, the shrine of St Thomas Becket yielded two huge chests of jewels, each needing six or eight men to move it. We may guess at the wealth grabbed from all the bigger shrines by what remains in some of the smaller: the Virgin of the Pillar, for example, representing the pillar on which the Virgin appeared to St James the Greater on his missionary journey in AD 40 at Saragossa Cathedral, many of whose pieces were sold to the Victoria and Albert Museum in 1870, was surrounded by some 550 pieces. Santa Agata in Catania Cathedral, a thirteenth-century reliquary bust, is festooned with so many jewels given by the grateful and the faithful over the centuries that only some of her face is visible, her neck, shoulders and head

being wholly encrusted with finery, a uniquely evocative display.

The second upheaving event was the Thirty Years' War which devastated Europe. The court jewelry of the Renaissance became a thing of the past, yielding, except in Spain, to smaller pieces for poorer people.

The earlier Renaissance pieces, probably made in Italy, were those with the largest figures. By 1550 the imagery of fantasy was paramount: birds and griffins and soldiers and saints, all distorted to fit the composition, often to use existing odd-shaped pearls and stones without cutting. Some places like southern Germany specialized in this sort of joke adaptation of materials. Others, like Venice and England, seem to have expressed their maritime energy by using many jewels depicting galleons and ships, more decorative than seaworthy. In Spain great bird pendants were widely used, with assertive enamels and pendant pearls. Perhaps inspired by the pre-Columbian cast gold condors from Veraguas, these eagles and parrots and even lizards and frogs, which had a certain magic in Central America, invigorate Spanish jewels as the human figure does Italian and German. In the northern countries monogram brooches made of the owner's initials, cameo portraits which had started in Italy, and miniature painted portraits, like those of Nicholas Hilliard or Isaac Oliver, became very popular: one wore one's lover's or ruler's emblem. Chain necklaces were enjoyed up in the north. In Spain heavy gold work and emeralds and solid size were the results of the New World bullion. All these examples are of course generalizations.

The convincing theory has been suggested that very big jewels, as now in India or the Middle East or then in Spain, indicate silent, suppressed womanhood: muted by convention, a woman has to speak through her jewels. Certainly in those countries today where most women still live in purdah, such as the Yemen or the northern Punjab, big jewels are festooned all over the head almost like water dripping from a shower. Whether or not Spanish Renaissance women were less talkative than they are today, their jewels, anyway by 1650, had a distinct national character, heavy, big, with rhythmical, almost monotonous, compositions, revealing large areas of gold, large emeralds and stones, and only small flashes of enamel,

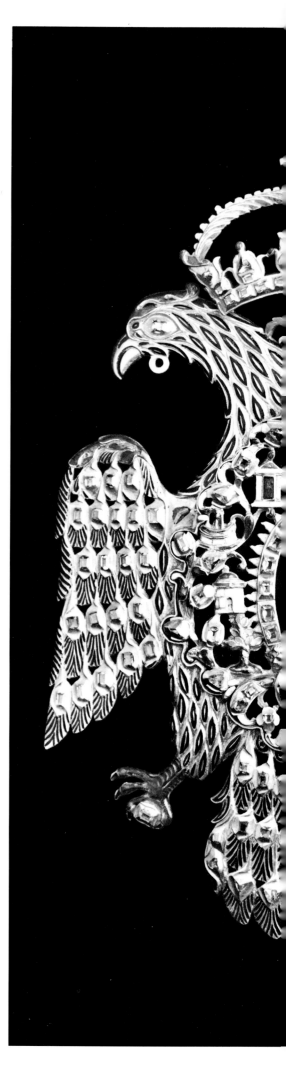

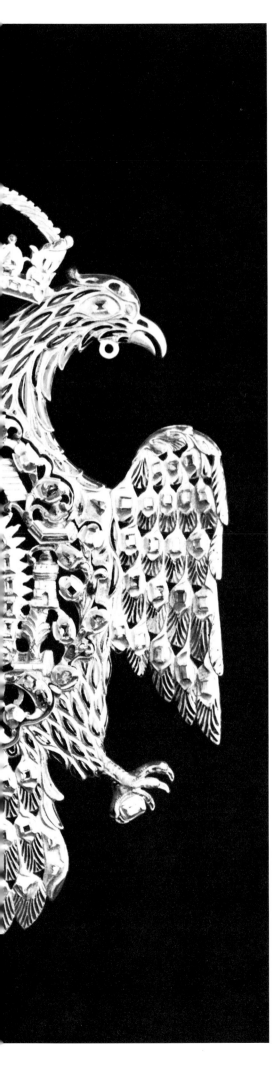

only a few human figures. Spanish dress was, of course, extremely heavy and formal, and Spanish manners too: ponderous jewels are especially associated with seventeenth- and eighteenth-century Spain.

Another Spanish preference, no doubt related to the terrifying power of the Inquisition, was the Christian token. It could be a simple gold cross picked out with flat-topped emeralds, some round, some square, deeply embedded in the metal. Or the cross could be composed of irregular square blocks of gold alternating with plain enamel and with the instruments of the crucifixion, nails, scourge, hammer, Judas' coins, even the soldiers' dice, painted in all their frightening detail. Sometimes these objects are cut *intaglio* into garnets or gold, themselves being then picked out in enamel. Spanish jewels, as the portraits show, were worn in splendid profusion. Spain remained feudal longer than other countries, and its feudal families, probably because of the American conquests, got richer too, compared with, for instance, England or Germany. It is tempting but probably misleading to identify rich jewels, as in Coello's portraits, with Roman Catholicism, and simple ones, as worn by German merchants' wives, with Protestantism. The distinction is class, not religion.

Technically, it would be idle to claim any advance in jewelry during the Renaissance: the goldsmiths' craft had had no technical limitations for thousands of years, unlike painting to which the Renaissance brought perspective, or music with its new form of opera. The big change during the sixteenth century was the growth in popularity of the precious stone which may now seem a move backward rather than forward, because it meant a decline in the jeweler's personal fantasy in favour of the new anonymous mineral glitter. Stones were more accessible than ever before, emeralds coming from South America, coloured stones from the east, diamonds from the huge markets at Golconda and the new mines around. Stone cutting and polishing were admired as a new science, the square table cut giving way to the subtler rose cut in the first half of the seventeenth century; the rounded cabochon stone was almost displaced by the sharper geometry of the lapidary. Benvenuto Cellini and Nicholas Hilliard, had both, in their sixteenth-century technical treatises, praised the

Portrait pendants were very popular in the Renaissance, often being worn by courtiers, or a lover of the subject depicted. Above Burgundian medallion, c. 1440, in gold with enamel and carved chalcedony, probably the portrait of Duke Philip the Good of Burgundy or Robert de Masmines; the chain and order of the Golden Fleece are just visible being worn. Diameter: 3.5 inches. Residenz Museum, Munich

Left *Ecclesiastical gold jewel in the form of the double-headed eagle of the Hapsburgs. The front is set with diamonds; in the centre is the figure of the Virgin of the Immaculate Conception, surrounded by emblems and symbols. Presented to the Convent at Caceres by King Philip II of Spain. Spanish, c. 1595*

Above *Finger ring, gold and enamel, with fashionable pointed diamonds. Perhaps Italian, c. 1570*

Right *Head of very large bird brooch (12.7 inches long) of gold and garnets. Some of the cloisons of this piece would have been filled with stones, stolen by the peasants who found this Petrossa treasure in 1837; others left empty in the style of perforation invented by the Romans—opus interrasile. 4th century AD. National Museum of Antiquities, Bucharest*

Below *Painted enamels from Limoges were much admired as table and wall ornaments. Here, Solomon turns to idolatry: probably the back of a small wall mirror; comparable enamels, usually of a religious nature, were sometimes worn as pendants. Limoges, 16th century. Walters Art Gallery, Baltimore*

stone cutter and the precise colour of polished stones: they can hardly have foreseen that within a mere century stones would almost displace not only tiny sculptures in jewelry, but enamels too.

At Limoges, an astonishing school of local painted enamels sprang up. In the twelfth and thirteenth centuries Limoges enamels with their dark mysterious slabs of colour were distinctive, but similar to the finer contemporary Mosan school which also produced opaque colours separated by small areas of metal showing through.

These early medieval styles were popular, and both may still have been trying to fulfil the original function of enamels: to give the varied colour of stones, without the expense. Now, in the fifteenth century, Limoges broke free and started an independent idiom; this time of painted pictorial enamel. Again, as in the Middle Ages, very few jewels were made, and these almost all either roundels painted with religious scenes or crucifix pendants. The palette, black, mauve and grey on white, was limited and distinctive; the subject matter, mostly derived from classical legends or Christianity, was almost as complicated as that on ancient Greek vases. As in the Middle Ages, copper was still normally used, though silver frames were common later in the sixteenth century. The French seem to have been the main patrons—this was a specialized product for a narrow clientele, comparable to the superb gold and silver inlaid pistols of the small town of Doune in Scotland, which acquired world fame in the early eighteenth century, or the beautiful scenes in pierced gold and green glass from Patubkar near Udaipur in India, so popular for arms and jewels over the centuries. Limoges enamels were the last great outburst of geographical individuality in jewelry; henceforth the speed of travel overcame all local boundaries.

The Renaissance was a time of unparalleled fantasy for jewels, with not only more variety in the styles, but also in the types of piece. The complete outfit or 'parure' of necklace, bracelet, hair ornament and earrings became by the seventeenth century a sign of success. Earrings, hardly worn in the Middle Ages, were increasingly common, like the *carcanet* (short necklace), the *cotière* (chain and pendant), and the *abillement* (suite). Hat badges and brooches were

hardly seen after 1570—complicated medieval head-dress had given way to flowing hair. Scented jewels or pomanders and flea furs to attract fleas often hung from the belt of the mistress of the house, a reminder that Renaissance enlightenment had not yet spread to hygiene.

The main developments in jewelry, however, were so big and so obvious that they are often forgotten: women quite rapidly began to wear more jewels than men, steadily translating jewelry from a set show piece into a flexible instrument of fashion which might be worn anywhere, any time. By 1700 most wealthy women probably wore more jewels than their husbands; among men it was only the greatest kings who wore big jewels at all.

Although diamonds and precious stones had always been treasured, it was not until trade with the east steadied, in the seventeenth century, that stones by their quantity alone began to oust the enameller and even to some extent the goldsmith. When the Duke of Buckingham, one of the richest men in Europe, went on official embassy to Madrid in 1623 to find a wife for King Charles I of England, he could hardly stand up under the weight of diamonds sewn all over his clothes. This was a problem which strained the physique of royalty with increasing frequency in the next century. Big stones had become the best way to impress. The stone dealer and the gem cutter started to inhibit artists; mineral values began to seem more important than the vision of pure art.

RICHES AND ELEGANCE

After the devastating Thirty Years' War (1618–48) European jewelry settled down first to a sort of baroque fatness, advertising that the wearer had survived the war, was no longer fighting or starving, was indeed becoming rich. All the Renaissance innovations continued: the named designer, the engraved pattern books, even the dominance of court patronage. But as civilization was reborn, so jewelry steadily became a mark not so much of wealth, but of wealth tamed, that is elegance.

One of the most extraordinary royal courts was France under Louis XIV. His mother, Anne of Austria, passed to him her own love of jewels; as a child, his toys were of precious metals, his model

Detail of large brooch in the form of a stylized bird from the Petrossa treasure. Gold inlaid with precious stones. Height: 5.9 inches. 4th century AD. National Museum of Antiquities, Bucharest

soldiers being made by Merlin, the court jeweler, from silver, with guns of gold. As king, he housed his principal craftsmen in his first royal palace at the Louvre and he always used jewels to show his own pre-eminence. That the *Roi Soleil* did not like competition was evident when with childish jealousy and unforgivable brutality, he sacked the brilliant Fouquet, and stole from Fouquet all the country's best talent. Nancy Mitford writes that at the opening of Fouquet's new palace, Vaux-le-Vicomte, in 1661 the king,

. . . with mingled admiration and fury, examined the establishment in all its sumptuous detail and decided that Fouquet's ostentation (*luxe insolent et audacieux*) was unsuitable for a subject and intolerable for a minister of finance. He did not modify this view as the evening wore on and such gifts as diamond tiaras and saddle-horses were distributed to the guests. Louis returned Fouquet's hospitality by clapping him in gaol and we seldom hear of other people giving parties for the King.

When the king married Marie-Thérèse he gave her a bouquet of emeralds with diamonds. His mistress, Madame de Montespan, was less fortunate. She made her fortune on percentages taken from meat and tobacco sold in Paris, but all the same she had her price. As Nancy Mitford drily remarks, 'She never would take jewels from the King. May this have been because the ones he lent her were even larger and finer than any he would have given away?'

Louis' second bride, Maintenon, 'had one great advantage in her husband's eyes—she did not care for diamonds, so that he was able to plaster his own clothes with all he had'. Men still often outshone women. Somebody asked the young Duc de Chartres if he was fond of dressing up. He replied, 'I like it better than Madame does, but not as much as Monsieur.'

Memoirs of the time are full of jewels. Madame de Sévigné refers to the Princesse de Soubise's emerald earrings, used as a green light signal to show the king that her husband was out of the way. She writes of Madame de Montespan being 'covered with diamonds', such a brilliant divinity that one's eyes were dazzled. When France was almost ruined by war, many people thought Louis XIV should have sold his diamonds. But he 'would never do that—he liked to see the women of his family covered with them, more covered as the

financial situation deteriorated, as a sort of defiance to the foreign visitors and ambassadors'.

Saint-Simon shed his usual lurid light on the strange proceedings at the French court. He wrote of the arrival of the Persian ambassador at Versailles:

The long gallery and all the state apartments were superbly decorated . . . no one was allowed in without full court dress. The king lent a set of pearl and diamond ornaments to M. le Duc du Maine for the occasion, and one of coloured stones to M. le Comte de Toulouse. M. le Duc d'Orleans wore a blue velvet coat embroidered in a mosaic pattern, overlaid with diamonds and pearls, which was a triumph of magnificence and good taste. . . . [The king] wore a dress of black and gold with the order outside, a fashion that was copied by those few knights who usually wore it beneath their coats. The coat itself was embroidered with all the finest diamonds in the crown jewels, to the tune of more than 12,500,000 livres. He stooped with their weight, and looked worn-out, thin, and vastly ill-favoured, as he seated himself upon the throne. . . . [When the ambassador arrived his] suite seemed miserable in every way, and the supposed ambassador highly embarrassed and very ill-dressed. The presents were beneath contempt.

Of his great friend the regent, whose diamond graces the Apollo Gallery in the Louvre today, Saint-Simon gives one of the first real insights into a big jewelry purchase in an almost modern manner:

By an extraordinary chance a worker at the Mogal Mines found a way of hiding a prodigiously large diamond up his bottom and, even more marvellous, of reaching the sea with it and embarking without being subjected to the normal precaution of being purged and washed. . . . Having arrived in Europe with his diamond, he showed it to several princes for whom it was too expensive. . . . A crystal model was made in England; the man, the diamond, and the perfect model then went back to Law [the Scots financier in France] who proposed a sale to the regent for the king. The king was terrified by the price; Law, who had big ideas, came in consternation to me with the model. I agreed with Law that it was unworthy of *la grandeur du roi de France* [the grandeur of the King of France] to be put off by the price. . . . The regent however emphasized that the state of his finances was a real obstacle. He was afraid of the blame which such a considerable purchase would arouse, at a time when one could hardly pay for necessities and so many people had to be left in suffering. I praised this sentiment but told him that one must not apply to the greatest king in Europe as if he were a private individual: the honour of the crown was at stake. . . . Law, before speaking to him, had emphasized to the merchant the impossibility of getting the asking price, the sadness of cutting the diamond into several pieces. . . . The deal was done. He was paid interest until he could get his full two millions, with other stones as security. The Duc d'Orleans was pleased to be proved wrong: the public applauded him for his beautiful and unique acquisition. The diamond was called the Regent. It is the size of a *reine-claude* apricot, almost round, of a depth suitable to its volume, perfect white, flawless, with admirable river and weight more than 500 grains. I congratulated myself for having persuaded the regent to make such an illustrious buy.

The distinction between *orfèvre* (goldsmith), *joaillier* (court jeweler) and *bijoutier* (small worker and jeweler) was not yet clear. Gold was as popular as diamonds. It would be unrealistic to write of eighteenth-century French goldsmiths without mentioning the snuff box, one of the few amalgams of craft and art which really got over the artificial hurdle erected by connoisseurs and snobs. These tiny boxes were as much treasured as the most fashionable paintings by Boucher, Fragonard and Watteau. The regent naturally had one of the best collections—when he died in 1723 it was worth over a million livres and he was one of several people supposed to have owned a different box for each day of the year. These boxes may have evolved from another sort of container—

the *drageoir*. Saint-Simon says that the king only took baths when in love; otherwise he just wiped his face with a scented handkerchief and dabbled his fingers in rose water and orange flower water: no wonder he had to keep with him a gold *drageoir* filled with aniseed! The scent dispenser may partly explain the later fashion for snuff: one marvellous container led to another.

Louis XIV's jeweler, Jean Pitan, succeeded from 1676 to 1714 by Pierre le Tessier de Montarsy, supplied the king with boxes containing suitable portraits, often for gifts. The royal appetite was regularly whetted by the arrival back from India of the adventurous stone merchants and travellers, Jean-Baptiste Tavernier and Jean Chardin. Jewels even went into battle: for instance at Fontenoy in 1748, where the king and the dauphin, covered with gold lace, their great diamond St Esprits glittering on their breasts, took up a position at daybreak. Women at court normally wore thickly embroidered satin skirts over enormous panniers, short muslin sleeves, and small white feathers, held in place on their lightly powdered hair with diamonds.

The French royal family was all-powerful. Compared with actual royalty the needs of their mistresses were

modest, though they hardly sound so today. In 1815 William Beckford wrote of Madame de Pompadour (Louis XV's mistress), 'No lady of the old or new world has ever been a better judge of the rare, the beautiful and the fine than Madame de Pompadour . . . I can assure you that Madame de Pompadour was the finest connoisseur of "objets d'art" and curiosities in the whole of Europe.' Nancy Mitford assesses her as the most beautiful of all the royal ladies, possibly the person who collected together the largest number of beautiful possessions in the whole of history.

When Madame de Pompadour was dying the king presented the queen with a beautiful gold snuff box with a jewelled watch set in the lid. The whole court knew that it had been originally intended for Madame de Pompadour.

Jewels were used for all sorts of intimate reasons. Pompadour made the king reward with a diamond necklace Madame d'Amblimont, 'the little heroine', for repulsing the royal advances. On another occasion the king nearly died in Pompadour's bed; after being rescued, without any scandal, he gave money to the maid and the doctor concerned, and to Pompadour herself a beautiful clock and a snuff box with his portrait on the lid. On the birth of a son

The early eighteenth-century courts of Europe spent fortunes on adorning their kings and noblemen. Far left and right two silver gilt sword hilts, with brilliant diamonds and emeralds, Paris, c. 1740, by Gouers, formerly part of suites of the Order of St George. Residenz Museum, Munich. Centre three walking-stick handles in wood, gold, crystal, tortoiseshell, enamel and stones, c. 1700. Grünes Gewölbe, Dresden

to the king, Pompadour gave him a diamond aigrette.

She was herself not only the most charming woman of her age, but also, unexpectedly, a craftsman, an engraver. She was constantly active over her possessions:

. . . thanking for cameos and asking for a piece of the 'True Cross', and the price of a rose diamond in which to set it—finally she put it in a crystal heart with a cross of rose diamonds . . .

Lazare Duvaux, who supplied her with bibelots, was called in to mend her crucifix. Among such items on her account with him, as a seal in the form of a negro's head, decorated with rubies and diamonds, a transparent blind in Italian taffetas, painted with bouquets and garlands, a chocolate box in rock crystal, we find a vessel for holy water in Vincennes china, decorated with cherubs, on black velvet with a gilded frame and destined for the Holy Father whom she loved so madly.

At the end of her life she sold her diamonds to endow the cottage hospital she had built. Jewels bulked large in her will: Nancy Mitford records that she left

her new diamond watch to the Maréchale de Mirepoix; portrait of Alexandrine framed in diamonds to Madame du Roure; a silver box set in diamonds to the Duchesse de Choiseul; a ring of pink and white diamonds set in a green bow and 'a cornelian box he has often

admired', to the Duc de Gontaut; a diamond the colour of aquamarine to the Duc de Choiseul; an emerald necklace to Madame d'Amblimont.

Voltaire, always a breath of fresh air, and an observer of Paris life under Louis xv, fell in love with Madame du Châtelet, who at her home at Céry 'glittered with diamonds like an operatic Venus'. Once this brilliant woman, one of the great scientific brains of her age,

showed Madame de Grafigny her jewels which are more beautiful than Madame de Richelieu's. Funny thing, when she was at Craon in the old days she didn't possess so much as a tortoise-shell snuff-box. Now she has at least twenty, some of gold with precious stones and some in the new fashion of enamel on gold which is so expensive, as well as jasper and diamond watches, jewelled *étuis*, rings with rare stones, in fact no end of trinkets. Madame de Grafigny was amazed, for the du Châtelets had never been rich.

Another jewel-loving court frequented by Voltaire was Prussia. King Frederick the Great's tastes were fastidious: he started a china factory; he developed the mines of Silesia in the 1770s, relying on Saxon help—his new minister was the Saxon, Heinz; he encouraged Swiss watchmakers to come from Neuchâtel to Berlin. He put Prussia in the forefront of rococo inspiration, with his

elegant building programme at Sans Souci. But his prime obsession was the gold box, a hobby which he probably inherited from his mother. His visitors complained that his fine furniture and clothes were continually stained with snuff. He is supposed to have owned more than 1500 boxes, and he, more than any of his craftsmen, is credited with the big diamonds and the generous, bulbous shape, for table more than pocket use, known as the Hohenzollern box. The Berlin crown jewelers, Jordan and Baudesson, supplied the boxes from 1752 to 1755: many were made by Jean Guillaume George Kruger, born in London in 1728, then working in Paris.

Count Brühl, one of the leading connoisseurs of the time, had over three hundred suits of clothes, each with a gold mounted walking stick and snuff box and each with its duplicate available for a complete change after the messiness of dinner. Frederick the Great dismissed Brühl as Prime Minister saying he had so many periwigs and so little head.

If Paris was the most centralized court and Berlin the most warlike, then Dresden, the capital of Saxony, may, even in this opulent company, have been the richest and the most cosmopolitan. The Saxon Elector, Frederick Augustus I was a big man. Called 'Augustus the Strong'

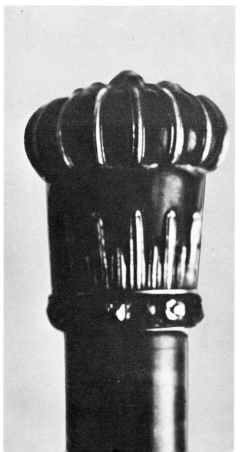

because he could bend in his hands a horseshoe or a ducat piece, he was also king of Poland as Frederick Augustus II. He filled his beautiful city with artists, musicians, actors, singers and dancers; so many immigrants were Italian builders that they formed their own colony, 'the Italian village'. Augustus undertook some of the most advanced building schemes in Europe, the leading artists being Pöppelmann, architect, and Permoser, sculptor; and he set up Europe's first factory for hard-paste porcelain, first in Dresden, where the process was discovered by Böttger, then in the privacy of Meissen castle, where the technical secrets were preserved as a Saxon monopoly for thirty years, giving immortality to the Kändler family of modellers.

In metal, Augustus nourished Johann Melchior Dinglinger, one of the truly great names. He worked with his brothers Georg Friedrich, the enameller, Georg Christoph and his son Johann Friedrich, the stone cutter; all were his partners. Johann Melchior, the chief, started at the very bottom as an apprentice, and rose during his long life to be one of the rich citizens of Dresden, building there a beautiful rococo house, alas destroyed in the 1945 bombing, except for its courtyard fountain. He must have been a brilliant all-rounder: extremely imaginative, in some ways the most advanced designer in Europe—it may have been he, rather than the French, who first grasped the nature of rococo; technically flawless, his jewels and table ornaments are probably the most elaborate and delicate of their time, and that is very high praise. He must have been a good team man because he worked with other leading Dresden artists like Permoser the sculptor, and he must have been a good time keeper to have kept his exacting clients happy for so many decades; one of his most intricate concoctions is the gold and porcelain tea-set perched on and among an *épergne*, which had to be 'shipped' by sledge right across central Europe in mid-winter from Dresden to Warsaw.

The decisive feature in the Dinglingers' life was patronage. The Court of Saxony stimulated art and spent vast fortunes not only on big sapphires and diamonds and stones from the local Erzgebirge mountain mines; that may have been good banking policy—money spent on stones is always a fair investment. But they also lavished their

wealth on fantastic workmanship whose only purpose was to give pleasure. The Dinglingers made sensational cups and jugs for the table, and jewels, combining size and purity of stones, brilliance of invention and perfection of craftsmanship, to decorate Augustus both by day and by night, when out of doors hunting or when at court. They dazzled not only his political visitors, but his enormous harem of lady friends, too. There are nine great suites of jewelry for Augustus, the feature of whose patronage was variety: he encouraged architecture and music as well as jewelry (to these his successor added one of the world's great picture collections). Dinglinger's most original work may have been the allegorical, useless table pieces like his 'Bath of Diana', or his fascinating miniature model 'The Great Moghul' showing the Indian emperor Aurangzeb at court. But his most numerous products were jewels.

The Dresden gold box makers each achieved their own personal style, mostly based on the exotic semi-precious stones like agate and carnelian from the Erzgebirge mines. Many of these were owned, like those round Cracow, by Polish noblemen. One version of Dresden's sudden blossoming is that Augustus brought to Saxony the wealth of Poland when he became king there. Anyway, with extraordinary enlightenment he realized that his prosperity depended on the miners in these nearby mountain ranges and treated them as minor aristocrats, giving them technical schools, a frock-coated uniform, which is still worn today in the mining region of Clausthal-Zellerfeld, and sophisticated

tools which rivalled the English pioneering in the Cornish tin mines. Throughout history miners had been slaves and prisoners of war, beaten with the whip right from ancient Egypt to Mount Potosi in Spanish colonial South America, from ancient Greece to Louis XIV's France. Augustus, unlike the mine proprietors of Wales or northern England a hundred years later, and unlike many mine owners even today, knew that mine workers, though their job might be the toughest in the country, were fundamental to it, and he nurtured them accordingly. The Green Vault (*Grünes Gewölbe*) Treasury remains today, and so do some of the buildings, as astonishing testimony to Augustus' generosity to art.

The Saxon culture which Frederick destroyed, by his constant wars of conquest, was a home of artistic quality such as is only seldom achieved, comparable with fifteenth-century Florence or Urbino, for instance, or even ancient Athens. In 1763 the elector's court dispersed on the death of Augustus III and the end of the Seven Years' War.

St Petersburg was probably the most artificial city of them all: during Catherine the Great's dictatorship artists and craftsmen were employed from the whole of Europe, apparently with almost no local helpers. Perhaps the Russian serfs were still too down-trodden to have made possible the evolution of skilled native labour. Peter the Great had brought some goldsmiths back with him from London in 1698, and others came from France in 1716, all helping to build a local school of metalwork which found expression first in the later eighteenth

century, in the distinctive tobacco boxes often depicting on their covers scenes of local life or architecture. At the end of the next century the exquisite trivia of Fabergé were the culmination of the tsarist quest for a mature Russian style.

In fact their jewels in the eighteenth century were more sumptuous than original. Peter the Great's own favourite snuff box, the Dutch three-masted schooner in walnut and gold, still survives in the Hermitage, Leningrad, a vigorous symbol, like his buildings there, of his maritime ambitions. But just as the empresses Elizabeth and Catherine were responsible for most of St Petersburg's ceremonial buildings, so it was these formidable women who commissioned Russia's very large but stylistically anonymous official jewels.

Catherine appointed Jeremy Pauzier as her goldsmith. Born in Geneva in 1716, he accompanied his father to Hamburg in 1729, then being apprenticed for years to Gavero a Frenchman in Moscow, opening his own shop in 1740, and returning to Switzerland where he wrote his memoirs before dying in 1779 —a typical international pilgrimage for artists of the time. Pauzier's great work was Catherine's diamond crown, commissioned for her coronation but not ready in time. Other Russian goldsmiths, Jean Pierre Ador from France, and Otto Samuel Keibel with his son Johann Wilhelm who came from Prussia in 1797, similarly made a living producing very large jewels for the very rich.

Vienna (whose master craftsman was Philippe Ernst Schindler) and Stockholm, Munich and Strasbourg, The Hague and Madrid and Lisbon—every capital had its own nest of luxury craftsmen, by now organized into efficient guilds with their number limited to whatever the community could support. But it was in London that a clear jewelers' personality emerged, different from continental Europe, the result of the wide dispersal of patronage through all the British landed families, of the power of the merchant classes, and of the new machine production, in short of England's liberal character. In England jewelry was emancipated from royalty: it had become a luxury in which the upper classes could all indulge.

One can scent the London scene from Horace Walpole's letters. In 1766, coming from Strawberry Hill to his Arlington Street house, he found a gold box on his writing table with a miniature portrait of Madame de Sévigné in the lid, and a mysterious letter inside. Walpole especially admired Sévigné—before her death in 1696 she had given her name to the lightweight bow brooch in diamonds and stones which is worn in many smart portraits of the time. As Sévigné was dead, Walpole hoped the box was a present from his next most favourite Frenchwoman, the Duchesse de Choiseul; alas, it turned out actually to be a joke from the blind and ageing Madame du Deffand—a strange incident illustrating the respect in England for fashionable France.

In 1791 Walpole wrote,

I should tell you that I have been at Sir Joseph Banks' literary saturnalia, where was a Parisian watchmaker, who produced the smallest automaton that I suppose was ever created. It was a rich snuff-box, not too large for a woman. On opening the lid, an enamelled bird started up, sat on the rim, turned round, fluttered its wings, and piped in a delightful tone the notes of different birds, particularly the jug, jug, of the nightingale. It is the prettiest plaything you ever saw— the price tempting—only five hundred pounds.

That economist the P. of W. [Prince of Wales] could not resist it and has bought one of those dickybirds. If the maker finds such customers, he will not end like one of his profession here, who made the serpent in Orpheus and Euridice, and who fell so deeply in love with his own works, that he did nothing afterwards but make serpents of all sorts and sizes till he was ruined and broke.

Apart from the wit and learning of French society, which gave a special lure overseas to everything French, no doubt the main attraction, the special appeal of French craftsmanship was its enamel work. Dresden was famous for its semi-precious stone work, Berlin for its big precious stones. The achievement of London around 1700 was the complex gold work, especially in its watches, at that time probably the best in Europe, and some decades later in its gold boxes, perhaps more robust and with less colour than those made on the continent.

In England there was no revolution brewing: that had been finished by the seventeenth-century Civil War and Restoration. Royalty did not indulge itself quite so splendidly as overseas, and the national wealth was already more evenly spread. Thomas, Lord Hervey, equerry to Queen Caroline of Ansbach, George II's wife, described her at her coronation in 1727—wearing not only Queen Anne's pearls, 'but she had on her head and shoulders all the pearls and necklaces she could borrow from the ladies of quality at one end of the town, and on her petticoat all the diamonds she could hire of the Jews and jewelers at the other quarters. . . . So the appearance and the truth of her finery was a mixture of magnificence and meanness.' The age of deception was at hand—jewels came to be worn often more for their effect than their reality.

Horace Walpole, describing the same coronation, noted that the queen's dress was so heavy with jewels that she could not even kneel; her skirt train had to be pulled up with two pulleys like a curtain. Even if her jewels were not her own, she still put on a comprehensive panoply.

During the long period from the terrible Thirty Years' War till the age of reform of the French Revolution (1789) and the British great reform bill (1832), one might expect European jewels to have become steadily less magnificent, as the wealthy classes felt less secure. There is no evidence of any such decline in ostentation—the most famous jewelry scandal in history is the affair of Marie Antoinette's necklace. Originally ordered by Louis xv for his beautiful but apparently feather-brained mistress, Madame du Barry, from the court jewelers Boehmer and Bassanges, it was not ready before the king's death in 1774 and was considered too expensive by Louis xvi. An officer's wife, Madame la Motte, persuaded the very grand courtier, Cardinal de Rohan, that the queen needed money for charity, and he lent it. She then persuaded him that the queen wanted to buy the necklace without the king's knowledge, using the cardinal to make the purchase. This he did, handing the jewel to someone he thought was the queen's servant. In 1786 the storm broke, the cardinal having to retire, the other guilty parties mostly being punished, with the queen herself, actually entirely innocent, receiving nearly all the public blame. The necklace was so expensive that the complicated intrigue centring round it helped to bring on the French Revolution. However, the whole dramatic tale shows that colossal royal purchases were still quite normal, otherwise de Rohan would not so easily have been duped.

Bapst, the nineteenth-century Paris crown jeweler, lists Louis XIV's personal jewels in 1691. These included two diamond 'parures', one of 123 buttons, 300 button-holes, 19 frogs or Brandebourgs for the *justaucorps*, 48 buttons and 96 buttonholes for the *veste*; the other correspondingly, of 168 buttons and buttonholes, 48 buttons and buttonholes. Both had a loop for the hat, garters, a diamond-hilted sword and Saint Esprit cross.

Joan Evans quotes Louis XV as late as 1759 still using jewels to influence politics: Augustus the Strong's daughter, Maria Amalia Cristina of Saxony, married Charles III of Spain; to enlist her sympathy for France, Louis gave her a pair of bracelets each with an enormous diamond in the clasp. In 1800, even in relatively democratic England in a great war, the *Ladies' Magazine* describes Queen Charlotte as follows:

Her Majesty was magnificently attired in a lilac crape petticoat . . . with five superb diamond bands, composed of collets, and fifteen large brilliant roses and stars, at equal distances on the bands; these bands were terminated at the bottom with four very magnificent bows and tassels of diamonds and large pearls, from which were also suspended festoons of beautiful pearls in wreathes; over the left side flowed two corners of lilac crape, caged with diamond chains and pearls, with pearl tassels at bottom, and fastened at the pocket holes with superb diamond and pearl bands and chains. The ensemble was completed by a diamond stomacher, necklace, bouquet and bandeau.

Up till 1618 jewels had shown the same sort of zest and unevenness as most other Renaissance art, music and literature. Pendants, brooches, hat badges and finger rings may have been the commonest pieces, and surprisingly often they show the same themes: pleasure in the human form, just unveiled from its medieval drapery; obsession with stories, both religious and, especially outside Spain, classical, lately released from those centres of church learning where they had been preserved for so many centuries; and, finally, a completely unsystematic boasting with whatever materials were to hand—the availability of stones was still so chancy that when used at all they, rather than the designer, tended to dictate the shape of the jewel. Before 1618 enamels and gold were the normal prerequisite for any piece, and they were used with the utmost fantasy and virtuosity. The strongest designs, with bold contrasts of plainness against intricacy, were the earliest, around 1500; the frenzied torments and strange mis-proportions of Mannerism appeared around 1550; after that the only simple spaces were to be the stones themselves, all the metal surface being covered with agitated elaboration.

During the next century and a half, till about 1800, the inspiration of jewelers faded under the new weight of precious stones. Stones which had been no more than an incident in most jewels assumed a new status; they were often the whole point. Instead of being surrounded by those exciting Renaissance creatures, snakes and masks, birds and animals, with arches and columns, pilasters and capitals, stones were often surrounded now by nothing more interesting than other stones.

The parure or matching set of necklace, brooch, earrings, bracelet and sometimes corsage ornament had existed since the sixteenth century, but it came into its own with the rise of the precious stone: Augustus the Strong in Dresden, for instance, commissioned no less than nine parures, in the first years of the eighteenth century, one with diamonds, another with sapphires, another with rubies, another with emeralds, one with garnets and so on, each of them far beyond the normal size for women, including as they did buttons, swords and watches, each of them rather a throw-back historically because by now the parure had become more a female than a male outfit. By the mid-eighteenth century, gem cutting had pretty generally become a precise science rather than an individual art; these parures were little more than walking gem collections, fabulous colours, marvellous groups of stones, sparkling geometrical patterns, but none the less completely unmemorable because they had no personality.

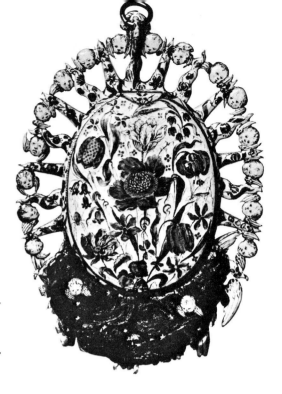

By the mid-seventeenth century precious stones, newly available from the east, were becoming steadily larger, carved gold and enamel simpler; but the flower became fashionable at the same time as the flower garden and the Dutch craze for tulips. The obverse uses one enormous 'baroque' pearl, whose name is misleading because these became popular about 1500, before the baroque period. Museum of Fine Arts, Vienna

From the mid-seventeenth century brooches and pendants often featured the prettiest of nature's gifts to us, strangely neglected in jewelry till then— the flower. Medieval gardens tried to be a tiny patch of 'paradise' in the midst of nature's jungle outside; they could only be afforded by the very rich, and the variety of plants was very modest, with probably an effect of mostly green herb plants and green trimmed hedges. During the Renaissance it was the human body and the explosion of interest in classical antiquity which intoxicated jewelers; then, around 1600, it was the turn of the precious stone from the new trade routes to America and the east. In 1637 Holland, Europe's leading power, suddenly succumbed to tulipomania, the cult of the tulip becoming the national gambling sport. About the same time Le Nôtre began his long career as French court gardener. Europe's taste for flowers, the result of more peaceful and prosperous times, developed quickly. So it is consistent that the pendulum of jewelry fashion should have swung briefly to flowers in the late seventeenth century, usually incised and enamelled in richest translucent colours rather than modelled in stones, before swinging back again to stones fifty years later, made more attractive as they were by the new polishing and cutting.

Solid lumps of stone, however, were not enough, even though they now represented reflected light instead of just colour as they had done throughout history. The heavy symmetrical group soon gave way about 1760 to a rococo elegance which in its turn yielded to delicate flower sprays and bouquets, now utilizing small stones for the middle classes. In the seventeenth century and before, stones had been contained in a golden cup usually with coloured foil inside to give more brightness; around 1630 this cup or collet became silver, easier to work and more secure; by the end of the eighteenth century the collet disappeared. The cult of light required transparency: stones were held by claw settings with an open gallery behind.

The main performer in this saga was, of course, the diamond with its miraculous light effects. The diamond market at Golconda, fed by its nearby mines, known since perhaps 600 BC but probably first visited by a European (the Viceroy of Goa) in 1565, became generally accessible in the seventeenth century. Tavernier, in his fascinating accounts of

the Indian scene, thought there were about 6,000 men, women and children working there, but he did not visit the outlying areas. Towards 1700 Indian diamond production slumped, probably because the supply of stones on the surface was exhausted. But in 1725 the first Brazilian diamond was authenticated at Diamantina and throughout the eighteenth and nineteenth centuries Brazil formed the world's chief source. At Ouro Preto ('Old Gold') Brazil had already established a huge source for gold. This was followed not only by diamonds but by massive supplies of topaz, amethyst, tourmaline and other semi-precious stones, making available to jewelers everywhere, a mineral wealth of previously unimagined variety. The dealer in stones and gold, and the gem cutter, began about 1700 to displace the all-round Renaissance artist-jeweler, reigning supreme until he in his turn yielded pride of place in the nineteenth century to the retailers.

The history of jewels in modern times can be summarized not unfairly as the rise and fall of the gem. Medieval stones were usually smoothed, not angled; in the Renaissance they were shaped in a most erratic way which absorbed light but reflected it back hardly at all. Then new scientific cuts came in—the old soft cabochon was superseded around 1500 by the flat table, around 1640 by the rose; then came the fifty-six-faced brilliant supposedly invented in Venice by Vincenzo Peruzzi about 1700. This aggressive, scintillating brilliant cut gave a new inhuman precision to gems, the result of polishing by simple machinery, which one can study in the French *Encyclopédie* of 1772, Diderot's fascinating technical manual. What seems today the beginning of a sad journey away from personal imagination towards impersonal technology was then thought to be the optimistic march of progress, and was used enthusiastically in almost all precious jewels of the later eighteenth century. The nature of the stone began to matter more than the nature of the jewel. It is no coincidence that the beginning of this period, 1652, saw the first English language 'history of precious stones with cautions for the undeceiving of all those that deal with them'—*A Lapidary*, by Thomas Nicols of Jesus College, Cambridge.

The machine, however, having just tidied up stones and promoted the diamond to its present supremacy, had a

Right *Hat badge of gold and enamels. Medieval jewelry was dominated by Christian imagery; in this case, the Nativity with Christ in the centre, the Virgin Mary and Joseph in the foreground, the manger with the two oxen and two of the shepherds above. The figures, embossed in thin gold sheet, are pinned to the gold back disk. The group, of Renaissance style, is in a circular frame, with Gothic foliage. It is a product of the end of the Middle Ages, c. 1510. Diameter: 1.75 inches*

Overleaf: left *Gold pendant with five table-cut rubies, two table-cut diamonds, one pyramid-cut diamond, green enamelled columns, enamelled scrolled base with the badges of two evangelists—a bull for St Luke and a lion for St Mark—a small table-cut diamond and a drop pearl. The central group shows the Adoration of the Magi with the Holy Ghost above God the Father, and a trumpet-blowing angel on each side. Such complicated allegories are typical of Renaissance ingenuity. Perhaps by Erasmus Hornick, the jewel of a type known as 'tabernacle' resembles a design published by him in Nuremberg in the 1560s. South German, late 16th century. Height: 4 inches.*
Right *Reverse of the 'tabernacle' jewel. Champlevé enamel. Nativity with the Virgin Mary and Joseph adoring Jesus. Above, the angel appears to the watching shepherds.*

sions of a story showing how good jewels helped people to rise socially even though, as Maupassant and Balzac suggest, 'top' people no longer always quite lived up to expectation:

The two outstanding beauties of the *demi-monde* were La Belle Otéro, a dark and passionate young woman with a strong blend of Greek and gypsy blood, who was always flamboyantly dressed to set off her magnificent figure; and lovely Liane de Pougy, who looked the *grande dame* she eventually became by her marriage to the Roumanian Prince Ghika.

There was rivalry between them and they were proud of the precious stones that adorned them as visible signs of the eminence they had reached in their profession. Fortunes were spent and lost for them and bets were exchanged on the relative value of their jewels. It was not surprising therefore that Otéro should challenge her rival by appearing at the Casino one night covered from head to foot with priceless jewels. It was a dazzling display, but in seeking to outdo her rival Otéro had sacrificed good taste and had lent herself to ridicule. Excited conjectures about Pougy's rejoinder were promptly answered. The next evening, appearing in a simple white gown without a single jewel, she was followed by her maid gorgeously arrayed in jewels that far outshone Otéro's.

Consuelo wrote of her impending marriage to the Duke of Marlborough:

My father had generously told me to get whatever I wanted as a gift from him, but I was surprised by the excess of household and personal linens, clothes, furs and hats my husband was ordering. Marlborough's ideas about jewels were equally princely, and since there appeared to be no family heirlooms, jewels became a necessary addition to my trousseau. It was then the fashion to wear dog-collars; mine was of pearls and had nineteen rows, with high diamond clasps which rasped my neck. My mother had given me all the pearls she had received from my father. There were two fine rows which had once belonged to Catherine of Russia and to the Empress Eugénie, and also a *sautoir* which I could clasp round my waist. A diamond tiara capped with pearl-shaped stones was my father's gift to me, and from Marlborough came a diamond belt. They were beautiful indeed, but jewels never gave me pleasure and my heavy tiara invariably produced a violent headache, my dog-collar a chafed neck. Thus bejewelled and bedecked I was deemed worthy to meet English society.

When Consuelo was painted by Sargent, he wanted her neck long, like, as he said, the trunk of a tree. For that aesthetic reason he refused to adorn it with pearls, a fact that aggrieved one of her sisters-in-law, who remarked that she should not appear in public without them.

Nubar Gulbenkian, in his autobiography, recorded some of the customs of international jewelry buyers: for instance, in Paris

Cartiers always remained open throughout the night because of Mantacheff's habit, in the early hours of the morning, of splashing out, thinking nothing of spending say, £3,000 on jewels for the favourite of the moment. He was a very good client of the night clubs and, like so many Russians, had a weak spot for the gypsy bands of which there were many, both before the [1914] war and again afterwards. He loved to take a handful of gold coins, louis d'or, from his pocket, throw them on the floor, and then watch the band scrambling for them. But old Mantacheff was a shrewder and much less generous man by day . . .

This was the world of fine precious stones, which continued up to the 1939 war. Since then it has been steadily eroded. The world-wide social revolution has led to a more equal distribution of wealth, and, equally important, an attitude of discreet restraint by rich people rather than of open ostentation. The trends of taxation, of fashion and morality alike, have led away from rich, formal clothing towards a new informality. But just as important as these changes in the nature of society is the rise of artist-jewelers. They launched the art nouveau style around 1900, exciting but short-lived and with almost no impact outside its own devoted circle of aesthetes; since 1945 they have reappeared in all the larger countries and this time they have come to stay.

ART NOUVEAU

Art Nouveau was a crazy but exciting reaction against convention: against big stones, big money, boring colours and conventional dress. The new style had a different flavour in each country, but all were inspired by a lanky, intertwined line which owed something to the new awareness of Japan. Its stylized sculpture and its dramatic mixture of precious and worthless materials suddenly became fashionable in jewels about 1895 and equally suddenly died around 1910. It was fascinating, obsessed with endless creepers and leaves, dream-sodden faces, soft, irregular low relief, dusky colours.

Art Nouveau was dependent on individual genius, and could not be mass-produced. Its own exaggerations killed it. Walter Crane recorded in 1903, 'L'Art

Brooch, formerly a pendant, showing Noah's Ark on Mount Ararat with the animals emerging and God giving blessing. Chalcedony cameo carved in high relief probably by Alessandro Masnago a famous gem engraver in Milan. Late 16th century (the gold setting is 19th century)

Left *Gold pendant. A ram decorated with table-cut diamonds, a ruby and enamels, with a large trapezoidal sapphire in a blue enamel collet surrounded by small pearls and another sapphire in an octagonal enamel collet. The geometrical arrangement of the open-work platform beneath the ram is in the style of Hans Collaert, rather later and more open than Erasmus Hornick's. The piece is of exceptional weight and size — height: 5.25 inches; weight: 3.3 ounces. South German, late 16th century*

Right *During the eighteenth century elegant living conditions spread rapidly, and with them the variety of personal ornaments: chatelaines, hung from a lady's belt, might include seals for letters, scent containers, portraits and keys. Early in the century they were often of solid gold, by the mid-century they sometimes had gold backs (which did not mark clothing) and base metal fronts or, as here, c. 1750, they were in the base metal called pinchbeck. Later they became popular in silver.*

much greater impact later on jewelry as a whole around 1760, with the beginnings of the Industrial Revolution in England. There was pinchbeck, invented by Christopher Pinchbeck, the London watchmaker (who died in 1732), a copper and zinc alloy almost like gold which was very widely used for the production of late Georgian everyday ornaments — necklaces, chatelaines, buckles. There was the first production in 1758 by the Viennese jeweler Joseph Strass of paste — silica, iron oxide, clay and soda, which despite the Empress Maria-Theresa's trying to suppress it, rapidly swept Europe as the poor man's substitute for diamonds; these were the latest and most successful attempts with glass and coloured foil, to imply intrinsic value where in fact there was none.

George Ravenscroft, the English glass-maker at London's Savoy Glasshouse, was one of the first experimenters in 1676. George Wickes, the famous court silversmith, also sold jewels with his partner, Netherton, and advertised on his 1759 trade card 'a variety of false-stone work' — no pride here about mixing fake and real. The Bohemian glass cottage-industries began to flourish: the seventeenth-century court jeweler Kaspar Lehmann cut glass as well as gems. Jiri Kreybich made thirty trips outside Bohemia from 1682 to 1721, trundling glassware and garnet jewels through Europe on his wagon.

The early eighteenth century saw the introduction of a dazzling volume of fashion accessories, walking sticks, spectacles and gold boxes, chains and seals, fobs and links, buckles and clasps, pencils and pens and portable watches which could be hung all over the person. Mourning and memento rings, an English innovation, have a touching sentimental character, containing the dead person's portrait or hair, or simply his expressed wish to be remembered by his friends (Samuel Pepys, for instance, listed no less than 123 friends he hoped would treasure his memory in this way). Launcelot Andrewes, Bishop of Winchester, left £300 in his will in 1626 so that twenty named recipients should each receive a mourning ring.

It was Matthew Boulton and the world pioneers of industry in eighteenth-century England who made these new trinkets accessible to everyone. Boulton's ideal of fine quality mass-

production began to knock the precious stone off its pinnacle and therefore make room for more variety. It was base metal costume jewelry that made possible the eventual re-emergence of the designer. For the first time cheap jewels, often made of cut steel and marcasite, were available to everyone.

Cut-steel jewelry is associated especially with Woodstock in England, partly with Salisbury; steel buckles with Wolverhampton. Diamonds had produced a taste for glitter, which cut steel helped to satisfy. The shoe buckle became very fashionable: in 1739 a surviving entertainment ticket card says, 'Gentlemen cannot be admitted wearing shoe strings.' In 1773 the great Boulton himself wrote to the Earl of Cranborne, whose button shanks had come out, 'We have hitherto delay'd answering your Lordship's favour in hopes of sending steel buttons to replace the former ones. We have at last got 'em done and send them p. the night's coach.' Boulton's success was founded not only on brilliant innovations, scientific, industrial, artistic, and human: he worked very hard, and gave personal attention to small details, even such an order for a few buttons. But by 1791 fashion was already changing. Makers of these 'toys' from Wolverhampton, Walsall and Birmingham had to petition the Prince of Wales for his help. By 1845 the boom was already over, but 5,300 'toy makers' were still registered in Birmingham compared with only 3,700 jewelers.

Cut steel was popular in continental Europe too; Napoleon gave a suite to his second wife Marie-Louise; in eighteenth-century Switzerland wearing diamond

Above left *The engraved hard stone cameo, popular with the Romans and during the Renaissance, was revived in the later eighteenth and early nineteenth centuries, as in this necklace; English, carved agate with gold and pearls, c. 1780*

Left *Enamel mourning rings, often containing the hair of the person commemorated, were another popular fashion of the late eighteenth century—like these English and German examples from the Jewelry Museum, Pforzheim*

jewels was made illegal, so steel and marcasite benefited. In Paris one of Marie-Antoinette's jewelers, Monsieur Granches, was supposed to charge higher prices in his Rue Dauphine shop for his steel than for his gold.

Berlin ironwork, made around 1800 because of the scarcity of materials under the Napoleonic conquests, also gave base metal a better social image. It was first made at Gleiwitz in Silesia: the Royal Berlin Factory opened in 1804. Black and gloomy, this ingenious stamped patterning had a certain vogue for decades with the formal middle-class fashions of central Europe.

From the mid-seventeenth century the team of people producing a jewel had begun to fragment, the direct result of the increasing value of stones. The financial aspect of jewels started to efface the art. The designer became separated from the craftsman, the jewel became sometimes the product of a team of specialized independent outworkers, no longer the direct child of one person's brain. The age of the entrepreneur was at hand, and we know very little about him: one of the first to declare himself in public was James Goddard, who could not possibly have himself fabricated all the delights on his trade card of 1765 which declared, 'Watch cases, snuff boxes, and other curious work in gold are enameld, either transparent or painted, in an elegant manner, by James Goddard, at the Dial in Denmark Street, Soho. Likewise makes dial plates of all sizes for clocks and watches.' It was indeed a sign of the times that advertising had at last become necessary.

The market for jewels expanded hugely in the eighteenth century not only because of mass production, more prosperity, more people, and habits more equally shared between the different social classes; a fundamental change was the new distinction between day and night. For the sun, one wore garnets and paste and cut steel and semi-precious materials; for the candle, one wanted refraction and reflection, gaiety and light, and that meant faceted precious stones.

The emergence of the English beau around 1800 put England in the fore-front of world fashion, not at all surprising as she was by then also the leader of political empires and factory technology. Men everywhere henceforth came to imitate the foppish but trim and under-ornamented English dandies. The male wig and frock coat were too fussy for the new practical life. Men came to be described by new words like 'dapper' and 'neat', and despised the thought of being decorative. It was now for women, not men, to decide the future of jewels.

COPY OR CREATION— THE NINETEENTH CENTURY

Art always grows from reality, but it is reality transformed by the artist's vision. Throughout history, art has looked backwards or outwards; inspiration in the Renaissance, for instance, coming from Greece and Rome, in the seventeenth century from the flower garden, in the eighteenth from the bouncing lines of rococo; but none of these was an accurate copy, for the simple reason that human knowledge was not suffi-cient. Only after 1800 did we know enough about the past to be able to copy it, a process clinched by the invention of the camera.

In so far as nineteenth-century jewelry had a style at all, it was imitation. Of course, aesthetes today, having said almost all that can be said about earlier periods, are trying to find the exceptional genius hidden under this load of nineteenth-century derivation, but so far without success. Whatever has emerged is either a survival of original eighteenth-century grace, such as the Biedermeier classical revival in Vienna and the English Regency work with its splendid crispness at the beginning of the century; or the revolution at the end, corresponding to Van Gogh and Gauguin, Cézanne and Manet, determined to revive the impact of the human spirit on jewelry. It is these Oscar Wildes and Aubrey Beardsleys of the work bench around 1880 who gave birth to modernism. In between, we see the result of a pious but futile wish to emulate in the present what everybody knows is good from the past, and the result of rising mineral supplies coupled with ever growing wealth: in fact, of Victorian imperialism.

Art is essentially creative: imitation is not. So the interest of nineteenth-century jewels lies not so much in their rather sterile artistic content, as in the way they reflect the social background. This is a much better documented scene than the eighteenth century, partly because several prominent jewelers made a record of their times: Germain Bapst, for instance, of the French jewelry family, who wrote on the crown jewels in 1889;

Berlin iron-work jewelry may have originated with the shortage of precious metals at the time of Napoleon's European conquests. Bracelet, c. 1800. Austrian Museum of Applied Art, Vienna

Watches inlaid with different coloured gold, and engraved partly by hand, partly by engine turning were a fashionable speciality of Liverpool. Gold pocket watch, hallmarked in Chester in 1829

Much nineteenth-century jewelry was imitative: the more original pieces were usually the cheaper, with powerful intertwined lines and often with ingenious articulation like this gold and garnet necklace, left, c. 1850. Once the property of John Horsley, designer of the world's first Christmas card

or Henri Vever, the distinguished art nouveau designer, who in 1908 surveyed the whole previous century. Then there were the fashion magazines like *Ladies' Magazine* and *Illustrated London News* in England with, latterly, the influential art paper *Studio*; in France appeared *L'Observateur des Modes, Art et Décoration, Journal des Dames* and *La Sylphide*; in Belgium *L'Art Moderne*; and in Germany and Austria *Die Elegante Mode, L'Iris* and the Leipzig *Allgemeine Modenzeitung*.

Another source of our knowledge is the great international exhibitions. The first, biggest and best of all was the brain-child of Prince Albert: the Great Exhibition of 1851 in London's Hyde Park was intended to prove to the world the blessings of machinery, especially if it was made in Britain. Queen Victoria notes in her copious journal of the opening on 1 May, 'I forgot to mention that I wore a dress of pink and silver, with a diamond ray diadem and a little diamond crown at the back . . . all the rest of my jewels being diamonds'. Then came the Paris exhibition in 1867. These huge displays normally inspired catalogues of excruciating ugliness. We can now recognize them as the epitome of machinery without art, though at the time they were mostly intended to demonstrate quite the reverse, namely that industry was becoming the culminating cultural asset of all. Whatever the art historians' verdict may eventually be, these international tournaments forced everyone to examine everyone else's products in a way that had never before been possible. Jewelers could copy each other not in the normal manner through using engraved sheets of patterns, or through the random travels of actual jewels themselves, but simply by looking at each other's pieces on exhibition. Hence the staggering speed with which the nineteenth-century eclectic fashions followed each other.

The complex story of nineteenth-century jewelry can be unravelled partly through the medium of what actually created it—better communications, that is better fashion papers, better international exchanges, bigger exhibitions and more travel. But there was one specific, picturesque and admirable force at work which probably affected jewels more than any of the other arts, and that was exploration. The fashion for 'Egyptian' styles was nourished by Napoleon's massive archaeological works in Egypt after his 1798 conquests; 'Etruscan', a particularly Roman craze, by the painstaking first opening of Etruscan tombs in the nearby hills; 'Greek' by the revelations of remote Aegean islands like Aegina, Rhodes and Crete, and later from Asia Minor; 'Roman' by the successive layers of personal relics dug out from the hardened lava in the houses of Herculaneum and Pompeii; 'African' by the French conquests of Algeria; 'Assyrian by Layard's spectacular forays with their massive and unexpected yield around Nineveh and Nimrud; and finally Schliemann with his wonderful gold found at Troy—all these had an influence on jewelry design which was at least unsettling: it helped to stop any one idiom maturing into a specific style for the century.

The late nineteenth-century fashion for jewels in black jet, much of it from Whitby in Yorkshire, is generally credited to Queen Victoria's long mourning for Prince Albert, during which her Court was expected to wear black. Hair ornament, 1898, made in Bohemia, where a big cottage jewelry industry grew up in the eighteenth century based on the local sources of garnet stone at Mount Kozakov. Jablonec Museum

The overwhelming fact after 1815, though, was simply money. The joint power of organized labour in factories, and of world-wide political empires, yielded unprecedented wealth. The prevailing materialist philosophy surprisingly tended to equate material riches with spiritual, and it was the same with jewels. The bigger the piece, the better the person because she has more money than you have, so the theory ran. As one could not actually talk about money—that would be bad breeding—one wore it instead; and the combined efforts of the gemmologist and retailers together made it easy because jewels were not often specially designed and therefore they had less individuality than before, and the relative size of the stones indicated with horrid precision the status of the wearer's bank balance.

Of course, each firm employed its own jewelry designer, but commercial conditions were probably too conventional to allow much enterprise. A battle of the styles enlivened architecture, swaying from classical in the early part of the century to Gothic later on and, once Gothic had won, from the fairy, light perpendicular of Pugin and his followers to the hard, heavy Early English of Street and Butterfield. There was nothing comparable in jewelry—no steady evolution, very little public discussion except in the verdicts of juries at the big exhibitions, who often lamented what they saw, without finding any better remedy than a nostalgic leaning to foreign products which, it was thought, being farther from home, must be more exciting. The most famous designers like Owen Jones, the British master of ornament and tableware, or Antoine Vechte, Belgian sculptor turned silversmith, seem not to have involved themselves in jewels. There were nevertheless some successful freelance producers, who achieved good reputations usually based on their technical ability.

Fortunato Pio Castellani opened his shop in Rome in 1814, first copying the London and Paris copies of antiques. Then, turning to the marvellous Etruscan treasures which were being unearthed on his own doorstep, he built up a team of craftsmen who could work more or less in the ancient manner, spreading their interest to Greece and Rome and then to Renaissance times. In 1851 Fortunato left the business to his son Augusto, whose scholarly interests secured for him the curatorship of the

Capitoline Museum; some of his collection of genuine ancient jewels is now in the British Museum. His work eventually became the inspiration of other leading European producers like Giacinto Mellilo of Naples, Eugène Fontenay and Robert Phillips.

Carlo Giuliano's name is usually coupled with Castellani's; both had a very big production of a very precise ornamental miniature style, both are still in demand today. Giuliano was born in Naples, settled in London, spread his interest perhaps wider than Castellani, and like Castellani left his business to his two sons, Frederico and Fernando, in Howland Street.

Another illustrious name which achieved art perhaps more through literature than through metal was Bapst. The first of this eminent dynasty of jewelers was Jacques, who in 1797 married the daughter of the court jeweler Ménière; his two sons Constant and Charles carried on the business as Bapst brothers, in 1820 remaking some of Napoleon I's regalia for Louis XVIII; Jacques-Eberhard supervised the designs with his colleague Seiffert, and Charles-Frédéric Bapst, manager of the workshop for fifty years, brought the ideas to fruition. They made Charles X's coronation regalia, including his sword now in the Galerie d'Apollon at the Louvre. The Bapst family established powerful sway over French court jewelry for a City of Paris fête. It was held at the Hôtel de Ville, to celebrate the christening of the new prince, and the Empress Eugénie was as usual overwhelming. Her white tulle gown was sewn with silver stars; she had a diadem and a double necklace covering her corsage made of diamonds and amethysts. She wore a diamond girdle and the comb *en pampilles* especially prepared for the occasion with some of the old Mazarin diamonds and pink 'peach blossom' diamonds.

Massin, a Liège apprentice, worked his way in Paris to become the foreman of the Rouvenat firm in 1854 when he was only twenty-six; in 1856 he visited London for eighteen months; in 1863 he refused offers from London and from Tiffany's in New York and continued to prosper. His career was not altogether different from other successful jewelers of the time like Fossin or Fontenay, or Boucheron, with more craft than art, and perhaps more skill than imagination. The scene was static and complacent:

nobody guessed it was in fact a stage, set ready for the sensational revolution of Art Nouveau and the modern movement.

To some extent Carl Fabergé in Russia epitomizes all that was right, and all that was wrong too, with this period. He had a spectacular career. The Fabergé firm was started by Gustav, his father (1814–93) at St Petersburg in 1842; the famous son Peter Carl (1846–1920), taking control in 1870, was joined in 1882 by his younger brother Agathon. In 1884 (this was the year when the first of the famous imperial easter eggs was made) the firm received the royal warrant of Tsar Alexander III. They achieved great success through their high standards of craftsmanship. In 1882 they won a gold medal at the pan-Russian exhibition in Moscow; in 1885 a gold medal at Nuremberg; in 1888 a special award at Copenhagen. In 1900 Carl Fabergé was awarded the Légion d'Honneur after the Paris exhibition. And there were many other awards. Branches of the firm were established in Moscow (1887–1918), Odessa (1890–1918), Kiev (1905–10), and London (1903–15). In 1910 the firm brought an unsuccessful test case against the Worshipful Company of Goldsmiths disputing British hall-marking laws. The business was closed by the Bolsheviks in 1918 and Carl Fabergé died in Lausanne.

At the height of their fame the staff numbered over 500, including some thirty designers, but Carl and Agathon Fabergé exercised close personal supervision and designed the great majority of the pieces made by the firm in the St Petersburg workshops. Exquisite craftsmanship, most clever and often original technique, high social connections, artistic delight and charm, a keen business sense—these do not add up to greatness. Fabergé's may be the biggest name of the epoch, but he was not a very creative artist: indeed he is the ideal illustration of the difference between artist and craftsman. His style is enchanting, captivating, but not original. It is too close to eighteenth-century Dresden and Paris, which he knew and loved. Perhaps his aristocratic international clientele thought the Art Nouveau designers not quite respectable; perhaps in retrospect we in our turn can now see that it was these dreamers with their fantastic invention who, more than Fabergé, were the real innovators of their age.

Some of the grandest old firms of the

nineteenth century have retained records right from the start, foremost among them perhaps Chaumet of Paris. F. R. Nitot once helped Napoleon to his feet after a coach mishap in Rue St Honoré and from that beginning went on to become the emperor's jeweler. He had, in fact, succeeded Foncier as the Beauharnais family jeweler, so Josephine, the first empress, probably introduced them. Nitot made Napoleon's beautiful crown of cameos now in the Louvre and the other regalia for the 1804 coronation, also resetting the old crown jewels. The crown was worn at the coronation, then again at Napoleon's wedding to Marie-Louise. Nitot set the Regent diamond in the state sword in 1803; with Marguerite, crown jeweler in 1811, he provided many official jewels including the plaques and chain for the Legion of Honour, and a famous ruby diadem with diamond laurel leaves for the emperor himself. In 1815 Nitot's politics drove him out; he left his business to his foreman Fossin, who was appointed royal jeweler in 1830 by Louis-Philippe; thence the succession passed through family marriage to the present Chaumet family in their Place Vendôme shop.

Garrard's (till 1950 the Goldsmiths' and Silversmiths' Company) in London's Regent Street, trace their descent back, this time by purchase as well as by marriage, to George Wickes who opened his Threadneedle Street shop in 1721. F. R. Wilm, now of Hamburg, supplied Bismarck at his most aggressive time in Berlin, and most of the Prussian aristocracy. Tillander, now in Helsinki, and Bolin of Stockholm were both big names in tsarist St Petersburg and Moscow. Other firms, like Auguste, who made Louis XVI's crown in 1774 and still miraculously survived the Revolution with no less than fifty craftsmen, or his contemporary Biennais, may be studied today in the Paris Bibliothèque des Arts Décoratifs or London's Victoria and Albert Museum. This was the time when good jewelers tended almost automatically to become wealthy commercial companies as well, and these companies naturally kept better records, just as they produced worse art, than the freelance artist-jewelers of the centuries before.

Probably the first recognizable retail shops were the *marchands-merciers* of mid-eighteenth-century Paris. Rich people came to them from all over Europe to buy *bijouterie* or luxuries. Diderot cruelly called them 'Faiseurs de rien et marchands de tout' but they filled an obvious need. Many of the biggest jewelry shops today grew up, however, not in the graceful tradition of eighteenth-century understatement but in the blatant mood of the later nineteenth. It is significant how many of the famous jewelers today began business in the nineteenth century. Some were started by artists and developed into big business; most started as they still are today, retail merchants.

The nineteenth century was the time of the rise of the retailer, whose main aim can be expressed in many ways: to satisfy the client, to glorify the jewel, to market efficiently what would otherwise die still-born, to gather patronage from the richest and most influential people, to sell someone else's work, or just to make money. Whatever the motive, and it was usually a mixture of all these, the retailer's increasing wealth inevitably caused loss of contact between jewelry designers and the general public: whether or not retailers wanted it, what in fact they caused was an increased respect for the material side of jewels—fine stones, fine cutting and polishing, fine designs and setting, fine boxes and presentation and, perhaps it is not unfair to add, fine profits all round—the whole a fine team job. The individual artist-jeweler was almost wholly suppressed under the load of the middleman and the profit motive.

One revealing document for nineteenth-century jewels is the Maupassant masterpiece *La Parure*: a suite of jewelry is borrowed for a grand occasion, the owner not admitting that it is paste, not diamond, the borrower assuming it is real. The suite is lost, the borrower's whole long life ruined earning enough money to buy a comparable real suite. The original owner meanwhile has had a lifetime of contentment, secure in the public estimation that she is rich and her jewels, therefore, of a suitable expense and quality. The irony and tragedy are, of course, too subtle to summarize: the essence is that, at this time, poor people still had the inborn instinct of quality, the rich no longer cared as long as they gave the right impression. Balzac hints at the same situation several times, particularly in *Cousine Bette*.

Consuelo Vanderbilt, the great American heiress and the Duke of Marlborough's wife, gives one of many versions of a story showing how good jewels helped people to rise socially even though, as Maupassant and Balzac suggest, 'top' people no longer always quite lived up to expectation:

The two outstanding beauties of the *demimonde* were La Belle Otéro, a dark and passionate young woman with a strong blend of Greek and gypsy blood, who was always flamboyantly dressed to set off her magnificent figure; and lovely Liane de Pougy, who looked the *grande dame* she eventually became by her marriage to the Roumanian Prince Ghika.

There was rivalry between them and they were proud of the precious stones that adorned them as visible signs of the eminence they had reached in their profession. Fortunes were spent and lost for them and bets were exchanged on the relative value of their jewels. It was not surprising therefore that Otéro should challenge her rival by appearing at the Casino one night covered from head to foot with priceless jewels. It was a dazzling display, but in seeking to outdo her rival Otéro had sacrificed good taste and had lent herself to ridicule. Excited conjectures about Pougy's rejoinder were promptly answered. The next evening, appearing in a simple white gown without a single jewel, she was followed by her maid gorgeously arrayed in jewels that far outshone Otéro's.

Consuelo wrote of her impending marriage to the Duke of Marlborough:

My father had generously told me to get whatever I wanted as a gift from him, but I was surprised by the excess of household and personal linens, clothes, furs and hats my husband was ordering. Marlborough's ideas about jewels were equally princely, and since there appeared to be no family heirlooms, jewels became a necessary addition to my trousseau. It was then the fashion to wear dog-collars; mine was of pearls and had nineteen rows, with high diamond clasps which rasped my neck. My mother had given me all the pearls she had received from my father. There were two fine rows which had once belonged to Catherine of Russia and to the Empress Eugénie, and also a *sautoir* which I could clasp round my waist. A diamond tiara capped with pearl-shaped stones was my father's gift to me, and from Marlborough came a diamond belt. They were beautiful indeed, but jewels never gave me pleasure and my heavy tiara invariably produced a violent headache, my dog-collar a chafed neck. Thus bejewelled and bedecked I was deemed worthy to meet English society.

When Consuelo was painted by Sargent, he wanted her neck long, like, as he said, the trunk of a tree. For that aesthetic reason he refused to adorn it with pearls, a fact that aggrieved one of her sisters-in-law, who remarked that she should not appear in public without them.

Nubar Gulbenkian, in his autobiography, recorded some of the customs of international jewelry buyers: for instance, in Paris

Cartiers always remained open throughout the night because of Mantacheff's habit, in the early hours of the morning, of splashing out, thinking nothing of spending say, £3,000 on jewels for the favourite of the moment. He was a very good client of the night clubs and, like so many Russians, had a weak spot for the gypsy bands of which there were many, both before the [1914] war and again afterwards. He loved to take a handful of gold coins, louis d'or, from his pocket, throw them on the floor, and then watch the band scrambling for them. But old Mantacheff was a shrewder and much less generous man by day . . .

This was the world of fine precious stones, which continued up to the 1939 war. Since then it has been steadily eroded. The world-wide social revolution has led to a more equal distribution of wealth, and, equally important, an attitude of discreet restraint by rich people rather than of open ostentation. The trends of taxation, of fashion and morality alike, have led away from rich, formal clothing towards a new informality. But just as important as these changes in the nature of society is the rise of artist-jewelers. They launched the art nouveau style around 1900, exciting but short-lived and with almost no impact outside its own devoted circle of aesthetes; since 1945 they have reappeared in all the larger countries and this time they have come to stay.

ART NOUVEAU

Art Nouveau was a crazy but exciting reaction against convention: against big stones, big money, boring colours and conventional dress. The new style had a different flavour in each country, but all were inspired by a lanky, intertwined line which owed something to the new awareness of Japan. Its stylized sculpture and its dramatic mixture of precious and worthless materials suddenly became fashionable in jewels about 1895 and equally suddenly died around 1910. It was fascinating, obsessed with endless creepers and leaves, dream-sodden faces, soft, irregular low relief, dusky colours.

Art Nouveau was dependent on individual genius, and could not be mass-produced. Its own exaggerations killed it. Walter Crane recorded in 1903, 'L'Art

Brooch, formerly a pendant, showing Noah's Ark on Mount Ararat with the animals emerging and God giving blessing. Chalcedony cameo carved in high relief probably by Alessandro Masnago a famous gem engraver in Milan. Late 16th century (the gold setting is 19th century)

Nouveau is already old. Its apotheosis was at Turin last year . . . the new art carried seeds of dissolution in itself.' The idea of 'eternal undulation', conceived by Mackmurdo in 1883, gave way to the straight line.

The most stylish manifestation of this strange phase in the history of design was, in fact, its jewelry. Art Nouveau was ornament, not structure, and therefore ideally suited to this most ornamental of the arts. Enamel was its chief medium, but already in 1902 the magazine *Studio* noted of Belgium:

Little by little enamel is being abandoned in favour of stones, such as onyx, agate, and malachite, materials of no special value, which can be cut in different ways, and whose colour gives fine effects infinitely preferable to those of inferior enamels.

It was an international age, with governments everywhere seeking to emulate the triumph of the machine in England by staging great industrial exhibitions, and with many of the public responding to refreshing new impulses after decades of social stagnation. Following the first and greatest exhibition, London's in 1851, the catalogue of the London 1862 show summed up the outlook: 'We may not be more moral, more imaginative, nor better educated than our ancestors, but we have steam, gas, railways and power looms, while there are more of us and we have more money to spend.' Then came the great expositions: in Philadelphia in 1876, New Orleans 1884–5, Paris 1867, 1889, and 1900, Chicago 1893, San Francisco 1894, Antwerp 1895, Brussels 1897, Munich 1897, Dresden 1897, Turin 1902, St Louis 1904, and Liège 1905. They showed the western world's instinct for unity and prosperity.

C. R. Ashbee of England, architect and goldsmith, exhibited at Vienna, Munich, Düsseldorf and Paris, and designed rooms for the Prince of Hesse's castle at Darmstadt, which was destroyed by bomb damage in the 1939 war. Mackintosh of Glasgow designed the brilliant Scottish Pavilion in the 1902 Turin exhibition, and showed also in Vienna, Budapest, Dresden, Munich and Moscow. Joseph Hoffmann of Vienna was born in Antwerp, died in Zurich, and worked in Germany, Switzerland, Holland and Belgium. Tiffany studied in Paris and won a *Grand Prix* at Turin 1902. The St Louis 1904 exhibition represented many of Europe's leading names.

Wolfers of Brussels had jewels reproduced in eighty-three art magazines all over the world from 1893 to 1908, and a showcase he designed, once at the Paris 1902 exhibition, now appropriately houses art nouveau jewels in the Darmstadt museum. The different artists showed an intense interest in each other's work without ever apparently wanting to copy it.

For Britain it may be said here, as in other fields, that she mothered the invention but could not cope with it when it grew up. A. H. Mackmurdo (1851–1942) started the Century Guild in 1882 to drive trade out of the arts, and his 1883 book cover is the world's first recorded art nouveau design, but he abandoned the lead he had won.

England was inspired by the writings of William Morris and John Ruskin, now known under the flat, uninspiring name 'Arts and Crafts Movement'. William Morris (1834–96) had a vision of workers enjoying their 'daily necessary work' and he wanted artists to express their own nature, not copy someone else's. In 1891 he started the Kelmscott Press, an offshoot of his own Morris & Co. 'The Firm' and he himself enjoyed some financial success. But the weakness of the British movement towards artistic creativity was simply expense: Morris' socialist convictions prevented him from realizing that artists' hand-made work, while it may be superior to the factory product, can only be bought by rich people. The British pioneers of Art Nouveau viewed business with some suspicion; it is not surprising that their enormous artistic influence failed to impress the world of commerce.

C. R. Ashbee (1863–1942), the most prolific metalworker of the time, started the Guild of Handicraft in 1888, as a craft co-operative, at Essex House in the Mile End Road, London; retaining a London shop, he moved the co-operative in 1902 to Chipping Campden in Gloucestershire where old houses were restored and agricultural work undertaken, and finally wound it up in 1908. Ashbee seems now to have been one of the quieter, less creative designers, but his reputation then was good: in 1912 his *Silverwork and Jewellery*, privately printed, showed his interest in, but also his rather limited appreciation of craft work. His jewels were usually clumsy and inelegant, made of silver and one of the translucent stones, blister pearl, moonstone, turquoise or opal, but always of much more metal than stone; and his silver followed suit.

If Ashbee made the most jewels, Henry Wilson (1864–1934) led in silver. Professor Pevsner surprisingly claims that Ashbee's silver is not Art Nouveau, in which case Wilson's, with its castellated romantic medievalism, is even less so. Both rather homespun stylistically, Ashbee was more designer, Wilson more craftsman, though he himself might not have liked the assessment, as he was an active author and lecturer. He made great quantities of church plate and regalia, for health reasons often doing his casting at Torcello. He made the enormous doors for New York Anglican Cathedral. He is a link with both the past and the future, because his style is almost as backward-looking as to be Victorian, almost progressive enough to confuse with Omar Ramsden and Alwyn Carr, the next generation of church-smiths. Wilson was a sensible, serviceable bridge between the nineteenth and twentieth centuries, with Voysey's or Dresser's austere unornamented functionalism at one extreme, and the exuberant Art Nouveau at the other. What he carried over the bridge is not now fashionable: it is William Morris's belief in the joy of handwork. Yet Morris's energies were not in vain, because England is now one of the few countries in the world where hand-made jewelry is still often commissioned from independent artist-craftsmen.

Next in importance probably comes the firm of Liberty, which was started in 1875 by Arthur Lasenby Liberty, partly to popularize unsold Japanese stock remaining from the first western showing of Japanese work at the London 1862 exhibition. William Morris managed the Farmer and Rogers' oriental warehouse and inspired his friend Liberty with zeal for Japan, whose influence on Art Nouveau was partly due to the novelty of the country, opened to the west in 1857. Liberty in his turn used many metalwork designers, his chief suppliers probably being William Hutton & Sons of Sheffield and W. H. Haseler & Co. of Birmingham; in 1899 he launched the 'Cymric' range of silver and jewels, still commonly seen in British antique shops, stamped with the trade name, heavily worked, and soberly but not brilliantly eccentric. 'Tudric' pewter followed. Unfortunately Liberty policy was to keep the names of their designers secret, no doubt in order to retain control over them; this means that, despite splendid researches by Mrs Shirley Bury at the Victoria and Albert Museum, we do not know what proportion of the work was machine-made, or how far the firm either wanted or achieved a union of art and industry. Archibald Knox (1864–

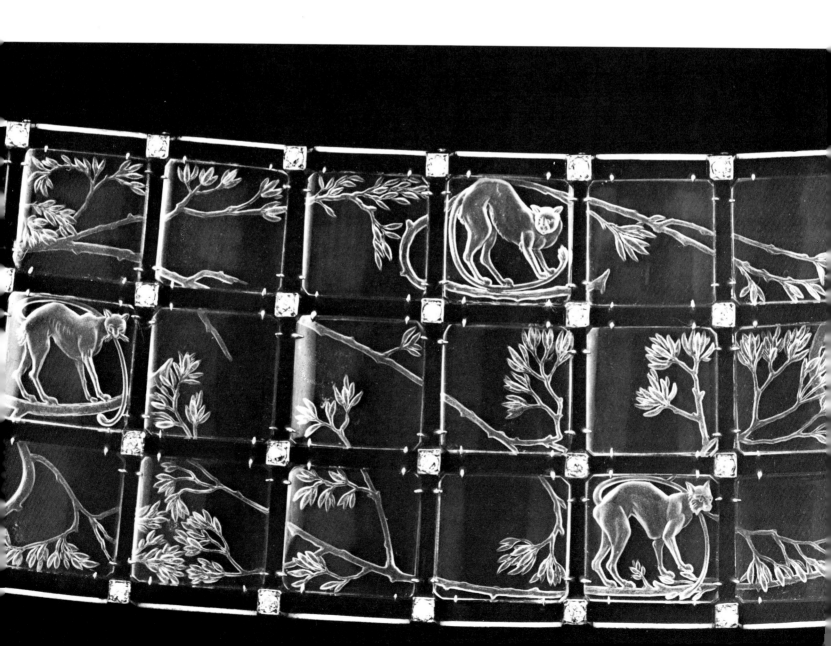

1933) was one of the more original designers; Bernard Cuzner (1877–1956) a typically devoted craftsman who looked back on his art nouveau work as a youthful irresponsibility, a whimsical betrayal of the solid materials he admired. Haseler himself, conversely, probably valued production for its own sake: his joint company with Liberty's was dissolved as late as 1927.

Charles Rennie Mackintosh (1868–1928) is now recognized as the world giant of the period, the one British designer whose invention never flagged, whose conviction was absolute, whose stature is comparable with van de Velde and Lalique. He designed tableware prototypes and architectural metalwork which have excited stylists everywhere, and those numerous austere art theorists who, as valid twentieth-century art forms, prefer doorknobs to jewels. Mackintosh was the catalyst for a group of artists who came to be centred on the Glasgow School of Art, including his wife, Margaret MacDonald (1865–1933), and her sister Frances (1874–1921), Jessie King (1876–1949), Nelson Dawson (1859–1942), Talwyn Morris (1865–1911) and others, all of whose jewels and metalwork are much commoner and less distinguished than their master's, though still dominated by his own personal idiom, as astonishing as it is logical. Only one Mackintosh jewel survives, inadequate testimony of his giant influence.

Sir Alfred Gilbert, another outstandingly original artist, was at the Beaux Arts from 1876. He designed half a dozen known jewels. He used to twist wire in his fingers as a therapy, a ready-made recipe for Art Nouveau, and was one of the few Englishmen to evolve a full-blooded version of the style in the plastic arts. Apart from the Glasgow School he made the most distinguished British contribution to Art Nouveau, although he characteristically would not admit that he belonged to any type: 'L'Art Nouveau for sooth! Absolute nonsense!' 'Vapid, disloyal, unhealthy', he called it.

British Art Nouveau was almost stillborn because of British reticence; as a nation we do not indulge in orgies of visual fun. Walter Crane (1845–1915) called the phenomenon a 'strange decorative disease' and 'the antithesis of the Morris school of decoration'. Morris himself was primarily a social reformer. Although his wallpapers and fabrics

Art Nouveau in Germany and Austria was called Jugendstil or Sezession; its style was angles and straight lines, rather than the curves of France and Belgium. Above Pendant in silver and semiprecious stones designed by Joseph Hoffmann, made in the Wiener Werkstätte of Vienna. Height: 1.7 inches. German National Museum, Nuremberg

Art nouveau jewels brought new vitality to jewelry not only through inspired originality but also through unusual materials as in this detail, left, showing Japanese influence, of a choker in gold, engraved glass and diamonds by René Lalique of Paris, 1898. Gulbenkian Museum, Lisbon

were commercially successful, his main artistic conviction was a sentimental one in favour of the individual as against the machine. He never reconciled the contradiction between his socialist and his artistic theories, the inability of expensive handwork to satisfy cheap mass markets to lighten the world's burden of poverty. The nearest he got was to praise sensible designs at the expense of fantasies. As he was a very powerful and popular personality, his ideas, which dominated the applied art world, may have helped to undo British Art Nouveau, at the same time giving a world impetus to conscientious workmanship.

In Denmark there was the work without the theory. Georg Jensen and Johan Rohde quickly grew out of the prevalent style, imitative and over-elaborate, and evolved their own personal idiom which has served the Jensen name so well ever since: more bulges than curves, more bulk than line, more fleshy than sinuous, more heavy fruits than light flowers, the idea was a steady success from the beginning. The material, as in Britain, was almost always silver, often with amber, the common Polish stone; and it may be guessed that jewels formed a much larger proportion of Jensen's output than they did of that of his contemporaries in England. Jensen designed with greater conviction than his British colleagues (and without the hampering influence of the Ruskin/Morris theories); moreover, precious jewelry and good silver hardly existed in Denmark before. In Britain, on the other hand, there were already hundreds of factories and retail shops: here the craftsmen's task was to convert an existing taste—a task which is only now nearing success.

In Norway, too, there was almost virgin ground. In the eighteenth century Bergen had been a great centre for filigree work, and Bergen smiths, such as the Reimer family, had exported all over the world. But it was not until the late nineteenth century that Norwegian silver, mostly from country workshops, was revived. The old firm of Jacob Tostrup pioneered not only filigree but a very fine, specialized transparent enamel—*plique à jour*—which won many international exhibition successes. The architect Torolf Prytz and later Jacob Prytz, head of the firm after 1918 and then head of the state art school, worked with the Oslo museum to bring a new vitality to applied art. Other firms like David Andersen followed, until Norway became widely famous for its modern enamels.

In Germany *Jugendstil* (from the Munich paper) was also a commercial success. In fact it was commercial from the start, and therefore different in detail, being adapted to semi-quantity production. Machine-made components were assembled in small, already existing factories, mostly at Pforzheim, since the eighteenth century the great centre for gold and silver jewels, but also at Frankfurt, Schwäbisch Gmünd and at Hanau. The products were small, unlike French and Belgian work, light, unlike British or Danish, and anonymous, unlike art nouveau jewelry in any other country. The great German pioneers of international modern architecture, Peter Behrens, Walter Gropius and Joseph Olbrich, killed the curve almost before it had appeared there. But, as in Denmark, German work around 1900 led to enormous commercial expansion in the 1920s and 1930s: the new Pforzheim Reuchlinhaus Museum has the most elegant jewelry display in existence, and shows the development from the sophisticated, pioneer, small-scale production of 1900 to the vulgar, meretricious work which today has gained for Pforzheim its undisputed place as the world's leading producer of cheap work.

Individual German metalwork designers like Karl Bauer (1868–1942) or Georg Kleeman (1863–1929) or Ernst Riegel (1871–1946) did not apparently have very personal styles, and the giants like Behrens or Riemerschmid, and indeed the whole artists' colony established at Darmstadt had more influence than the craftsmen themselves on silver design. The Darmstadt museum, brilliantly rebuilt and completed in 1965, shows this German *Jugendstil*, in many media, at its best.

Vienna was one of the first capitals to meet Art Nouveau, but one of the last to digest it. Of the founders of the anti-historical *Sezession* group in 1897, which gave its name to Viennese *Jugendstil*, Joseph Hoffmann (1870–1956) and Koloman Moser (1868–1916) both designed jewels. Many of the leading artists, including Hoffmann and Dagobert Peche (1887–1923) supported the Wiener Werkstätte, started by Hoffmann in 1903, a society of artist-craftsmen with furnished workshops which survived till the 1930s' slump, having made, over three decades, much of the best Viennese craftwork. The style was that

Necklace of gold and rubies, perhaps German, c. 1760. The bouncing interwoven lines are typical of the gay rococo style.

of 'chequerboard' Hoffmann, small squares and triangles and dots, much richer than the German, often using gold or pearls or ivory, or enamels, often producing rather large pieces for the wealthy classes. The great achievement is Hoffmann's Hôtel Stoclet in Brussels where many of the craftsmen worked from 1904 to 1911, and where some of the best of the rare *Sezession* pieces are still preserved.

It was in Belgium that jewels in the 'modern style' as it was called, first became fashionable, through the influence of Philippe Wolfers (1858–1929) a very substantial artist. His firm, Wolfers Frères, were and still are the Belgian crown jewelers, with all the power which that responsibility carries. It must have been this power, so seldom well exercised by its holders, that enabled Wolfers to produce a signed series of precious jewels; the finest group is now venerated by the Brussels couturier L. Wittamer-de Camps. Wolfers studied at the Beaux Arts in Brussels, joined the family firm which, however, had no retail shop, and was much impressed with Japanese work at the Vienna International Exhibition 1873; around 1890 he established his own workshop in Marie Louise Square, and about 1893 started using ivory from the Congo offered to artists by Leopold II. From 1905 he became increasingly interested in sculpture, abandoning jewels, his first love, and interior decoration, his second, and in 1910 Victor Horta built the firm's splendid workshops and showrooms.

Henri van de Velde (1863–1957) was born in Antwerp, worked as architectural adviser to the Grand Duke of Weimar from 1899 to 1917, then taught at Ghent and Courtrai, also working intermittently in Holland and in Switzerland. Unlike Mackintosh, with whom his strength and originality are comparable, he must have particularly enjoyed silver and jewels: his surviving pieces are almost all of austere silver or base metal—architect-jewelers do not seem to respond to the joys of luxury— but van de Velde's work makes up in exquisitely elaborate linear chasing what it loses in intrinsic lustre. He strikes the perfect balance between an architect's perfectionism and a jeweler's fantasy, a rare combination of qualities which gives his metalwork unique distinction. He seems to be one of the few great architects to have concentrated on

and really found pleasure in jewels.

The name La Maison de l'Art Nouveau was invented by Samuel Bing of Hamburg for the shop he opened in Paris in 1895, from which he must have sold much of Europe's best Art Nouveau, particularly to the museums in Paris and Copenhagen with whom he developed strong links. Always a jewel centre, Paris was seething with change at the turn of the century, much more so than London, its sister in wealth and politics. Impressionism in art, Proust, Victor Hugo, de Musset and symbolism in poetry, Diaghilev, Stravinsky, Debussy and Ravel in music, the Franco-Prussian War of 1870 and the Haussmann replanning on a huge scale afterwards—all these made women ready for a change, and indeed they expected it.

René Lalique (1860–1945) is the most sensational figure in the field. He always wanted to draw. He was the son of a merchant, and on his father's death in 1876 his mother apprenticed him as jeweler to Louis Aucoc, and he started courses at the Ecole des Arts Décoratifs, which he abandoned for lack of time. From 1878 he studied at Sydenham, and in 1881 returned to work with various Paris firms, designing wallpapers, fabrics, and an industrial art journal with etchings as a guide to jewelers. By now he knew some of the customers of the firms for whom he had worked—Cartier, Boucheron, Aucoc, Destape—and in 1886 he was left Destape's business. From 1890 to 1893 he studied glass techniques in his Rue Thérèse workshop, and, equally important, attracted Sarah Bernhardt who commissioned two groups of jewels for *Iseyl et Gismonda*.

In 1895 his first display at the Salon made him well known—he won third prize there. The same year he first used the female nude in his jewelry. In 1896 he first used horn encrusted with silver; horn was his great innovation. In 1897 he became *Chevalier* of the Legion of Honour. In 1900 he showed in the great Paris exhibition from which Queen Victoria bought two pieces. In 1903 he designed and built his shop at 40 Cours Albert I, with a great doorway in glass and pinewood by Saint Gobin, followed in 1905 by his main Place Vendôme shop. The same year Thomas Agnew, the the British art gallery, gave him a one-man show. In 1909 he leased and in 1910 bought a glass factory at Combes-la-Ville, glass becoming more prominent in his jewels, till he finally abandoned

113

jewelry in 1914. He employed as many as thirty craftsmen—a big producer as well as a fertile artist. Eugène Feuillâtre (1870–1916) worked for him, researching into the problems of enamelling on silver; Lalique himself was a great technical innovator, using machines to reduce his large models to actual working size. The superb group of pieces commissioned by Calouste Gulbenkian from René Lalique, and now in Lisbon, shows the style at its best and most personal. Lalique was indeed the giant of the movement.

Georges Fouquet (1862–1957), the eldest son of Alphonse Fouquet, jeweler

of Avenue de l'Opéra, had a stylistic affinity with Lalique, and seems to have operated on a similar scale. We know of him from his family because his son Jean is now one of the foremost Paris artist-craftsmen. Georges started work with his father at eighteen; in 1895 he inherited the business and immediately modernized it, working with Tourrette, Desroziers (1905–8), Grasset and Mucha. After prizes in the Universal Exhibitions of 1900 and 1901 he asked Mucha to design his new shop at 6 Rue Royale, which was demolished in 1920. He showed in Milan 1906, was president of the jewelers at the Paris 1925 and 1937

exhibitions, and a member of the Union Centrale des Arts Décoratifs, thus being one of the few designers to remain in practice having outlived the epoch. His most significant connection was no doubt with Alphons Mucha, to whose designs he made many pieces, and through whom he must have met some of the most exotic women in the world.

Henri Vever (1854–1942), author of the history of French nineteenth-century jewelry, inherited his firm in 1874 with his brother Paul (1851–1915) from their father, Ernest, a figure of standing who had been President of the Chambre Syndicale. Henri studied at the Ecole

Left *Dragonfly corsage ornament in gold, ivory, stones, chrysoprase and enamel of the specially fragile unbacked type called* plique-à-jour; *by René Lalique, Paris, c. 1898. Bought by Calouste Gulbenkian and lent by him to Sarah Bernhardt. Width: 6.1 inches. Gulbenkian Museum, Lisbon*

Below *Comb in perforated gold with a large amethyst which was originally a diamond, c. 1898. Bought by Calouste Gulbenkian from the artist, Lalique, in 1904. Length: 6.1 inches. Gulbenkian Museum, Lisbon*

des Arts Décoratifs in the evenings, and by day at the ateliers of Loguet, Hallet and Dufong. In 1889, at their first exhibition, the brothers won one of the two *Grands Prix*; in 1891 at the French exhibition in Moscow, they won the *Croix de la Légion d'Honneur*, and studied the crown jewels of the tsars there, and of the sultans in Istanbul. In 1893 Henri was Commissioner at the Chicago exhibition; in 1895 he won prizes at Bordeaux, in 1897 at Brussels, in 1900 a *Grand Prix* at Paris. Vever's work was much heavier and less spontaneous than Lalique's or Fouquet's, and he probably did not pride himself as the others did on producing outstanding special masterpieces.

So much for the biggest French names; foremost among the others was Alphons Mucha (1860–1939), painter, graphic designer and decorator, the best known and most prolific of all. He started his studio with Whistler. From 1894 he had a six-year contract for Sarah Bernhardt's posters and décors and published portfolios of designs which were disseminated so far that *le style Mucha* and Art Nouveau were for a time synonymous. He worked in Paris, Berlin, and his native Prague, and designed rather lightweight jewels for Georges Fouquet from 1898 to 1905. He was more facile than inspired. Then there was Lucien Gaillard (b. 1861), known for his interest in Japan, who exhibited at the Paris 1900 and the Glasgow 1901 exhibitions; Eugène Grasset (1841–1917), another Japanese enthusiast, who visited Egypt in 1869, studied with Viollet-le-Duc and designed for Vever, was more popularizer than creator. Victor Prouvé (1858–1943), pioneer of exotic glass made at Nancy under the inventive lead of Emile Gallé (1846–1904), Paul Liénard (1849–1900), Georges de Ribaucourt (1881–1907), L. Gautrait, Henri Dubret, and others hardly established their personalities in this most personal of styles. All these artists followed the giants, but Art Nouveau was a medium for creators, not for followers.

Smart shops for this metal and glass existed in Paris as nowhere else in Europe. Lalique's, in the Place Vendôme, was where the group La Haute Joaillerie de France now mostly are; Fouquet's, designed by Mucha, was in the Rue Royale near the present shop bearing Lalique's name but not his philosophy. Some of the Fouquet–Mucha parts preserved in the Musée Carnavalet (but not on show) give an idea of the luxuriant fittings which must have made the exhibits seem quite normal. The big old firms like Cardeilhac hardly swallowed the new style—proof, if any were needed, of its limited appeal.

Elsewhere the seed was sown but did not take root. In Italy it was called the *stile Liberty* from the firm whence the imports came. Architecture was hardly affected, and silver not at all, if one is to judge from such works as 'Liberty a Napoli' by Renato de Fusco, 'L'età di Liberty' by Italo Cremona, or the 1965 display at the Galleria Milano. The large and expanding firms, Calderoni, Bulgari and Buccellati, retained their static dignity in the face of all temptation.

Gaudí of Barcelona lavished coloured glazes on his buildings, and they too have a jewel-like quality because of their creator's devotion to hand-made detail. It is sad that no actual jewels survive by him, one of the most creative spirits in this age of dazzling originality.

In the USA Louis Comfort Tiffany (1848–1943), with his original iridescent glass techniques and jewels in a style somewhere between Lalique and Henry Wilson, alternating surprisingly between the very elegant and the overthick, was a lone phenomenon. He designed bronze and iron lamps and table decoration, but very few jewels—perhaps only half a dozen in all, compared with thousands upon thousands of lamps.

Louis Sullivan, the famous Chicago architect, pioneer of the skyscraper, is not so well known as a brilliant draughtsman of profuse and exotic ornament. He was at the Paris Beaux Arts in 1874; and the Chicago Auditorium, his first big building, shows his personal art nouveau style as early as 1887. Sullivan may reasonably be claimed as an originator of Art Nouveau; his large-scale architectural metalwork decorations are a revelation, colossal virtuoso jewels.

But, alas, he never designed real jewels and his brilliant architecture with its lavish art nouveau details never caught on. The Americans preferred either heavy period reproductions, or building based on economy of structure. This rough new society was not yet tired of artistic orthodoxy, nor yet settled enough for a *belle époque* high society to establish mannerisms of its own.

The Artist-Jeweler

Jewelry today represents beauty and money; it is related to love and sex; it is intimate and mysterious. To some extent one can even judge a person by the jewels she wears: taste is an ancient fundamental streak buried deep down in all of us, and jewels now more than ever before show our subconscious selves.

This was not so even as recently as ten years ago. Fashions then were more personal than jewels: usually, a girl would choose her wardrobe to suit herself, whereas her jewels would simply be for glitter. Now a revolution has occurred. Jewelers everywhere are trying to be different, more modern, more personal than their competitors, and there are now many successful artist-jewelers expressing their own creative imagination. In the 1920s and the 1930s the world of fashion was suddenly intoxicated by the great designers who emerged—Schiaparelli, Balenciaga, Chanel, Dior; names were identified with particular idioms, and the trend continues with designers like Mary Quant. But now there are big names in jewelry too. Jewelry, like fashion, is steadily becoming more stimulating and more individual.

This change is partly the result of the market's turning upside-down: very rich people no longer constitute the main part of the jewelry industry's custom. In the developed countries ordinary people buy jewels as never before, and jewelers of all sorts therefore cater for an unprecedented range of income and age, fashion and function.

There are other reasons for the change too. The unsettled state of the world shows in all its modern art; the speed of travel means that we all keep up with each other's ideas, so that a new trend in one country very quickly appears in another; modern journalism, with its vast coverage for women's pages, not only flatters the emancipated woman but also pounces upon and publicizes the smallest tremor of novelty, even magnifying its significance, and often causing other producers to envy or copy it. It is probably true, too, that the whole world is giving more conscious attention to art.

The main and final reason for the big jewel shake-up is the new prominence of designers. One launching pad for them was the world's first international exhibition of modern jewelry, 1890–1961, held at Goldsmiths' Hall in London in 1961. Nine hundred jewels were exhibited, from twenty-eight countries, mostly from small workshops, and the impression of vitality was overwhelming. The gulf between the possible, in the shape of these artists' products, and the actual, in the shape of normal smart retail stock, was painful and obvious. The £10,000 ($26,000) competition organized by the Worshipful Company of Goldsmiths and De Beers put some solid backing behind the artists. Since then many of them who were little known have become famous, like Andrew Grima or John Donald in England, Friedrich Becker or Reinhold Reiling in Germany, or Bruno Martinazzi and the Pomodoro brothers in Italy.

Jewelry design has turned back from being simply the harmonious use of stones. Now it tends to express a conscious wish to be oneself, to be distinctive. Jewels have no easily recognizable national characteristics, but they show the original and, later on, the echoed ideas of just a few dominant designers and producers: style no longer varies according to country as it once did, however elusive the change was to pin down.

One supreme job stands as a good symbol for the whole world's jewelry. Louis Osman's coronet for the Prince of Wales is typical of the best modern work. It is a noble design, finely proportioned and obviously in the contemporary style of 1969, as a great public memorial of that date should be. Its details make the most of the piece's historic association, adding enormously to the general appeal. The orb on top suggests the world and worldly influence, and is engraved with the wearer's attributes (Welsh dragon, corn stooks of the Earl of Chester, feathers of the

Left *Hatpin in gold, silver, diamonds, horn and glass; the sunflower is a carved opal; by René Lalique. Bought from him for 1,500 French francs at the Paris World Fair, 1900, by the Kunstindustrimuseet, Copenhagen.*

Below *Detail of the cross of nails in gold and diamonds from the coronet (see p. 123) given by the Worshipful Company of Goldsmiths to HRH the Prince of Wales for his investiture in Caernarvon Castle, 1969. Designer, Louis Osman*

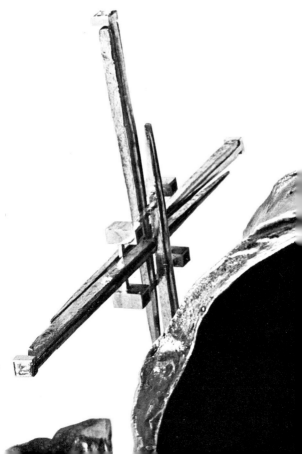

Prince of Wales and Black Prince, bezants of the Duke of Cornwall). Superimposed diamond stars, arranged in the shape of Scorpio (Prince Charles was born in November), suggest space and there are seven stones to suggest the seven deadly sins and the seven gifts of God, under the domination of the cross above. On top rises the cross for Christian spiritual power, round the sides are crosses for protection and the fleur-de-lis for purity. All over are seventy-five diamonds of tiny size—a show of huge stones to imply wealth would be out of keeping with today's duty-burdened monarchy. These sparklers are simply to relieve the soft peach sheen of the burnished gold. This is an elaborate story-piece. It will surely compare in centuries to come with the great historical documents.

But it is more than that. What makes it not just a supreme freak but a good representative piece of work is its technical accomplishment—a splendid mixture of old and new techniques. Much of the work could have been done centuries ago: the stone setting, the hand burnishing and bright polishing, the assembly of the parts by soldering and, of course, the sketch of the original idea on paper. All these highly skilled contributions were made from small craft units, workshops of usually three or four people such as form the basis of jewelry production all over the world. Jewelry, of all industries, is normally least sympathetic to mass production and big business groups.

But this crown is exceptional: although from a hand workshop it also used new factory technology. It was made by electro-forming whereby an electric current deposits a layer of gold onto a resin mould. Had it been hand-forged in the traditional manner it might have weighed more than twice its present three pounds and been almost unbearably heavy. The matching stones were chosen from a selection infinitely greater than has ever been possible before: the London stone market now offers an astonishing variety of stones from the whole world, and cuts from such diverse places as Antwerp and Tel Aviv, Amsterdam and Idar-Oberstein, even India and Brazil. The temperature for the enamel and the solder had to be precise, to retain the shape and texture of the metal.

New science has percolated into the old art of fine jewels, and both are richer

for it. On all points, therefore, jewelry is changing; new design and manufacture, marketing and wearing, are all transforming the world's oldest art.

JAPAN

If the ripples started in London, they have now reached the furthest point, Japan. Always sensitive to outside influence, Japan nevertheless still remains extremely different from Europe. In some spheres of life—for instance, the theatre—Japanese traditions are so old that they are almost impossible for a westerner to understand. But in jewelry the situation is almost equally surprising for the opposite reason—there is no history at all.

For centuries Japanese women have worn their magnificent embroidered costumes in place of jewelry—the kimono is often sewn with metal braid and almost constitutes a walking jewel. Anything worn on that would have been superfluous. Then there is the hair: as admirers of the old prints will know, Japanese women, being of small build, always enjoyed building their hair into wonderful concoctions held together with tortoise-shell combs often surmounted by delicate laquer and steel inlay, or with flimsy danglers of foil to catch the light. Japanese jewelry habits, as one might expect, are still dominated by the ancient social structure of this, one of the world's most rigid cultures.

In Europe jewelry has always been considered an ancient practice; every jewel sold in Japan, conversely, is a sign of new emancipation, a break with the past. Japan allowed in western trade and ideas only as late as 1853, and only since 1945 has the Japanese 'miracle market' enticed large numbers of westerners into this fascinating country.

Jewels are a new idea here, and no doubt partly the result of this western invasion. So, amazingly, are artists: until perhaps twenty years ago there was no social distinction whatever between painters, sculptors, industrial designers, jewelers and, say, bricklayers. All were earning their living by doing a sensible job. All craftsmen were greatly respected, almost as Europeans might respect, for instance, a sergeant in the army, a foreman in the factory. The astonishing rise of modern industry in Japan has created an entirely new breed: the creative Japanese designer. Kenmochi, who runs what is perhaps

Left *Symbols of earthly and heavenly power from the coronet above; on the orb, engraved by Malcolm Appleby, are badges from the Prince of Wales' coat of arms.*

Below *Group of combs and hairpins in horn, tortoiseshell, lacquer, and,* top left, *iron gilt (terminating in an ear-pick). Until recently the rich embroidery on Japanese kimonos was a substitute for jewelry for Japanese women; in their elaborate hair styles, however, they often wore sets of three or more identical decorated combs or pins. Japanese, perhaps 19th century*

now the world's largest design studio, handling objects as diverse as motor-cycles and cutlery, jumbo jets and paper lamp-shades, is one of these. No longer the imitator, Japan has become a leading creator, not only of modern industrial processes but inevitably of styles as well. The designer has moved from his very ancient position of responsibility to an entirely new one of prominence.

Not only is the wearing of jewels a very recent development, not only is it quite strange for a Japanese artist-craftsman to think of himself as a fine artist with individual vision, but the methods of selling jewels in Japan are bewildering and are changing very fast. Japan is now the world's second largest importer of diamonds, after the USA.

There are altogether in Japan about 30,000 retail jewelers, some of them big chain groups. One of the best of the small surviving family firms is Nakai in the smart arcade of the Okura Hotel. Started in 1892 by the grandfather of the present owner, Mr Katsuyama, half the turnover was always in diamonds bought from Indian traders at Yokohama. Up to ten years ago stock was bought at the private trade auctions, which are a mysterious prop of Japanese business, and sold wholesale to other retailers.

Rings are still the easiest jewels to sell because anyone can wear them with anything—they are equally good for weddings and funerals, for dinner and for washing dishes; but there are combs, too, and buckles for the *obi*—the central sash of the kimono—and, a new development, some pins and earrings. Pearls still account for about sixty per cent of sales: they used to come from Toba, the area fertilized a hundred years ago by the young pioneer, Mikimoto, but the sea here is now too polluted for oysters. The best sources are from Omura Bay by Nagasaki, and from further away by Kyushu, and, most spectacular, from the huge new fields by Thursday Island, and Cape York off northern Australia. Pearls are now considered rather old hat, though everybody likes to have them. Diamonds are becoming more popular: at Nakai's, small stones of 0.3 to 0.5 carats go best, and Nakai sell only the best quality. Synthetic rubies and sapphires are popular too, nearly all the stones being imported.

The routine settings and jewels are made at Kofu, a small inaccessible sec-luded city eighty miles west of Tokyo, in Yamanashi Province. This is the old

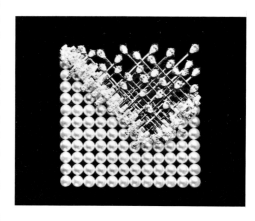

Japanese jewelers are not only creating new designs but also using new materials in addition to their traditional pearls and lacquer:
above *gold, pearl and diamond brooch by Yuji Takahashi of Tokyo. Diamonds-International Award, 1969*

Right *The random fantasy of some modern handwork is often tempered with the hard discipline of industrial design; many free-lance jewelers, like Weckström and Persson, also run studios for general industrial design.*
Top *Four finger rings, some of the earliest modern jewels in the permanent collection of the Worshipful Company of Goldsmiths, at Goldsmiths' Hall, London, now the world's largest collection of modern jewelry. From left to right: gold and smoky quartz by Björn Weckström, Helsinki; white gold and diamonds by Sigurd Persson, Stockholm; gold with flake granules by Bruno Martinazzi, Turin; gold with coloured gold and niello inlay by William Haendel, Illinois; all 1961*
Bottom *Gold flower with leaves beaten thin and springy, ruby stamens; by Henry Shawah, Boston, USA, 1970*

centre of gemstone carving, the nucleus of a large cottage industry where crystal mines and stone cutters were active a hundred years ago; the home of jade and rose quartz, of dyed agate and carnelian. The emphasis is on gemmology more than craftsmanship.

Nakai get their best work by their own staff designer Ogawa made in some of the dozens of tiny top quality work-shops in Tokyo, many with two or three craftsmen, none with more than five. As in every other country, the best work is found in the smallest workshops. In fact, even the big firms are small by western standards. The firm of John Jerwood, the Englishman who started Australian pearls, and now dominates Japanese production and sales too, is, it is true, enormous, handling over seven tons annually and now undertaking world-wide promotion schemes; but he is exceptional in that respect, as in almost every way, not least in his inter-nationalism and his energy.

Taiyo Pearls have substantial fishery interests in the South Seas but their excellent small Tokyo shops are con-fined to only three in number, one of them in the New Japan Hotel, another in the Palace Hotel. Mikimoto, despite their world fame, have only one shop and, since the death of their founder, their pearl interests have dwindled and they are concentrating on diamonds. All these, and the other smart retailers like Miwa or Uyeda by the Imperial Hotel, would fit many times over into Tiffany of New York or Asprey of London.

Japanese jewelers are still fragmented and unco-ordinated, waiting for their Jean Jacques Cartier. By far the most im-portant places for jewelry are the depart-ment stores, an entirely Japanese phe-nomenon. Especially in Tokyo—the world's biggest city with a population of some fifteen millions and very much the country's business centre—these stores are prodigious and the main force in Japanese consumer goods. One of the newest and quickest-moving is Seibu: thirty years ago it hardly existed, now it is the fourth largest store in Japan, with a turnover bigger than Britain's huge Marks and Spencer group. Seibu expects about 300,000 visitors to see each of its shows. During the British Week Tokyo in September 1969, the store had no less than four shows running concurrently, including one about Queen Elizabeth I, with beautiful antique jewels, in the main store, and, at the Shibuya suburb,

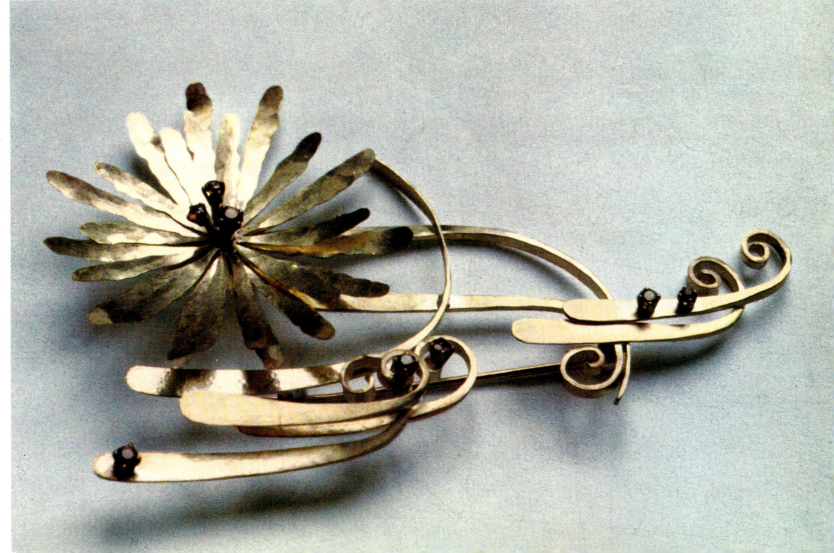

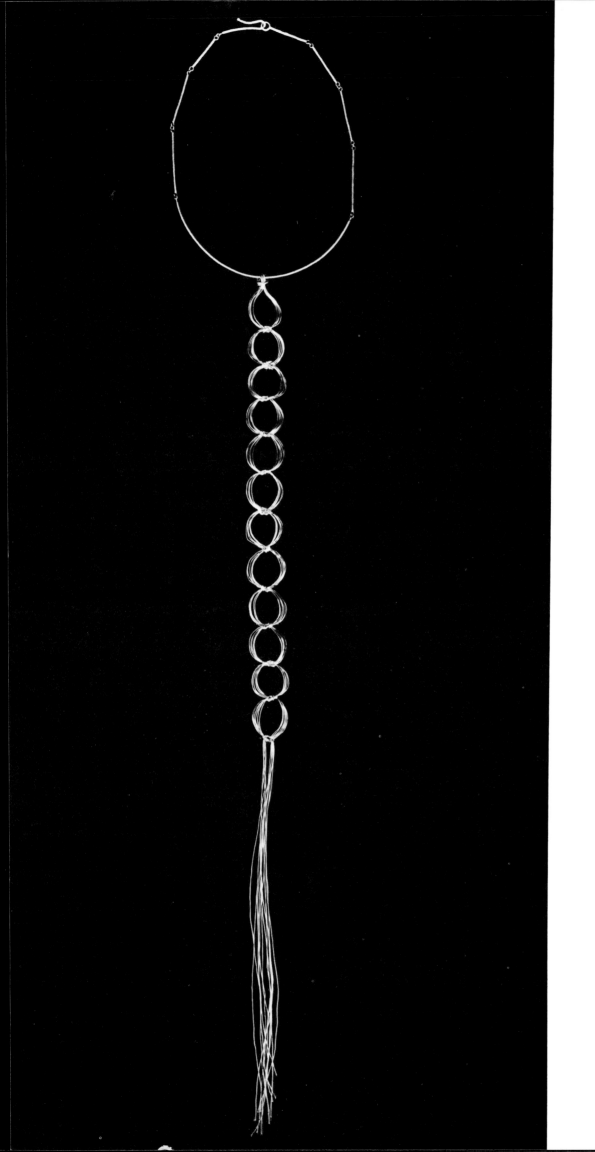

The Japanese taste for exquisite, rather lightweight detail shows in this distinguished gold necklace by Suki Hiramatsu of Tokyo, 1967

of Japan but whether it will lead to the diversity and delight of really distinguished jewels remains to be seen.

The Jewelry Design Association indeed gives the show away by its tiny size: it has only some sixty members, of whom two-thirds are part-time jewelers —not many for a country of more than 100,000,000 people. But there are some 20,000 amateur jewelers in Tokyo alone who make jewels as a hobby. Japan is entering the diamond age and it is anyone's guess whether it will do so in a thrilling oriental manner, developing a new idiom to suit its extraordinary background, as it has done, for instance, with its magnificent pens and paint brushes, or whether it will slide along behind the west with rather thin, lightweight re-interpretations.

At the moment there is evidence both ways. Yasuki Hiramatsu, professor at Tokyo University of Art, has evolved a delicacy and sophistication entirely his own: he beats his gold extremely thin, he crumples and roughens and torments it, he makes it crackle, and, by putting baubles inside his brooches, he even makes them tinkle. Here is the miraculous grace of Japanese calligraphy, each stroke quick and exact, both fine and firm, turned into gold. It is memorable, and it has been modestly distinguished in competitions at Pforzheim and elsewhere, but it has never won—perhaps it is too eastern in character for western eyes. The tragedy is that it may be too eastern for eastern eyes, too. One of the main aims of many Japanese philosophers is to be not Japanese but universal. Japan, so the argument goes, wants to prove it is no longer an emperor-worshipping or *shinto*, militaristic, feudal state, but a modern democracy on the western model. The way to prove this, it is said, is to be like, and to behave like, the west. Hence the amazing snob value and easy saleability of western goods, and the sometimes surprising affinity between Japanese designs and our own. It is not only imitation, it is flattery.

Koji Iwakura runs a powerful workshop of forty people, with contacts throughout the Tokyo trade. His speciality is casting and there is no magic here: his equipment is small in scale and orthodox in type, his factory is a small converted private house in a back street. His designs are mostly derivative, a mix-up of many European ideas which he makes in order to sell, a good motive for a manager but a dispiriting one for a designer. In fact he employs two or three draughtsmen and modellers in addition to himself, and the strength of his business is its range of designs: several rooms have their walls lined with used rubber moulds for casting, efficiently indexed, carefully stacked in order, and ready for re-use at any moment to suit the requirement of any of the myriad customers in the world's largest city—a good example of the power of Tokyo retailers who carry a minimum of stock and expect immediate supply and service from the wholesale warehouses and factories, often ordering only on consignment, that is, borrowing not buying. This top-heaviness in the balance of trading power would be intolerable in Europe or the USA and is already changing in Tokyo, particularly with the newer stores like Seibu; but as long as it persists small producers like Iwakura will remain inevitably rather uncreative, slaves to the crushing burdens of high interest rates on the one hand and the vagaries of public demand through the retailers on the other.

One of the most active forces in Japanese jewelry design is Yasushiko Hishida. As university teacher, as writer and propagandist, as head of the jewelry designers and organizer of the Seibu 1970 international show, he is influential. With some Italian training, he has travelled more than most designers. His opinion of Japanese designs is hopeful, but rather less than reassuring. In 1968 he wrote that Japanese modern jewelry design started only ten years ago, that his and Hiramatsu's are the only two university design classes in the country, that there are in all Tokyo only some thirty studios where apprentices can learn chasing and other heavy metalwork skill. It seems the gargantuan Japanese appetite for jewels of all sorts will almost certainly overwhelm those few idealists like Hishida. He, like most other Japanese designers in media which are strange and new to them, is feeling his way towards his own idiom—pleasing patterns of narrow spiky strips— but in commerce the bad often chases out the good. The Japanese demand for jewels, with its unformed taste, may overlook the stirrings of individuality and succumb to the cheap and trivial.

One hopeful landmark is the Japan Craft Centre founded five years ago by the distinguished Finnish-trained architect Kenji Fujimori, who is now helped by half a dozen other artists, each in his own field. Housed in the Maruzen store, the centre's aim is to foster native Japanese skill—for instance, in cast iron, ceramics, knives and bamboo, all peerless throughout the world—and to establish a similar standard of local excellence in other consumer goods, including jewels.

Whatever happens artistically, Japan is going to dominate commerce in perhaps only twenty years, becoming the world's richest country. So the last words on the quality of Japanese jewels must be a financial postscript. There are about one million marriages a year in Japan; in 1966 about seven per cent of them involved a diamond engagement ring. De Beers' publicity programme there, though started only in 1967, is already one of their biggest, and they expand the programme by some ten per cent annually. Sales of jewels in the stores are expected to multiply three times in the next five years.

Probably it is that old mystical force, gold, which provides the most significant factual news. In 1969 its local price was about £1 ($2.60) per gram; the small Japanese mines' production was about three times as expensive as the imported South African, and satisfied only some three per cent of the nation's consumption. To stabilize the bullion and currency situation, and to protect the local mines, the Japanese government, which has a notoriously obscure protectionist policy, has hitherto made the import of 18 carat gold jewels almost impossible. As this is the very type of work in which modern European designers excel, Japan has denied herself access to the best examples which might have proved a catalyst for her own workshops. Eventually the Japanese government will no doubt admit progressive influences. The Japanese favourites so far have been white metals—platinum which is now too expensive, silver which is very common, and white gold. The new idioms in yellow gold, if it were admitted in quantity, might provide just the right tonic at the right time. Meanwhile, Japanese jewels have not yet realized the dazzling potential of Japan as a whole.

AUSTRALIA

Australia and Japan are now probably each other's biggest trading partners, but there the similarity ends. Australia, with a population of only fifteen millions, is very under-populated, close to Britain in its thinking, relaxed in its trading. Its jewels do, of course, use the local opal mostly from Lightning Ridge, and there are a few specialized opal shops as at the Menzies Hotel in Sydney, but generally the picture is of a spacious version of Europe.

In Sydney one of the half dozen leadings firms is Prouds, who also have other branches throughout the country. George Proud likes to recall his success with expensive Patek Philippe watches. Ten years ago their total sales in Australia were one and a half watches annually. Proud bought twenty-five, found he could at first sell five annually and is now selling over a hundred every year, including one in 1969 for the price of two Rolls-Royce cars. The tale carries several messages, the main one being a tribute to bold trading policy; Australia is steadily becoming a luxury market. Prouds have five craftsmen in their own Sydney workshop, buy from some fifteen other local factories and import perhaps a quarter of their stock.

Also in Sydney, the huge David Jones department store is one of several stores to start a diamond counter on their ground floor. Only recently introduced, it sells conventional pieces at reasonable prices, taking most of the production from a typical local studio of two Italians, one Swiss and three Australian craftsmen. The manager is ex-president of the local Gemmological Association and has spent thirty-three years at the bench with Hardy Brothers, the old family silversmiths. It is sad that retailing so often seems more profitable than being a skilled craftsman.

One of Australia's strongest designers is Gary Bradley of Melbourne. After a six-year local trade apprenticeship, he worked in London for two years with John Donald, to whose inspiration he says he owes his subsequent success. Behaving with the independence of a true artist, he rode to Kabul on a motorcycle, sold it there, hitch-hiked to Saigon, teaching the craft to Nepalese tribes *en route*, got via Japan to Vancouver, worked there for a few months making cheap cast jewels for the firm Jacobi, and then went home to his first exhibition at Melbourne's Princes Hill Gallery. There he met the Prime Minister's wife, Mrs Holt. She, and then her successor Mrs Gorton, placed important commissions with him, including gifts by the Australian government to six

Perhaps the only golden bra ever made, with diamond pinnacles. Intended to attract publicity, the piece proved difficult to finish with the right degree of tension in the wire. An outstandingly graceful composition by Sven Boltenstern, Vienna, 1970, acquired by Spritzer and Fuhrmann of Curaçao

Asian heads of state. Later he made a pair of earrings for Lady Bird Johnson, and in 1966 he opened his little shop in Toorak Road. In 1967 he made twelve pieces for the Australian display at Expo, Montreal. With his two or three craftsmen he has now been producing in Australia for two and a half years and reckons he has made at least 780 pieces without ever once repeating himself. He sells his work as unique art, and hates the idea of limited editions of even as few as two or three. What is good enough for most sculptors, who readily allow editions of other bronzes, will not do for Gary Bradley. He prefers the struggle of a painter, and struggle indeed it is: his profit from the job is not counted in dollars in the till but in the pleasure it gives him.

Just down the road again in South Yarra, Melbourne, is Alan Shaw, perhaps the only craftsman in Australia to call himself 'goldsmith': nothing but gold for him. After a trade workshop training followed by a spell at Gabriel Lucas, Montreal (no art school—he is too practical) he worked at home for four years. In 1969 he opened his shop. Most jewelers use casting, but in a rather furtive way: it is not so strong as hand-forging, so they keep quiet about it. Not so Shaw: he has developed waste-wax casting to a state of refinement so the thin lines are really thin and the bits needing to be strong will really stand a strain. He reckons about one-third of his production is very boring, but that is all the wholesale buyers will take from him: the other two-thirds he sells in his own shop which, naturally, is what interests him. Buying stones, he spends two-thirds of his money on diamonds and much of the rest on Gilson emeralds. He uses only 18 carat gold, so is pure in his materials, even if the fight for survival compels him sometimes to make what he did not enjoy designing.

Compared with literature, music and painting, the Australian jewelry field is sadly uncreative. Other good designers may be no more than ten in number in the whole country. Near Melbourne there is Tor Schwanck and Macham Skippers; in Sydney, Darany Lewers and Helge Larsen are attached to the University of New South Wales and are active in the Crafts Association of Australia; and, perhaps most original of all, there is Emanuel Raft, who has both learnt and taught with great success round the world, recently exhibiting at the Crafts Centre in Covent Garden, London, at the fine Bonython Gallery, Sydney, and at Jensen, New York. Andrew Grima, of London, opened a daring modern shop in Sydney in 1970. Rex Steele Merten, the Australian winner of a 1969 Diamonds-International Award, came back from New York with the comforting news that Australian design seemed much more lively than American.

Perhaps it is at Perth in Western Australia, newly become a big communications centre and a mining boom town, that the best future lies. Geoffrey Allen in Stirling Highway trained himself as a painter, then as a jeweler. He is somewhat rugged; his favourite material is 18 carat gold, and he is happy to be unfashionable, declaring 'I am a caster and I work slowly'—both tendencies deplored by most jewelers. He made his own centrifugal casting machine from a child's chair and part of a refrigerator. Only twenty per cent of his production is in gold (all of it Australian) and the biggest diamond he has ever used was 0.6 carat, in an engagement ring for a gold-mine owner's son; only one piece in a hundred of Allen's uses diamonds. He avoids trade firms in the city because he thinks they are uninterested in design. The biggest piece he ever made was a necklace in gold with precious stones. He is sad that his own customers so often ask him, 'how little can you do it for?'—that inspires a nervousness about price.

De Beers started their Australian advertising in 1968; perhaps this, together with the steady conviction of people like Allen, will suddenly cause the market to explode.

SCANDINAVIA

Scandinavia is the home of modern design. The Stockholm exhibition in 1930 startled Europe into the enjoyment of simple shapes and almost made us forget our human instincts for pattern and personality. This was not northern emptiness but disciplined restraint. Seven years after the First World War it was Sweden that won more official honours than any other country at the Paris World Exhibition. Between the wars many designers all over the world responded to the Swedish initiative: function, so the theory went, was the same thing as beauty. But because jewels, unlike tables or tea-pots or curtains,

Above *Ring, silver and amethyst by David Dunne of Sydney, Australia, 1970. He, like many artist-jewelers, trained as a painter.*

Left: top *Gold and baguette-cut emerald ring designed and made by Alan Shaw, Melbourne, Australia, 1970. The gold framing was cast, then given its ingenious texture by hammering to catch and reflect the light.*
Bottom *Bracelet in white and yellow gold with rubies and sapphires by Elizabeth Defner and Helfried Kodré, Vienna, 1970. Under the joint name Kodré–Defner these two distinguished sculptors have built up a leading reputation on the rounds of international exhibitions.*

have no structural use, they neither contributed to nor gained from these austere aesthetics.

Since 1945, however, personality has re-emerged. In 1951 it was not Sweden but Finland which won the most honours at the Milan *Triennale*; and Finnish designers were inspired not by the logic of the ball-bearing and the geometry of the snow-flake, but by human imagination enjoying a new political freedom.

Luxury came late to Scandinavia, with the arrival of industry no more than fifty years ago; so there are very few antiques. Designers started with a clean palette, in contrast, for instance, to Japan where the clothing traditions are old and deep-seated, or Australia where a yearning for historic Britain is a drag on artistic change. In the northern countries, neither the habits nor the metalwork of the past were strong enough to make a precedent.

What emerged was a mixture still not resolved. On the one hand are the angular straight-sided shapes of the older school in Sweden, such as those of Wiwen Nilsson of Lund, now aged seventy-four, much admired by functional architects and by the apostles of mass production. On the other, probably sparked off by Finland, the smallest of the four nations, is the erratic personal fantasy which seems to express the true untidiness of human nature. Pioneered by Tapio Wirkkala with his striated glass of 1946, this new informality was spread by him and others into metalwork and jewelry twenty years after.

Finland is unexpected in many ways, not least in how its artists live. Wirkkala himself is to some extent the grand old man of Finnish design; grand because it is he who has won most awards, who is the most famous both at home and overseas, and who has the largest range of clients, from the Finnish Government with its art education projects, to the big factories like Rosenthal china in Germany, Venini glass in Venice, or the local Iittala glassworks or Hackmann cutlery, down to the small Westerback jewel workshop in Helsinki. Wirkkala is old only in the sense of inheriting the mantle of the Finnish Art Nouveau giants, Louis Sparre and Axel Gallen. Born in 1915, he startled the world by the originality of his products, a world already amazed by Finland's achievement of new independence from both Germany and Russia. But Wirkkala is the most unassuming of men, and he is

Left *Pendant head in white, red, yellow and green gold, carved, chased and engraved in Helsinki, 1970, by Tapio Wirkkala, who also works as architect, sculptor and industrial designer*

Right *Gold pendant head with chain by Tapio Wirkkala, Helsinki. Makers, Tapio Wirkkala and Westerback Oy, 1970*

one of the youngest in outlook; to hear him talk about design is to be convinced that design is not all labour but fun. His office is a mess, the reflection of his view on life: not for him the empty table and silent telephone of some sterile theorists. The prototype models of many of his jobs—the entrance feature for the magnificent costume jewelry exhibition at Jablonec, Bohemia, in 1966, commissioned by the Czech Government, or his own log-house to which he retreats in far northern Lapland for two months in the summer, as he says, to get rid of problems, and concentrate on real thinking—decorate his room. There are papers everywhere, his four or five colleagues often eating or drinking as they draw, Wirkkala himself expressing with his actions, and with his own huge, hairy person, his primary feeling which is enjoyment. But when he gets angry, he retreats to the basement, and this is how the Wirkkala jewels have happened, beaten out by himself on his own workbench.

Wirkkala's experimental sheets of chased patterns are embossed perhaps with more determination than patience. Banging at this sheet metal is his personal therapy, giving him not the indirect satisfaction of an industrial designer, but the direct pleasure of a craftsman. He calls it 'anti-design' because it is instinctive, not intellectual. His first jewel, a wild head, was made in 1969 by Westerback from his prototype. Its elfish quality descends directly from the two religious table pieces by Wirkkala, made by Westerback for the jewelry exhibition at Goldsmiths' Hall, in London in 1961.

If jewels represent Wirkkala's inner nature, they are for another most original Finn absolutely everything. He is Björn Weckström, also of Helsinki, born in 1935. He is self-taught—he began as a jazz trombone player. In 1956 he sold his trombone in Paris in the middle of his four years of evening classes at the Helsinki Apprentices' School, determined to become a jeweler. In 1959 he started a small shop, the only one in Finland, he claims, concentrating on new jewels made by him and his friends. In 1961 he took part in the Goldsmiths' Hall exhibition, soon afterwards abandoning his restrained, geometrical style, and starting to experiment with casting, which he saw not as a cheap imitation but as a brilliant new opportunity.

In 1964 he began to change from a brave pioneer into a big success. He made some designs for the tiny local company Kruunu (Crown) Koru (Jewelry) which then employed only three craftsmen. The owner of the firm, Mr Anttila, had concentrated on producing endless chains of the type known as Bismarck, and, as an antidote, solid boring bracelets. With no high school education, no university, no language except Finnish, he had established himself on his own as a goldsmith as recently as 1962. He was his own designer, craftsman, and, most unusually, commercial traveller. Soon after, with the uncomplicated strength of vision one finds so often in the far north, he realized he could not expand unless he proved himself distinctive, and he could do this only with the inspiration of an artist—hence an ideal partnership, which has now made its impression on the whole of Scandinavia.

After three years Weckström had proved to Anttila what most trade people with broader experience refuse to believe: that enterprise and adventure can be lucrative. Customers in half a dozen countries were buying jewels, but the larger the purchases the more the complaints about the Finnish language. A new name, Lapponia, was invented so that everyone could remember it, a typically sensible concession to buyers' needs. Weckström made nine per cent royalty on sales and continued to get more pleasure from his own studio pieces than from factory production. Now he is not so sure. Lapponia have grown to seventy-five craftsmen, perhaps the biggest team in the north. Lapponia prices are about ninety per cent lower than gold prices for Weckström's own personal work. Each design is produced about fifty times over—a bigger series would bore the craftsmen—and there are about 250 patterns in production at any one time.

It is every artist's dream. Weckström's only grumble is that he now sees as much as one-third of his production being copied by other small factories. He is bursting with confidence, undimmed by setbacks like his one-man show at Maison Clerc in November 1969 in Paris: it was covered by French, Italian and Spanish television and by Twentieth Century Fox, yet he sold only ten per cent of the exhibits. In London's Rosenthal he did a little better in 1971. He is honest enough to admit that his own prices were too high, and that part

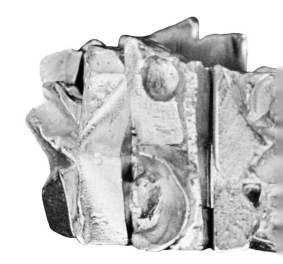

of the Lapponia legend is simply due to low wage rates and efficient production bringing this fabulous gold within reach of almost everyone.

He travels sparsely—twice to the USA, once to England, once to Africa; he says there is no need to meet other artists—one can understand them by seeing their work. Weckström won the international competition sponsored by Stern, the chain jewelers in Rio de Janeiro in 1968; but even this did not lure him from his beloved lakes, snow, forests, and, above all, his sailing and the magnificent colours of the ten-day *ruska*, the Lapland autumn.

He models his personal jewels just as a sculptor models for bronze casting, using wax and sometimes plaster. When the gold comes out of the mould, he often works over the surface by hand, drilling the metal till it is little more than half a millimetre thick—surprisingly light and easy to wear—in a way that is sometimes not economic for the large-scale production at Lapponia. He takes his art seriously, using names for his pieces like 'Shadow in the Forest', 'Homage to Henry Moore', or 'Well of Mariba' (where Moses beat the rock). He does not especially concentrate on local stones—pearls are probably his favourite, but he also likes the rich colour of African tourmalines and Spanish pyrites. He sees jewels not as a social status symbol but as sculpture. 'The only thing that limits my art is its size—otherwise jewelry has all the freedom in the world,' he says. He hates the polishing of stones which, he finds, removes their character.

For him, as for most artists, character is everything, turnover only an incidental frill. His most pleasing surprise was from the ancient and respected Helsinki retailers, Lindrus. When he first showed them his jewels, their advice to him was 'Come back again in a hundred years' time!' They are now among his best customers.

The Finns may be the most surprising people in Europe. Herbert Tillander has made himself one of the world's leading gemmologists, and precious stones are probably more popular in Finland than elsewhere in Scandinavia. Tillander's firm, in fact, owes its luxurious tastes to its origins in tsarist Russia; they worked with Fabergé, and with Bolin, now of Stockholm.

There are half a dozen established workshops, too, from Kaija Aarikka, who continues to make spheres and squares and triangles elegant as well as cheap, to Kalevala Koru, the factory with some sixty workers, with their heavy reproductions of prehistoric tribesmen's work, as well as their modest excursions into new designs; they export to seven countries (half their products are brass, almost none in gold). Kaunis Koru are typical with their stubby abrupt pieces, often using the local smoky quartz.

But, of course, Finland's greatest asset is the fertility of its designers: architects like Sarpaneva, all-round creators like Kaipiainen, daring young women concentrating on jewels like Aarikka or Paula Haivaoja and Liisa Vitali, a farmer, self-trained as jeweler, whose pierced circlets adorn the Wester-back showrooms.

The Finns have paid off their debt to Russia and earned at last a stable identity of their own. Inspired by Wirkkala, Weckström and others, and tantalized by the court glamour of nearby St Petersburg which some can still remember, Finnish women can at last afford jewels. The next big moves in the jewelry of the north may well be here.

If Finland is surprises, Norway is tradition. The oldest firm, Tostrup, was founded in 1832 by Jacob Tostrup, and is managed today by his great-grand-daughter, Greta Prytz Korsmo, and her two Tostrup brothers. Even their building is in the family—designed by her architect grandfather in 1892, it dominates Oslo's central shopping area. The special contribution of Norway is its enamels, evolved by the Tostrup firm in the 1880s, perhaps because of the pure local water. Whatever the cause, the result has been a continuous stream of international prizes, beginning with the Paris Exhibition of 1900, and still going strong today with the Milan *Triennale* 1954 *Grand Prix*.

Greta Prytz Korsmo herself loves this distinctive, transparent enamel, though she finds it easier to use in its most difficult form—on large cups and dishes, often made in stainless steel by the partner workshop Catherine Holm. But she makes her biggest and best silver pieces and jewels at home, engraving beautiful grains and rhythms onto her silver and then enamelling with much the same breath-taking drama that the great sixteenth-century Cellini himself describes for the casting of his Perseus: will it work or not? Many craftsmen have failed to keep to deliveries and

Bracelet in cast and textured gold, designer Björn Weckström, 1970; makers, Lapponia, Helsinki

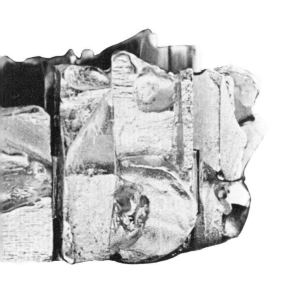

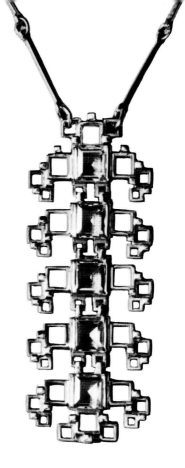

Above *Silver pendant made from mass-produced strip scrap bar and tube, an ingenious way of reducing the price of handwork to make it generally marketable; by Uni David Andersen, Oslo, 1969*

Right *Pierced silver pendants by Tone Vigeland of Oslo, 1969, whose workshop is near the museum devoted to her father's sculpture; she sometimes works for the Norwegian craft co-operative Plus at Frederikstad.*

price because their enamels have cracked at the last moment: Greta seems at last the master of this craft. Introducing visitors to the dozen craftsmen in Tostrup's attic workshop, she looks lovingly at their vividly coloured enamels but dashes past the replicas of the ninth-century Viking ships in all sizes from brooches to tables, and says powerfully, 'I hate it'. Nevertheless, the best craftsman in the firm is reserved for it in deference to tourist taste.

The other leading Oslo firm is David Andersen, founded in 1876 and also still in the family. Ivar runs the firm and his daughter, Uni David Andersen, is one of their designers, supplying modern jewelry from her workshop at home, which she has built up during the past nine years. She says, 'work by hand is fun, but we found we could not sell it'. So she bought a range of mass-produced balls and tubes, and found she could assemble these into fascinating jigsaw puzzles cheap enough for the international market. She modestly does not believe she is a great artist, and enjoys being usefully in demand. She works only in silver, and evidently relishes human contact with her three or four craftsmen; presently she is training the daughter of the Hingelberg family, who run the main firm of silversmiths in northern Denmark. David Andersen's are perhaps more international than Tostrup: they buy from 150 different sources, world wide.

Christian Gaudernack trained at Pforzheim and designs revolutionary jewels for Andersen's in his studio at Son; his father won many prizes also for Andersen's, then starting his own private company at Sandvika. Christian is going the same way: rather expensive, rather exclusive, very spectacular. In Norway, as everywhere in Scandinavia, there is the happiest friendship between artist and commercial companies. Such embarrassments as designers selling direct to the public from their private studios rather than through their retail shops are solved calmly to mutual advantage.

Norway is rightly proud of the magnificent interlaced ornaments of the Vikings a thousand years ago; patterns were still a passion when the remote wooden medieval churches and houses were being carved with their fascinating zigzag shapes. Today, Norway seems less ostentatiously modern than its neighbours, its jewelers less precious in every sense of the word. One of the most

interesting artist's studios is Tone Vigeland's; she, like the Tostrups and the Andersens, is one of a famous family—indeed the Vigeland museum is in her village next to her own house. She makes simple, unsophisticated enamel jewels, using silver with foil to give enamel its underlying sheen. For ten years she has designed for the enterprising art colony called Plus at Fredrikstad, the old fortified town. Led by the experienced entrepreneur Per Tannum, Plus has scored splendid export successes, partly at the expense of original distinction. As Tone says, one cannot have it both ways—small workshops, to achieve world-wide sales, either have to become large factories so as to reduce their prices, or adapt their designs to the deadening demands of middle-men.

One solution has been found by Paul Hughes, who met his Norwegian wife when they were students together in London, set up on his own with her in Oslo fifteen years ago, and now has one of the biggest wholesale import/export firms there, selling many of the gaudy enamelled teaspoons which everybody likes. On this business structure Elsa and Paul have based their own amazing growth: their casting of silver jewels and sculpture may be technically the most efficient in the north, here again the Norwegian taste for richness being in sharp contrast to the self-critical Swedes. Paul's turnover has risen fiftyfold in the past decade.

Where Norwegian jewels are rough, Swedish are smooth; where Norwegians want to be different, Swedes are correct. When Finns are startling, Swedes are critical; when Finns delight, Swedes think. It is no chance that Sweden has the biggest and oldest art school (founded in 1844). Probably the most famous Swedish goldsmith of all, Sigurd Persson, being told that art schools sap vitality, ruefully and reluctantly agreed. Sadly, because he is himself helping now to set up throughout the country as many as three schools for artists, and three others for designers. He prefers to keep his own concerns small and private, with an occasional big splash which ensures he keeps in the news as one of Sweden's foremost prizewinners, perhaps the designer with the hardest touch of all.

He uses gold and diamonds; he is not afraid of price—his most expensive diamond and platinum rings may reach £10,000 ($26,000) in the Stockholm

Gold and diamond bracelet by Sigurd Persson, Stockholm, 1968; Persson is also prominent as a silversmith and industrial designer.

showroom of his agent. One can tell Persson's work by its harshness and strength: very clear, impersonal and architectural. He has made special collections of silver, at three yearly intervals—bowls in 1969, for instance, shown at Goldsmiths' Hall in London, of subtle angular variations with hammer marks on the basic squares and hemisphere. In this context of elevated abstraction, and of industrial design for saucepans and army equipment, for furniture and for building ornament, jewels are Sigurd's recreation.

Persson (born 1914) is the ideal art school product: he is highly educated (he studied in Munich as well as Stockholm), speaking several languages, often travels to Germany and elsewhere, knows the leading international art figures, and, perhaps most impressive, he is the master of many consumer goods. But he likes silver best. For jewels, liking is not enough—he feels a secret adoration because they liberate him. He limits his workshop to just three or four craftsmen—not the dozens which one might expect to result from his fame. Appropriately for such a citizen of the world, these craftsmen are one Canadian, one Irishman and one from Holland. This is the area where he finds extremes are valid; in his other products he would equate such charm with weakness. The rings he made for the Seattle World Fair in 1960 startled the world: Persson, like most Swedes, proved himself much more complicated than he appears.

Self-trained and inward-looking, by contrast, is Olle Ohlsson; he and his wife Barbro are on their own with no helpers. Born in 1928, he was apprenticed at fifteen with a big group of seventeen smiths in the Hallberg factory, worked at the crown jewelers Bolin, then at Borgila, another respected silver shop, then at Raström for one year, and three years at Geka Co., including evening classes. In 1961 he joined Persson, but their styles were too emphatic for each other; in 1962 he started on his own, teaching at a small private school. He had his first show at Fahlström's retail shop, then in 1964 and 1967 at the huge Nordiska store, and in 1968 and 1969 in Hantverket. All the while he evolved his own exotic approach to melting and drilling, yielding surfaces reminiscent of Botticelli hair imposed upon lava flowing from a volcano.

Ohlsson is a master of traditional

technique and therein lies his strength: he can rise above it. He opposes the bright, cold style of our times—his ideal is soft and curvy both to sight and to touch. He uses acid etching extensively: he heats the metal until it is almost molten, then blows on it to make it ripple, or often at this point mixes two metals, usually gold and silver, to achieve spectacular richness with an almost translucent surface; then he may gouge out willowy lines in the art nouveau manner, using his formidable selection of dentist's drills. Drilling, like any other process, has its hazards: Olle's face has a few little black marks where silver chips have temporarily oxidized and stained him! He does not mind: indeed he is one of the happiest of craftsmen, determined never to repeat his designs, always to make them himself with his wife, never to be inspired by other people's work, but rather by the overwhelming excitement of natural forms and everyday life. Although in the last three years his work has been bought by several museums and churches, and he is now generally considered a phenomenon, he remains a very small producer in a shabby back room, and likes it that way.

The walls of heaven are, so says the book of Revelation, made of jasper. In central Sweden, at Kopparberg, one can pick up a wonderful range of local stones: amethyst and rock crystal, topaz, opal and smoky quartz, molybdenum and wolframite. It is sad that such splendours are not much reflected in Swedish jewels. Lars Arby, one of the promising starters, prefers to work his silver in high-relief stalactites and stalagmites, picking out the shapes in green or blue enamel; Bengt Liljedahl gets interesting effects using asymmetrical polished stones from Germany. But most younger designers, like Kerstin Ohlin, seem to prefer a rather impersonal geometry. Dahlquist and Barve, another charming husband and wife team with outlets in Malmö and Visby, now working in Stockholm, seem almost alone in using prehistoric fossils and the other glories which they pick up on the beach. For them, as for most Swedes, silver remains the favoured metal; gold and diamonds have not yet arrived.

Danish jewelers are probably the richest in Scandinavia. There are more retailers in Copenhagen than in the other capitals. Although the Swedish group of Hallberg/Guldsmeds Aktie-bolaget may be the biggest, Jensen are the only Scandinavian firm which consistently maintains and refreshes its international reputation for top-quality design and finish. Indeed it was Georg Jensen himself who revived the idea of silver as an art form at the turn of the century, and it is quite suitable that the Lunning prize, Scandinavia's premier design award, should have been endowed from the earnings by Lunning himself as the first head of Jensen's American enterprise.

The Jensen firm is a summary of the whole of Scandinavian design. Denmark being nearest the centre of Europe, Danish designers tend to be cosmopolitan travellers, much aware of outside influences and perhaps not enough obsessed by their own ideas. They concentrate mostly on simple, beautiful, functional shapes for sensible household use, knives and forks, teapots and candlesticks, all in silver. Jewels for them eighty years ago were a somewhat exotic foreign fantasy which did not quite catch on, though old Georg Jensen's gold gem-set pieces, then made only in very small quantities, are much admired today. His successors are a changing team of distinguished designers too numerous to mention. Henning Koppel has managed to introduce his gorgeous flowing forms into his silver jewels as well as his ewers and bowls; never sharp or jagged, looking almost like overlapping islands, in some Baltic archipelago, Koppel's jewels are almost too smooth for the rough ways of the 1970s.

A newcomer to Jensen is Torun Bülow-Hübe. Having worked in Sweden and France, she now lives at Wolfsburg in Germany and enjoys the help of the Jensen craftsmen. As she says, 'after twenty-three years of hard struggling on my own, I eventually found that five craftsmen are not enough for the seventeen countries to whom Jensen sell.' Torun's Jensen jewels have already had world-wide orders. She is unusual in Scandinavia in putting jewels first; 'table silver', she says, 'is so static, so upper-class'; jewelry is 'a mystical, not a fashion thing. The moment it is out, it takes on life of its own. Its silver is a mirror of reality.' She thinks her jewels should be without time—still modern twenty or forty years later, and she is proving her point—some of the 'new' Torun/Jensen collection was first made by her a generation ago.

Two gold bracelets designed by Henning Koppel, made by Georg Jensen, Copenhagen, 1969; examples of the firm's enlightened policy of semi-quantity production of excellent designs. The twenty-fifth anniversary of Koppel's joining Jensen was celebrated by his one-man show in the Kunstindustrimuseet, Copenhagen, 1971, then in Japan, and at Goldsmiths' Hall, London.

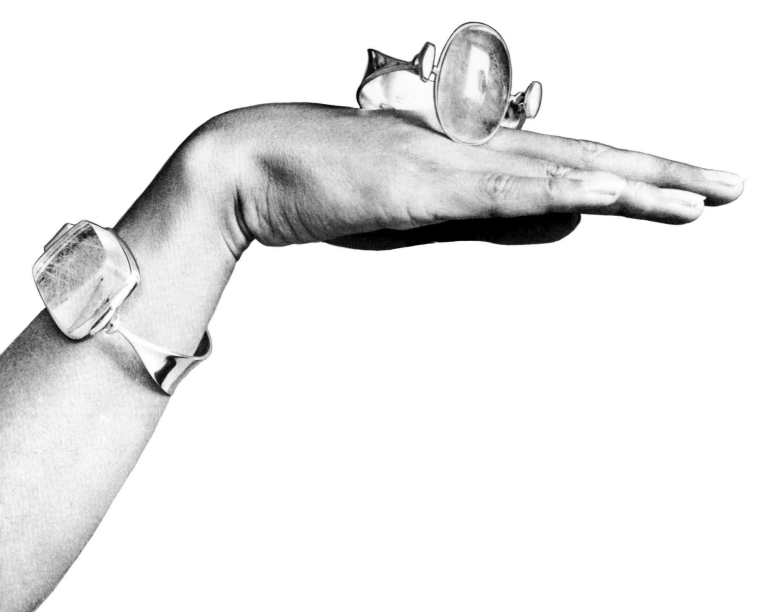

Other Jensen designers are Nanna Ditzel, now married to an Englishman in London, and Astrid Fog. The firm's production is one-half cutlery, one-quarter tableware, one-quarter jewels; New York is its best outlet, with London next and then Paris. There are some twenty-five craftsmen, three hundred workers altogether, including the very important die-sinkers. Stainless steel becomes steadily more important with one factory already outside Copenhagen, in addition to the main silver works in the city, and a new factory for forty men just open at Hjørring in the north, specializing in filing and finishing. Jensen's own retail limb, in Europe's most alluring shopping street, Strøget, sells foreign jewels as well as Scandinavian: Jensen, like everyone, are becoming more international. The Jensen group shows an impressive approach to quality often at the expense of profits. But their very seriousness seems to deny the sort of amusement and whimsy which can make jewels irresistible.

Two other distinguished Copenhagen firms have at various times patronized excellent designers: Michelsen, lately acquired by Royal Copenhagen Porcelain, and Dragsted, who almost specialize in precious jewels. At one time they employed Karen Strand, with Torun one of the very few Danish designers who is also a maker.

In Denmark, particularly, architects and industrial designers sometimes pretend to universal talent, to the envy of their colleagues overseas and the annoyance of those artists at home who can actually make jewels with their own hands. Distinguished families of craftsmen still produce fine work, often acknowledging gratefully their debt to Jensen in whose workshop their father or grandfather may have trained. Among them, Hans Hansen of Kolding, Hingelberg of Aarhus and Just Andersen are outstanding.

A bubbling tonic on the Danish scene is Arje Griegst, the young Jewish jeweler, winner of the Lunning Prize 1968, who has worked in Israel and elsewhere. Not for him super-critical uniformity. His wild, convoluted gold conceals the time and care needed to make it structurally sound. Arje likes to be on his own. Scandinavian jewelry needs more of him, but with the present pace of communications and the weight of critical opinion here, only the strongest, like Arje, can survive as themselves, uninfluenced by others.

At least in modern jewels, Scandinavian design is rather quiet. There have been only five De Beers Diamonds-International Awards: Hans Klintz of Sweden in 1965, Matti Hyvärinen of Finland and the Swedish Mema Guld & Silver A/B in 1967; and, naturally, for Denmark, Georg Jensen in 1966 and 1969.

The Scandinavian contribution to modern design has been just as important as, say, the ancient Romans' was to law. But one feels now that there may be up north a danger of too much talk and too little private inspiration.

SOUTH AFRICA

Centres of production seldom manage to attract conspicuous consumption. In Europe the world's biggest concentration of industry, stretching solidly from

Düsseldorf through the Ruhr and Holland to the sea, is rich in blast furnaces and rolling mills, but the best jewelers are on the fringes outside, away from the toil and dirt. In Scotland, Glasgow has the industry, Edinburgh the shops. Leipzig before the war was the trading centre, but it was lovely nearby Dresden that provided pleasure. In Brazil, people make money at São Paulo, and spend it in Rio de Janeiro. In America, spending follows the pleasure route to Florida, where many of the best jewelers open high-season shops.

This pattern is to some extent true of South Africa: she produces the materials for jewelry, but it is in other countries that South African tourists seem to make their finest buys. Perhaps all travellers automatically become impulse buyers, leaving their cautious instincts at home; perhaps it is that if one behaves extravagantly one likes to be anonymous; perhaps it is simply that the South African jewelry industry offers more problems and fewer rewards to its workers than heavy industry and mining. Attempts to establish silversmithing production failed because the market was too small and European imports too aggressive.

However, South African jewelers are certainly thriving and expanding; in Cape Town the family jewelers Murdock are selling more and more luxury goods. Founded in 1897, the firm is still managed by two Murdock brothers, Bob and Graham. In Johannesburg Ike Schwartz have grown with enormous confidence; Mappin and Webb (founded 1891) and Charles Greig (1899) are big old firms, very active; Katz and Lourie (1895) have outgrown no less than four retail showrooms—they now have an ambitious exhibition policy with many overseas contacts. And yet when one considers the wealth of South African mines the jewelers still seem surprisingly modest. 'In Africa,' said Cecil Rhodes, 'think big': his message has evidently not affected the local wearers of gold and diamonds as strongly as their producers.

One of the best designers, Kurt Jobst of Johannesburg, who died in 1971, spent a lifetime in design and got rather depressed about it; maybe his customers were so conditioned by carat weight and tonnage of rock that their aesthetics were overwhelmed by logistics. South Africa's concentration on her subterranean problems had till recently made her jewelers quite understandably reluctant to play with the imponderables of art. Kurt Jobst brought with him a fine mature style from his beloved Austria, and built for himself an impressive shop in Johannesburg. Another 'senior', as the German goldsmiths' journal called him in 1969, is Erich Frey of Pretoria and the University of Stellenbosch. Also from Stellenbosch is Eberhard Dechow. Otto Poulsen from Denmark worked in Durban for fifteen years and now employs five craftsmen there, an impressive success.

Most of the larger South African cities have their resident artist-jeweler. Perhaps the most significant development is the new interest throughout the country in semi-precious stones. In Strand Street, Cape Town, the enterprising Gem Stone Gallery gives genuine and delightful local colour with its tiger-eye crocidolite, its agates, carnelian and jasper, chalcedony, its amazonite and amethyst, rose quartz and achronite and garnet and jade—all lesser cousins of the diamond but, like the diamond, the hard-won dividend from South Africa's mining skill and adventure.

SOUTH AMERICA

The first stop on the new air route from Johannesburg to New York is Brazil. It is an exotic place in every way: for instance, in 1963 inflation exceeded 120 per cent. Here Hans Stern has made himself the *Reader's Digest* 'king of coloured gems'. Born in 1923, he might have inherited the biggest electrical firm in the Ruhr. But he and his father had to leave their native Essen to escape the Nazis in 1939. His father for three years worked in Brazil's provincial electric supply industry; there was not enough money for Hans to complete his engineering studies. He began in a lapidary firm mainly buying stones and quartz on horseback in the country, sometimes himself polishing the stones. So his present empire is well and truly founded on intimate craft knowledge. In 1945 he decided to set up his own shop as a wholesale stone-broker, his capital being the $200 proceeds from the sale of his ancient accordion (he still plays the organ). He was amazed at the small value people attached to the local semi-precious stones; he first came to love them when going on plant inspection trips with his father in the interior; and people, especially his own customers, were amazed at his honesty. His love of coloured stones, together with a very straight trade policy, are the guide lines of his life; a tremendous gift for mastering a complex organization, his dominant characteristic. Soon he was expanding so fast that he absorbed his own father into his staff. One of the jewelry world's most spectacular success stories was under way.

Stern's today are much the biggest group in South America, trading in fourteen countries, employing 600 people; they have a noticeable command of the continent's trade. Many of the 140 outlets are small shops in luxury hotels, for instance at Frankfurt, Tel Aviv, Lisbon, Rome and Mexico; but they are also in airports and ocean-liners, in shopping centres and arcades. Stern's have exhibited for the past three years at Hanover Fair where it is a thirty-kilometre walk to see all the stands. Olympia office equipment have a staff there of 300, Stern's only two, one of whom is usually Stefan Barczinski, Hans' right-hand man. Hans Stern, like every jeweler expanding his trade, laments that his increased profits always seem to be swallowed up in increasing stock. This rapid overseas growth can be a mixed blessing.

Stern's special and formidable character—zip with integrity—was Germany's loss and is Brazil's immeasurable gain. Hans Stern himself likes to feel he is repaying the very generous Brazilian people for their hospitality when he desperately needed it. Stern's pay nearly one-third of the jewel taxes in Rio de Janeiro, but ruefully know that they do not handle one-third of the total business; three-quarters of all Brazilian women buy their jewels at the door from freelance commission salesmen—known in Europe as Knocker Boys.

Hans Stern's passion is topaz and aquamarine, tourmaline and quartz, even diamonds, of which Brazil was the world's almost only source till a hundred years ago, and of which she still produces perhaps one-tenth of the world's supply. The organizing brilliance of Hans Stern and his colleagues, the novelty and charm of these native stones are the recipe for the Stern saga—expansion and success. But with so far only one award in the De Beers Diamonds-International contest, and with a sensible clear commercial eye, Stern's routine products are not yet breathtaking new designs: true there have been some huge exhibition compositions like the three-foot-high tableaux shown at the Goldsmiths' Hall, London, International Modern Jewelry exhibition in 1961, or another group especially made for the New York World Fair. But a big business needs a huge turnover. It is usually the smallest studio which gives its time to generate new ideas, and which has the personal loyalty of a few customers to provide the necessary occasional sales.

One such is Haroldo Burle Marx, one of whose brothers, Roberto, has achieved fame bringing Brazil's fantastic tropical vegetation into the context of modern landscape gardening. Haroldo, the jeweler, with his twenty-foot-square shop in Rio, laughs about his eminent brothers, the gardener and the composer: 'I don't care about names,' he says, 'it is what I do that counts. I have tremendous pride in my new invention of free form stones—that is a real contribution by me—I have contributed something.' He adores handling his sculptured gold pieces with their tribal flavour, a little Aztec, a little Inca, some modern architecture, mostly Burle Marx. There may be three or four people ragging with him in his workshop. 'They are my friends and sometimes they work for me,' he says, teasing everyone: they are actually his craftsmen, who have wandered down for a chat from the workshop upstairs. Fun is vital to him, but with his three or four craftsmen he is meticulous as well: he avoids casting because it does not give enough strength. He gets his ideas from the lovely Copacabana beach, with its endless rolling waves a hundred yards from his front window; and from the richness of the inland forests. It is rewarding to find so close together Stern and Burle Marx; they could not be more

different, yet each obviously finds jewelry thrilling, each enjoys his own rewards, one perhaps more financial, the other more in art.

Far to the north is Caracas, centre of the vast South American oil wealth; the Venezuelan economy has recently expanded even quicker than Brazil's. The famous architect Villanueva has stimulated an awareness of new design with his huge Caracas University, rather as Niemeyer did in Brazil with its new capital, Brasilia. But the opportunities for Venezuelan modern jewelry are still rather modest: there is almost no technical education available, and the several excellent modern art galleries in Caracas concentrate, as they do almost everywhere else in the world, on painting and sculpture, which with their large size and obvious qualities are more profitable and less troublesome than tiny jewels. Jewels need security, they involve elaborate taxation, and in South America they often require factual verification of the weight of stones and the quantity of metal. It is sad that Venezuela which now has the money has no precious stone deposits, whereas neighbouring Colombia has the world's best emeralds without the consumer wealth to found a local modern production. Some of these marvellous emeralds find their way over to Caracas and they are the nearest approach one finds there to a local flavour.

One of the best and biggest firms is Herbert Fischbach's Taller Suizo: sensibly they have promoted in both their branches the work of Harry Abend, one of the leading architect-sculptors of the country. His displays in Taller Suizo distinguish that firm from all the others in the capital and represent one of those sadly few ideal marriages between art and commerce that have given pleasure and profits in equal quantity to all concerned. Abend himself has one of the truly hair-raising histories which fortify one's faith in human nature. Born in 1936 at Jaroslav in Poland, he fled with his Jewish family to Siberia where they then found themselves imprisoned, working in forced labour camps. In 1945, during a short fortnight's relaxation by Stalin of the Russian political repression, the Abends rushed to Fürstenfeldbruck outside Munich, Harry still having been denied almost all education. In 1948 they went through France to Venezuela determined to start a new life. Harry's father, with a small import/export business, managed to train his son as architect and sculptor; Harry began to make jewels to make a living while still a student, but in 1965 started seriously. A wealthy friend commissioned first one piece, then a whole collection of jewels which were shown in 1966 in the Museo de Bellas Artes. The only existing modern jeweler to influence Harry was the very flamboyant Gallofre who died in 1969; but Harry from the start had his own personal style, not related to the South American love of show and colour; he has by nature the restraint of a serious north European.

Now with several large sculptures in public places, a constant demand for his gold jewels and an exhibition at Goldsmiths' Hall in London in 1972 and other European centres, he may achieve his ambition: to establish modern jewelry design in a country with almost no metalwork history at all. He has allies. The leading Venezuelan painter Soto, now in Paris, is constructing jewels inspired by his gigantic outdoor sculpture, a fascinating interplay of rods and planes. Perhaps less encouraging, in some of the spectacular modern office buildings like Caracas' Torre Caprillo, the modern shops are questing for novelty; the tiny Forum Gallery there shows artists' silver jewels like those of Manuel Ratto.

The most cheerful personal phenomenon in South America is Charles Fuhrmann, head of the big chain Spritzer and Fuhrmann in Curacao. He is an endless source of gaiety: most of all he enjoys people, but he has a fine appetite, too, for the excitement of putting up new buildings and for the glitter of jewels. In 1927 he left Bokowina, east of Vienna, equipped with enormous energy and a watchmaker's expertise. Thirty-four years ago he married Mr Spritzer's daughter, still his chief supporter. Now the group employs 550 people with some seventeen stores in the Antilles Islands and one in New York to keep contact with their customers there. The firm sends buyers to Europe at least three times a year, sometimes buying designs from one source and initiating manufacture somewhere else. They make almost nothing locally and are probably the biggest importers in the whole world of jewelry retailing. Thus they are not only very popular visitors in Europe's workshop centres; they can even, with their great purchasing power, be a somewhat critical influence in manufacturing trends as, for instance, when they placed an order for tens of thousands of dollars with Sven Boltenstern, the Viennese artist-jeweler, who was then struggling for survival.

It was a very solid tribute to Charles Fuhrmann when, in 1967, the jewelry industry of Valenza near Milan gave him an 18 carat gold key weighing over a pound and measuring ten inches. He is very proud, too, to be an Officer of the Order of Orange, an honour bestowed on him by the Dutch Government because of his liberal use of local coloured labour. Winner of three Diamonds-International Awards, he thinks he knows, like so many experienced retailers, that expensive modern designs can only be a small part of his whole activity. He has staff from most European countries; he represents almost all the Swiss watch companies; almost all the modern jewelry makers from Denmark to Italy, from England to Austria, from Holland to Germany.

THE UNITED STATES OF AMERICA

What are the 'jewelers of the Caribbean' doing in New York? So questions one of Fuhrmann's tourist advertisements; the question is almost superfluous. Anyone ambitious in jewelry must be active in New York. Stern of Brazil are there. So are Van Cleef and Arpels of Paris, very noticeable with two wonderful tiaras given by Napoleon I to his two successive wives in 1806 and 1811, both normally on show in the Fifth Avenue windows. So are Boucheron and Chaumet of Paris with their office. Buccellati of Rome have a large shop; Cartier and Jensen are there, though each now is independent of its European parents. Then there are the astonishing native phenomena: Harry Winston, Julius Cohen, Tiffany and Schlumberger, David Webb, Fulco Verdura, Arthur King, and Carlos Alemany who makes the Salvador Dali jewels in the St Regis Hotel. All of these, and many others, too, in the few hundred square yards round Fifth Avenue and 59th Street in Manhattan, put on the greatest show imaginable of wealth without ostentation.

Then there are the dozen or more department stores, many of which run diamond and jewelry counters. In the Gimbel store the jewelry counter, like some thirty others throughout the USA, is run by the Marcus Purchasing Company, who may, half a dozen times a year, sell a piece for $10,000 or $15,000. Add to this the hundreds of small manufacturers, dealers and retailers on 47th Street, and the many suburban stores like Marsh of Millburn, whose turnover in 1969 was bigger than Jensen or Cartier in New York, and you realize why many jewelers talk of New York by mistake instead of the United States; why trades people treat it as a challenge bigger than in any other whole country; why a survey beginning with South Africa, the world's biggest producer of gold and diamonds, can suitably end with New York, by far the biggest consumer.

Fortunately for the rest of the world, the high power of American salesmanship, mostly conducted by men, is almost matched by their dynamic buying, mostly by women. Money is nothing to be ashamed of in this exciting city, and if a man has it, he prefers his wife not to conceal the fact. In a way it is like India and Pakistan, where your jewels are your bank balance, and you buy jewels instead of paying money into the bank; but the wealth of New York is such that the rich do both together. The wonder of jewelry in New York is not in startling modernity—the unique skyscraper architecture has not exploded traditional ideas of personal ornament—the wonder is simply the confident richness, the large size of the pieces, the large number of stones and the splendid resource of the window displays. If a modern jewelry designer dislikes the razor-sharp attitude of the New York shops (one must be modern and exclusive, they say, but, still more important, one must be fashionable not just crazy) the designer may be forgiven, but he has probably forgotten the primary purpose of jewels, to give pleasure as ornaments on ordinary human beings.

Arthur King had an amazing shop on 59th Street—with its rough-hewn slate, fish-filled aquariums, seemingly armoured safe door, and craggy quartzes all around—for which he substituted his new and overwhelming fantasy in the next block on Madison Avenue, a continuous web of sinuous black metal fronds with small lozenge-shaped showcases suddenly appearing where you least expect them to be. His own extraordinary history is a good prelude to this wonderful eruption. Born in 1921, he taught himself jewelry in the United States Navy in the 1939 war, where his duties as an overseer of an empty and

Belt of feathers inspired by ancient Aztec work, with buckle of silver gilt and sliced tourmaline. By Arline Fisch, San Diego, California, 1971. Primitive tribal work often provides inspiration for modern artist-jewelers.

unused troopship made him yearn to do something useful with his hands. He is not the only brilliant modern jeweler now making the most expensive work who formed his judgment and learnt his craft on scrap metal. He opened in Cuba, in Miami, Florida, on Madison Avenue and at Fortnum and Mason in London with the help of some backing from the singer Lena Horne, and surviving several frightening set-backs. The worst was after a one-man show in New York, on the sleeper-train taking the same show on to Chicago: he answered a knock on his apartment door, opened it too wide, and found himself a few moments later strapped up with adhesive tape and minus his jewels, unable to utter, lying furious on his bed. Two years of fruitless investigation followed. It all made Arthur more determined about the permanent value of art, more wise about the unimportance of money. He does his design work for one person: himself. If there is a difference in taste with a customer (there rarely is—they are all his friends) he feels, and sometimes even says 'there are lots of you and only one of me'. He is determined not to abandon his personal style. His jewels are as uninhibited as his life: enormous black

pearls, which he buys in Bombay or Japan, jostle with ferocious uncut emeralds straight from Bogota. His settings are mostly cast tendrils of coloured gold, flowing in a rather random way; critics sometimes find him too exuberant, but his is a tonic, valuable quality in today's denigrating times. There are too many critics today and too few creators. Arthur King, with his colourful fantasies, helps correct the balance: he is one of the liveliest creative people in the country.

For unassuming magnificence there is David Webb. His designs are on the sober side of avant-garde, his shop is not one of those where you cannot see anything because of the showmanship. There are brilliant windows each containing its own group of ideas: diamond star brooches in one, carved colourless rock crystal in another, bright emerald and sapphire bracelets in another; then there are life-size golden frogs with enamelled skins and precious stone eyes and nails; similar on a smaller scale are his famous bracelets with coloured dragon-heads chasing their tails, perhaps the most admired type of jewel in all of New York high society. Webb has in the last fifteen years changed the style of American jewels more than any other designer; if

he owes something to the delicacy of Schlumberger and Verdura in the 1940s, the whole of the USA is now indebted to his vitalizing influence, from Ken Lane the costume jeweler up to the expensive firms outside New York and Palm Beach, his only two fields of operation.

David Webb, like Arthur King and many others of the world's leading designers, had no formal training in jewels. His greatest asset has no doubt always been his own personality: it is as compelling as his finest object. And it is of course his own ability that enabled him to grasp his chance and charm his customers throughout the whole continent. Born in 1925, he started work at eleven in his uncle's workshop at Ashville, North Carolina. At sixteen he went to New York, worked in several trade firms and in 1946 started his own workshop. Steadily he sold more to private customers, less to trade retailers. In 1963 he opened his shop. Now he uses about three hundred craftsmen, himself no longer working at the bench but concentrating on his endless flow of heavy and convincing designs, and on meeting his customers. What he understandably seems to enjoy most is sharing pleasure in his superb pieces. This is indeed

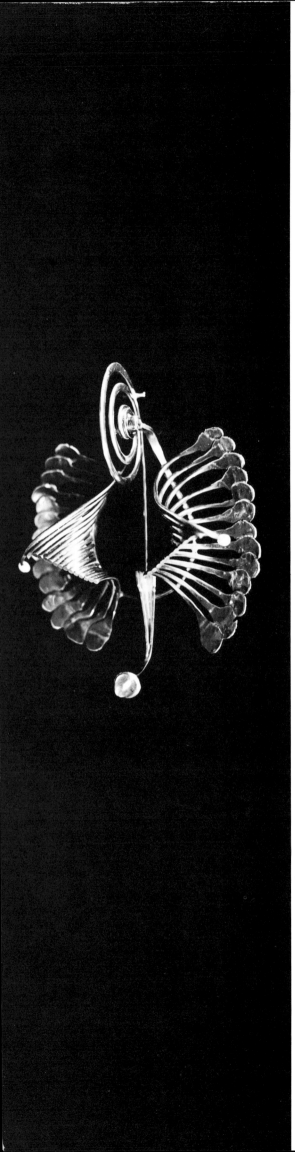

an original artist-craftsman—he will flourish tray upon tray of important jewels in the private rooms behind the shop as if the supply of wealth is endless. Perhaps it is. The whole enterprise is privately owned, and Webb himself intends to open new branches as soon as he is able to train the necessary staff. Webb bears convincing and encouraging witness to the good taste of fashionable America.

David Webb and Arthur King are each so obviously exceptional that they would hardly fit into any normal pattern. But it is typical of America, the country of extremes and contrasts, that these two brilliant people should be so obviously successful, whereas their friends, contemporaries, and competitors, each different to only a tiny degree, should be so very ineffective either in art or in trade.

Nothing succeeds like success, and in America until one achieves real success the alternative seems very close to failure. Most American craft designers have given up the struggle of making a living from their work; they are professors of design at the many universities which believe in the value of skilled work as a sort of therapy: like Arthur Paley of Rochester Institute of Technology, Olaf Skoogfors of Philadelphia College of Art, Dane Purdo of Lawrence, Wisconsin, Arline Fisch of San Diego, with her beautiful feather work, Philip Morton of Salt Lake City or John Paul Miller of the Cleveland Institute of Art, Dr Robert Coleman of San José in California, William Haendel of Illinois or Charles March at Wayne in Detroit (both of them impressive pioneers in the use of gold solder and granulation). Most of these admirable artists, earning a university salary, are able to make occasional jewels for an occasional craft fair or their local art gallery like, for instance, the Little Gallery outside Detroit, or for their own American Craftsman's Council. But American economics are almost hopelessly loaded against handwork, which is so much cheaper when it comes from Europe and so much easier to find. There are almost no craft schools as such—Cranbrook Academy in Michigan or the Haystack Mountain Summer School in Maine are exceptions—so there are pitiably few serious designer-craftsmen being trained. Designers from the university there may be, but these are almost none of them craftsmen. The fertilizing influence spread in Europe by young designer-craftsmen is lacking. The cut

Left *Fibula or decorated safety pin, silver parcel (partly) gilt with two pearls. Length: 3.5 inches. By Arthur Paley of Rochester, USA, 1969. The safety pin's history is long and interesting; beginning as a bent pin it evolved over centuries to be a brooch.*

Right *Two rings, two brooches and a necklet in gold, silver and plastic by Juli Guasch, Barcelona, 1970. Perspex or Plexiglass, because of its rather harsh colours and its susceptibility to scratching, has not yet widely realized its obvious potential in modern jewelry.*

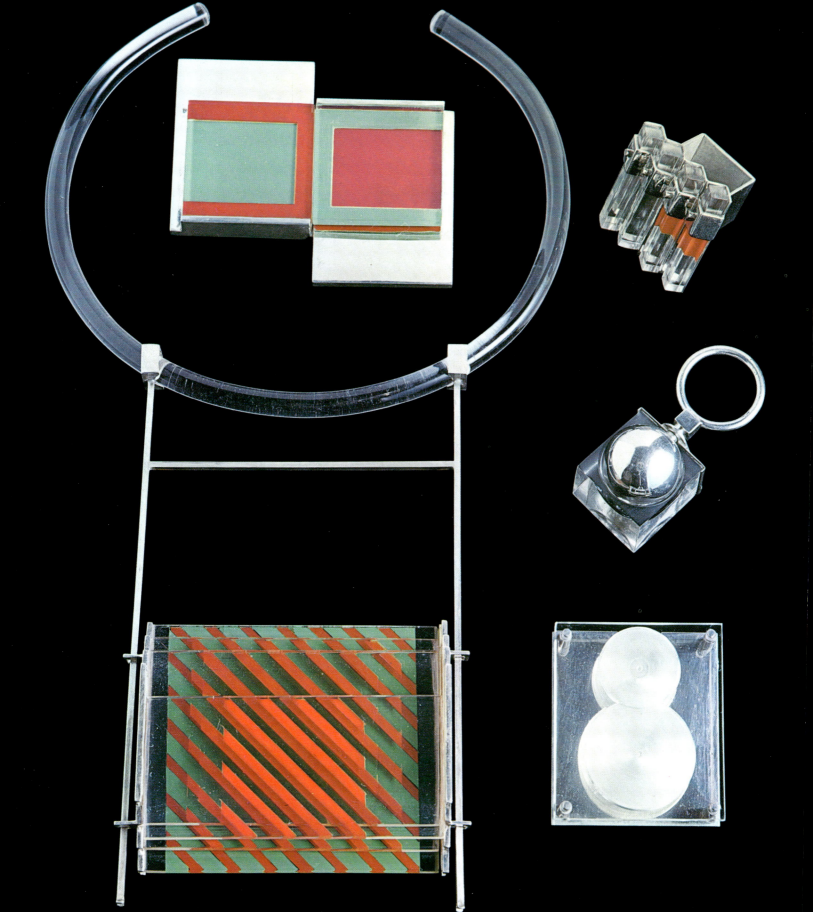

and thrust of American commerce with its extraordinary vigour and enterprise is no substitute.

Rodeo Drive in Los Angeles has dozens of smart jewelers, all probably doing well, but where is the individuality? The Dayton Corporation of Minneapolis have bought the world's biggest store—J. L. Hudson of Detroit; they also bought Shreve of San Francisco and Caldwells of Philadelphia, hitherto two of the really big old family firms surviving; the giants in jewelry grow bigger, newcomers cannot get started at all. Shreve, Crump and Lowe in Boston, Douglas Cooper in Philadelphia and Montego Bay, Charles Warren, a Hudson subsidiary in Detroit —all hold enterprising exhibitions, but all reach the same conclusion: modern craftsmanship is not so profitable as modern mass production. Even in mass production, new design does not bring nearly so big a money dividend as new technique. Carl Bross of the Traub Company near Detroit tried everything before his death in 1971: a devoted art patron, a flawless scientific innovator (he made space equipment), a most perceptive connoisseur of design, he built up the world's biggest engagement ring business—Orange Blossom—not by being memorable visually, but by being unexceptional. His recipe was simple, if soulless: high precision casting, efficient but unmemorable designs.

How refreshing to meet the small men who still make a living working with their own hands—Irena Brynner, for instance, of New York, or Henry Shawah of Boston. Henry is the only 'goldsmith' in the Massachusetts telephone book. He knows only eleven others working in all of the USA and thinks he may be the only one making his living from his own hands. He graduated from teaching goldsmithing at Boston University, into the more difficult career of running his own one-man studio at a profit. He is constantly inspired by the Boston Museum collections, especially their Hellenistic gold; and infuriated by his neighbours in Cambridge—the Harvard Museum who, like many owners of gorgeous jewels, refuse for security reasons to show their pre-Columbian gold to the public. He loves the feeling of beating the metal. He says, 'If the machine is making a piece of jewelry it has to follow a blueprint. If I'm banging on a piece of gold, I can make any number of changes . . . A little quirk you stumble over sometimes opens up whole new vistas of de-

sign—or you get a design in your head that calls for the development of a brand new technique.' 'To me a work of art has more meaning when it is intimate with its owner,' he professes; 'seen in the showcase, it is hard to discern its essential quality. It must be worn to be appreciated.' Perhaps he shows some ancient atavistic streak from the Middle East, where gold rules all, inherited from his Syrian parents. Life became easier when he met a Rockefeller and, later, a Du Pont; in 1970 he was the first American ever to have a one-man show at Goldsmiths' Hall, London, which obtained more honour for him in the USA than anything he had ever done at home. He promptly registered his hallmark there, to be recorded with the great names in the British archives. His distinctive, much-hammered gold has the strength of a spring and the lightness almost of air: as fabrication, very refined; as design, very whimsical.

He had studied at the Pratt Institute and at Columbia University and, though he moved to the academic quiet of Cambridge, and now has his one-man studio workshop there, he, like everyone, responds to the magnetic draw of New York. A recent project was his day-long display in the ornate old Plaza Hotel on Fifth Avenue.

Another excellent craftsman is Stanley Lechtzin; unlike Shawah he is not quite on his own because he teaches at the Tyler School of Temple University, Philadelphia. With the laboratory resources available, he has pioneered in the USA the use of electro-forming, the basic achievement of the Elkington factory in England in the 1840s. An electric current deposits gold or silver on a master form in some easy material like wax or wood; the metal result can be at once light and complex, accurate and original. As Lechtzin says, electro-forming has opened formal and structural possibilities which he could not have predicted before beginning his work in this technique. He has developed light, delicate objects which normally would have been unwearably heavy. Lechtzin's response to New York's hypnosis was at the Museum of Contemporary Crafts in 1965 and the splendid Lee Nordness Gallery in 1969.

The last word must be with two of the jewelry designers who helped to give New York its fashionable panache. Fulco, Duke of Verdura, born in Palermo in 1900, trained himself as an amateur

Brooch in gold, cast and chased, with emeralds of a full colour known as jardin; *some are of rounded cabochon form, some cut irregularly, so the piece shows off the beautiful stones with exceptional variety. By Arthur King, New York, 1970*

Right *The Tiffany diamond, perhaps the biggest and finest canary-coloured diamond in the world, set in gold, platinum and diamonds by Jean Schlumberger of Tiffany, New York, 1964. It is rare to find such enormous stones in wearable jewels because of the difficulties they present, artistically, financially and socially.*

Below *Pin, silver gilt with eight baroque pearls and thirty fresh-water pearls by Stanley Lechtzin of Philadelphia, who has pioneered the use of electroforming in jewelry like this: an electrical current deposits the metal, rather as with electroplating, sometimes producing exciting crystalline growths.*

painter. In 1931 he began jewelry design with Chanel of Paris, started jewelry on holiday in America in 1934 with Paul Flato, opening his jewelry shop in the unaltered first-floor Fifth Avenue show-room—a suite of three or four rooms carved and panelled—where Cartier themselves had begun their American life in 1911. Verdura keeps steadily on: if 'elegant' or 'charming' no longer sound like words of praise in the context of today's high-powered art jargon, this is our fault, not his. He makes different colours of gold, he uses the hard stones—*pietre dure*—so beloved in his native Italy: malachite, lapis lazuli, porphyry. He has always loved the tiny: many of the famous families possess a minute metal creature, perhaps a unicorn, camel or rhinoceros, by him. Recently he has created larger table ornaments. As he says, 'I have tried, in my own way, to re-vive the concept of the *objet de vertu*. Small objects of no functional use what-ever existing only for the pleasure of the eye. Things one would like to touch.'

Jean Schlumberger was born in 1907 into the famous Alsace textile and oil family. He tried a silk factory in New Jersey, art publishing in Paris, costume jewelry, much of it for Schiaparelli; eventually, like everyone, he began to find precious stones more satisfying than their imitators, and set up his own jewelry shop, first in Paris and then in New York. In 1956 he joined Tiffany's as a vice-president, the second time in that firm's highly successful financial career that art has unexpectedly appeared on the assets rather than the liability side of the balance sheet. The first occasion was when the founder's son, Louis Comfort Tiffany, invented his fabrile glass in his own studio around 1880, introducing Art Nouveau and changing the taste of a continent. Schlumberger cannot claim quite as much, but then he is more closely integrated into the company, with his own set of rooms on the second floor and the use of his name in much Tiffany advertising. His jewels are often inspired by coral formations, fishes and the sea—no coincidence that his villa is away on an island, Guadeloupe. To get a really good piece from him nowadays, when he is much in demand, you may have to go specially to the West Indies. Of all the modern designers Schlumberger prob-ably mixes precious and non-precious materials with the greatest freedom, and on occasion uses the biggest stones; in fact in every way he behaves as one

of the Tiffany team is expected to do.

Farnham Lefferts says—and he has been with Tiffany's for twenty years and is now their president—'we are strong enough to withstand that'. Actually re-ferring to Tiffany's rather tentative naming of the designers of their stock, which in fact is usually unnamed and comes from all over the world, Lefferts might have been referring to life itself. In six years to 1969 the Tiffany profits in-creased more than threefold; and they spent seven and a half times as much on advertising, using such catch phrases as '25 rings that deserve a hand'. Their dis-play director, Gene Moore, startled even Fifth Avenue with the ingenious quaint-ness of his miniature window displays; they recruited young designers such as Donald Claflin, Sonya Yonnis and Donald Berg; they opened branches everywhere —in San Francisco, Houston, Chicago, Beverly Hills, even in Atlanta in Georgia. Under their new chairman, Walter Hoving, whose son is head of the Metro-politan Museum, the firm has boldly decided to sell cheap as well as expensive work: they have solitaire diamonds for as little as $225; they may have sold as many as a thousand of one gold and enamel bracelet design by Schlumberger at $1,500. If Tiffany's are the grandest of the big firms in New York, this may be because, more than any other, they use creative art and artists.

The Diamonds-International Awards contest started with mostly American prizewinners, but now, despite its American home, it is proving even more of a stimulant outside the USA than in-side: in 1964, for instance, only three of thirty prizewinners were American; in 1970 America produced three compared with six from Japan. Some of the biggest names in America like David Webb, twice a winner, or Marianne Ostier, Julius Cohen and Coleman Adler, with three awards each, have won so often that they no longer enter. The statistical message is clear: young designers, thirst-ing for the honour of a win, are scarce in the USA but very numerous elsewhere. In modern jewelry, American wearers may pay the piper, but, surprisingly, it is not American designers who call the tune.

WESTERN EUROPE

Western Europe is the great power-house of ideas. A short survey of the modern jewelry scene can hardly hope to cover

all the best and the worst, all the survivals from the past and all the future hopes; but, after studying some of the leading performers place by place, one can perceive how they differ from their colleagues outside Europe, and how quickly the nature of their achievements is changing.

Italy is perhaps the wildest case of all. With comparatively few art schools, she has at Valenza Po, outside Milan, one of the world's great jewelry factory complexes; with almost no welfare state or technical training, she maintains probably the world's biggest store of technical craftsmen; with a very big gulf between rich and poor, and almost without the personal taxation which should bridge that gulf, she nevertheless manages to launch and nourish a steady succession of new artists and designers of startling quality. Despite the heaviest load of survivals from antiquity—not only the Etruscans, the Greeks and the ancient Romans, but the great popes and

princes of the Middle Ages and after, who have all left a splendid wealth for posterity to see and imitate—Italy manages to remain one of the most unexpected modern markets, one of the most fertile sources of modern fashion and design.

Leaving aside the normal trade production, which is exported from Milan and Arezzo, it is as usual the smallest studios that show the real vitality. Milan generated the explosion of modern design in Italy after 1945, and Milan, with its dozens of artists and private galleries, is still the catalyst for Italian artists. Perhaps this dazzling post-war revival of Italy was due to her abandoning her Fascist ideas of militaristic greatness, much as Britain's present artistic upsurge has coincided with the loss of the British Empire. Perhaps in Italy it has been due to the *Triennale* exhibition, the foremost presentation of modern designs throughout the world, collected and shown every three years in Milan. Per-

haps it was due simply to the activity and faith of a few rich patrons, some of them also leading industrialists; for a young craftsman today the situation is still much as it was for Michelangelo with Lorenzo de' Medici in 1490—he has to find his patron and train as an apprentice in his workshop.

Whatever the cause, in the 1950s a small group of Italian sculptors became the envy and inspiration of jewelry designers throughout the world. The family retail jewelers in Rome, Masenza, sold their work; Neiman Marcus, the luxury store in Dallas, Texas, staged an exhibition. This modern art jewelry was not designed for women, it was simply modern abstract sculpture in miniature, fascinating to see but often uncomfortable to wear, often very intricately worked but of small intrinsic value, usually made of gold without stones, because the painters and sculptors who made it were not used to microscopic lapidary complications.

Famous names in fine art shone, and mostly still shine, their lustre on jewels: Lucio Fontana the painter, Pietro Consagra the sculptor, Afro and Dangelo, Bruno Martinazzi, Capogrossi and Kiky Vices Vinci. They have been repeatedly featured at Italian government displays, notably at the Montreal Expo '67. Today bad marketing has deflected some of them back into fine art; a few at least, however, qualify as real jewelers.

Foremost among them, certainly in reputation and probably in production too, are the brothers Arnaldo and Gio Pomodoro. Both run big sculpture studios and regularly win international competitions and commissions; as jewelers they have been very usefully harnessed by the husband of their sister Teresa, Gian Carlo Montebello. He left his job in furniture in 1970 and now sells artists' jewels throughout the world, mostly at small temporary exhibitions in art galleries and clubs. In his first year he attacked Brussels, Naples, Verona, New York, San Francisco and London. This is more than just a family concern: Montebello, under the name 'Gem', hopes eventually to concentrate leading painters and sculptors from all over Europe, and persuade them not only to give jewels as trivial presents to their girl friends, but also to use them as a stimulant, different in scale and finish from their larger output, but no less important. Gem now employs only three or four craftsmen to make up these fine art jewels, the small number of useful artisans contrasting rather poignantly with the flood of visionary artists who provide sketches and prototypes: the idea is excellent, the realization still conjectural.

Italian artists are very status-conscious: reputation means more in Italy than almost anywhere. Right at the top is Ettore Sottsass, perhaps the leading Italian display architect and industrial designer: he and his poet wife, Nanda, share a passion for jewels. Ettore has already hand made a collection of some thirty or forty pieces in gold with brightly coloured enamelled circles and rings. Some artists immediately tire of their own creations once finished: not so Nanda. One day the Sottsass jewels will be shown as an entire and magnificent statement.

If Sotsass is the king of geometry in jewels, Mario Pinton of Padua represents extreme subtlety. His work, all made by himself and one or two helpers, is among the most delicate in Europe: very thin

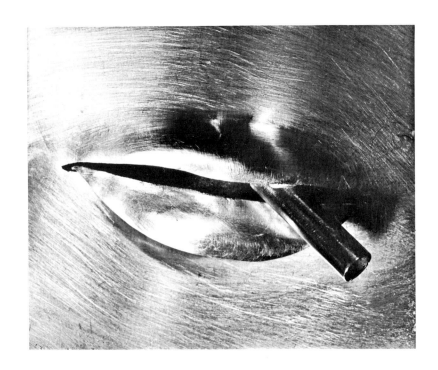

Above *Gold brooch by Bruno Martinazzi, Turin, 1969; hitherto an abstract sculptor and jeweler, his jewels have recently taken the form of human details.*

Left *Gold necklace by Arnaldo Pomodoro, Milan, 1965. With his brother Gio, Arnaldo is recognized as one of Italy's leading modern abstract sculptors; their jewels are similar in feeling to their large-scale work.*

wire, very low relief, exquisite modelling, often of the human face or of animals, with a soft finish; almost always gold, often with one small diamond or precious stone—here is the obsession with intricacy of the ancient Etruscans, far from Sottsass's clash and harshness.

Pietro Gentili, born in 1932, stands outside every group. A painter and sculptor in Milan, he makes his own jewels on his dining-room table. In 1969 he exhibited as far afield as the Oslo city museum and he straddles Italy. He has a second home in Florence and has shown in the past two years in the Milione and the Stendhal galleries in Milan, the Fiori in Florence, at Foligno, in Rome and in almost every other Italian city; in 1969 he won the prize given in Cefalù by Marucelli, the couturier, for the best integration of jewels with dress.

Inspiration is one thing which Italy gives the world through the rare visions of these few artists; production is something quite different. One can sense Italy's primitive obsession with gold and precious stones, walking through jewelry shops on Milan's Via Monte Napoleone, where there are some of the grandest shops like Faraone; or on the Ponte Vecchio in Florence. Here is delightful manipulation, and energetic commercial verve, but it is rather sad to find so little modern work to correspond with the big names in Italian couture, like Pucci, for instance, artistically so brilliant yet also so closely integrated with big textile business. The huge new Omega shop under the shadow of Milan cathedral, which has already shown spectacular work by Gilbert Albert of Switzerland and Andrew Grima of England, seems the one place in Italy which may transform artists' dreams into effective turnover. The legendary Bulgari of Rome, founded in 1881 and still run by the Bulgari family, certainly handle the biggest and best stones in the country; their power is overwhelming, their dignity impressive. But one wonders how long this sort of grandness, reminiscent of the past, can continue to rise to the challenge of the present.

France, with Italy, is probably the country with the richest ancient aristocracy, and at the same time with the biggest spending on jewels by the new industrialists. Probably even more so than Italy, France is proud of its classical jewelry tradition. The great old firms who claim no less than perfection are therefore suspicious of restless modern

ideas, which certainly are not perfect. The five leading Paris shops on and around the seventeenth-century Place Vendôme—Boucheron, Cartier, Chaumet, Mauboussin, and Van Cleef and Arpels—have formed themselves into an *élite* group called *La Haute Joaillerie de France*, and together they do indeed represent an astonishing continuity of history (the oldest, Chaumet, was founded in 1780) and an almost blinding wealth of stones. This group used to present a monumental unity. In June 1970 the situation changed suddenly. Pierre Chaumet, the young head of his own firm and at present of *La Haute Joaillerie* too, staggered Paris with a whimsical new shop, *L'Arcade* in the Place Vendôme, next to his fabulous headquarters; as a German fashion magazine put it, 'the future has already begun'. Huge triangles and squares of silver, gilt and gold and—quite different—elaborate carved stone bowls and chess sets (first made in 1969) adorn the glistening showroom; downstairs it has audio-visual salesmanship with colour films showing blown-up details of the new stock, to make the challenging shapes seem irresistible. Pierre himself says, 'When we are copied that means we have succeeded'; this is admirably philosophical, as the flattery of imitation is much too widespread in modern jewel design. But every successful designer is always imitated, and always will be; his only protection is always to be a move ahead of his followers, and this will give him a unique reputation, the magnet which keeps his clients. René Morin, sculptor, has been seven years with Chaumet and is chiefly responsible for the big flat neck-pieces. He is under no illusion: this must be the beginning of a new era in French jewelry, not just a chance firework which momentarily illuminates the glamorous past.

Each of the main Paris firms has at least one other branch, for instance at Cannes or Monte Carlo. All of them, even with only two branches, have world-wide business connections. The broadest spread is probably Van Cleef and Arpels, with shops now in Cannes, Monte Carlo, Deauville, New York, Palm Beach and, recently, in Geneva and Beverly Hills. Pierre Arpels explains how they have achieved their almost unique strength:

I don't like anything booming, I like to see things go steadily along. We thought about it eight years before we opened in Beverly Hills. We do not advertise, but we do lots of publicity with direct personal contact: I myself am always travelling . . . I don't like a style that is too brutal or disrupting. We sell precious things, imperishable, untarnishable; continuity is fundamental to us. If our jewels are not everlasting, we betray our faith.

Pierre Arpels has formidable confidence in this middle-of-the-road policy; he himself is one of the most impressive, intelligent assets in the whole world of jewelry. His sales ideas seem to work incredibly well: he does not like to force a sale. The firm was founded only in 1906; but it now has probably the biggest Paris showrooms. A Mr Van Cleef married a Miss Arpels, and Louis Arpels of the first generation is still going strong, surrounded by his descendants.

These big retailers each maintain two or three designers, with a workshop for fifteen or twenty craftsmen; they also buy from suppliers everywhere, and they share the skilled facilities of Paris to get their designs made up outside. It is surprising that with so many art galleries there are almost no independent artist-jewelers in France; the Galerie du Siècle on the Left Bank in the middle of the art gallery region is the only one of this kind, and even there jewels are only part of the whole effort. Madame Scaperda founded the enterprise in 1947. Her main jeweler for years was Torun, lately removed to Jensen in Copenhagen; now it is Jacques Lacroix, who comes from near Grenoble. Trained in Brussels at the Beaux Arts, Jacques has six workers; he sells at Lacloche, of Cannes and of Rue de Grenelle in Paris; and in small shops in most French cities like Lyons, Nice and Toulouse. It is unhealthy that Jacques has so few competitors in such a big country; probably only in the south, in tourist centres like Les Baux, do they exist at all (Jacques Moniquet and others make a summer living there).

Austria under the Hapsburgs was, of course, the world's jewelry capital, and it still preserves magnificent treasures in its museums. Although family habits die hard, and the Austrians are a conservative race, they have changed more than most since 1945. Probably the most distinguished contribution to Austrian jewelry is being made by Elizabeth Defner and her husband, Helfried Kodré, born in 1940 in Graz and self-trained. Defner-Kodré, as they are now known, contribute to the ever increasing art jewelry exhibition syndrome: more and

Left *Gold necklet and pendant by Pietro Gentili of Milan and Florence; distinguished painter and sculptor, he shows in galleries, not shops. He dislikes solder which gives his jewels some affinity with the earliest known metalwork.*

Below *Necklet in white and yellow gold by Chaumet of Paris. One of the world's oldest and grandest retail firms, founded in 1780, they have recently launched a new and imaginative range of modern work.*

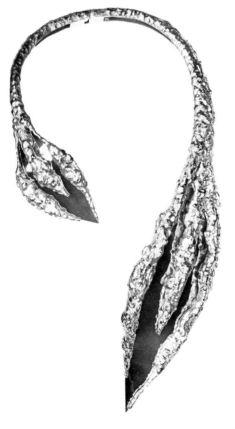

Above *Sun burst pendant watch in coloured gold and pearls, by Gilbert Albert, made with Patek Philippe, 1960*

Right *Circular brooch in white and yellow gold by Gilbert Albert of Geneva, 1971. Typical of the enterprising designs without great intrinsic value, which many artist-jewelers—and ordinary jewel wearers throughout the world—now prefer to big stones*

Overleaf *Pendant jewels in silver and Australian opal by Emanuel Raft, the truly international sculptor-jeweler: born in 1938 of Greek parents he was brought up in Cairo, practised in Sydney, Australia, and briefly in New York, and now works in London. He cast and burnished the silver, achieving the exciting clashing stone shapes simply by smashing a large opal under a hammer. 1967. Pendant, right, from Goldsmiths' Hall, London*

more exhibitions in museums throughout Europe lead to more and more talk, to write-ups (especially in the German trade papers), and to a wholly misleading impression by outsiders that modern art jewelry provides a prosperous livelihood. Defner-Kodré—just the two of them in their small Vienna workshop—are honoured in the art world: in the past four years they have shown in many parts of Europe. They have also achieved distinction in a wider, more competitive field; in 1970 they won a De Beers Diamonds-International Award.

More orthodox is Sven Boltenstern, also of Vienna. He worked for ten years at the leading Vienna manufacturer and retailer, Hügler, who have some eight craftsmen in their workshop, and acquired there some impatience with conservative Viennese tastes. He recalls the eminent modern Viennese painter, Hundertwasser, dramatically taking off all his clothes on the platform at the opening of a new school, as a protest, because, he declared, there is no modern architecture in Austria. Nor is there any jewelry school. Sven shrewdly suggests that the 'dead' state of culture may be because there are virtually no Jews left since the brutal Nazi extermination programme. Sven was originally apprenticed to his uncle's firm, Godina; he now has a workshop with half a dozen craftsmen partly making traditional jewelry; he struggles to sell his modern work in Graz (at Schulin), Linz and abroad. He has three Diamonds-International Awards, in 1965, 1967 and 1968. His most spectacular effort was a fashion show in Bonn and Cologne where he gained good publicity with his golden bras; he took three weeks to make them, with the intention of shocking the press into noticing him.

Particularly popular are the semi-precious, carved stone flowers evolved by Professor Stengl and his son at Zell am See, and now offered by many retailers, first among them probably Paltscho. Austria's first goldsmiths' gallery was started in 1969 by the young craftsman Manfred Stubhann in Salzburg; there he mounts successful and enterprising international events during the festivals.

Switzerland's economy is always buoyant; the same is true of Gilbert Albert, the most stimulating mind in jewelry today, who has won three Diamonds-International Awards, in 1963, 1964 and 1969. He has been the top designer, first for Patek Phillippe where he managed their workshop for seven years, and then for Omega; but he prefers his present life, on his own with twelve craftsmen, overlooking Lake Geneva. He was an orphan at thirteen and went into a munitions factory; he is proud to be the son of a workman and a trades union member. Born in 1930, he won his first competition at nineteen with a shell piece. He has continually offered himself seemingly impossible challenges, by abandoning salaries and openings which would be most craftsmen's dream, and he has won through. After his recent break with Omega, he revived his fortunes by selling five hundred rings—with interchangeable stones packed as a set, a brilliant new idea—not through a great jeweler but in a local drug store. He says that rich people no longer dare to show off their wealth; and that capitalism provides badly distributed wealth, communism, marvellously well distributed poverty. He is critical of art education: 'To educate is not enough—one must give technique and one must know how to sell.'

Perhaps his most admirable characteristic is his generosity. His ideas, like the interchangeable stones for rings, are very quickly copied everywhere, but he wryly accepts this as inevitable. He considers competition good, and with his new sales network for medium-priced pieces throughout Europe, the USA and Japan (many of them locally manufactured, and cast, not hand made) he will obviously continue to dominate the scene. No modern jeweler today has earned a bigger and better reputation, and nobody deserves it more.

Othmar Tschaler of Berne builds his jewels mostly out of flat strips of different coloured and textured metal. In his small studio by the medieval cathedral, his artist's vision has an ideal setting. If Albert's business might conceivably become a factory, Tschaler's seems likely always to demonstrate the pleasures of being small.

It is in Germany and Britain, two rich countries so different in character, that the biggest impact of modern jewelry design can be seen. Both countries have a wide-ranging art and technical education system, both a long history and a respect for the past, both an urgent awareness of the need to map out a civilized future; most important, both have a very big consumer market of relatively intelligent buyers.

Badge and chain of office of the President of the Praesidium of the German jewelry societies, the winning design in an open national competition. Gold, carved rock crystal and amethyst. Each link in the chain bears the impression of a maker's mark of a German master goldsmith of the eighteenth, nineteenth and twentieth centuries. By Peter Tauchnitz, Berlin, 1965

In Germany the idea of investment is much discredited, after ghastly and repeated money and political crashes since 1914. Enjoyment of the present moment may be more accepted as a valid aim there than in Britain, because caution has proved unwise. Britain, on the other hand, is still the world's financial centre and still has more continuity of activity than any country in the world, and so big jewelry collectors still have their eye on the steady increase in value of big stones.

There are three main metalwork schools in Germany: Pforzheim is the country's centre for jewelry, Schwäbisch Gmünd for silver, and Hanau, outside Frankfurt, probably the main centre for light industry. Each competes with the other. Such is the interest in modern jewelry that two German trade papers, the best in the world, also jostle for leadership, and have just started publishing features about students' work in each school—beneficial for the students immediately, but perhaps not in their best long-term interest, because students should be learning, not performing.

More evidence of the current German frenzy for novelty and distinction is the number of competitions. If jostling is a sign of health rather than of anxiety, Germany is well. The wealthy and beautiful resort town of Baden-Baden last year gave its first 'Golden Rose'; the Hamburg-based Society for the Goldsmiths' Art *(Deutsche Gesellschaft für Goldschmiedekunst)*, awards its Golden Ring of Honour from time to time to designers who are considered to have made an epic contribution; Degussa, the huge Frankfurt metal merchants, have started a student contest; the Society of Gemmologists *(Edelsteinfreunde)* last year elected Paul Hartkopf, the distinguished Düsseldorf craftsman, as their 'jeweler of the year'. Paul Hartkopf, born in 1925, has indeed made a fine contribution: solid, distinguished and public-spirited. He now has a dozen craftsmen. One can trace his progress in a colourful record in his beautiful small Düsseldorf shop—the rather unusual wall covering of masses of certificates won by him.

German goldsmiths are organized into complex groups—each city has its *Innung* (local society), and representatives of each *Innung* frequently meet each other and their mayors, and even state and national ministers. Paul Hartkopf makes time to play a big part in this structure of craft government (which does not exist in any other country), as well as carrying off many awards; and the main purpose of it all is to enchant his own customers.

Georg Lauer, one of the few top-quality Pforzheim factories, celebrated their seventy-fifth birthday in 1970, with an international competition. Lauer's are managed by two young cousins, Georg and Bernhard—it is sad how seldom big jewelry names have youth at the helm. Here, their Lauer dynamism has led in recent years, with a staff of about 120, to a thirty per cent annual sales expansion, and is now constructing a strong bridge between real art and successful trade. The Lauer competition judges included three of the world's most powerful retailers—Fuhrmann of Curaçao, Schilling of Stuttgart and Kern of Düsseldorf—but the winners were not all 'trade' people. Klaus Bohnenberger, now probably the top competition winner of Pforzheim, received several prizes; the Lauer collection also includes unknown names, who will benefit from the factory's backing.

Retailers usually get scant sympathy from aesthetes, who blame them for pandering to less-than-fastidious public taste, and give them none of the credit for making a successful living. But whereas designers often satisfy nobody but themselves, retailers are absolutely bound to the consumer. The phenomenal rise of René Kern has a moral for us all. His father was the engraving teacher at the Pforzheim school and then worked at Cartier, where René learned good French. The Nazis placed him in the most dangerous part of the German front-line because he had a Jewish grandmother. His division was the first into Kharkhov; he remembers being unexpectedly welcomed as a liberator of the Ukraine, by flower-throwing girls. Sometimes, because of his French, he was sent to France on exotic shopping missions to buy scent for the High Command. After the war he started as a manufacturer in Schwäbisch Gmünd, with only three craftsmen to help him. He used to sell his drawings to retailers and other manufacturers for about five marks each. In 1956 he started his retail shop simply because he had to take over one of his retail customers, who could not pay his bills. His own skill as a metalworker was slowly overwhelmed by his administrative responsibilities. Now, with eighty employees, including

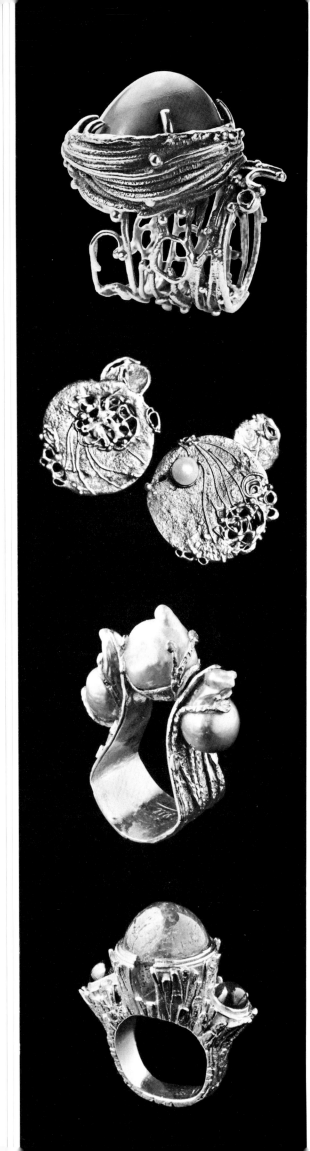

and with exhibitions of the winners in the major capital cities, rotating among them year by year. In 1965 there were only 264 entrants; in 1970 a record 793 (showing 2,351 designs) from thirty-three countries: interest and support seem to be increasing steadily. De Beers advertise diamonds in most of the wealthiest countries and have set up diamond publicity committees in eleven of them.

Giant corporations have the same power today as the great princes of the past. All credit to them for showing the same public spirit! But what they cannot have is personal taste, often so necessary to harness an artist's vision. Competitions are the substitute, and they are a matter of luck: nobody knows what the word 'best' means, nobody can foretell what will be the corporate opinion of judges who do not know each other; nobody can be sure how the selected drawings will look when made up, nobody can know whether the made-up prize-winners will in fact be sold, or prove commercial tragedies. If a competition is run by experienced retailers, who think they know what sells easily, the results will be unexciting and will achieve no publicity; a jury of aesthetes may make a startling choice and get the publicity, but the results may not be to the taste of the shoppers in Bond Street or Fifth Avenue. Artists are helped much more by a precise, personal brief from their client than by the chance verdict of a jury thousands of miles away which did not know what it was looking for, and which often does not even see its finished selection. So competitions and committees are not a universal panacea; they are no more than the appetizer which should create better private patrons.

De Beers have helped to spread the lure of diamonds throughout society: it is no longer a matter of 'diamonds for duchesses'. Similarly, the Chamber of Mines of South Africa may revive the fortunes of gold. Gold is often linked with Fort Knox and with money, and often seems too precious and awe-inspiring to impinge on ordinary life; the Chamber may transform this fear of the legendary into a desire for the charming. Whatever the future, precious jewelry is now recognized as art, exhibited and enjoyed not as a menial disguise for minerals, but as a positive facet of human nature.

Left, from top to bottom
Finger ring in silver and gold with cabochon turquoise by Gerda Flockinger, 1971, Goldsmiths' Hall, London; she was the first woman jeweler ever to be honoured by a one-man show at the Victoria and Albert Museum, London, in 1971.
Pair of cufflinks, silver, gold and moonstone by Gerda Flockinger, 1971, Goldsmiths' Hall, London; her personal style fuses the surfaces of her metals to achieve unique plastic interest.
Finger ring, gold and pearls by Nevin (Mrs Nevin Holmes), 1972, Goldsmiths' Hall, London
Finger ring. Gold, emerald, crystal and sapphires by Nevin, whose work shows an almost Byzantine richness of colour, relief and texture. Goldsmiths' Hall, London

Right Finger rings in gold with lapis lazuli, on a plastic display mount, by Wendy Ramshaw, London, 1971. New conceptions in jewelry are of course very rare: this is one of them—a new type of dress ring, turned by lathe and worn in a cluster on one finger. Wendy Ramshaw won a London Design Centre award for it in 1972. Goldsmiths' Hall, London

Technique

To the art historian technique may provide a useful clue to general understanding—an artist's scientific skill may be the key piece of evidence by which his work can be dated, placed and pigeon-holed. For instance, in painting there are milestones like the Romans' not having perspective, the Van Eycks' discovering oil paint and Antonello da Messina's introducing it to Italy, and Rupert of the Rhine's inventing the aquatint. But for jewels there are almost no such laboratory finger posts to show us the big crossroads.

'Thermoluminescence' is the new key to the pedigree of pots and potsherds; radiocarbon dating is now sorting out the muddle of many old museum collections. Archaeological finds can often be dated only by their relationship to each other; so although neither process works on metal, they do nevertheless sometimes help simply by dating neighbouring objects or indeed the strata level in which the metal is discovered.

For metal the best dating process is spectographic analysis, something like an X-ray, which records the density of the various metallic elements in a piece of metal. As metal refining was not developed until the nineteenth century, most antique jewels use their local metal with all the impurities found locally: for instance, Asia Minor jewels in Roman times contained as much silver as gold, giving it a white colour, often being called electrum, a local mixture; and South American Inca gold similarly included copper, giving it a red colour. But the only proof provided by the spectrographer is that if the jewel is of pure metal it is probably of nineteenth-century or modern date, and as all makers of fakes no doubt know this, the proof is something less than positive.

The history of technique is the history of human ingenuity except that, with jewels, it is already almost finished before history begins; the very earliest civilizations, 5000 years old or more, seem to have made their jewels exactly as we do today. Jewelers seem from the very beginning to have been masters of their craft. They were never, so far as we can tell, subject to any crippling limitations, as were ancient architects who made do without the wheel. For some five thousand years jewelers have used almost the same tools and metals, stones and apparatus as they do today: the means of production have been constant. It is only the ends, the appearance of the actual jewels, that have continually changed. At different times and places fashion gave prominence now to enamels, now to plain sculptured shapes, now to extreme detail; but in most periods throughout history jewelers seem to have had about the same range of capacity as one finds today in London's Hatton Garden, and New York's 47th Street.

Basically, metalwork is the problem of changing a flat piece of metal brick or sheet into decorative relief. It may be done by raising, beating with a hammer on a hard metal or wood stake; by casting, pouring molten metal into a sand mould; or by the waste-wax method, pouring metal into a cavity left by melted wax between plaster moulds; or, more recently, with the aid of pressure from centrifugal force, pushing molten metal into a revolving mould. Carving, unpopular because of the wasting of metal, is more often used as specialized engraving—cutting a thin line from the metal surface. Chasing, with which it is often confused, digs a groove into the metal, impressing the line, removing nothing; *repoussé* is the same done from behind. Chasing and *repoussé* are normally used together to emboss pictorial designs, like people or heads. Flat chasing leaves the main surface flat, just impressing into it a pattern of lines, like arabesques or heraldic cartouches, more used for table plate than for jewels. Burnishing is polishing with a hard surface, not a soft mop; it implies the use of a flat, smooth tool, often of hard agate or steel, to press the surface flat and smooth. Polishing often removes a microscopically small film from the surface, using abrasive with a revolving or moving mop. Enamelling is the melting

Left *Brooch in gold and diamonds by David Thomas, London, 1971. Many artist-jewelers have their own personal idiom: here, very thin gold wire and dots. The sun-burst effect re-interpreted in this jewel was most popular in baroque ceremonial jewels, especially those of Louis XIV of France, the Sun King.*

This ring (two views below) *was probably cast in a sand mould, the surface cleaned by chasing with a hammer and punch; the inscription 'joy sans fyn' (joy without end), the flowers and the crucifixion were engraved with a sharp tool. Perhaps connected with the Earl of Warwick, c. AD 1350*

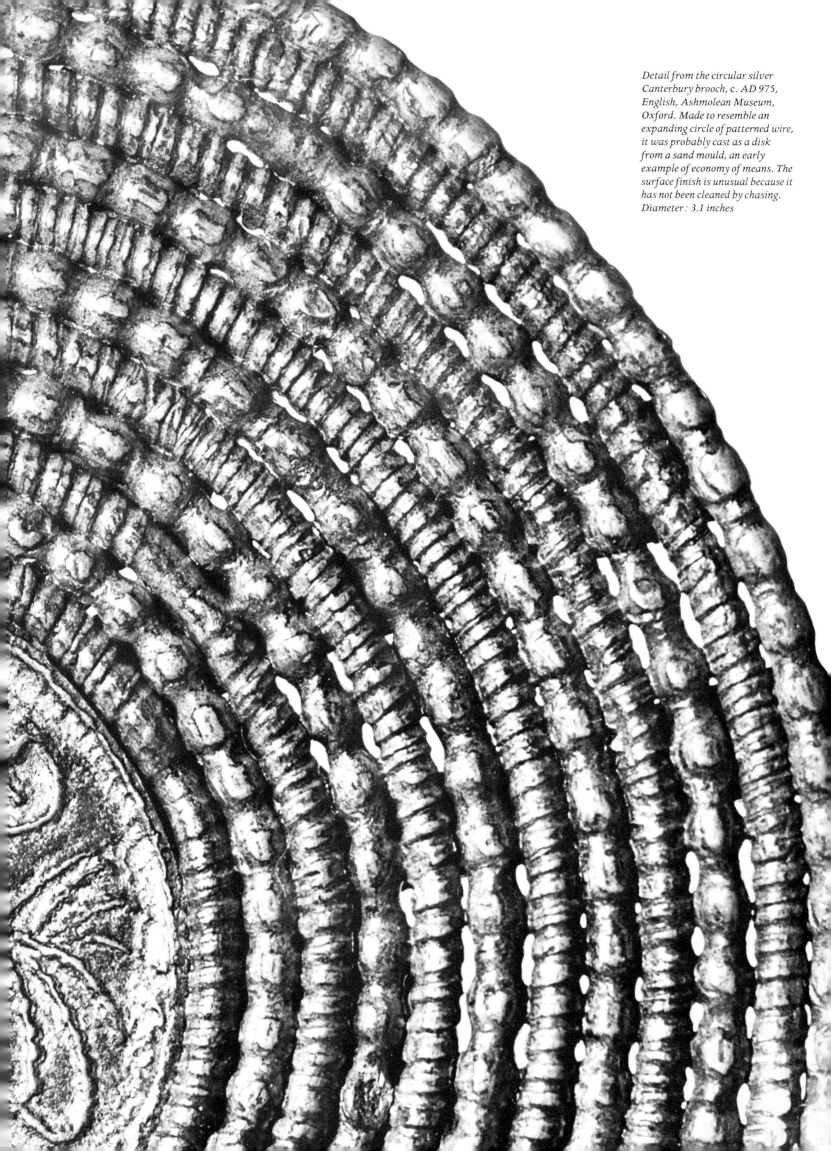

Detail from the circular silver Canterbury brooch, c. AD 975, English, Ashmolean Museum, Oxford. Made to resemble an expanding circle of patterned wire, it was probably cast as a disk from a sand mould, an early example of economy of means. The surface finish is unusual because it has not been cleaned by chasing. Diameter: 3.1 inches

of a specially fine glass composition powder into a prepared hole or onto a prepared surface, from which the enamel is always likely to spring away. It is often impossible to distinguish this from inlays of cold coloured glass into its setting under heat. So much then for the basic vocabulary.

Machinery—with its stampings, banging metal into a hand-carved steel die with a sudden blow, and its pressings, by the imposition of enormous force—was probably introduced to the world of jewels by Matthew Boulton, the Birmingham pioneer of the industrial revolution in the 1770s. During the past two centuries industry has begun to create its own style; in the past generation vacuum evaporation, spark eroding, spot welding have, alas, usually succeeded only in a poor quality copying of hand work, not in evolving a new language of their own. Jewelry remains the craft with the least apparatus, the most portable tools, the oldest opportunities of them all.

Statements as to how jewels were made are only valid where enough pieces survive to give a fair spread of what was customary. The most distinctive aspect of Sumerian work, for example, is certainly the clever chasing, of uniform depth on very thin metal, sensitive but not a great manual problem. Schliemann's Trojan hoard from a thousand years later, perhaps about 1600 BC, shows a comparable use of chasing which, of course, before the arrival of hard steel and easily sharpened tools, was the normal system for patterning. But whereas at Ur the metal is usually thin, at Troy it was thick. A surprise in the history of goldsmithing is Knossos, which seems to have become rich in gold just when Troy became poor, perhaps because Crete conquered Asia Minor about that time, around 1500 BC. The Minoans achieved sensitive models, probably cast and chased, which would have done professional credit to any Renaissance master. If Mycenae in its turn conquered Crete about 1300 BC, its gold work shows little trace of the contact: cruder than Minoan, it is the inspiration for many modern craftsmen. If the Cretan smiths evolved casting of a modern professional standard, the Mycenaean contribution was chasing in high relief of thick metal, maintaining the thickness throughout, not, as is the danger, weakening the metal into thin patches.

Necklaces in carved lapis lazuli and in thin chased gold, c. 2450 BC. Found by Sir Leonard Woolley at Ur. Metal may have first been used in the fourth millennium BC in Anatolia; the Sumerians may have invented the alloy now called bronze.

Horse in gold by Benvenuto Cellini; famous for his autobiography and treatise, almost none of his gold survives. This detail is from his salt-cellar planned for Cardinal Ippolyto d'Este, made for Francis I of France at Fontainebleau and given in 1570 by Charles IX to the Archduke Ferdinand of Tyrol, at Ambras Castle; in 1806 it went to Vienna, and is now in the Museum of Fine Arts there. Superb modelling in gold is finished by chasing and engraving with a jeweler's precision.

Thus one can point to general trends. But to try to trace detailed accomplishment, age by age, is on present evidence too presumptuous.

Some of the arts depend upon civilization, that is upon a fine balance of human organization, of law and rights and science and art, usually centred on urban life, usually with the help of the written word. It is arguable that great architecture cannot be achieved without such a high all-round civilization. But with metal it is different: one of the astonishing aspects of the goldsmiths' craft is its technical perfection over so many degrees of civilization and barbarism alike. The earliest Egyptians, the painters of the Dordogne, even the wandering tribes of central Asia would probably today be called savages because they did not have so-called civilized values; but each was its own strong culture and each culture seems to have succeeded in the field of human ornament, even if it failed with the larger problems of human organization. Surprisingly, one cannot claim that the finest cultures produced the finest jewels: finery was a feature of almost every powerful culture, good or bad, from the very beginnings.

The Sumerians probably made the earliest jewels now known. By the fourth millennium BC they had not only invented writing and the wheel which they used for transport and for pottery; they had evolved their own system of casting, either solid or with a hollow core, by *cire perdue*, and they used quite a range of alloys like electrum. One of them, bronze, seems to have been unknown elsewhere for centuries to come. They had mastered inlay of coloured stones into *cloisons* or compartments. From Ur and its neighbours there are splendid pieces of semi-precious stone inlay, especially lapis lazuli and carnelian. Amulets in the form of birds and animals were carved in the round with superb grace, sometimes pierced as pendants, sometimes with a geometrical symbol—square, triangle or star—engraved deep on a flat bottom for use as a seal. Sumerians used sweating and soldering, achieving delicate elaboration beyond the reach of simple melting and hammering. They understood how to beat gold to use its unique capacity as thin foil for their so-called beech leaf necklaces (actually beech trees were unknown; these represented a sort of willow); they could chase delicate veins

onto leaves and grooves onto beads; and they used casting to make some of the small, heavy, doubled beads. Many of their larger artefacts like jugs and cups were beaten to shape, or raised, from a flat sheet—a process involving continual heat treatment to anneal the work-hardening and brittleness in the metal, coupled with manual skill to keep the metal moving with constant thickness. Sometimes the foot was in the form of a disk soldered or sweated to the bottom. Soldering had already replaced riveting as being stronger, smoother and more harmonious. The Sumerians could make gold ribbon and fix it onto other elements. Sumerian work is flavoured with an amazing sophistication—delicacy of touch, fluency of line, a variety and charming use of coloured beads, a general elegance of conception. All suggest that the goldsmiths' craft emerged almost fully fledged in early Mesopotamia.

Put another way, this marvellous early work proves that Sumeria was in fact not the world's first civilization, nor were the Elamites of southern Persia with their stylized animal charms; nor, with their beautiful lapis lazuli snake jewels, newly discovered by the Danish expedition there, were the Delmun people of Kuwait, hitherto known only from references in the tablets of Babylonia and Assyria. All these must have been heirs to the ancestral skill of still older peoples in Asia Minor or in the Middle East of whom we know nothing.

There is little to be said about ancient Egypt itself technically, except that almost every piece was a masterpiece. If Egyptian art and architecture seem stiff and formal, now that we value spontaneity so highly, their goldsmiths' work, being more supple in its design, strikes a more sympathetic chord today; it showed the strongest blend of colour, rhythm and form that anyone had yet achieved. Blessed with rich supplies of gold, carnelian, lapis lazuli and agate, the Egyptians seem to have been the first people to use colour as a primary element in their jewelry design. It was the need to identify jewels with gods, or with the wearer's name or office, however, that really explains the extraordinary variety of these jewels. Very often they incorporate hieroglyphs or symbols telling some story, very often the magic scarab is used with its amazingly detailed low-relief carving of the beetle's wings and head on one side

The Sassanian dynasty in Persia left more carved stone seals than any other civilization: usually, as here, they were engraved, probably by wheel, with great style in cream-coloured chalcedony. c. 3rd century AD

and, on the other, the lettering and signs which made the piece important to its wearer, sometimes immortalizing his name or office, more often praising a god. Perhaps there is one specialized craft in which the Egyptians especially excelled, and that is inlay: cutting myriad fragments of stone and glass, and setting them so as to give an ordered richness never again achieved before or since.

The rainbow colours of Egyptian jewelry became, as one might expect, more haphazard and less geometrical as the hieratic nature of Egyptian society relaxed until, under Roman influence, Ptolemaic Egyptian and Roman jewelry ideas merged into a new, soft, rather heavy treatment of gold specially associated with Syria. The meticulous Egyptian craft of inlay, which may have lasted as long as three thousand years, simply faded away.

In Mesopotamia the geographical and historical heirs to the Sumerians were the Babylonians and Assyrians. Their jewelry is almost all lost except for the splendid seals made of local hard stone like carnelian, amethyst and agate. For the early Babylonians these were often oval or round, with a precisely drawn group of one or two figures in simple dress; for the Assyrians they were usually cylindrical, much more elaborately executed, often with shading and full regalia; for their successors, the Achaemenid Persians, Greek influence was strong. But their very few surviving jewels are much heavier and more robust than the Greek, no doubt because there was much more gold in the centralized kingdom of Cyrus and Darius than in the diverse democracies of Attica. These Persian jewels are simple and crisp, like the Persepolis sculptures. Next, around the time of Christ, were the Parthians whose distinctive product was their seals, shaped like an almond with one end chopped, rather confused natural and abstract geometrical symbols being deep cut into this flat face. For the Sassanians seals may have been especially attractive, to judge by the great numbers and confident, original style of the survivors. They were extremely beautiful, made often of delicious honey-coloured chalcedony or tawny carnelian, shaped almost like a ring, but with a small hole big enough only for thread, the drawing by now, the third and fourth centuries AD, being almost like a pencil sketch, feathery and im-

pressionistic. Occasionally these stone seals fitted over the finger, but it was the early Greeks—Mycenaeans and Minoans—who adapted the idea of an independent seal into a seal and ring combined. They made the seal ring customary, often using stone scarabs inspired by Egypt, with gold mounts. They carved into both gold and into hard stone, like carnelian, scenes of epic sagas, cut with more depth and precision than ever before or since.

The Greeks and Etruscans were obsessed with granulation, a decorative effect of incredible delicacy, so difficult to achieve that even today nobody quite knows how it was done. It sounds simple enough: thousands of tiny, almost microscopic balls of gold soldered to the surface of the object to provide a contrast in texture and light. The background may be polished or just burnished to give a softer sheen, against which the granules, which are so small that they never shine, stand out; normally they form a pattern such as a swastika (the old Persian sun device), or an animal or bird in silhouette, or simply a zigzag border round the edge of a circular brooch, for instance, or round the lower half of pendant earrings. The Mycenaeans used granulation in a relatively crude manner towards the end of their empire about the thirteenth century BC. Homer compares an earring presumably of about that time to a mulberry, showing vividly how large its grains of gold must have been. Granulation became steadily more fashionable until, in the great period of ancient jewelry in Hellenistic times, from the fourth century BC, the gold drops became bigger and less regular; by Christian times, granulation had died out—perhaps its secret was lost simply because the craftsmen who could do it were killed in the tribal invasions. It was revived sporadically and attractively in the Roman colonies of Syria and Asia Minor and later under Byzantium; but by then each sphere on the knobbly gold surface was as big as a pin head, whereas early granulation produced a surface textured as finely as human skin.

Granulation provides a matt, opaque finish of great charm; just as one wants to feel as well as look at fine glazed porcelain, or silver or gold with an antique patina, so granulation provides an effect of subtlety and tactile value. The finest granulation, that is to say the smallest particles of gold used to create

Early granulation: serpent's head enlarged perhaps twenty times, one of the alternating serpents and balls hanging from an Iberian gold necklace in the Javea Treasure, 6th century BC. Archaeological Museum, Madrid

the most intricate network of patterning, was probably made in Greece from the sixth to the fourth century BC, when one tiny earring might have on its surface a carpet of as many as 5,000 to 7,000 individual grains of gold, almost as fine as vapour. But gold was so rare there, and surviving pieces are so few, that granulation is usually, even if incorrectly, reckoned to be an Etruscan invention.

Just as in archaic bronze sculpture there is some uncertainty as to what the Greek colonists inspired the Etruscans to do, and what the Etruscans themselves invented, so with jewels we do not know how much, if at all, the Etruscans used Greek craftsmen. Anyway granulation is much commoner in Etruria than in Greece, probably because gold itself was more easily available, possibly because Etruscans valued their women more than the Greeks did. Gold jewels found in central Italy, what was the Etruscan empire, use granulation with perhaps more body than in Attic Greece: the pieces are more beefy, the patterns stronger; perhaps Etruscan work was not only heavier than Greek, but more imaginative. So much has been discovered that it is even possible to define two different fashions: in northern Etruria, for instance, in the city of Vetulonia, grains were used to silhouette the object or figure—it would be all grains, or all polished with the background granulated. In the south, by contrast, as at Praeneste or Caere the grains were used as outlines, round the edge, not all over.

The mystery is simple: how were the blobs held in position? Any bits of metal if placed beside each other tend to turn treacly just before melting. Their edges soften and, at the point of junction, they fuse together over a large area. But with ancient granulation the balls of gold hardly touched each other and hardly touched the surface. What was it that fixed them in position and who had the patience to do it?

Since the 1930s the world has become pre-occupied with technology, the one direction in which we may claim continued 'progress'. Jewelers and historians alike have therefore become increasingly frustrated by the fact that they simply cannot do granulation as well as the Etruscans, although the Etruscans had no temperature control, no high precision tools, no refined metals, no metallurgical science, no accurate drills, cutters or measuring equipment and no accurate magnifying glasses with which to survey the details of their superlative work.

The first modern theory was evolved suitably enough by H. A. P. Littledale, who in the British Museum, London, was in daily touch with one of the world's best collections of granulation. His research was formulated in a lecture at Goldsmiths' Hall in 1936. He believed the explanation was in the solder: he evolved a method of using copper, with a very low melting point, so that it did not soften the crispness of the gold surfaces it joined which had a higher melting point. It may be that the granules themselves were heated until the copper alloy in the gold oxydized, covering the gold with black copper oxide; then when glued onto the gold background, the join was effected by evaporating the glue and the oxide, leaving the copper which, while molten, flowed where it was most needed—between the two gold surfaces. Alternatively, if the gold contained no copper, as was frequently the case in ancient times, it is possible, as Littledale suggests, that the copper oxides were present not on the granule but in the gum. Probably they originally got there quite by chance, as a result of contact with copper or bronze utensils which were of course normal during the Bronze Age. The granules themselves may have been made by melting fragments of gold suspended in powdered charcoal; they could then be picked up either one at a time or in clusters on a brush moistened with gum. There is no evidence that any preparatory patterns were established on the gold background by scratching or indenting—the granules seem to have been just laid onto the surface.

The Munich goldsmith Michael Wilm experimented also before the war. Mark Rosenberg evolved a highly technical theory, crediting ancient craftsmen more with elaborate devices than with their obvious prerequisite, infinite perseverance. At Cologne the goldsmith

Gold safety pin or fibula in the form of a bow. The filigree and granulation are much finer than on the earring opposite, but of random pattern which would have been unlikely in earlier times. From Campania, Italy, c. 300 BC. Length of whole: 3.1 inches. Cleveland Museum of Art

Elisabeth Treskow has summarized the matter efficiently, most recently in the Dürer Nuremberg centenary catalogue of 1971.

Whatever the exact truth may be, the spectacular intricacy of ancient goldsmiths' work must owe more to the nature of the metal used than to any technical or chemical complications. Native gold, as used by the Greeks and Etruscans, always contained silver and its melting point was substantially higher (about 1,000°C) than that of modern alloys (about 900°C) which contain little or no silver. It is this high melting point which gave room for manoeuvre to the ancient smiths. Even though they could not judge their temperature accurately, even though they heated their piece more than they might have intended, they still would not melt it in the way that they would do today. Even so, there are occasional examples of Greek jewelry where the metal has immersed or flooded itself, losing its clean edges, having approached too closely to its melting point. The greatest worry for any jeweler is that he will by mistake melt his masterpiece before he has finished it. Working heat might be the melting point of solder, or whatever was needed for annealing or softening metal hardened by continual hammering. Anyway, the closer the margin between this working heat and the melting point of the jewel itself, the greater the danger. It was a kind provision of providence that gold throughout the Greek world, contained in its natural state lots of silver. Its high melting point compensated for the almost complete lack of what we would now consider rudimentary equipment, and made it possible for jewelers to express adequately in their own idiom one of the great moments in human history.

One cannot explain the Greek and Etruscan achievement simply by saying it was easier for them than for us because their gold had a higher melting point, any more than one can say Ictinus was a better architect than Corbusier simply because he did not have to cope with the motor-car. The mystery of pure art was the main challenge to both of them, technology only one of the many influences forming the context for their work. The Greeks and Etruscans had vision, and that is the reason for the triumphant nature of their jewels. Their patience and microscopic precision were not unique to gold. In the

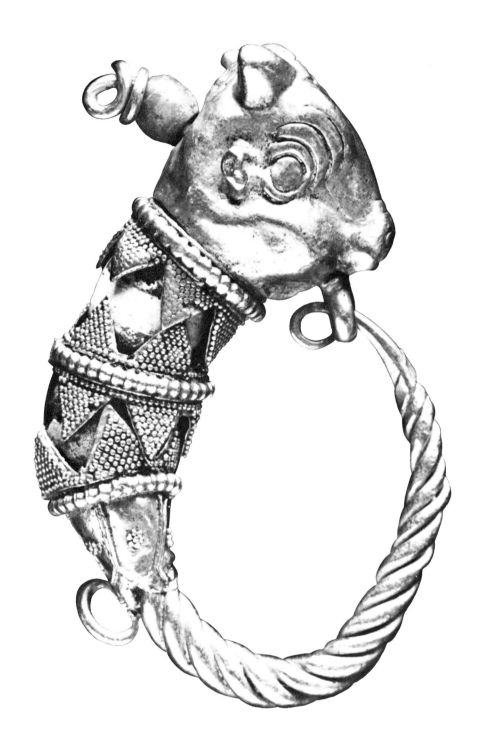

The fineness of gold dots in granulation increased steadily from the Sumerians' proto-granulation in the third millennium BC till its peak in the Etruscan, sixth century BC. Here, as often, filigree—wire ornament—is also used. One of a pair of gold earrings from Sidon, Greek, 6th or 5th century BC. Archaeological Museum, Istanbul

great Hellenistic mosaic picture from Pompeii, of Alexander defeating Darius, there were originally some 1,374,516 pieces of stone. Such persistence puts us to shame!

In addition to their pet speciality granulation, these early jewelers achieved an even more astounding feat of compression: great sculpture reduced to the size of a finger nail. Ancient seal engraving on gold, and still more so on stones like carnelian, gives us the same shudder of humility today as granulation does. But here perhaps the achievement is even greater: the degree of finish almost forgotten today, the way to polish interior surfaces of incisions into hard stone hardly dreamt of, and the mounting of burnished silver leaf behind the bezel of a ring to give the stone better transparency—all these show dexterity; but, much more, they show creative imagination, almost defiance of the limitation of the material.

Gem engraving—*cameo* if in relief, *intaglio* if recessed—is a marvellous feature of ancient jewels from early Babylonian seals on. How was it done? We really do not know. Gisela Richter of the New York Metropolitan Museum lists some of the very scant ancient records: of Theophrastus, for instance, who wrote,

There are some stones which can be engraved, others which are worked by the aid of the drill, still others which can be sawn; upon some an iron tool makes no impression; upon others again only slightly and with great effort;

and of Pliny,

There is such a difference in the hardness of gems that some cannot be engraved with an iron tool, others only with a blunt graver, but all may be cut with the diamond. The heat of the drill is of great assistance in engraving. . . . When a diamond by good luck happens to break, it separates into particles so small that they can hardly be seen. These are in great request among engravers, who set them in iron and by this means are able to hollow out any hard surface with ease.

There are very few old pictures of gem engravers, and the stones themselves do not help much. One can deduce that variously shaped drills rubbed the holes by grinding abrasive powder between the drill and the gem; probably they used the same sort of 'Archimedes' bow' drill that is still favoured by modern jewelers today. The gem was probably fixed and the tool moved around on it, whereas today it is the drill

or wheel (often mounted in a table) which remains steady, and the gem which is moved—one explanation of the great fineness of old work compared with new. Broad lines which finish bluntly were drilled; those which taper to a sharp point, cut with an engraver, and consequently found more often in the softer stones where hand engraving was easier. When lines cut into stone fade to almost nothing, we may be sure the cutting tool revolved and was armed with hard powder like diamond. Magnifying may have been used—there is a Greek reference to the magnifying effect when one looks through water in a bottle. But, the expectation of life was probably only thirty-five or forty years, so craftsmen's eyesight would have been comparable to that of superb young athletes today, and the need for magnifying therefore less.

A third phenomenon of Greek and Etruscan work is its use of wire as border, as chain, as applied geometrical ornament weaving all over the surface. A favourite use was filigree, a pattern made of wires. Sometimes a tube was twisted from a long narrow strip, like a child's drinking straw; sometimes it was hammered and rolled from a thick sheet; sometimes when square, which was rare, solid wire was cut from a chunk. Often, spiral and double spiral effects on the smallest scale challenge one's eyesight. Then there is beaded wire—appearing to be small beads fastened in rows, or spools of varying shapes like cotton reels. The last is rather mysterious because such a small complicated shape as a spool will become round when heated for solder. Perhaps some ingenious tool was used for swaging, that is shaping a continuous wire, but more likely no such tool could have been made hard enough; all these wires were simply an extension of granulation—infinite variations on the humble dot, workaday solder elevated to the level of poetry. All our evidence is that the incredible actually happened—there were no scientific aids, no short cuts; artistic and technical values were the same thing. If an artist wanted a result, he took what today would seem incredible pains to reach it.

Engravers used tools of obsidian, copper or iron, bronze or flint. In Greece itself the gold was so thin that if one cut deeply into it, one went right through, and tools, too, were not sharp enough before the days of steel to give engraving much impact artistically.

Right *Pair of gold hairpins. Chinese, probably Ming Dynasty, c. AD 1500. Chinese jewels were extremely intricately worked, usually in the form of pins for the hair because clothes, like the Japanese kimono, were so heavily embroidered as to leave no room for brooches.*

Overleaf *From top to bottom and left to right:*
a) *Agate, carved* intaglio, *pendant in gold enamel frame, perhaps Italian c. 1590. Some carved lines taper to very fine points which means they were carved by hand with an engraving tool. The strange proportions of the figures show the provocative influence of Mannerism. Height: 3.2 inches.*
b) *Sumerian technique differs little from our own nearly 4,500 years later. These head ornaments were discovered by Sir Leonard Woolley at Ur about 1925. The gold leaves have thin grooves impressed into the metal, probably with the help of a wooden die. The roundels are probably cast. Iraq Museum.*
c) *Detail of a bracelet showing the rich variety of Brazilian semiprecious stones: tourmaline, topaz, garnet, aquamarine, opal, chrysoberyl, amethyst and gold. Hans Stern, Rio de Janeiro, 1971.*
d) *This carved jade knife handle, inlaid with carved rubies, represents table jewelry which may have been as popular as personal jewelry. Indian, probably 18th century. Salar Jung Museum, Hyderabad.*
e) *In most countries gold is kept thin so as not to be too heavy and expensive. In India, conversely, the thickest and heaviest jewels are the most desirable. Similarly with diamonds—in India, unlike most of the world, irregular cuts which absorb rather than reflect light are normal, and the stones are often cut shallow and flat at the back, hence the name 'plate cut'. This detail is from a gold and diamond bracelet; probably Delhi, 18th century.*
f) *Spanish late Renaissance and seventeenth-century jewelry sometimes resembled Indian because it enjoyed a great wealth of gold (from South America) and pleasure in birds and animals (often inspired by South American exploration) at a time when other European countries' jewels had turned to classical mythology. Swan earring, gold.*
g) *Painted enamel was more versatile than the earlier* cloisonné *and* champlevé *techniques. The repetitive cumulative lines express baroque feeling. Spanish gold, diamond and emerald pendant, 18th century.*
(continued on p. 185)

(continued from p. 180)

h) *Gold and emerald necklace, perhaps Jaipur, 18th century.*

i) *Reverse of gold and jargoon brooch. Probably Hyderabad, 19th century. The rather coarse champlevé enamel may be compared with much finer Jaipur work above.*

j) *Superlative Italian Renaissance ring, gold, enamel and pyramid diamond: the bold design, intricate fantasy, and impeccable technique make this ring a masterpiece. First the frame would be cast, then chased, then engraved, then enamelled. Note the square stone which was often used to carve names in glass. Mid-16th century.*

k) *The technical ability of craftsmen who had no scientific resources is a constant surprise: detail from the Tara ring brooch showing the Celtic love of ornament, hatred of plain surfaces. The frame is gold, the triangular spandrel of silver perforated and laid on copper. 8th century AD. National Museum of Ireland, Dublin.*

l) *Translucent enamel allows the metal beneath to be seen. In Turkey, metalwork was more gaudy, less subtle than in India or Persia, with which it was related. Translucent enamels from the throne given by Nadir Shah of Persia to Mahmut I, 18th century. Topkapi Museum, Istanbul.*

m) *In the Renaissance courts, the armourers, like the Negroli family in Milan, were as important as the jewelers and painters. Ring, iron with decoration in gold and silver leaf, at the centre, a human head. Italian, c. 1550.*

n) *Chinese intricacy practised by the Memon Moslem community in Bombay, 19th century. Central panel of bracelet.*

Left *Detail of an ancient Greek gold earring, one of the most delicate pieces of surviving gold-work anywhere in the world. Behind the circular disk was a hook to attach to the ear. Included in the design are a gold quadriga with winged genii on each side, and a boat-shaped pendant with granulation beneath, with gold chains and pendant urns (not illustrated). The whole, right, is 3.5 inches long and was found at Theodosia. Greek colonial, perhaps 5th century BC. A late nineteenth-century replica, commissioned by the Tsar to show the excellence of Russian craftsmanship, is exhibited near-by; in fact it proves that Russian goldsmiths a hundred years ago worked much more coarsely than the ancient Greeks. Hermitage Museum, Leningrad*

Deep-cut seal engraving in thick blocks of gold or stone remains a miracle; for ornamental jewels, by contrast, engraving was too shallow, the grooves were not cut sharp enough to throw the light back with the necessary brightness. Much more common was chasing, when the line, instead of being cut from the metal, is impressed into it with a hard tool, either wood or metal. More common still, especially in Greece itself, was the use of dies, where a pattern would be carved into the die, probably hard wood, and the very thin sheet gold, thin as paper, for instance for the front of a diadem, or the centre of an animal head brooch, would simply be rubbed into the crevices of the die. Although the Greeks seem to have painted their sculpture the brightest colours (thus, according to our present ideas, vulgarizing and spoiling it) they do not seem to have used much colour in their jewels: it was the Romans who did that, when they synthesized all these activities into a complete Mediterranean style.

Ancient Greek and especially Etruscan jewels showed the most extraordinary virtuoso technique, but many of the pieces are so thin that they can hardly have been intended for regular wear. Probably they were made as ornaments for the grave: Etruscan excavations certainly suggest that much of their sculpture and painting was intended for the dead rather than the living, being situated as it is on and around their tombs, and often having the character of a memorial. Hellenistic jewelry from the age of Alexander the Great showed more vigour in its design, and was usually of a better weight, so that it might have withstood everyday wear and tear.

But it is Roman jewelry from the time of Christ onwards that begins almost to have the solidity of modern work. No doubt this is partly because the Romans were much richer than the Greeks. The Greeks had almost no gold in Greece itself, whereas the Romans developed sources all round their empire—in the east in Dacia (now Rumania), in the west in Spain, in the south in Egypt—and they were also heirs to the wealth of Persia, which had been captured by Alexander the Great. The Romans did not acquire their gold by chance: they positively wanted to be rich in a way which hardly occurred to the Greeks, for whom other ambitions seemed more important.

It is not unfair, for instance, to compare two dinner parties: the Greek, imagined by Plato in his *Symposium*, where the all-male company indulged in a cerebral fencing match, discussing great truths such as the nature of life and death; and the early Roman imperial, when Petronius describes Trimalchio calling for scales in the middle of dinner, to weigh his own and his wife's jewelry to the general delight of all. The Greeks either could not afford, or did not need, the satisfying weight of bullion on their bodies. They used solid metal so sparingly that they even found it sufficient to coat the surface of the famous statue of Athene on the Acropolis with gold leaf, rather than making her of real gold; and they made jewels, which for all their cleverness often verge on the tinselly and give little satisfaction in handling. In the Hellenistic period, weight and intricacy reached an ideal balance. Under the Romans, mere weight came eventually to be more important than decoration.

But, quite apart from the lust for gold, there is another factor, which is usually overlooked: the status of women. Just as classical Greek homes were very humble compared to the glories of their civic temples and centres, so Greek women seem to have been almost slaves,

by necessity quiet and retiring. So it is very likely that, even if they wanted jewels and even if their menfolk could afford to buy them, their need was simply neglected.

For the Greeks it may be surmised that all the important needs of life, except for procreation, were satisfied outside the home, in public, without women. Only in Sparta do women seem to have achieved even a minor place in public affairs, participating as they did in the chorus and even in some games. Only as far afield as Lycia in Asia Minor does society seem to have been partly matriarchal. Elsewhere it seems to have been men who ruled the roost throughout the ancient Greek world. There is no recorded prestige for a Greek who ran a successful home and family in preference to public life. For the Romans it was different: the forum was a centre for commerce as much as for politics and religion, but it was not everything. The Romans regarded the size and beauty of one's private home somewhat as a thermometer of success, and to this, of course, the Roman matron was vital. Roman jewels are more sensible and easier to wear, tougher and heavier than Greek, and this must partly reflect the new power of Roman women.

Roman work also suggests Roman

Pair of gold earrings with enamel round the neck and eyes, and a big garnet set above, from Asia Minor, perhaps Lydia. Hellenistic, perhaps 3rd century BC. Diameter: 1.4 inches. The work is less fine, but more spirited, varied and wearable than the rigid earlier style of the piece on p. 179.

wealth. The law of the twelve tables in the fifth century BC, as R. A. Higgins tells us, limited the amount of gold that could be buried with the dead, and the *Lex Oppia* of the third century BC fixed at half an ounce the amount of gold a Roman lady might wear, specifically excepting the gold *bulla*, worn as an amulet particularly by children. Under the Republic, the wearing of gold rings was reserved for special classes of occasions and people, such as senators and knights. But by 30 BC Rome had absorbed Egypt and with it a great source of materials and, in Alexandria and Antioch, great and continuing centres of production.

The quantity of gold available for use increased rapidly as Rome became more powerful. The old Greek mines had been on the islands of Siphnos, and on Thasos with its accompanying mainland. The alluvial deposits of Asia Minor had helped to make rich Phrygia and Lydia, for instance, and even tempted the dictator of Miletus, too, so that he tried to rebel against mighty Persia under Darius. Then in the fourth century BC Philip of Macedon exploited his alluvial deposits and founded the mines at Philippi to which he gave his name; and his son Alexander the Great opened the treasuries of Persia. The history of the Roman empire's establishment and expansion six centuries after can be told not only in terms of conquering troublesome barbarians round the edge, but of securing new sources of gold and minerals. So the simple dignity of Roman jewels expresses not only the important status of women and the fact that the jewels were worn more actively; it also shows that more gold was available.

If Egyptian jewels were all colour, and the Greek all intricacy, the Romans' represented mass and form. For some strange reason, although these qualities are much admired today in sculpture and in art, aesthetes have neglected them in Roman jewels. These are usually supposed to be a coarse imitation of what went before, not a creative and satisfying re-interpretation of a universal theme. Perhaps the Romans themselves would have taken the same slighting attitude towards our Renaissance imitations of ancient Rome as we do to the Roman vision of Greece and Egypt.

One specifically Roman innovation is *opus interrasile*, which means making patterns in sheet gold by cutting away geometrical fragments, successions of triangles or squares for instance, probably done by chisel. The effect was partly evolved by the early Etruscans but probably used too much gold and yielded too little delicacy for their extraordinary, fastidious taste. It did not become really popular until the second century AD, giving an effect almost like perforated embroidery or lace, which was to remain an exciting jewelry technique both for the Byzantines and for the migrant tribes. A comparable sort of fretwork treatment was a feature of seventeenth-century English table silver under the name 'cut-card ornament' and it is still attractive to designers today as the art of exploiting not only stones and metal, but the cavities between as well.

The Romans developed niello both for their table silver and for their jewels; it may have been invented for use on plate by the Greeks and before, but it was the Romans who discovered how to work it. Comparable to enamel, niello is black, made of metal sulphides or graphite powder; it was rubbed into engraved patterns on the surface of the metal, more often silver than gold, and then heated till it adhered.

The Romans did not make such beautiful coins as the Greeks, but they were the first to think of putting coins in jewelry—a simple way both of using the decorative value of the coin and of showing everybody something of the wearer's own richness and sophistication. Often no doubt the portrait incorporated might represent somebody whom the wearer wished to flatter. It was a habit followed later by the Byzantines.

Filigree and granulation almost died out; their place was taken by the varied textures of different degrees of polishing and burnishing, possible with thick Roman metal, impossible with the thin early Greek foil. The love of polychrome effects, originating in Mesopotamia and in Egypt, took the form under the Romans of widespread use of stones. For the Greeks stones meant engraved gems, carnelian and agate and all their beautiful variants. For the Romans the seal was no longer so important—perhaps because the house itself, rather than the treasure box or tablet, represented the owner's security—and stones came to have the same function as in the east: simply to give colour, sometimes engraved with an amusing picture of an

Gold pin; the thicker work, with more solid castings, may be compared with the much more intricate but less wearable Greek wire work on p. 179. By Hellenistic times gold had become much more common—one reason why jewels were much heavier. 1st century BC. Benaki Museum, Athens

athlete or lion, a dolphin or pattern, very often simply rubbed smooth. Garnets were one of the favourites and, in much increased numbers, the harder stones like sapphire, emerald, topaz and even uncut diamond.

After the Romans one may guess that there were no further craft inventions, only new adaptations of old ideas. Perhaps indeed this was true even before the Greeks: round their provincial Black Sea colonies the Greeks seem to have mastered almost everything: laminating, *repoussé* work, chasing both with hammer and punch; welding (sweating two surfaces together without solder), soldering. Perhaps filigree and enamel were two of the last techniques to filter out from the most civilized centres. If so, the barbarians certainly concentrated on the first, the Byzantines on the second.

The word filigree comes from the Latin *filum* (wire) and *granium* (grain) meaning a combination of these components soldered into a composition. As a surface decoration, filigree was used as an extension of granulation—filigree did for lines what granulation did for masses. Both depended upon the high melting point of ancient gold alloys, and the low melting point, however it was achieved, of the adhesive between. The Etruscans, and to a lesser extent the Greeks, especially loved filigree and it was usually applied as a surface decoration, made, as Castellani notes in his technical investigation of 1861, by soldering together and building up the gold, rather than by chiselling or engraving.

But filigree achieved a new emphasis as it became obviously wire rather than a succession of almost microscopic spots in sequence. At the time of the great migrations after the Roman empire, it may be that the tribes started to use the draw plate, that is a metal plate with a small tapering hole through which gold wire is drawn; the wire, once at the required thinness, can then be hammered to give the sort of morse code effect which is the essence of filigree from Carolingian times right up to the present. Reliquaries of Charlemagne's time, the interlacing patterns of Irish and Northumbrian gold work all use wire, sometimes free standing, sometimes applied in knotted or strip form. Bosses and borders of filigree continue through the Middle Ages into the Renaissance until the craft surprisingly left the highways for the by-ways: no

Above *Prehistoric sophistication: this gold helmet shows the amazing grace of Sumerian hair styles— here, a bun with varied curls, combings and patternings, rendered in delicate chased and repoussé embossing, c. 2450 BC, from Ur. Iraq Museum, Baghdad*

Right *Modern filigree: few craftsmen today have the patience to apply wire to a surface, and to solder it into a lace network. Detail of a finger ring in white and yellow gold by Sue Barfield, 1972. Goldsmiths' Hall, London*

longer fashionable, filigree became the preserve of rather remote, almost peasant workshops, for instance in Malta and Albania and the Greek islands, and Bergen in Norway. The history of filigree is still to be written. The teasing technical question is what changed filigree from a synthesis of grains into a patterned wire, and whether it was in fact the migrant tribes of the sixth century AD who had this bright idea, whether they brought it from the east, or whether it was dictated simply to make filigree bigger and stronger.

The invention and evolution of enamels is easier to explain: R. A. Higgins at the British Museum has made an interesting study in his *Greek and Roman Jewellery*. He detects a distinctive Mycenaean invention of enamel, blue slabs of colour sunk in hollows, rather in the manner later called *champlevé*, around 1425 BC, which seems to have died around 1300 BC. More delicate enamels, with different colours separated by dividing wires, the type later called *cloisonné*, appeared in the eastern Mediterranean about the twelfth century BC after the fall of Mycenae. Fine filigree enamels, tiny dots of colour, for instance on flower rosette petals like those from Ziwiye now in the Tehran Museum, seem to have started in Assyria in the seventh century BC, arriving in archaic Greece in the early sixth century BC and then being adopted by the Etruscans. According to Higgins it is quite possible that these three different types of enamels were in fact invented independently one from the next, the result simply of glass working and metal working combined. But one may suspect that these ancient peoples could in fact achieve whatever effect they wanted: it was fashion, not the crafts, which changed.

From the third century BC dipped enamel became common: a pendant from an earring or diadem would be immersed in molten enamel which then covered the whole surface. The subsequent history of enamel work is too complex to trace in detail, nor has it yet been properly unravelled. What is clear is that Syria became from Hellenistic times the great centre of glass working, and that glass was originally used there more for beads and enamels than for cups and jars. Ptolemaic Egypt became one of the richest consumers of this gay coloured glasswork; no doubt the Romanized Egyptians were trying

to satisfy a taste inherited from dynastic Egypt for coloured beads and inlay of both glass and faience. But by Roman times it seems that the inlay of cold particles, which was probably the ancient Egyptian practice, had been superseded by hot enamel. Certainly Syria and Egypt in the early centuries after Christ produced chromatic glass scent bottles and beads, often with coloured glazes on a white ground, whose luxuriant colours suggest all the sensuous appeal of Cleopatra.

Enamels were used by the Egyptians and others in just the same way as stones, as geometrical patterns of inlaid colour. No doubt they were considered cheap substitutes for stones. In fact there is no proof that the Etruscans, or indeed the Mesopotamian countries before them, melted powder: they may have simply sweated it into position under heat. The Byzantines, however, promoted the craft from imitation to creation, using it in their jewelry rather as they had mosaics in their buildings, providing a luminous patchwork. Their method was to create a picture whose colours were separated with wires or *cloisons*, and then melt into each compartment a different colour, each with its different melting point. By the twelfth century the parallel technique of *champlevé*, when the cavities are not created with wire but simply scooped from the background, emerged, both along the Rhine and the Moselle and at Limoges, to produce more delicate shadings of colour. The stiff, hieratical quality of these enamels owes a lot to Byzantium. Perhaps the connecting link was the marriage of the German emperor Otto II to the Greek princess Theophania from Byzantium in 973.

By the fourteenth century, the idea of *basse taille* had caught on: translucent enamel allowed not only luminous effects like medieval stained glass but also low relief sculpture on the metal seen behind. By the fifteenth century enamelling in the round became the fashion and remained so till the rococo period three hundred years later. First a figure was carved, then either immersed or painted so that only its face and hands, for instance, would be gold metal, all the clothes being enamel; it was an amazing feat to make the molten glass stay in place on its various planes especially as each colour had a different melting point and therefore needed its separate firing.

By the fifteenth century the new idiom

The Byzantines elevated enamel from a substitute for stone to an independent art form, of equal importance to mosaic and painting. This gold and enamel medallion shows the cloisonné process: each colour is in a cloison or compartment separated from the next by a gold wire. 10th or 11th century AD. Cluny Museum, Paris

of painted enamel became popular both in Italy, where for instance gold and silver and copper chalices from Siena often had enamelled panels attached to them depicting religious scenes, and in France. Limoges again became the great European centre, as it had been for *champlevé* work in the late twelfth century, when it seems to have stolen the initiative from the Rhine area. It may have been the depredations of England under the Black Prince, who sacked Limoges in 1371, which caused the decline and virtual extinction of enamel production there, but the family traditions must have lived on.

In the second period of greatness most of the metal was again copper or plate, only occasionally silver, and probably never gold; a white enamel ground on a copper plaque formed the base onto which the design was drawn and glazed. Then the colours were painted on with brush and spatulas, and fired, usually with a characteristic palette of violets, greys and turquoise blues. Often the resulting miniature picture would be given a gilt metal frame. Limoges's enamellers in the twelfth and thirteenth centuries concentrated mostly on reliquaries and pyx boxes for church use, and in the sixteenth century mostly on decorated tableware, doing for the French princes' dining-halls what engraved rock crystal did at this time for the Germans'. But these enamels with their sophisticated perspectives and colours were never popular in jewels as *cloisonné* had been in Byzantium.

Just as in Milan certain families cornered their chosen skills of gem cutting and armour making and inlay, so in Limoges there were the great names like Pénicaud, Loudin, Courteys, Pierre Raymond and perhaps most famous, Jean de Court. A higher point was reached when Léonard Limousin was invited by the bishop of Limoges to the French court at Fontainebleau, becoming King Francis I's valet in 1548, and there falling under the influence of the resident Italian mannerist painters like Primaticcio. But by the seventeenth century, fashions changed again, enamels lost their importance in favour of the new cult of the precious stone, and Limoges fades from the scene.

Enamels were not, in fact, killed by the precious stone, indeed they survived through the eighteenth and nineteenth centuries as a delicate complement to the stone. But the enamellers created an entirely new outlet for themselves: eighteenth-century dress ornaments, especially pendant watches. Claude and Jean Bérain and Jean Roberdey, pioneers of the French rococo and chinoiserie, were some of the earliest of the many names that have come down to us: sometimes they both designed and made their own pieces, usually somebody else made them up, from time to time even using compositions from the leading painters like Boucher, Greuze, and Fragonard. Painted enamel remained very popular during the seventeenth century, possibly because it was cheaper and easier than *champlevé*. The taste was for bright colours and crowded scenes, quite different from the muted Limoges style. Portrait miniatures became a recognized art form used as pendant jewels, two of the early masters being Jean Tutin and Gribelin at Châteaudun.

But there was no real change in technique until the mid-eighteenth century. Then *basse taille* transparent enamels exploited the new engine-turning machines—*tours à guillocher* so that, instead of seeing through the transparent enamel onto a low-relief, hand-carved scene, one saw a fascinating network of geometrical patterns. Again this charming work hardly impinged upon wearable jewels—it was part of the cult of the gold snuff box—though as it was often made by jewelers and as it represented a mania for very rich collectors, it provided one of the rare instances of artisans getting across the price hurdle into art and charging for their ideas as well as for the use of their hands.

The last ploy of enamellers was *plique à jour*—transparent enamel with no backing, held in place simply by wires round the edge. It was a sort of refinement of *cloisonné*, using the wire *cloisons* without a metal frame, so that the jewel became all enamel and almost no metal. The result is extremely fragile and seldom lasts for long: it was a favourite toy for the art nouveau jewelers around 1890, a *tour de force* with which they seduced their clients away from the precious stone.

Gem cutting was not very popular under Byzantium and in the Middle Ages; but in the Renaissance it became a snob symbol in the German countries, like Limoges enamel in the French. Vasari, in his *Artists' Lives*, 1568, said the new prominence of gem cutting at court, was due to the passion for collecting of Lorenzo il Magnifico and of his

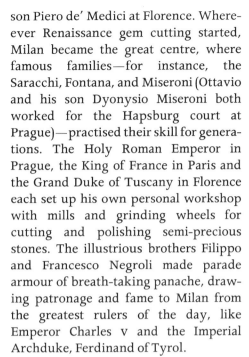

son Piero de' Medici at Florence. Where-ever Renaissance gem cutting started, Milan became the great centre, where famous families—for instance, the Saracchi, Fontana, and Miseroni (Ottavio and his son Dyonysio Miseroni both worked for the Hapsburg court at Prague)—practised their skill for genera-tions. The Holy Roman Emperor in Prague, the King of France in Paris and the Grand Duke of Tuscany in Florence each set up his own personal workshop with mills and grinding wheels for cutting and polishing semi-precious stones. The illustrious brothers Filippo and Francesco Negroli made parade armour of breath-taking panache, draw-ing patronage and fame to Milan from the greatest rulers of the day, like Emperor Charles V and the Imperial Archduke, Ferdinand of Tyrol.

The eighteenth-century French en-graver L. Natter sums it up rather tragically:

Certainly the art of gem engraving is more painful and discouraging than all others. For besides the knowledge of drawing, which is as necessary to an engraver in stone as to a sculptor or painter, he is obliged when he does whole figures or groups to regulate his design or composition according to the method of engraving; he must avoid, for example, perspective, which is so great an advantage to a painter, and the foreshorten-ing of the parts of the body—he must always strive to give his figures a light and easy posi-tion. . . . Another difficulty attending this art is that the engravings are commonly done on such small stones . . . that it is scarcely possible to draw the just propor-tions with the diamond point, which greatly fatigues the eyes; nor can they be cut after-wards without excellent eyesight and very good light. Furthermore, you cannot have the assistance of another to forward your work; and the least mistake in executing the design is very difficult if not impossible to correct. You must also form your idea of the design for the reverse of the engraving and engrave deep what is to appear in relief. Add to this that the stone is liable to be spoiled by many accidents. All these reasons discourage people from cultivating an art that requires so much precaution and labour, and which is at the same time not patronized by the rich and great.

The history of stone cutting and faceting and polishing, as opposed to their pictorial engraving, can be viewed as an evolution from dark magic to dazzling light. For thousands of years coloured stones were considered to have magic properties—they were amulets and talismans. It was not until the six-teenth century that stone cutters began

systematically to let in the light. Eric Bruton in *Diamonds* locates the first diamond polishing in Venice around 1330, then in Bruges and Paris, and by the fifteenth century in Antwerp. In 1582 a charter was given to an Antwerp guild, and stone polishing features in sixteenth-century Nuremberg and Augs-burg. When the Spaniards sacked Ant-werp in 1585, some stone cutters went to Amsterdam and the craft began to disperse. By 1636 there were 186 registered diamond cutters in Venice. Lisbon was a sixteenth-century centre because of direct Portuguese imports of stones from India; for the same reason stone cutters found a living in seven-teenth-century London with England's acquisitions in the east.

Whatever the exact chronology, the processes may involve cleaving or split-ting, a difficult and rather secret knack of hitting the stone with a punch and mallet so that it falls apart according to its crystal structure; grinding the faces and then polishing them; and bruting or cutting one stone with another. For polishing, stones from as early as the sixteenth century were fixed with lead to a stick, then held on a revolving grinding wheel or scaife. A stick or tang holds on its end a dop or knob of lead solder; in the nineteenth century a precise metal clamp began to replace it, and the grinding wheel was harnessed to a motor—hence the accuracy of modern cuts.

Our knowledge of craftsmen and how they worked over the centuries is very scanty, although Pliny gives some details about stones and their supersti-tions in the early second century AD. The next milestone is the only discourse on metalwork by a medieval craftsman, *De Diversis Artibus*, written in the first half of the twelfth century under the pen name of Theophilus, actually Roger of Helmhausen, an outstanding goldsmith whose portable altar survives in Pader-born cathedral and Franciscan monas-tery. He surveys the making of a workshop and its tools and furnaces. Of all the arts goldsmithing was his favourite. From this and from other con-temporary texts like the writings of Abbot Suger of Saint Denis, it is clear that goldsmiths were considered the most important of the artists serving the glory of God. The next technical manual is Benvenuto Cellini's 1568 treatise upon which any modern workshop could still base its activity; then comes the

Right *Rajah's button of gold,
mauve enamel and plate diamonds
with irregular facets and flat backs
in contrast to the deep backs of
European stones. Diameter: 0.8
inches. Perhaps Lucknow, 18th
century*

Below *In some Indian jewels, gold
was used to hold stones in position
rather like builders' putty. This
archer's ring shows carved stone
with entwined patterning as on the
great Moghul buildings like the
Taj Mahal; jade, with small
rubies, sapphires and emeralds
inlaid in gold. Probably Delhi,
18th century*

eighteenth-century French *Encyclopédie* edited by Diderot, which is especially interesting in its coverage of obscure details like gold leaf, gold wire drawing, and stone cutting.

But the crafts are indeed a mystery. Many craftsmen always prefer to keep secret the fruits of their experience for fear of imitation. It is no coincidence that there are so few written records: the London medieval guild of goldsmiths includes in its title the word craft or 'mystery'—the French word *métier* has the dual meaning of job or mystery; one can learn how to be a craftsman not by reading manuals but only by practising and working with one's hands.

The most memorable polished stones in antique jewelry are the pyramid-shaped, pointed diamonds, still almost in their natural crystalline form. With black foil behind them, as was customary, their cold, straight precision

makes a dramatic contrast with the warm undulating gold and enamel surrounds. Before 1538, the first true cut appeared: the table cut which was just such an octahedron crystal with the top point cut off to form a square 'table'. Sometimes early table stones had a small flat facet on the bottom, too, then being known as Indian cut. Till the early seventeenth century table stones became more popular, not only diamonds but sapphires, emeralds and others too, and the pointed diamond lost its appeal.

The rose cut may in fact be the oldest of all: famous old stones like the Kohinur, cut in its original form before 1530, were simply faceted all over, in the manner of the later rose cut. 'Rose cut' used to mean little more than simply tidying up the actual surface of the stone, and might be a double rose cut; or diamonds could be faceted all over, enjoying such exotic names as *briolette*

and *pendeloque*. Cellini in his 1568 treatise describes rose as well as table cut and pointed stones. But it was not until the seventeenth century that the rose cut—supposed to resemble an opening rose bud—became more or less systematized, with usually six facets on top (the crown or star) and outer groups of six each (the teeth). Antwerp and Amsterdam each evolved their own treatment, which became very popular in the eighteenth and nineteenth centuries. These rose-cut stones have nobility but almost none of the modern, much sought-after fire.

An early variation of the table cut was the Mazarin, according to the Finnish expert Herbert Tillander, introduced about 1620. It was probably given the name of the famous cardinal of France because he was a great diamond lover, buying many stones from Tavernier, including the Sancy, and leaving them

Below *The brilliant cut, which evolved in the seventeenth century, became normal in the nineteenth and twentieth centuries, as in this detail from a diamond brooch with gold back and front of silver to give more brilliance; once the property of Mrs Caroline Weston, English, c. 1855. Whereas the diamonds in the ring,* right, *have metal behind them, in this brooch they are open behind to let in more light, an innovation of the late eighteenth century which accompanied more scientific stone cuttings.*

Above *In the seventeenth and eighteenth centuries, the rose cut (bottom stone) table cut (centre stone) were customary with diamonds and other precious stones; less precious stones were still cut erratically (side stones). Gold ring, English late 18th century with silver surrounds to the stones to give more glitter*

This treasure trove is in England the subject of elaborate case-law, but, especially when gold or silver, it usually ends up in a national museum. In France, Germany, Italy and Spain it is divided between the owner of the land and the finder; in America the government in theory gets it all, but in practice the finder usually keeps it.

Under-sea law, by contrast, has hardly yet begun. The ever increasing depredations of modern submarine skin-divers, encouraged as they may be by the free-for-all atmosphere, have established an urgent need for order in place of chaos, so that history beneath the waves can be organized as carefully as it now is under the ground.

Of course, ancient hoards were continually found and lost, such as Alexander the Great's loot from the Persian Darius' capital at Susa; this and other Persian treasuries, minted into coins, brought vast new trade and prosperity to its users. Plutarch recalls the aftermath of Alexander's victory at Issus in 333 BC:

Alexander . . . took the chariot and the bow of Darius, and then went back. He found the Macedonians looting the enemy camp and carrying off an enormous quantity of booty despite the fact that the Persians had left most of their baggage in Damascus and had come to the battle with light equipment. For Alexander they had reserved Darius' tent with his servants and furniture and all the treasure it contained . . . When he saw the bowls, the pitchers, the bath-tubs and the scent bottles, all of gold and the finest workmanship, and smelt the heavenly aroma of the perfumes that filled the place, and when he had entered the tent, wonderful in its height and splendour and its elegant furnishings, he looked at his companions and said: 'This, it seems, is what it means to be a king.'

One of the first and greatest permanent discoveries was Peter the Great's. In October 1715 at St Petersburg, his newly founded capital, his courtiers hurried to congratulate him and the Empress Catherine on the birth of their son. Nikita Demidov, who had worked his way up in a serf's family from being a blacksmith to become the richest mine owner of the Urals, gave her 100,000 roubles in coins and a collection of golden objects, whose only history was that they came from burial mounds in Siberia, regularly plundered by greedy outsiders to the embitterment of the superstitious natives. Peter's insatiable curiosity was aroused by these superb animal figures and plaques: he ordered

the collection of all similar finds for the crown; an imperial decree was issued to protect antiquities, ages before other western countries developed a serious respect for their past. Two months later the first new consignment arrived from Tobolsk, containing ten pieces for the new 'cabinet of curiosities'. The Governor of Siberia, Prince Gagarin, had bought all the gold he could find—fifty-five larger and twenty small pieces weighing nearly 53 lb. The Dutch scholar Nikolas Witsen received about forty pieces from Russian friends: the emperor was not the only grave robber but, fortunately for the Hermitage Museum in Leningrad today, he was by far the biggest.

Another later Russian find, also in the Hermitage, is the grave goods from the frozen tombs of Siberia at Pazyryk. High in the Altai Mountains rich farmers buried their chiefs with their concubines and horses in pits below huge stone cairns. The climate and the freak construction formed a permanent ring of ice round each grave, so that all the textiles and ornaments have survived through two and a half millennia. Grave robbers found the human corpses, but the rest remains, a tribute to the universal passion for ornament.

Russia was exceptional in its early concern for pre-history; elsewhere in the eighteenth century anything before classical antiquity was hardly respectable. It was not till the 1840s that the Danish antiquarian revolution began to make some sense of the huge archaeological vista. Henry Layard, after studying in Copenhagen, was one of the first great discoverers to think the unknown thrilling rather than revolting.

He saw in Assyria a desert queen, Rathiangah, who jingled with earrings and amulets and bangles:

Hanging from each ear, and reaching to her waist, was an enormous earring of gold, terminating in a tablet of the same material, carved and ornamented with four turquoises. Her nose was also adorned with a prodigious ring, set with jewels, of such ample dimensions that it covered the mouth, and was to be removed when the lady ate.

Such was the hot nineteenth- and twentieth-century setting from which many of our cold unattractive museum displays were painstakingly extracted.

There is evidence that all the Mesopotamian peoples were in fact great jewel wearers: the huge carvings and friezes brought to England by Layard

Detail of one half of a gold ornament, perhaps a collar or breastplate. This type of gorget derives from the earlier 'lunula', about 1800 BC, and spiral torc, about 1500 BC, of similar size. The original use of all these early pieces of Irish gold is unknown—only one of them was found in a grave. This collar shows the great technical skill of Bronze Age Irish smiths who used elaborate chased and repoussé designs, to achieve their favourite circular rhythms, and efficient solder for the hinge. Irish, from Gleninsheen, County Clare, c. 700 BC. Maximum width of whole piece: 11.8 inches. National Museum of Ireland, Dublin

Gold pendant jewel. Large pectoral ornaments like this were very popular in ancient Egypt, using local semi-precious stones and, in later centuries, glass. The symbolism in Egyptian jewelry is usually complicated. Here is a winged scarab (representing Khepri the Sun God at dawn, a symbol of resurrection—the sun about to be reborn) in chalcedony. The scarab is pushing, instead of the more usual ball, the sacred wedjet eye—the left eye of the Sky God Horus—in a celestial bark. Within the crescent and disk of the moon is a figure of King Tutankhamen supported by the ibis-headed Thoth (God of the Moon) and the falcon-headed Sun God Re, the first two wearing the crescent and disk of the moon, the last the solar disk. To the left and right, serpents symbolize the north. Lotus and composite buds form the base; the bird's claws hold the heraldic flowers of Lower and Upper Egypt—the lotus and the flowering rush. The red stones are carnelian, the blue, lapis lazuli; there are also calcite, turquoise, obsidian, and green, red, blue, black and white glass (faience). Length: 5.8 inches; width: 5.7 inches. Found by Howard Carter in the tomb of Tutankhamen. Egyptian, c. 1350 BC. Cairo Museum

after 1847, including the human-headed bulls 'whose ice-cold eyes had gazed on Nineveh', and, since then, other great loads of carving, for instance from Khorsabad, now in the Louvre at Paris, the Oriental Institute, Chicago, or Berlin and, thankfully, still *in situ* in Iraq, show the important figures wearing some of the most resplendent jewels of antiquity. We even know many of the colours from the eighth-century BC frescoes at Til Barsip, and the sixth-century BC description by Nabonidus, the last king of Babylon, of the lavish gold chains and gems he put in his mother's tomb.

It is chagrining that systematic pillaging over the millennia has deprived us of nearly all the actual pieces. One fine exception is the 'Nimrud Jewel' recently found at Nimrud in Fort Shalmaneser by H. A. L. Mallowan and now in the Baghdad Museum. The excavators naturally assumed that this jewel made between 681 and 669 BC, with its beautiful gold, but rather poorly cut *intaglio* chalcedony, must be no less than royal, because it is so extremely rare. It is one of the few surviving gold jewels from either Babylon or Assyria, that is from about two millennia, 2500 BC till 500 BC. The Nimrud Jewel cannot have been unique even if it was royal: Assyrian generals and officials, all obsessed as they seem to have been by the idea of military parade, used the luxury of their dress to impress friend and foe alike.

What do survive in very large quantities are the hardstone cylinder seals, used originally to close the clay writing tablets which helped to run the bureaucracy. Sometimes, surprisingly, these clay 'signatures' enclosed a complete private inner copy of a clay inscription, presumably to confirm to the recipient the authenticity of the outer version. Found in many digs the seals are some of the most tantalizing of all jewels, not only because their meaning is obscure, but also because one cannot see the whole design carved in the gem—it has always vanished round the circumference, and the hieratic figures with tiny heads (often sitting on their sparse Bauhaus-like furniture) preferred by the early Babylonians, or the formal processions of Assyrian animals and rulers, lose some of their beauty when transferred from the circular stone and rolled in a flat pictorial sequence onto mere clay.

Heinrich Schliemann (1822–90) caught the gold fever so badly that many people

still say he was not a proper archaeologist. Son of a poor German pastor, grocer's apprentice working eighteen hours a day for five and a half years, cabin boy on the *Dorothea* which was wrecked on a voyage to Venezuela, office attendant and book-keeper in Amsterdam, he became obsessed by the Homeric sagas, and by his personal need to live a larger, richer life (for which purpose he learned about eight languages). Schröder's Bank eventually sent him in 1846 to St Petersburg where he became successful dealing in indigo as an independent contractor. He further prospered from the Crimean War. He went to California when it joined the Union in 1850 during the gold rush, and as an American citizen he visited Greece, Tunisia, India, China and Japan, in 1868 returning to his chief love, the sites of Homer.

He wrote to try to prove his theory that Hissarlik, and not as was generally supposed Bunarbashi, was ancient Troy; and furthermore that the tomb of Atreus at Mycenae (seen by Pausanias, the Baedeker of the second century, but subsequently lost) was in fact within the fortress walls there. Two years later he started digging at Troy; by 1873, having plunged much deeper than he needed, he discovered a great hoard of

gold jewelry, over 9,000 pieces in all. When, without adequate evidence, he declared it to be the 'Treasure of Priam [King of Troy]' (in fact it was about five centuries too early) and had his young Greek wife, Sophia, photographed wearing it, Europe was naturally intoxicated.

Of course he was unscientific; he tore down whole walls if they got in his way, and he dug so impatiently that he went right through the layer containing remains of the Homeric period without even noticing it. His contemporary, Captain E. Botticher, even said in 1883 that Schliemann had manufactured the palace instead of discovering it. But he did pave the way for truly scientific work.

Later, at Olympia in Greece, was established the precedent upon which most digs are conducted today: a foreign government, in that case Germany, provides finance while the host government, there Greece, keeps any treasures discovered except for duplicates. The earlier practice slowly died of the host country keeping nothing and the visiting archaeologists taking everything found, as, for instance, when the French in 1895 paid 50,000 francs to Iran in exchange for all their loot from Susa. Schliemann's Turkish jewels were divided between the Archaeological Museum at Istanbul

where they still are, and East Berlin, from which the Russians removed them in 1945, since when they have vanished without trace.

In 1876 Schliemann opened the graves at Mycenae, finding an immense treasure buried with sixteen corpses, which is now to be seen in the National Museum at Athens. He cabled the King of Greece, 'These treasures will fill a great museum, the most wonderful in the world, and for centuries to come thousands of foreigners will come to Greece to see them'. He continued these impatient hunting operations in Greece notably in Tiryns, Alexandria, Knossos and Cythera, but with no further thrilling revelations, and died in Naples in 1890.

Less picturesque, but establishing an equal hold on the public imagination, was Sir Arthur Evans (1851–1941) of Oxford University. Son of the famous palaeologist Sir John Evans and brother of the jewelry scholar Joan Evans, he inherited a love of jewels and of collecting which influenced his whole life. In 1896 he began his investigations on Crete. Italian and other archaeological teams worked there, but none with the same persistence as Evans. Because of the political instability, he sensibly acquired the ownership of the freehold site of some of the Knossos palace. (He

subsequently gave it to the British School at Athens, and they to the Greek government.) He rebuilt and repainted great areas of it with almost too much confidence, but because he made these remains look so vivid and complete it is perhaps due more to him than to anybody that archaeology became the popular science it is today. The splendour of Knossos can be guessed from the number of rooms: over 700 have been counted, and there may have been as many as 1,200 at the height of the Minoan civilization. In the multi-storied 'Palace of Minos' the murals illustrated jewels even more splendid than those now in the Heraklion Museum, Oxford's Ashmolean Museum and in the British Museum, London. Evans, incidentally, was very short-sighted and could therefore enjoy close-up, detailed vision more than most people. Hence his love of tiny seals, not then usually much respected. His fortunate myopia is reflected today in the wonderful display of Cretan seals given by him to the Ashmolean Museum.

The most spectacular find ever made was the Tutankhamen tomb in Egypt. It was opened on the afternoon of 25 November 1922. Howard Carter, the archaeologist, had looked for it for thirty years; his patron and companion, Lord Carnarvon, had spent a fortune backing him for eight years previously. Carter called this 'the day of days, the most wonderful that I have ever lived through and certainly one whose like I can never hope to see again.'

He succeeded just in time, when he was already discouraged, and when the government concession to explore had only a few weeks still to run. On 4 November, the last rubble-covered corner of the neighbouring Rameses VI tomb was cleared, and Carter saw the beginning of a step cut in the rock. Further steps led to a screen of stones, plastered over and bearing seals of the royal necropolis. He then prepared for the ceremonial opening of what he knew to be a tomb. Inside he found funerary objects made of alabaster, ebony, gold, lapis lazuli, turquoise and ivory. There were also jewels scattered on the floor, presumably left hurriedly by grave robbers disturbed centuries before. Madame Desroches-Noblecourt of the Louvre describes the succeeding drama:

The opening of the first coffin on 10 October 1925 marked the beginning of a most exciting period for the archaeologists and their

Above left *At Mycenae from 1876 Schliemann discovered one of the world's greatest gold hoards— justifying Homer's phrase 'Mycenae, rich in gold'— including this necklace of surprisingly modern aspect. Mycenaean, c. 1350 BC. National Archaeological Museum, Athens*

Right *Three gold roundels, from among hundreds discovered by Schliemann at Mycenae, especially by the legs of the dead. Many archaeological survivals, common in their time, are like these, of unknown use: they were perhaps dress ornaments, but there are no means of attachment. Mycenaean, c. 1350 BC. Diameter, butterfly roundel: 2.7 inches. National Archaeological Museum, Athens*

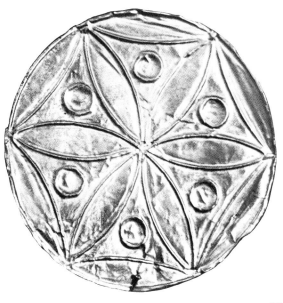

guests. A mummiform sheath, wrapped in a red linen shroud, was revealed where the priest had left it, with only the face exposed to the darkness of the tomb. A necklace of flowers on a backing of papyrus plants still lay on the breast and the side-pieces of the wig. The coffin, of solid gold, was incised with a religious pattern . . .: the interlaced wings of the goddesses Isis and Nephthys, and then, in gold cloisonné and shallow relief upon the king's arms, the great goddesses of Upper and Lower Egypt, Nekhabet, the vulture, and Wadjet, the serpent. This golden coffin . . . revealed the extraordinary gold death mask—a most striking portrait of the king . . .

Then there were chests crammed with jewels and treasure; nothing like it had ever been uncovered before—there were altogether nearly two thousand fabulous objects. Madame Noblecourt continues:

The mummy was literally covered with treasures and it is an irony of Tutankhamen's fate that its deterioration was not due to theft but to the superabundance of oils destined to give it new vitality. However, the hundred and forty-three precious objects tucked between the bandages were in an excellent state of preservation: golden finger-stalls, sandals, gold rings, necklaces, bracelets, diadems, daggers, pendants, pectorals and amulets cut out of gold leaf. The incorruptible metal endowed the protected creature with its own power, and everything united to make a god of the mummified prince.

All this was to deter the demons and help the king's rebirth to a new life.

Work at the tombs finished in 1928, and all the treasures were retained for the Cairo Museum. In recent years the Egyptian government have generously lent some of them to Paris and Tokyo, London and the USA; they have always attracted enormous crowds of visitors, fascinated no doubt by the vividness as well as the beauty of this journey back to ancient Egyptian times.

After Schliemann's great finds at Troy and Mycenae, Sir Arthur Evans' at Knossos and Howard Carter's at Thebes, came Sir Leonard Woolley's at Ur, some 220 miles south of Baghdad. It is, as he wrote in 1934, 'a rolling expanse of gravel with limestone outcrops which sometimes rise to the height of hills; but from the top of the Ziggurat of Ur, the great brick tower which has dominated it for four thousand years, one sees nothing but the alluvial plain of the Euphrates Valley.'

Cyrus of Persia was the last monarch to restore the monuments of Ur in the late sixth century BC: the last date re-

Pectoral of the vulture goddess of the south, Nekhabet, in gold, cloisonné, lapis lazuli, carnelian and green glass, the bird holding in its claws the ring of infinity. Found by Howard Carter in the tomb of Tutankhamen after 1922. Width: 4.5 inches. c. 1350 BC. Cairo Museum, Egypt

corded on any tablet is the twelfth year of Alexander the Great. In 1853, over two thousand years later, the British Museum started unsuccessful excavations on the site, at the same time as Layard was finding his colossal bulls and friezes in Assyria. Then Ur was left again to the jackals for over half a century. After 1916 the British Museum resumed work, helped by the British troops in Mesopotamia. They achieved such promising results that in 1922 the University of Pennsylvania joined the British team and Woolley's famous digs began. After eleven successive seasons a maze of walls and well-laid pavements of burnt brick were uncovered, suggesting a city of perhaps half a million people. The Ziggurat four-square tower with its triple staircase and other city buildings were clear for all to see. Only the royal cemetery, discovered in the first week of the joint expeditions' work in 1922, and the great death pit, from which the gold treasure eventually came, remained so crumbled as to be obscure. Woolley, with enormous patience and subtlety, using whisk, spatula, painter's brush and his own hands, not only found fantastic treasure, but also unearthed no less than 1,850 graves. For the first time he established the Sumerian chronology, rather as Evans had already done for Crete.

The Sumerians may have used magnificent jewelry to decorate queens and priestly women already dead; indeed, much of the treasure discovered by Sir Leonard Woolley in the royal graves at Ur seems to have been used as an accompaniment to mass human sacrifice. Woolley had found the bodies of sixty-eight women, heavily bejewelled, with that of Princess Puabi in the great pit of death. They all died about 2450 BC. Woolley imagined the awful scene:

Down into the open pit with its mat-covered floor and mat-lined walls, empty and unfurnished, there comes a procession of people. Members of the court are there, soldiers, menservants and women, the last named in all their finery of brightly coloured garments and head-dresses of carnelian, lapis lazuli, silver and gold. There are officers with the insignia of their rank, musicians bearing harps or lyres, and then, driven or backed down the slope, the chariots drawn by oxen or asses with their drivers and grooms. All take up their allotted places and finally a guard of soldiers forms up at the entrance. Each man and woman has brought a little cup of clay, stone or metal, the only equipment needed for the rite that was about to follow.

Such is the background to the splendid displays now in the Iraq Museum at Baghdad, the British Museum and at the University of Pennsylvania in Philadelphia.

Such shattering revelations seem unlikely to recur: archaeological finds, although more numerous as the pace of research steadily increases, have not produced quite the same bulk nor quite so many shocks about the strangeness of human nature: human sacrifice, for instance, at Ur in the midst of wonderful works of art, of the highest metalwork accomplishment and of sophisticated city organization. But nobody can foretell what lies in store. At Mohenjo Daro one square mile of the Indus Valley city is now revealed, and it may be the oldest fired-brick city in the world; seven cities exist, one on top of the next, but only one part of the three latest layers—dating from perhaps 1800 BC, 2000 BC and 2500 BC—is uncovered. The few dozen beautiful beads and gold jewels are mostly in the Karachi Museum, some at New Delhi, having been subjected to the political division between Pakistan and India.

Less spectacular, because it fitted into a known historical context, but none the less probably the most famous discovery ever made, as well as almost the first, was the unearthing of the Roman towns of Pompeii and Herculaneum. In 1748 the clearance of Pompeii began, using convict labour, and revealing with undreamed of intimacy details of everyday life. Goethe wrote of these excavations, 'Many disasters have occurred in the world, but few have given following generations more pleasure. I am hard put to think of anything more interesting.' Winckelmann and others stole whatever they could find—all wealthy excavators thought of art as treasure.

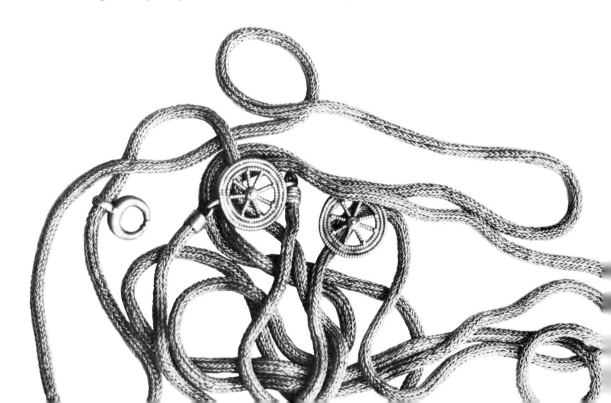

Some of the more recent discoveries are now being kept in the smart museum on the ancient site at Pompeii itself, but most of the gold jewels—many dozens of pieces—are now in the National Museum at Naples. They include the 115 pieces of table silver with gold jewels, too, found in 1930 in the cellar of one average-sized house—it was named after the Greek poet Menander, whose portrait was also found there. These pieces fill three large rooms, making the most complete collection of Roman goldsmiths' work.

The Sutton Hoo ship burial in the British Museum is Europe's most magnificent recent find, illustrating vividly how well appointed a great king might be even in the Dark Ages. This funeral deposit or ship burial of about AD 625, with its pagan vigour, was discovered on a sandy heath in rural Suffolk near Woodbridge; in 1938 three barrows were opened, then in 1939 a larger, taller one still only nine feet high. Rows of iron nails immediately suggested an intact ship burial deposit. It was of the same type as the later Viking ship burials in Oseberg and Gokstad in Norway, whose boats form wonderful abstract sculpture in their special Oslo museum. But this was earlier Anglo-Saxon work—the richest treasure ever found in Britain, and one of the most important European historical documents of the era of the great Teutonic migrations.

The Old English *Beowulf*, which was composed about AD 700, the earliest epic poem of the Teutonic peoples, describes just such a burial:

> . . . the people of the Wederas upheave
> A barrow on the steep, which was high and broad,
> Far to be sighted by men who pass the wave,
> And had built in ten days that landmark for their lord:
> Round what fire left they turned a sodded wall
> As the wisest could plan it, most worthy of him and fair:
> Into the mound they put ring, jewels, — all
> That skilful work . . .
> They left it to earth to keep the precious lot,
> Gold under dust, where to this day it sits,
> Not used by men . . .

Evocative words to describe those mounds of earth which constitute the burials of chieftains, priests, and kings the world over.

In 1952 at Vix, near Châtillon-sur-Seine, a gigantic bronze vase nearly five feet high was discovered. Some of its decoration is applied, and the letters indicating on the surface which piece goes where are not in Attic Greek, but in the Spartan alphabet. The now famous crater of Vix was thus, in fact, a sixth-century BC export from Sparta. The supposedly inartistic centre of the Dorian warrior migrants is now proved, because of this chance discovery, to have produced not only war but beautiful art too, as beautiful as even the artistic Athenians themselves ever did, with their less warlike tradition and Ionian ancestry. Perhaps the difference between success in art and war is not so great as we may like to think.

What spectacular deductions this one discovery has stimulated! Perhaps a Gaulish chieftain bought the urn and other objects in the rich Greek colony at Marseilles, as a wedding present for his daughter, who then died. Also in the burial chamber, surrounded by gifts and offerings for the journey to the next world, was a woman's skeleton with a heavy, plain gold headband of unique conception. It was designed to wear over the top of the head, with a lion's paw at each end gripping a globe almost as big as a golf-ball, decorated with filigree. Nothing like this has ever been found anywhere—perhaps it is 2,500 years old, and came all the way from Scythia.

Words like 'treasure' and 'hoard' are over-used today to describe the modest outcome of incredible coincidences. Deep ploughing with modern powered tractors, penetrating perhaps eighteen inches beneath the earth and until recently impossible, turns up some of the happiest chances. It uncovered the Roman Mildenhall treasure, now at the British Museum (but which the landowner at first tried to retain quietly at home, overwhelming ornaments for his mantelpiece) and the five enormous Celtic torcs found in 1958 near Ipswich, eastern England. In 1919 at Traprain Law in Scotland, near Haddington, the Edinburgh Royal Scottish Museum director records the triumphant moment in an excavation:

As the foreman was cautiously picking away at the remaining few inches that overlay the second floor level, he was suddenly conscious of the fact that his tool was in contact with some strange substance. The removal of the crust for a couple of feet around revealed a wonderful sight, a mass of dingy

Above Europe's most spectacular recent archaeological discovery was the ship burial at Sutton Hoo in Suffolk—a Saxon royal king's tomb uncovered in 1939; the treasure included this gold buckle with niello inlay. 7th century AD. British Museum, London. Comparable discoveries continue today: the hoard of Bronze Age torcs at Snettisham, Norfolk, now also in the British Museum, found in 1948, is still growing—further pieces were found in the same field in 1968.

Right Chinese burial crown for an empress, probably late Tang or early Sung dynasty, perhaps 9th century AD; gold, pearls, rubies and cat's-eyes. Metropolitan Museum of Art, New York

white metal resembling tarnished pewter. Further excavation showed that a pit had been discovered about two feet deep and of similar diameter, dug undoubtedly from the last level of occupation, and into this had been emptied a hoard of silver vessels.

It was a late Roman collection of table plate, coins and jewels, presumably stolen by Teutonic pirates from northern Gaul. The Esquiline treasure at the British Museum was found in 1793 on the Esquiline Hill, Rome, in the vaults of a house which must have fallen in; it comprised silver brooches and ornaments, horse trappings and plate. The treasure of Chource, similarly at the British Museum, was found in a field in 1883 near Montcornet in France, wrapped in a piece of cloth.

The investigation of Etruscan tombs, one of the chief depositories for jewels, was transformed as recently as 1953. Then Carlo Lerici, an Italian expert in boring for oil and water, turned his attention to archaeology. Using partly the English equipment evolved at Oxford by Edward Hall, he probed into the past with geophysics of the future. Round Tarquinia he found in one season more graves than had yielded to conventional searches for the past two centuries. The Florence Archaeology Museum and Rome's Villa Giulia, the civic collections at Orvieto, Cortona and elsewhere, are obviously going to enrich their already dazzling Etruscan displays. One of the first known Etruscan tombs, called Regolini-Galassi after its discoverers, was opened in 1836 at Cerveteri (Caere), and among its rich contents were a golden fibula or clasp over a foot long, with an oval plate, five lions, two hinged joints, and a smaller pin with minute ducklings, now one of the masterpieces in the Vatican Museum, Rome.

Further afield, in 1966, one of the latest of the magnificent groups of twelfth-century gold bracelets from the rich trading island, Gotland, in the Baltic, was dug up there by the farmer Per-Anders Croon. In 1968 dozens of Bronze Age buckles and jewels were found at Vognserup in Jutland, Denmark. Discovered because one of the bronze pieces stuck to the mud on a tractor wheel, the hoard lay forgotten in a farmer's sack until 1971 when an archaeologist heard of it by chance. In Vienna's Kunsthistorisches Museum is the savage ninth-century Bulgarian gold from Nagyszentmiklos found 200 years ago, and the wonderful Germanic necklace of about AD 1000 from Szilagysmlyo. In the Bavarian National Museum at Munich are the jewels of a seventh-century Alemannic noblewoman whose grave was at Wittislingen. Breath-taking is the Petrossa treasure of the fourth

century AD in the Bucharest National Museum. Buried during the Hun invasions, it was found in 1837 on Mount Istritza by two peasants looking for building stones. Originally the twenty-two golden objects were mostly ornamented with stones and coloured glass; alas by the time the authorities heard of the discovery, many of the pieces were mutilated and destroyed, and only twelve eventually reached the University Museum at Bucharest. Thence they were moved to Jassy to escape the German invasion in the Great War, only to be captured by the Bolsheviks thereafter, remaining inaccessible to anyone till 1956. Even now this splendid group is not always on view in Bucharest.

At Tehran is the Ziwiye treasure, found by chance in Kurdistan at the fortress of Ziwiye in 1947 in a bronze cauldron; the pieces were immediately pillaged, cut up into bits and shared out among the neighbouring villagers, which partly explains their present disorder. But they were anyway of diverse ancestry; they were probably plunder made by a Scythian nomad chief called Bartatua, Heroditus' Protothyes. At Amlash just south of the Caspian all sorts of bronze ornaments are being dug up; at Marlik gold was found in a royal tomb in 1963. The mysteries of Luristan are still to be unravelled in northern Persia.

A hundred years ago a queen's tomb, at Novocherkassk near the mouth of the Don, yielded staggering riches of the first and second centuries, including a famous Sarmatian crown now at the Hermitage, Leningrad: in this context, Strabo's comment that the Sarmatians 'could afford to wear gold ornaments' seems an understatement. Russian excavations continue: in 1971 a great gold Scythian pectoral of nearly twelve inches diameter, from about 400 BC, was found with dozens of smaller jewels at the Tolstoi Burial (the 'Thick Grave') at Ordzhonikidze in the Ukraine.

Perhaps the most extraordinary underground secrets of all are in China. Between the Tiger and Dragon Mountains, thirty-five miles north-east of Peking, are the subterranean Ming emperors' tombs, at least thirteen of them, of which only one is so far opened: that of Cheng Tsung, called Ting Ling. Scarlet and gold gateways with wide courtyards and pavilions are the overture to the mausoleum, which was finished in 1490 after six years' work. The king and his empresses were laid to rest with their royal treasures banked around them, then the mausoleum itself was buried sixty feet underground, the first shaft being sunk to it in 1958. The two empresses' peacock crowns of gold, enamel and pearls partly coated in kingfishers' feathers of dazzling colour, dangle like cobwebs in metal. They could almost be coiffeurs' work, not goldsmiths'. There is no end to the variety of this metal. This is probably the second richest of the tombs. When the Chinese, who are in no hurry, have uncovered the other twelve, the craft will probably have received a whole new dimension.

Chinese jewelry is still almost unknown. Ancient work is nearly all lost, and new jewels are not made there, perhaps being thought decadent. For the Chinese more than for anyone else jewelry was the art of the pin. Elaborate embroidery on the swaddling clothes took the place of dress ornaments of the west, just as it did also on the kimono in Japan. What was needed was not brooches (there are none) but intricate pins to keep the hair in place. Sometimes carved in hard jade for which the Chinese had a passion, sometimes constructed from myriads of wires, they often featured the divine dragon. In later times, at least from the Ming dynasty (1368–1644), the normal finish for metal was the flashing blue of the kingfisher feather. Nobody knows how it was cut up and glued into position—the technique is as mysterious as its provenance and its dating. In its frail gaudiness this feather decoration is typical of all Chinese jewels: built to enchant more than to endure, and attracting pleasure more than reverence.

In the early 1930s the Nubian treasures found at Ballana and Quotol were some of the most dramatic ever made in Egypt: Herodotus' 'City of the Sun' of 500 BC to AD 300 was revealed at last with the dreary scientists' label 'x group'.

Zimbabwe is Africa's great archaeological teaser; capital of the Rozwi tribe, the citadel may have flourished for 2000 years before being sacked by the Zulus in about 1830. Imports are found there from as far away as Flanders and China, and thousands of small holes in the ground suggest that this may have been the now vanished but once famous central African source of gold. It seems to have been a huge fourteenth-century complex of Mashona strongholds.

Heads of wild beasts, dragons and snakes have always been a favourite theme for bracelets. The less settled the tribe, the more vivid the animal imagery in its jewels, none more so than the Scythians of western Russia in ancient Greek times. This gold lion's head, with a ram's head each side and amber inlay down the back with granulation, is a detail from a pair of cylindrical objects, found in 1904 at Kelermes, whose use is unknown—perhaps not wearable jewels but parts of a throne. Length: 7.5 inches. 6th century BC, before the Scythians absorbed Greek influence. Hermitage Museum, Leningrad

Top *Five engraved gold seal rings.
Left to right, top row:*
a) *A goddess seated under a tree in
the sacred grove is surrounded by
her hand-maidens with two
women paying homage. The heads
of the principal figures are
decorated with lilies. The double
axe suggests a holy place; the
moon, sun and wavy line suggest
heaven. Perhaps the scene shows
the mother goddess and tree
worship. The grace and charm and
the prominence of the women
suggest the civilized palace life of
Minoan Crete. Minoan, 15th
century BC. 1.3 × 0.7 inches.*
b) *A lion fight. The subject is
common on Mycenaean seals;
nobody knows if it reflects the
myth of, for instance, Heracles or
Theseus, or an incident in everyday
life. This seal, found in the royal
grave circle on the Acropolis at
Mycenae, is typical of the vigour
and toughness of Mycenaean art.
16th century BC. 0.7 × 0.5 inches.*
c) *Tree worship. A man shakes the
'sacred tree' with his gaze averted;
a woman bowed over a bench sings
or laments while another dances
ecstatically. Rituals combining
lamentations with joy are known
in Cretan, Mycenaean and other
civilizations, and are connected
with the annual cycle of nature, the
fall of leaves being succeeded by
renewal. Found in the chamber
tomb in the Lower Town at
Mycenae. 15th or 14th century BC,
by which time Mycenaean art was
influenced by Minoan.
0.7 × 0.5 inches.*
bottom row:
d) *A ritual scene. A seated goddess
raises a chalice, perhaps
containing the liquid which would
increase the fruitfulness of nature.
Lion-headed genii of fertility hold
libation jugs to catch the precious
liquid. Saplings between the
genii, ears of corn and raindrops in
the sky all hint at soil cultivation.
Mycenaean, late 16th century BC,
found in the Lower Town at
Tiryns. 2.2 × 1.3 inches.*
e) *A battle scene. Four men in
ferocious stance. Mycenaean,
found in the royal grave circle on
the Acropolis at Mycenae,
16th century BC. 1.3 × 0.8 inches.*

Bottom *A large but flimsy gold
diadem. Found by Schliemann at
Mycenae in the women's grave in
the upper grave circle, it is one of
the most magnificent ancient
creations ever discovered anywhere. Length: 25.5 inches.
16th century BC.
All at the National Archaeological
Museum, Athens*

Perhaps this was the source of wealth for the fabulous land of Ophir, the 'land of Solomon's gold'—the First Book of Kings recounts how Solomon plastered gold both in and outside his temple, and gave his troops shields of beaten gold, with cherubims in gold and golden chariots. Rider Haggard, who lived in Natal, was fired by the vision, and caught the world's fancy with *King Solomon's Mines*. Cecil Rhodes and his colleagues, in the 'Ancient Ruins Company Limited', alas sold and thus dispersed much of the excavated evidence. New radiocarbon dating of wood fragments at Zimbabwe suggests the second or third century A D. Here was possibly one of those paradises of wealth known as Eldorado.

Then there is the deep water—in 1964 divers working at Lucayan Beach in the Grand Bahama Island found an unusual early type of anchor, then two cannon, and coins: a boat had grounded between two reefs half a mile off shore, ripping its bottom away and scattering nearly ten thousand silver coins. They turned out to be from the Mexico mint, set up as the first in America by the Spaniards in 1536. Herman Cortes used a private house for it, also making in his foundry there bells and cannons. Probably the coins were from a Spanish treasure-fleet aiming to take them on the 'golden road' from Havana back to Spain; but on 8 September 1628 Piet Heyn captured the fleet in Mantaza Bay, and these coins were almost certainly part of the loot. Piet Heyn became a Dutch national hero, whereas the Spanish captain general was executed and the admiral banished to north Africa.

Kip Wagner, the American, using magnetometers and modern diving equipment, located all ten of the Spanish galleons known to have been wrecked in 1715 by an out-of-season summer hurricane at Florida. That time it was all coins.

At Lake Guatavita in Colombia, the Chibcha Indians for centuries threw gold and emeralds into the circular lagoon, presided over by their high priest whose body was covered in gold dust and whose name was therefore Eldorado—the golden man; it was an extinct volcano, more than 10,000 feet up in the Andes, and received the Indians' tribute to the Sun God. The Spaniards failed to reach the bottom even though, by cutting a cleft in the side of the bowl, they lowered the level by seventy feet. The Mexico City underground railway is penetrating where the Spaniards failed, burrowing towards the treasures of Montezuma, some of which the Spaniards took in 1514, most of which eluded them.

In the Mediterranean several rooms at the fine Kyrenia Museum in Cyprus have been filled with the amphorae, jars, jewels and treasure taken from an ancient Greek ship found only two hundred yards off shore. A similar hoard was scooped from deeper water off the Greek colony of Marseilles whose museum it now graces. Diving expeditions off the islands of Hydra and Mykonos are disclosing yet more evidence of the vitality of Greek trade two and a half millennia ago.

In Britain King Charles II's beautiful yacht *Mary*, wrecked off the coast of Anglesey in 1675, was discovered in 1971. The Dutch eighteenth-century merchant-ship *Amsterdam* is still engulfed in the quicksands off Hastings where she ran aground in 1748; discovered only in 1969, she still has not yielded any relics such as the *Vasa*, the Swedish seventeenth-century flagship, disgorged in Stockholm harbour in 1961. The wreck of the eighteenth-century British East Indiaman *Hollandia*, which sank containing two million pounds' worth of gold and silver, was found in 1971 by skin divers off the Scilly Isles. At Stoura Stack in the Shetland Isles, divers in 1971 started investigating the Dutch spice trading ship *Kenemerlandt*, wrecked in 1664 on her way from Holland to the East Indies. The Spanish Armada of 1588 has proved more rich in legend than in fact, but since 1969 one of the Spanish wrecks at Spanish Point by the Giant's Causeway in Ulster, has revealed a dozen fine sixteenth-century cameos from Milan.

All these random hints lead to the same conclusions: ancient men were much cleverer than we think. Archaeology is piecing together the whole human race from its warring fragments; showing that similarity between different peoples is often the result not of chance, but of systematic contact.

The most exciting discoveries penetrate the unknown. Re-creations of forgotten civilizations such as Woolley achieved with the Sumerians, and such as is now continuing throughout the Middle East, at Mohenjo Daro in Pakistan, with the Elamites at Susa in Persia, with the Delmun people at Kuwait, or with the great tribal movements around

Lake Van in Turkey—these are all quests which may lead to yet another 'oldest culture'.

The element of mystery has a strong appeal to all of us: as some aspects of our environment become less mysterious with the spectacular advance of modern science, so the question marks of archaeology exercise a stronger magnetism. What, for instance, became of a strange revelation by Sir Arthur Evans to the select Society of Antiquaries in London in the early years of the century? He and his French colleague, Gillieron, showed a set of large gold engraved seal rings, picturing for instance Ajax falling on his spear, and Oedipus with the Sphinx, all said to be from Minoan Crete; but how, it was asked, could these legends have been illustrated in Crete, if Homer in fact wrote them after the end of the Cretan civilization? Why is the best Minoan jewelry in the British Museum known as the Aegina Hoard, when everybody knows that in fact it did not come from the Greek island of Aegina, nor was Aegina part of the Cretan empire? More recently, what became of the sensational treasure from Dorak which the British archaeologist James Mellaart saw in Smyrna in 1947, but which, when he returned to verify it, had vanished together with the buildings in which its owner lived?

Activities in Russian territories are unpredictable. Francis Meynell smuggled jewels from Russia, given by the Soviet government to subsidize the *Daily Herald* for which he worked; some of the Russian crown jewels sent by the Bolsheviks for sale at Christie's in 1927 were withdrawn at the last moment. The Russians took many treasures from East Germany after their 1945 conquests. Why have they returned the coin collection to Berlin, for instance, and the magnificent Saxon crown jewels to Dresden, but retained, in hiding, the jewels discovered by Schliemann at Troy a hundred years ago? Most recently of all, what is the origin of the Boston Museum hoard of Greek and other jewels, hailed by the museum in 1970 as a great new treasure comparable to Schliemann's from Troy, frowned on by others as a load of odd bits and pieces and fakes illegally smuggled from Cilicia? There is a gold cylinder seal of Egyptian style, dated about 2500 BC: it is unique, so nobody knows if it is genuine.

Archaeology and discovery show up human frailty and uncertainty. Our constant probing penetrates the chaos of the past which destroyed so much. Jewels, now associated with present life and joy, have ironically survived best with the dead. As our curiosity about the past becomes keener, so our vision of jewelry as one of the world's great pleasure givers will become fuller.

Gold pendant from the 'Aegina Hoard'. Despite their name the pieces are of Minoan or Cretan style, c. 1500 BC. Purchased in 1892 from a sponge fisherman, who may have wished to conceal his source. Height: 2.3 inches. British Museum, London

The Collections

Public displays of jewelry are almost always disappointing: what could be more absurd than a jewel you cannot wear—a jewel, the embodiment of personality and instinct, embalmed in a show case, immovable and inaccessible? Jewels more than any other art need movement, and that is the most important thing they lose in a museum.

Then, secondly, there is the question of feel. Any enthusiast wants to touch his treasures: how else can he enjoy the tactile effect which the designer intended? One reason why ancient Etruscan granulation, for instance, is so much finer than we can now manage must be that the ancient Greeks and their contemporaries could sense more through their finger tips than we can today. Our loss of sensitivity, compared with our forebears, may partly be due to our changed attitude to our treasures. Locking away one's most prized possessions instead of wearing and enjoying them means that we cannot appreciate old jewels as was originally intended.

A third sadness in museums is the light. Until perhaps the eighteenth century, nearly all jewels everywhere were enjoyed most in daylight. Then, in the age of faceted stones and cut steel, came the night-time jewel designed to catch the shimmers of candlelight. But in place of Mediterranean sun or soft flickering candles, we have to make do in museums either with harsh, modern nakedness in lighting, fluorescence and all, or, much more often, with gloomy shadows and dust.

The truth is that jewels, once they cease to belong to the human beings for whom they were made, to some extent lose the joy from which they take their name. Museums nearly always put jewels at the bottom of their list of priorities. They are a worry for security, continually getting lost or stolen. Very little is known, or ever will be known, about them, so they do not provide much bait for the detailed art historians. And they are much more difficult to show correctly than, for instance, paintings.

It is hardly surprising, therefore, to find that some of the world's best collections are open to the public only in theory, not in practice. The best of all, London's Victoria and Albert Museum, was closed first for repair, then for redesign, then amazingly for a second redesign, for five out of eight years till 1972. Much of the British Museum jewelry has been in storage for years while bigger objects, supposed to be of greater public interest, are re-organized there. The Medici treasures in the Pitti Palace at Florence are usually inaccessible. The wonderful Farnese cameos at the Naples National Museum have been locked away in store for four decades. The Musée des Arts Décoratifs in the Louvre keeps its vaults well stocked with jewels at all times. The reason? No room upstairs. The Madrid Museo Arqueológico is rebuilding. Result: the great early treasures of Aliseda and Javea have been inaccessible for years. The Baghdad Museum shows only some of its marvellous seals, and many even of those are invisible in the shadow. The Kremlin Museum in Moscow is accessible only two or three days a week; its neighbouring diamond display less often, and then only after a three-month wait. At Leningrad the Hermitage Museum gold rooms can be penetrated only with special permission and escort. The crown jewels in Prague are given a semi-mystical appeal by being shown only once every ten years. The Hungarian crown jewels, including the oldest constitutional crown—Stephen I's of 1001—are never shown. Perhaps they never will be now. Some were sold at Christie's in 1867, the crown itself has been in secret American military custody since 1945, the subject of political feeling between communists and patriots. The Moghul jewels in the New Delhi Museum, having been once stolen in 1968, are now locked away to prevent such another resurgence of human cupidity over security. In Cairo the Tutankhamen treasures have been inaccessible in storage for years, though the most outstanding of them have been occasionally exhibited outside Egypt.

The Kiani Crown. The royal crown of the Qajar house; gold with a velvet cap, and thousands of gems —diamonds, pearls, emeralds, rubies and red spinels, often backed with pink metallic foil. Some of the units are sewn together with thread, perhaps having been used in different combinations for different occasions. Old pictures often show this crown, surmounted by a large jiqa *(aigrette or turban ornament) and three black heron plumes which only a shah could wear, being worn by Fath Ali Shah in the early nineteenth century. The two* jiqas *in the illustration are not original but were affixed probably for the coronation of Muzaffar-ud-Din Shah in 1896. The spinel on top may have once adorned the throne of the Moghul emperor, Aurangzeb, and formed part of Nadir Shah's loot, taken by him from Delhi in 1739. After his death, it came into the possession of his blinded grandson, Shahrukh, who after hideous tortures surrendered it to the Aga Muhammed Khan, the founder of the Qajar dynasty. Height without jiqa: 12.5 inches. Tehran Crown Jewels, Melhi Bank, Tehran*

The Peabody Museum at Harvard, USA, hides its magnificent pre-Columbian gold.

Museum jewels are on their way to joining coins—in a backroom safely locked in dark drawers, the almost private preserve of a small international band of scholars. And museums themselves, like airports, never grow fast enough to 'accommodate the traffic'. The effect on museum practice is lamentably to keep out the public, often the reverse of declared museum policy.

The displays which give the most pleasure today are probably those which in one way or another have the most personality—either, as with royal treasure, reflecting the outlook of the country or royal family concerned, or, as with archaeological hoards, reminding us of far distant peoples whose jewels are often their most vivid memorial

A quick summary of existing collections is not quite fair to the history of jewelry, because it neglects those which have almost vanished, like those of King John the Good of France (d. 1364) with his four sons at Paris, Angers, Bourges and Dijon. One of them, Jean de Berry (d. 1416), commissioned wonderful manuscripts from the brothers Limburg; these are famous because they still exist, but the jewels are now forgotten because lost. Or there is the English King Henry VIII, world renowned for his riches. Only three of all the objects from the Tudor royal inventory in the sixteenth century now survive: the royal gold cup in the British Museum, the royal gilt salt at Goldsmiths' Hall in London and the 'Holbein' cup at the Munich Residenz, and no jewels at all.

MUNICH

The first museum to be established north of the Alps was at Munich; Duke Albrecht of Bavaria (who ruled 1550–79) decreed that seventeen of his treasures were to be inalienable state property, housed in the Munich Residenz of the ruling family, Wittelsbach. Albrecht V's original collection of antiques was seen in 1611 by Philip Hainhofer of Augsburg, owner himself of a cabinet of rarities. He said there was nothing so good even in Rome and Florence, and the Munich treasury was only one of many starting throughout Europe at that time.

The idea of the ruler was to establish a *Kunst-und-Wunderkammer*, partly to show his friends what good taste he had

in art, partly to encourage scientific investigation, mainly no doubt to beautify the palace and to enjoy the varied fruits of human genius, which quicker travel was making better known. But probably the main incentive in all these old family treasuries was simply the enjoyment of art. They expanded very spasmodically, lying dormant for decades and sometimes centuries.

The counsellors of Duke Albrecht of Bavaria, surveying his finances in 1557, criticized the idea that 'Anything precious, strange or unusual that has been seen must be acquired. Two or three goldsmiths are working constantly and exclusively for the duke; what has been made one year is broken or pawned the next'.

Many of the treasures made in Prague for the Emperor Rudolph II adorned the Roman Catholic cause until Gustavus Adolphus, the great Swedish Protestant leader, conquered them in the Thirty Years' War; others later went from Prague to Skokloster Castle in Sweden. Queen Christina of Sweden dispersed some; many of them went to the Saxe-Coburg-Gotha family, some to the Gotha Museum, most to Vienna's Kunsthistorisches Museum.

Gustavus Adolphus said Munich was a golden saddle on a sorry mare: what he meant to imply, presumably, was the unfortunate gap there between the very advanced court patronage and the humble life outside; the merchant classes and craftsmen, so important to the Hansa cities, hardly existed. It was Nuremberg and nearby Augsburg which provided the Wittelsbach electors with their skilled craftsmen, but they never built up a really big local workshop activity—their own sixteenth-century craftsmen like Hans Reimer or Isaak Melper or Andreas Athemstett seem to have provided only a minority of the big jewelry collection recorded by the court painter Hans Miehlich.

For a time, Albrecht V's successor Wilhelm V (1579–97) had two lapidaries and the goldsmith Battista Scolari working for his court at Trausnitz Castle in Landshut. But most of the pieces continued to be bought or commissioned from outside, often through the Fugger family bank; the local nucleus of production always remained surprisingly small. This isolation of the ruling-class applied to most of the big collectors, and had its advantage: the patron himself could do exactly what he wanted—in

The crown of the Swedish crown princes which was made in Stockholm in 1650 for Karl Gustav as the Hereditary Prince at Queen Christina's coronation. Although she refused to marry, she decided that Karl Gustav should be her heir. The crown was made largely from an older crown of Queen Christina the Elder by the goldsmith Jürgen Dargeman, who received the order only seven days before the coronation. The Swedish crown jewels and the royal regalia were for the first time put on public view in the Royal Treasury at the Royal Palace, Stockholm, in 1970, having lain in the Bank of Sweden vaults for the past sixty years. The crown is made of gold and precious stones with a cap of pale blue embroidered satin. King Gustavus III added a black enamelled sheaf, the badge of the Royal House of Vasa, in the eighteenth century.
Height: 5.7 inches

the case of sixteenth-century Munich, for instance, introducing ancient Rome to Germany; in the case of the eighteenth century, using the French repertoire of rococo forms with more purity and enthusiasm than anywhere else in Germany.

In 1777, Max Joseph III, the last Wittelsbach Bavarian elector died. His successor was the Elector of the Palatinate, Karl Theodore (died 1799), who altered some of the Munich pieces and sold others to pay debts, but much more than made up for this after 1779 by bringing with him his own treasure from Mannheim. What began as dynastic routine ended as an escape operation from Napoleon's armies. There were some notable losses *en route* but the marvellous fourteenth-century crown arrived intact after its journey to England with Anne of Bohemia from her native Prague, and so likewise did much of the Palatine treasure from Düsseldorf including the Holbein bowl originally ordered by Edward VI and completed in 1550 for Henry VIII of England.

In 1803 the Bavarian abbeys and monasteries were secularized, many of their treasures going to Munich; the Bavarian rulers, dukes until 1623, became electors until 1806 and then kings until 1918. Their palace rooms were first open to the public from 1920, and the treasury for two years before the war. It was not until 1958 that the church treasures, including the Duchess Gisela's tenth-century cross and the altar of her son the Emperor Henry II, joined the treasury. The final partition between church and state, between the Wittelsbach family, now private citizens, and their magnificent museum, was complete.

Many stones have enthralling associations but few of the legends can be proved, and very few survive to the present day. The Elector Karl Albrecht (1726–45, later Emperor Charles VII), provided us with one of the few: the famous Wittelsbach 'Blue Diamond', no giant at $33\frac{1}{2}$ carats but very choice. It was his through his wife, Maria Amalia of Austria, who had in turn inherited it from her grandmother. In 1923 the Republic of Bavaria liquidated some of the old family assets to counteract inflation, offering this diamond for sale at Christie's in 1931, withdrawing it because the auction price was too low, showing it in the 1935 Brussels World Fair, and eventually selling it privately.

Acquired by the Amsterdam dealer I. Komkomer in 1962, it was shown in several shop windows such as Gübelin of Lucerne. Meanwhile the poor Bavarian royal crown, made by Guillaume Biennais of Paris, has a lump of blue glass in the key position.

It was always the early pieces, however, that impressed the tourists, like Johann Georg Keyzler in 1751. Today the first three rooms of the treasury are sensational with their four medieval crowns: that of the Empress Kunigunde, c. 1010; the crown, c. 1280, which formerly surmounted the reliquary of the head of the Emperor Henry II, canonized in 1146 in Bamberg Cathedral—too large for a human head, just right for the reliquary which covered the head; the silver gilt and gold filigree crown, c. 1350, perhaps of Margaret of Holland, second wife of Emperor Ludwig of Bavaria; and, most memorable, the fourteenth-century crown, c. 1350, perhaps made in a Prague workshop, taken from Prague by Queen Anne of Bohemia as part of her dowry to the English king Richard II, then brought to the Palatinate residence in Heidelberg Castle in 1402 by Blanche, daughter of Henry IV of England, then to Munich by Karl Theodore with the other Palatine treasure. The Bavarian crown jewels in a later room, the eighteenth-century insignia of the Order of St Hubert and of the Golden Fleece, the nineteenth-century regalia for the Order of St George, are by comparison characterless. By then, the spiritual power of the medieval goldsmiths had passed into sculpture and painting, leaving jewels for the lapidaries. The carved stone jugs, the table silver, a case of Renaissance jewels, and a jewel casket by Wenzel Jamnitzer, c. 1560, a piece itself as precious as a gem, round off what is one of the memorable experiences of Europe.

DRESDEN

Saxony had the richest mines in Europe. It was not, however, until the eighteenth century that the duke electors really showed their strength as art patrons. This was partly because the mines could not be exploited with efficiency before the invention of mining machinery. Partly also because the greatest of the electors, Augustus the Strong, Frederick Augustus I of Saxony, was also King Augustus II of Poland, thus achieving new wealth and power. As early as the sixteenth century, the Wettin family were already commissioning and buying work by the Jamnitzers, the Nuremberg masters, and by Elias Geyer, the only really notable smith ever to come from Leipzig. The Art Cabinet, created in 1560 by the Duke Elector Augustus, may have been the first of its kind in Germany—in contrast to the system at Munich, it was a miscellaneous jumble of curios including fossils and minerals, tools and scientific instruments. A rare gold and silver wire drawplate on an inlaid wood stand has found its way from this group to the Paris Cluny Museum; it is beautiful furniture as well as useful machinery, a good symbol of sixteenth-century Dresden's remarkable sophistication.

The Green Vault—*Grüne Gewölbe*—at Dresden became a gorgeous and amusing setting; it spread during the next two centuries into an eventual eight rooms, and Augustus concentrated into them what is probably the most extraordinary group of goldwork ever made by one man: the life's work of one of history's great goldsmiths, Johann Melchior Dinglinger. It is he who gave the treasury some of its special individuality.

Heinrich Taddel, expert box-maker, probably inventor of the *Zellenmosaik* effect of mounting local stones in a mosaic between gold wires, became director of the Green Vault; so did Johann Christian Neuber, another world master of the eighteenth-century box-maker's craft, with his own style of radiating lines of geometrically cut stones. The display hardly changed from the 1730s right through till 1942, except for the addition of a marble fireplace by the same great jeweler, Neuber, some re-arranging of exhibits, and the addition of an eighth room by the twentieth-century director Sponsel, who produced the standard catalogue. Right up till 1942, most of the objects were shown without glass protection, without burglar alarms: visitors were welcomed and shown round by custodians. The appeal was extraordinary.

In 1921 Saxony became part of Germany. The Wettin family lost their inheritance by the *Fürstenabfindung* and took with them some of their personal possessions, but none of the most famous treasures. In the war the collection was stored in the Castle of Königstein, with French prisoner-of-war officers; in 1945 almost the whole Dresden Castle interior, together with most of the old setting,

was tragically destroyed by bombing, after which the Russians took all the collection from Königstein, restoring it to Dresden in 1958. Then the present director, Joachim Menzhausen, was suddenly summoned from his job as curator of paintings in the gallery to a dim bank basement with one light bulb hanging from the ceiling. There he unpacked crates, one after another, revealing colossal treasure which to him at that time was almost unknown. Only one small emerald ring had vanished; the rest are now effectively shown in the Albertinum, the old home of the ducal antiquities, a building now mostly of nineteenth-century appearance. The castle is being rebuilt; during the next decades, the Green Vault will be restored to its fascinating eighteenth-century appearance, in its original rooms which have some of the first and finest rococo effects in Europe, themselves housed in their original position at the corner of the sixteenth-century castle wall, ten feet thick for safety. It should be a good permanent resting-place: it was the only part of the castle interior tough enough even partly to survive the 1945 bombing, and, miraculously, it had also lived through the Prussian conquests of Frederick the Great in the Seven Years' War, the French invasions under Napoleon and the national upheavals under Bismarck and Hitler. The Dresden Treasury has proved almost as indestructible as it is historic.

VIENNA

Very different is the *Schatzkammer* in the old Hapsburg Palace at Vienna. High up a small baroque staircase in this *Hofburg* one goes through an ancient iron gate slap into the Holy Roman Empire. On one side, mostly housed in the Empress Maria Theresa's eighteenth-century showcases, are the church ornaments, flamboyant trappings of the Roman Catholic counter-reformation, the spiritual or *geistlich* indication of imperial holiness. On the other side is the *weltliche Schatzkammer*: one walks backwards through history to Charlemagne. There is his crown with the insignia of the Holy Roman Empire: the gospel, St Steven's *bursa* (purse) and the sabre of Charlemagne, found, so legend says, by Otto III in Charlemagne's tomb; with the addition of the robes used at the coronation of Frederick II, 'Stupor Mundi', in 1220, they came to Nuremberg where in the National

Above *Crown of the Empress Kunigunde, perhaps made at Metz, c. AD 1010–20, of gold with filigree, precious stones, pearls and paste. From one of the world's best displays of medieval crowns, in the Residenz Museum, Munich*

Below *Noblewoman's crown, silver gilt, gold filigree, copper, stones and pearls, German, c. 1350. Perhaps the crown of Margaret of Holland, second wife of Emperor Ludwig of Bavaria. Residenz Museum, Munich*

Museum one can still see the beautiful medieval silver casket chest in which they lived.

By the fourteenth century these were supposed to be the actual crown jewels of Charlemagne and were occasionally used at imperial functions. In 1424 the Emperor Sigismund recognized that the pieces belonged not to him personally but to history: he gave them to the city, where they remained for four centuries. Occasionally they were displayed for pious contemplation at coronations and for great ceremonies: their significance becoming steadily more constitutional, less religious. The last emperor to be crowned with them was Charles v. They were finally evacuated to avoid Napoleon in 1794; from Paderborn they reached Vienna in 1801, staying there except when Hitler returned them to Nuremberg from 1938 to 1945.

Less numerous and also less numinous are the fifteenth-century Burgundian masterpieces, associated with the Order of the Golden Fleece. Founded in 1429 for Duke Philip the Good, this was a knightly society designed to bring together the independent rulers within Burgundy who were vassals of the duke throughout his odd-shaped empire, and, of course, to impress them with the glory of the Burgundian dynasty. It was always a very select body. The character of the pieces, part religious, part secular, is typical of the late Middle Ages: what is astonishing is the quality of their design and craftsmanship. The cross of the oath originally belonged to Duke Jean de Berry of France, and most of the other pieces came to the Order similarly from an earlier owner, like the unicorns' sword of Charles the Bold and an exquisite small brooch. The herald's chain seems to be almost alone in having been specially made for the Order. Philip the Good's goblet was a present from Charles IX.

Most of the Burgundian empire's portable jewels were lost when the empire itself collapsed at the three disastrous battles fought at Grandson, Murten and, in 1477, Nancy. The few pieces in Vienna became what is now Austrian property by the marriage of Maria, daughter of the last duke, Charles the Bold, to the Hapsburg Archduke Maximilian, later Emperor Maximilian I. Other vestiges of the treasure are still at Madrid, Brussels and Berne.

A third room in the Hapsburg Palace

contains some of the most marvellous products of the Prague workshops, set up in the Hradčany Castle there by the extraordinary impulse of Emperor Rudolph II. His crown, probably the most elaborate hand-worked crown ever made, was finished in 1602 and is covered with the finest chasing: low-relief scenes of Rudolph himself receiving the crown of the Holy Roman Empire in Frankfurt Cathedral; riding on the hill at Pressburg (Bratislava) after his Hungarian coronation, and then going in procession to the Hradčany after his Bohemian coronation; finally, inevitably, a scene of a ferocious battle—the Hapsburgs defeating the Turkish infidel. Rudolph's successors wore the crown as emperors of the Holy Roman Empire, though for actual coronations the tenth-century 'crown of Charlemagne' was preferred. In 1804 Austria becoming itself an Empire, Emperor Franz I chose this as the official crown.

Also on show at the Vienna Treasury is work commissioned by Rudolph's successor Matthias—official robes encrusted with jewelled embroideries, redolent with history. Finally, there are the nineteenth-century relics of Napoleon and his wife Marie-Louise, daughter of the Emperor Franz I. Nowhere else is there so long a span of history on show with so wide a European spread. The treasures are supreme examples of work from the greatest courts over a period of nearly a thousand years.

MOSCOW

There are now two great jewelry collections in Moscow. The first, an organic growth which has been there for centuries, is known as the Kremlin Armoury, jammed with an extraordinary mixture, including arms and armour; ceremonial coaches, many of them given by the sovereigns of Europe; thrones of ivory and ebony, gold and stones, made for Ivan the Terrible, Boris Godunov, Michael Feodorovich, Peter I and his brother, Ivan; table silver such as the enormous pieces given by Queen Elizabeth I of England, to imply that her small country was as big as her plate, and thus gain favours for her new Muscovy Company; ikons, often enamelled with perforated silver frames. Then there are the souvenirs, nineteenth- and twentieth-century, of the Romanov dynasty, artistic trivia which hint at their awful detachment from reality.

Left *Perhaps the world's most
evocative piece of gold : the crown
of the Holy Roman Emperors. 10th
century, Ottonian, in gold, stones
and enamel; for centuries the
symbol of the greatest worldly
power. Perhaps made for the
coronation of Otto the Great in
Rome in AD 962. Gold and stones,
frequently altered. Perhaps made
at the Abbey of Reichenau.
Height: 6.1 inches. Weltliche
Schatzkammer, Vienna*

Right *Crown of the Holy Roman
Emperor Rudolph II; an obsessive
patron of goldsmiths' work and
having an outlook that was very
international even in those
international times, he collected at
Prague some of the best craftsmen
from many European countries.
Used at many coronations, the
crown, made in Prague c. 1602,
shows great technical virtuosity.
Height: 11.2 inches. Weltliche
Schatzkammer, Vienna*

The intermingled jewels include a rich inheritance from old Byzantium, and a splendid group of crowns. The weight of it all may be guessed from the experience of Ivan the Terrible (1530–84): fearing a second assault from Khan Devlet Girai in 1572, he was forced to move to Novgorod; his two baggage trains containing his treasures consisted of an almost endless 450 sleighs.

The grand dukes had built a permanent home—the court treasury—inside the Kremlin in 1484–5; it was destroyed by fire with some of its contents in 1547, then rebuilt with workshops incorporated for harness makers, bedmakers, armourers, saddlers, seamstresses and gold-embroiderers. The silver workers became a separate unit and so, in 1624, did the goldsmiths. By the late seventeenth century, this treasury was almost like an art academy, with craftsmen coming from all over Russia to study there. In 1711 Peter the Great moved many craftsmen to his new St Petersburg, where he started his extraordinary public museum of curiosities. In 1812 it acquired its new building just in time to evacuate to Nizhni Novgorod to escape Napoleon, soon after going on to Moscow. After the 1917 Bolshevik revolution, the armoury instead of being the tsars' private stock of goodies, which they were always free to give away or melt, became the public museum which it still is today.

Most interesting, because most Russian, are the crowns. They accompany the coronation robes of gold and silver brocade, mostly eighteenth- and nineteenth-century, made not only in the Kremlin, but in private workshops of princes, boyars and monasteries. Oldest is the fur and filigree gold 'crown of Monomachus', probably an oriental piece of about 1300, supposed to have been given by the Byzantine Emperor Constantine Monomachus to his grandson Prince Vladimir Monomachus of Kiev. With it is Ivan the Terrible's sixteenth-century golden crown, the cap of Kazan, the early seventeenth-century insignia of Tsar Michael Feodorovich; then in the late seventeenth century the progression from fur to gold culminates with diamonds in the late seventeenth-century diamond encrusted crowns of Peter I and his brother Ivan.

Moscow's second great jewelry offering is the new USSR Diamond Fund, opened in honour of the fiftieth anniversary of Soviet power, in a modern, subterranean display, next to the ancient armoury. The least beautiful part is the jewelry made in recent years. Then there are the old stones, the original Diamond Fund established officially by Lenin in 1922, mostly large diamonds from Yakutia, and gold and platinum nuggets, like the 'Big Triangle' found in the Ural mountains in 1842. The general glitter is a powerful attraction for the luxury-starved Soviet people, but to most visitors the height of the collection is the eighteenth-century crown jewelry of Catherine the Great, and pieces associated with her court, all brought to Moscow from the Hermitage Museum in Leningrad in 1968.

This is really a woman's collection—Russia was ruled for seventy-one years by tsarinas, beginning with the Lithuanian ex-chambermaid, Peter the Great's rollicking widow, Catherine I, who succeeded to the throne for two years in 1725. The collection is a monument not so much to her, nor to Anna whose crown is in the armoury, but to Catherine the Great (1729–96). Her jewels are a magnificent tribute to the selfish vanity of one woman. She got herself crowned not in the nave, but in the inner choir of Moscow cathedral, a place hitherto forbidden to women. She wore her crown on her head, whereas previous tsars had seen their crowns carried before them. It was she who acquired nearly half the colossal Russian collection of crown jewels. Indeed, she got so much that her jewels for two centuries were housed not in the Kremlin Museum in Moscow with the other tsars', but separately in the Hermitage Museum in Leningrad. This was once called the Winter Palace, and it was here that Peter the Great had started his own considerable hoard in the 'Brilliant Room'. Some of his pieces are now in Moscow, some dispersed: it is fitting that it should eventually have been Catherine who monopolized the place.

She bought with rapacity and determination. The famous 'Moon of Mountains' diamond was typical: once the property of Nadir Shah the great Persian looter, Catherine saw and coveted the stone when an Armenian dealer offered it to her. But it was too expensive. So she sent her Count Pania to teach the Armenian the extravagant ways of dissolution which led him, of course, into hideous debt. She then ordered this

A Turkish masterpiece: crown, in gold with dazzling coloured enamels, rubies, turquoise, pearls and enamels, of Stephan Bocskay, the Grand Duke of Siebenbürgen, given by Sultan Ahmed I in 1605 (the Turkish armies were beaten back from Vienna in 1683). Height: 9.2 inches. Weltliche Schatzkammer, Vienna

Armenian to pay up and forbade him to leave the country until he was solvent. Naturally her scheme was for him to have to sell the stone, not at his price but at hers. She had learned the convenience of having a population of serfs—despite her occasional liberal speeches, she did nothing to relieve the appalling state of the Russian peasants.

The great Orlov diamond was another expensive historical token. Originally 300 carat weight, subsequently cut down to 190 carats, it is now in the Russian imperial sceptre in the Moscow Diamond Fund. Three hundred and sixty years ago it was probably owned by Shah Jehan, builder of the Taj Mahal, and known after him as the 'Great Moghul'. It was stolen by the same Nadir Shah and became known in Persia as the 'Sea of Light'. Then it turned up in the Bank of Amsterdam, was bought by another Armenian dealer, and sold in 1773 to Count Gregory Orlov, one of Catherine's first ministers.

To Potemkin, who for seventeen years until his death in 1791 was her steady paramour and sound adviser, she gave a famous black pearl, the 'Azra'. He in turn gave it to his niece, Princess Tatania Yusupov, from whose family it eventually emerged in the 1935 Russian exhibition in London. Among the many stones Catherine discovered from the Urals was a huge amethyst, 'gleaming by night like red fire'. She responded to the romance of stones: it is no chance that the pendant portrait of her which Potemkin used to carry was surrounded by diamonds.

The richest of all the surviving crowns of Europe is the splendid Russian imperial crown. Commissioned by Catherine for her coronation in 1762 it was not ready in time. One wonders how the lady took the news. The court jeweler, Jeremy Pauzier from Geneva, anyway lived to tell his tale. He arrived in Moscow with six assistants a week before the coronation, and picked out

the biggest stones from existing jewels so that the empress would feel his crown worthy of keeping unchanged during her life. He wrote, 'in spite of my greatest care to make the crown as light as possible by using only the strictly necessary materials to fasten the stones, it yet proved to weigh five pounds'; but he had underestimated Catherine's waywardness: of course she had to change the piece, removing the stones and substituting diamonds, of which she squeezed in no less than 4,936. The huge spinel on top, once the property of the Chinese Emperor Kang Ksi, gave contrast to the dazzle. And so it now remains, one of no less than eleven Russian royal crowns in the treasuries of Moscow.

Jewels played a big part in Russian aristocratic life. When Potemkin took his court to Bender (and Catherine called it condescendingly a *basse cour*) it included six hundred servants, two hundred musicians, a hundred embroiderers, and no less than twenty jewelers. In the

1755 conspiracy, it was the jeweler Bernardi who acted as vital intermediary, and who was subsequently arrested. Earlier, in 1697, when the Tsar Peter set off on his epic European journey, he took with him among his retinue two goldsmiths.

The last public occasion on which the imperial crown was used was the opening of the Duma by the tsar in 1906. It was in 1913 that Agathon Fabergé persuaded the tsar that the jewels needed repair and cataloguing; but the job was only just begun. During the Revolution, Agathon was twice arrested; on release Trotsky invited him to Moscow, but he excused himself on health grounds twice. The third time, at three in the morning, two Red soldiers brought Agathon a friendly note from Trotsky. Whether or not it was the friendliness of the soldiers that proved irresistible, Agathon agreed to catalogue the jewels on condition that he was comfortably housed. In 1922 the jewels were shown to a suspicious world in Moscow in the Hall of Columns of the Trade Union Centre, to prove that the Bolsheviks had preserved their treasures, whatever they had done to their country. But in 1927 their resolve faltered with the need for foreign currency, and some of the more ordinary jewels were sold at Christie's. When Greta Garbo saw them in London for that sale in the film *Ninotchka*, she called them 'the tears of all Russia'. The Moscow displays do indeed proclaim a story of frightening brutality and turbulence.

PARIS AND MADRID

On the 15 June 1530 King Francis I of France made his royal jewels state crown property. The queen made her state entry into Bordeaux a fortnight later, and received from him these crown jewels, one of Europe's first inalienable state reserves, an example subsequently widely followed. Francis, of course, kept many pieces for himself, but the collection grew steadily from then, with gifts and bequests by Mazarin, Louis XIV (the Blue Diamond), Louis XV (the Regent Diamond), until this became a précis of French history. Louis XIV established the jewels' present home in the Galerie d'Apollon in the Louvre, and although most of the jewels were dispersed by the Revolution, much of his carved, stone tableware is still there

today. So is Louis XV's crown, alas without its stones; Napoleon's crown; and another, very different, given by St Louis to the Dominican Friary at Liège in 1257, which the gallery acquired in 1947, following its post-Revolution tour to Parma and then to Saxony. There, too, is the Order of the Holy Spirit Cross, commissioned by Louis XV as a copy of Louis XIV's bigger version, acquired by the Louvre in 1951; and Charles X's diamond coronation sword, made mostly from stones preserved in the state treasury by Napoleon—the jeweler was Frédéric Bapst. Last and most sumptuous is the 'reliquary brooch' made by Alfred Bapst in 1855 for the Empress Eugénie, using two flat yellow diamonds from among the eighteen bequeathed by Cardinal Mazarin on his death bed.

In 1791 the collection, already mostly of carved stone rather than jewels, was valued for the National Assembly; many jewels seem to have vanished, but most of the carved stone survived, an interesting example, just as with the Bolsheviks in Russia, of radical revolutionaries respecting their country's aristocratic past.

Almost more evocative, though much smaller and less spectacular, is the Merovingian treasure found in 1653 at Tournai in the tomb of Childeric I. Most of it was stolen in 1804, the remains being in the Cabinet of Medals today in the Bibliothèque Nationale. For Louis XIV these pieces represented the very beginnings of France, and they were one of his favourites in the King's Cabinet at Versailles.

To complete the ancestral picture, it is necessary to visit the Prado Museum in Madrid, to which Louis XIV's son, the Grand Dauphin, father of Philip V of Spain, took some of the hard stone and glass. The Dauphin died in 1711 and Louis XIV decreed that the Dauphin's treasure should remain in Spain, as if the Dauphin had been a private citizen. Napoleon got them back to Paris and some were damaged on their return in 1815. This sumptuous group of strange decorative fantasies remains today in the Prado to remind visitors of the dynastic snakes and ladders which helped to give Europe its present shape.

FLORENCE

Visitors to Florence seldom penetrate beyond the fine art and architecture.

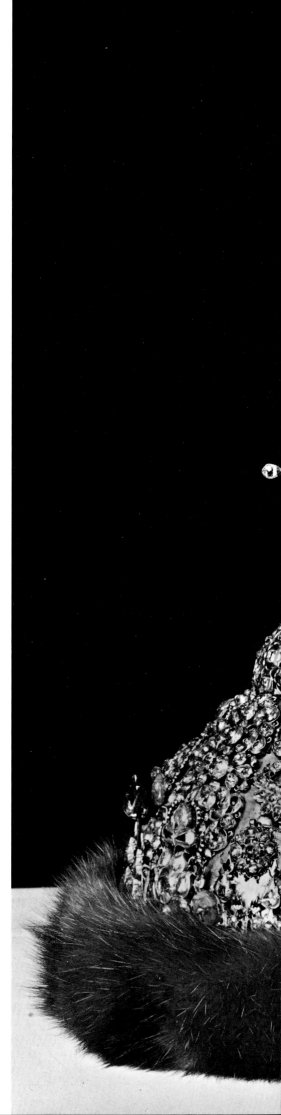

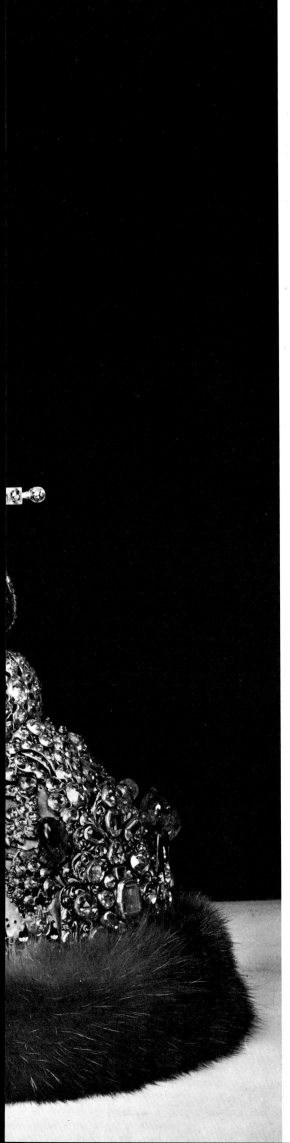

The purity of their taste today is confirmed by that of the Italian Renaissance princes: during the miraculous fifteenth century, when it seemed that man could again, as in ancient Greece, do anything he wished, and be the master of his destiny, jewels seem to have been no more than an unimportant accessory (much the same as they were to the Greeks).

On the ground floor of the Pitti Palace is the Museo degli Argenti, literally the Silver Museum; it is the treasury of the Medici family and of the later Austrian Grand Dukes of Tuscany, and it is housed in sixteenth- and seventeenth-century rooms of appropriate magnificence. But the contents are surprising and perhaps a little disappointing.

The fact is that the best patrons at the best period of the Italian Renaissance were not especially keen on jewels. The first Medici bankers, for instance, instead of jewels collected all sorts of other art for their pleasure: splendid tableware for special occasions and precious religious objects. Lorenzo il Magnifico loved antique stone carvings and the vases he bought are the greatest asset of the treasury today—many were mounted by his own goldsmiths. Luckily some escaped the looting of the Medici Palace in 1494. But, partly perhaps because of that uprising, mainly because rich Florentines lived rather frugal private lives, very little jewelry from that early time is now preserved, either in Florence or anywhere else.

The Medici were restored in 1530 and the treasury developed steadily from then till Napoleon's time. Cosimo I came into power in 1537, and was grand duke from 1569; the present collection is as much a monument to him as to anyone. He himself moved to the Palazzo Vecchio with his treasury; his son Francesco I established a small room—the *Studiolo*—in the Uffizi, decorated by Vasari for the best pieces; he actually practised craft work himself, and with his brother Ferdinando I set up the *Botteghe Granducali*—which by the 1580s was on the first floor of the Uffizi; on the top floor there the *Tribuna* was built, like the *Studiolo* to provide a setting for the most exquisite work, and it is still there today.

Christine of Lorraine, Catherine de' Medici's favourite granddaughter, married Ferdinand I in 1589, bringing from France some of the carved crystal and stone tableware. Benefactions continued

Above *Lorenzo de' Medici of fifteenth-century Florence was such a creative collector that he helped to start the Renaissance. He loved stones and had them engraved 'Lor Med', like this agate cameo of Athene (showing in her shield the Medusa head given her by Perseus). The gold ring setting dates from the eighteenth century.*

Left *The Kremlin Armoury in Moscow contains relics of most of the famous tsars. This crown was made in 1682–9 in the Russian style, which evolved from a fur hat.*

through the centuries, helped by the Medici inheritance procedure: the main estate of each prince went to the next grand duke, not to his private estate. The last Medici, Anna Maria Ludovica, married the Elector Palatine, bringing from his Düsseldorf home many German Renaissance jewels, probably the bulk of the present collection, possibly even the beautiful golden bowl with the monogram D H, which may have been falsely identified with France, Diane de Poitiers and her lover Henry II. Anyway, Anna left the whole of her treasury to the city of Florence when she died in 1743.

The Hapsburgs acquired Florence when the Austrian Empress Maria Theresa's husband had to exchange his own Lorraine for Tuscany in the mid-eighteenth century. By this time most of the precious gold and silver objects were kept privately in the Pitti Palace, the Uffizi display concentrating on objects of decorative value. In 1799 Napoleon's armies arrived. They took many of the Medici pictures to Paris, whence they were retrieved in 1810 and 1814, but they looted the gold and silver for melting in Paris, and it vanished. Mrs Piacenti, the present director, laments the difference between the 1783 and 1793 inventories and those of 1800 and 1805. Only the gems and carved crystal escaped the French, and they are still there for us to enjoy today.

In 1814 Ferdinand III (who had inherited the secularized principality of Salzburg in 1801, and in 1805 the former archbishopric at Würzburg) returned to Florence with that city's second fine German benefaction: those of the treasures, and they were many, which he had not himself melted down from those great old cities. The Bourbons succeeded the Hapsburgs as rulers of Florence in the nineteenth century. The Austrian grand dukes, when they needed money, melted huge table pieces from the Pitti Palace and their civil servants surprisingly recorded it. The kings of Savoy inherited the collections and the state in 1865, but it was only after 1918 that the present Pitti Palace Treasury was started.

Despite the sentimental hopes of Medici admirers, the Museo degli Argenti is now little more than its name— a museum of silver containing fantastic table ornaments in silver, carved ivory, crystal and hard stone, many of them made in Germany. The most delightful exhibit is the large crystal casket, perhaps used to contain jewels, carved by the greatest man in this field, and one of the earliest, Valerio Belli of Vicenza; it is called the *Cassetta dei Belli*. It was made in 1532 for Pope Clement VII to give to Francis I when Francis I's son (later Henry II) married Catherine de' Medici, returned to Italy as part of the dowry of Christine of Lorraine, and probably given in 1626 to the Grand Duke Ferdinand II by his grandmother, the dowager duchess. The box in its wanderings is a symbol of the whole museum, an ideal spot for the study of the backwater diplomacy of the minor dynasties of Europe.

LONDON

The British crown jewels incorporate the longest history of all, though not, alas, the oldest metalwork. The early regalia were the relics of St Edward (Edward the Confessor, d. 1066) kept by the monks at Westminster Abbey. From being possessors of relics, the monks exercised an early takeover bid and, in the twelfth century, made themselves managers of the coronation: the coronation could not be effective without the relics and, to use the relics, one had to acknowledge the monks' power. Hence the prominence of Westminster Abbey.

Oliver Cromwell no doubt had an eye on the $289,768\frac{7}{8}$ ounces of plate and jewels surrendered by the Church to Henry VIII. He was aware of Henry VIII's prodigious acquisitions and inheritances, further embellished by the extraordinary Queen Elizabeth. In 1642 King Charles I left London, and lost control of his Jewel House at Westminster; his wife Henrietta Maria, when she went to France in 1644, took only some of the royal jewels. The Commonwealth Parliament under Cromwell liquidated the rest, melting most of it down into coin because of their Puritan belief that goldsmiths' work represented immoral vanity. The Clerk of the Jewel House and the Dean of Westminster both finally were forced to surrender their charge, and the regalia were 'totallie broken and defaced'.

Charles II was crowned on 23 April 1661, his new regalia being made, so far as we know, by Sir Robert Vyner in greate haste for the occasion. So the Tower of London collection today is mostly of Charles II character, and, being an impetuous production, of un-

Gold crown, probably cast and repoussé, height: 9.8 inches. Thraco-Getian of the pre-Roman period, showing the wonderful vigour of the tribal animal style. Discovered in 1931 at Cotzofanechti, 5th century BC. National Museum of Antiquities, Bucharest

inspiring quality. There were further additions—and alarums: for example, in 1815 a woman poked her hands through the iron grill of the regalia cage in the Jewel House, and wrenched the arches of the state crown apart. Today, many of the great kings and queens of England are represented (Mary of Modena's crown is, however, in the London Museum): what they add up to, these Stuarts', Hanoverians' and Windsors' jewels are conventional metalwork, lots of sentiment, and absolutely fabulous stones and diamonds, the biggest and best in the world.

In the cross on top of the orb of St Edward's crown is a sapphire, rose cut, so it must have been altered at least as late as the sixteenth century; the original stone is said to have been taken by the Abbot of Westminster in 1269 from St Edward's finger ring on the second occasion that his body was moved. It was supposed to have the power of curing the cramp.

Next oldest is the Black Prince's ruby, in fact a very large spinel, uncut, said to have been taken by the Black Prince from the King of France at the battle of Crecy in 1346, and worn thereafter as a jewel in his breastplate. Another tradition says it was given to the same Black Prince by King Peter the Cruel of Castile after the battle of Najara in 1367, and later worn by Henry v in his helmet at the battle of Agincourt in 1415. Perhaps King Peter did in fact, according to a further embellishment, murder the King of Granada to get his jewels, among which was his ruby. Peter then gave it to the Black Prince to thank him for his victory at Najara. The huge stone is said, finally, to have been worn by Richard iii at the battle of Bosworth in 1485. It is pierced through the top in the eastern manner. Whatever the truth, the stone is one of the few legendary specimens in London not to have been recut in modern times.

Under the arches of the Imperial crown are four pearls which may have been Queen Elizabeth i's earrings. The Stuart sapphire was probably worn by James ii, and crossed the Channel several times; it was seen by Greville (dining with the king at Devonshire House) in 1821, being worn by Lady Conyngham, and later found its way back into Queen Victoria's possession. The Timur ruby, or 'Khiraj-i-alam'—'tribute to the world'—associated with Tamberlaine and with Nadir Shah, was a present from the Lahore Treasury given to the queen in 1851 by the East India Company. The Kohinur diamond has a history going back 500 years: when the first Moghul Emperor Babur defeated the Rajah of Gwalior in 1526, this diamond was part of the booty and was valued at half the daily cost of running the world. The Persian marauder Nadir Shah took the stone back from India to Persia. By inheritance it returned to the Moghul treasury at Lahore, until taken by the East India Company in 1849 during the Sikh war. They, in 1850, gave it to Queen Victoria who had it cut as a brilliant, reducing it from 186 to 106 carat weight: the 'Mountain of Light' thus lost its ancient appearance in exchange for a better colour.

Discovered in 1905, the Cullinan diamond is one of the largest brilliants in the world. Captain Wells found it at the Premier mine near Pretoria; it was named after Sir T. M. Cullinan, Chairman of the Premier Diamond Company. As a peace and loyalty gesture after the Boer war, it was given to the King of England by the Government of Transvaal, being divided to its present two 'Stars of Africa' and other smaller stones, by the Amsterdam cutter, J. Asscher.

These rather gaudy pleasures have been on public show in the Tower of London since the seventeenth century. In 1970, after several adjustments, they came to rest in their present fine, vaulted room deep in the medieval masonry; with detailing designed by the young architect Alan Irvine, these great stones and silver gilt table plate are shown and lit to their best advantage. They have become one of the great tourist attractions of Europe.

TEHRAN

The crown jewels of Iran are also the country's currency reserve: the Fort Knox or New York Federal Reserve Bank of the ancient kingdom of Persia. How sensible to buttress one's coins and bank notes not with gold bars which nobody can see or enjoy, but with objects of fantasy and beauty to delight the public!

These Persian jewels were seen by several wanderers over the centuries: George Mainwaring, an English traveller, described the throne of the greatest builder and art patron in Persia, Shah Abbas (1587–1629): 'the King's chair of estate . . . [was] of silver plate set with turkies [turquoises] and rubies very thick, and six great diamonds which did shew like stars, the seat being of rich scarlet embroidered with pearl, and the multitude of lamps hanging about it were innumerable'. Tavernier and Chardin, the two jewelers who traded with India, both recorded their impressions. But most of the early treasure was lost in wars and revolution. Nadir Shah brought back from India in 1739, booty which took a hundred labourers fifteen days to melt down into ingots for transport. 5,000 chests were filled with gold rupees and 8,000 with silver, not counting the precious stones. Jonas Hanway, an English businessman, describes Nadir Shah's horse furniture in 1744:

He had four complete sets, one mounted with pearls, another with rubies, a third with emeralds, and the last with diamonds, most of which were so prodigious a size as hardly to merit belief; for many of them appeared as big as a pigeon's egg. I could not but regard them with wonder, not more for their immense value, than for the barbarous taste in which they were set; for some of them did not appear to have any art at all bestowed on them.

Napoleon's emissary, Pierre-Amédée Jaubert, describes the Shah at a levée in 1806:

The throne was supported on several marble columns seven to eight feet high. Four other columns covered with gold and enamelled plaques were placed above the former and supported a canopy. Thousands of diamonds, rubies, emeralds and sapphires sparkled from all sides. A sun, formed by a very large number of great diamonds, gleamed behind the shah, who was seated, his back supported by a cushion of white satin embroidered with pearls, dressed in a robe of the same material over which fell the long beard of this prince. Cuffs formed of a fabric of pearls bordered with rubies and sprinkled with roses or coloured stones extended almost to his elbows. The shoulders and half the surface of the robe were covered with a similar fabric. Two great circular bracelets, worked in precious stones, ornament the upper part of each arm. The diamond to which the Persians give the name Kouhi-Nour (mountain of light) was set in the middle of one of these bracelets; and that which they call Deryai-Nour (ocean of light) embellished the other. . . . Instead of a turban, the shah wore a sort of tiara of which a fabric of pearls, sprinkled with rubies and emeralds, formed the border. An aigrette of gems was placed on the front of this headdress, and above it rose three heron plumes. A rope of matched pearls as large as hazel-nuts, and of the finest water it would be possible to see, crossed over his breast and passed twice around his body. A dagger embellished with gems was stuck into a girdle decorated with fine emeralds from which was hung a sabre entirely covered with pearls and rubies.

Lord Curzon characteristically concealed his passion for antiques and recorded rather more coldly the scene in the Golestan Palace in 1889:

Here are the enamelled and bejewelled arms of the great Sefavi kings, here the swords of Timur, Shah Ismail and Agha Mohammad Shah, here the magnificent Abbas' coat of mail. A square glass case contains a vast heap of pearls, four or five inches deep. . . . At the upper end of the room, beneath glass cases, are a number of royal crowns, dating from the Sefavean days to modern times, prominent among them being the mighty head piece, pearl-bedecked, and with flashing jika or aigrette of diamonds in front, which is worn by the King at No Ruz [The Persian New Year] . . . Here, too, is a superb tiara, manufactured by order of the present Shah, in Paris. The number of jewelled swords, scabbards, epaulettes, and cups, vases, boxes and kalians, is enormous.

The jewels were hardly ever seen by anyone, however, until 1960 when the present huge cave was opened in the basement of the National Bank. A team from the Royal Ontario Museum, V. B. Meen and A. D. Tushingham, in their admirable catalogue, found they could not trace the history of many pieces before Nadir Shah—that is, for longer than two hundred years—and had the usual difficulty with oriental art that it remains almost the same over the centuries, not striving for constant novelty as in the west. Outstanding are the plates piled high with huge diamonds, emeralds and rubies, the dozens of big diadems and tiaras, and the three royal crowns. Van Cleef and Arpels of Paris made the newest, and it caused Pierre Arpels to visit Tehran no less than fifty-six times during the 1960s—such detailed concern is a good indication of the significance of the job. For unexpectedness, this big room designed by Boucheron of Paris has no peer. For those who like to dream of history without bothering with the facts, it is perfection.

EUROPE, smaller displays

Any student of jewelry has to decide whether to search for it in its original setting where he will get the atmosphere but not the detail, or to go to a modern display which usually has no period

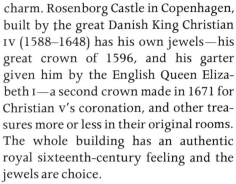

charm. Rosenborg Castle in Copenhagen, built by the great Danish King Christian IV (1588–1648) has his own jewels—his great crown of 1596, and his garter given him by the English Queen Elizabeth I—a second crown made in 1671 for Christian v's coronation, and other treasures more or less in their original rooms. The whole building has an authentic royal sixteenth-century feeling and the jewels are choice.

The Stockholm crown jewels in the great classical palace there, built in the late seventeenth century by the French architect, Tessin, were put on public view for the first time only in 1970, before then having been jealously guarded in a bank. Here again, the palace still contains some of the personal treasures of the royal family. Gustavus Adolphus (ruled 1611–32), for instance, is represented by a gift, from the city of Nuremberg which he entered in 1632, of huge drinking globes: one of Hercules carrying the world, the other of Atlas carrying the celestial sphere, made by the famous Nuremberg smiths, Christoph Jamnitzer and Jeremias Ritter. Alas, the art cabinet made by Philip Hainhofer of Augsburg (who cornered the specialized market for choosing royal treasures and then housing them in exquisite miniature chests of drawers), which was given to Gustavus by the city of Augsburg also in 1632, subsequently passed to Uppsala University, and so is now separated from its brother piece. Queen Christina assembled in Stockholm the loot taken by her armies under General Königsmarck in Prague Castle in 1648. Most beautiful are the three royal crowns, a fascinating study in showmanship.

Many museums are turning into treasuries, as their magpie instincts fructify, but they will never have the old personal quality. One which has, is the superb Monza Cathedral treasury near Milan: there are the personal jewels given by Theodelinda, sixth-century queen of the Lombards. Some of these glowing fantasies are carved in stone above the cathedral west porch, a romanesque record, clearly recognizable, of the magpie collector queen surveying her hoard around her. Among the crosses and bible covers and strange model animals is the iron crown of the Lombards, whose iron strengthening ring may be one of the nails from the 'True Cross'. Used from earliest times to crown the kings of Italy, wearers include the German Emperor Frederick Barbarossa

in 1155 at Pavia, Charles v in 1530, Napoleon in 1805 in Milan, and Ferdinand I in 1838. Frederick II of Sicily was crowned in Palermo Cathedral in 1198; his marvellous jewels are still there.

At Naples is the greatest assembly of Roman archaeology, housed in the National Museum. It contains many jewels from Pompeii and Herculaneum, and some fine Hellenistic pieces. It was started by the Bourbon King Charles III under pressure from his wife Maria Amalia Cristina of Saxony. In 1731 he formed his inheritance from his mother, Elizabeth Farnese, into a museum of antiquities, first in the royal palace of Portici, then in the new Capodimonte Palace. In the restoration in 1816, having moved to Naples university, the collection was re-named Real Museo Borbonico. In 1817 the Bourbons bought Cardinal Stephen Borgia's collection, with much excavated material from Velletri; in 1838 the Ficco collection; and thereafter the fruits of regular later excavations. From 1816 to 1943 the collection remained static; then, for better war-time safety, it went to Monte Cassino Abbey; the Hermann Goering division stole it first to Berlin, then for safe keeping to the salt-mines at Alt Aussee. In 1947 it was restored to Italy, and after a year in Rome re-installed in its noble old sixteenth-century home.

The National Museum in Athens has by far the best Mycenaean collection and, new in 1972, one of the best classical Greek collections too—until lately privately owned by the Stathatos family. The Benaki Museum at Athens probably has the best classical Greek jewels. At Heraklion, Crete, is the surprisingly sophisticated Minoan work. The National Museum at Taranto contains the strange, enormous, poetic fantasies of the rich Hellenistic colony there, while in Rome's Villa Giulia and the Archaeological Museum at Florence, one can see the world's best Etruscan pieces. Other glories are at Rome's Alto Medioevo and Vatican museums.

At Berlin and Hamburg there are good ancient jewels; and in the Munich National Museum of Bavaria, interesting, rather ordinary, medieval pieces with four aristocratic jewel chests. The Cologne Museum and the German National Museum at Nuremberg have medieval work, as has Essen Cathedral; so, wonderfully, has Aachen Cathedral, with the real feel of Charlemagne's time.

Mainz shows Frankish tribal pins and one of Empress Gisela's jewels, worn at her wedding to Conrad II in Rome in 1027, found in a cellar in 1880, and mostly lost in Berlin before 1945. At Pforzheim, the German jewelry factory centre today, there is a rather good ancient collection with some light Renaissance pieces, and one of the best modern groups anywhere, housed by the architect, Lehmbruck. In Switzerland the Berne Historical Museum and the Basle City Museum have good Alemannic barbarian hoards; one of the greatest early collections of gold plate, much of it seventh- and eighth-century AD, is at the abbey of St Maurice d'Agaune. Later pieces are at Anechs church, Bavaria. Vienna's Kunsthistorisches Museum has a fine range of high Renaissance pieces and Roman stone carving. Memorable are the 'Gemma Augustea' and other great classical cameos, the Renaissance heads of Charles V, and the Bulgarian gold. Despite the continual rape of

Poland—the Polish crown jewels were stolen by the Prussians as early as 1786—a fine historic jewelry display remains at Wawel Castle. Cracow shows the lovely order of the White Eagle, made in Saxon Dresden, given by Stanislas, the last king of Poland, to Potemkin in Russia, and finally bought by a Polish count; a fine symbol of the international nature of eighteenth-century aristocracy. Prague, Brno, Bucharest and Budapest have Dark Age tribal work. At the Hermitage in Leningrad is the world's best survey of ancient Greek and Scythian gold.

At Amsterdam's Rijksmuseum is a treasure room with some good Renaissance pieces. At Madrid, in the Archaeological Museum, is some of the most exciting barbaric jewelry—six dangling votive crowns from the seventh-century AD Visigothic Guarrazar treasure, found near Toledo; here also is the only big Phoenician treasure of the seventh century BC—a huge gold diadem band and other pieces found at Aliseda, sur-

prisingly delicate in finish for a people supposed to be artistically sterile. The later Javea treasure of similar size and type, from the pre-Roman Iberian period, makes an intriguing comparison in barbaric decorum. Three more Guarrazar silver crowns are at the Cluny Museum, Paris, with some other important Merovingian pieces. At the Cabinet des Médailles in the Bibliothèque Nationale are the ex-royal collections of cameos and the few surviving relics of the first French King, Childeric. At the Musée des Arts Décoratifs there is good middle-class work, especially of the eighteenth and nineteenth centuries and the art nouveau period; and in the Louvre, apart from the crown jewels, there are some Renaissance pieces, and seemingly endless rows of Louis XV gold boxes.

Dublin's National Museum is unique and thrilling: a whole room, the best in the world, of heavy, beaten prehistoric gold torcs and fibulae, with the finest early Christian group, too. The Scottish crown jewels deep in Edinburgh Castle, include Robert the Bruce's crown partly of the fourteenth century, lost from 1707 until 1818, in store and on public view there for the past 150 years. St Ninian's jewels are at the Edinburgh National Museum of Antiquities. The Fitzwilliam Museum, Cambridge, has choice watches; so has the Ashmolean Museum, Oxford, with some of Sir Arthur Evans' discoveries from Knossos, Crete.

But the richest all-round collections are probably in London. The British Museum is particularly strong with classical antiquity (the fruits of countless archaeological forays in the east) and Renaissance pieces. The Victoria and Albert Museum, partly owing to gifts from the great jewelry scholar Joan Evans, has a well-balanced survey, emphasizing the Renaissance and Georgian times, and including the best

Spanish group anywhere. Thanks to the British Raj in India, this is about the only place outside India where one can see good Moghul pieces. At Goldsmiths' Hall is the world's biggest collection of modern jewels, many of them foreign.

BEYOND EUROPE, smaller displays

At the Metropolitan Museum, New York, the few Egyptian and Renaissance pieces are outstanding, with good small finds of Greek work from Karavas in Cyprus and from Vrap near Durrës. The Boston Museum of Fine Art has noble Greek pieces. Toledo, Cleveland, and the Walters Art Gallery, Baltimore, have strong Renaissance sections. At the Washington National Gallery are some of the biggest and best Renaissance

jewels anywhere. In the new Anthropological Museum in Mexico City are some early stone pieces, but the wonderful gold from Monte Alban is at nearby Oaxaca. At Bogota are more than 10,000 pre-Columbian pieces, by far the best spread anywhere, beautifully shown in the new gold museum. At Lima in four great underground rooms in the garden of Señor Mujica Gallo, is his private collection of old Peruvian gold.

The Delhi National Museum has fine Moghul work. Salar Jung, the Prime Minister of Hyderabad for much of the twentieth century, bequeathed his very varied collection to his state. The new museum there, which bears his name, shows probably the richest collection of inlaid Moghul stone work anywhere; as a whole it probably gives the best idea surviving of the extraordinary mixture of good and bad, of

Crowns from Guarrazar near Toledo, for hanging over a votive shrine rather than for wearing. Left to right Crown of the Visigothic King Recesvinth (AD 653–72), gold and stones, with another silver crown, Archaeological Museum, Madrid; two silver crowns from the Cluny Museum, Paris

Indian, oriental and western taste, which made up the private fortunes of the Indian princes. At the new museum in Karachi there are the breath-taking pieces from Taxila of Hellenistic date, and, thousands of years earlier, from Mohenjo Daro.

The marvellous Tokyo National Museum has very little jewelry because jewels have only recently displaced armour and embroidery as dress embellishments in Japan; but there are exciting gold crown decorations there of c. 1000 BC from Gilan in Iran; and, from Japan's old adversary Korea, fantastic tiny crowns excavated at Yangsan and Changnyon. At the Taiwan National Museum in Formosa are the few jewels from the Peking Imperial Treasure, quite unknown in the west till the Boxer Rebellion of 1900 opened China to foreign observers.

At Beirut are the relics of Byblos, once famous for its papyrus and from which the Bible takes its name. In Ethiopia at Axum, the 3,000-year-old 'capital of the Queen of Sheba', the ancient cathedral of St Mary of Zion contains one of the strangest imaginable groups of gem-encrusted gold crowns: gifts from succeeding emperors right down to the present Haile Selassie. At Ankara's Archaeology Museum are sparse and rather crude Hittite relics. At Tehran's National Museum of Archaeology lie the fruits of Iranian archaeology, the jewelry again being disappointing in relation to the might of the Persian empire. The Iraq Museum, Baghdad, is one of the great glories, beautifully shown, spanning products of the cradle of western civilization, Mesopotamia, over 8,000 years—the Sumerians, Babylonians, Assyrians and especially the Parthians and Sassanians are all there. The Cairo Museum in normal times shows not only Tutankhamen's grave treasures in a special room but an incomparable range of gems spanning perhaps 4,000 years from pre-Dynastic to Ptolemaic times.

Lastly, at Istanbul are two special pleasures: the Archaeology Museum with much to remind us of Troy, and, perhaps architecturally the most beautiful of all, the Topkapi Museum, housed in the old Sultans' Harem, with fine marble traceries, ancient clothes, turbans and armoury, all helping to show how the jewels were worn. This place still pervades the lucky visitor with the spirit of the old conquerors, like Sulei-

man the Magnificent, 'Sultan of the Ottomans, God's Viceroy on Earth, Prince of the Most Happy Constellation, Possessor of Men's Necks . . .' Suleiman, like many of the great art patrons, was ruthless: as a fighter it may have been, if not admirable, at least necessary, to chop off men's heads and cause death to one's enemy; as a princely patron, erecting some of Istanbul's splendid buildings, he certainly helped artists to live. For all their human failings, it is to the patrons who actually commissioned jewels, having them specially made, that we owe our art.

Collectors of antiquities are not consistent either: they are a mixture of knowledge and covetousness, of the owl and the magpie. The founder of the world's biggest museum, the British Museum, stands as a good representative of the breed: Dr Hans Sloane (1660–1753). He was the only man to hold the double distinction of being President of the Royal Society and President of the Royal College of Physicians, both of them exclusive societies only open to men of the highest ability. London's Sloane Square and Sloane Street are reminders of Sloane's financial streak. His friend, Dr William Stukeley (1687–1765), in his commonplace book, gives a touching description of this great man to whom the world of knowledge owes so much:

Sir Hans is an instance of the great power of industry. [He] has had this piece of luck too, that being a Vertuoso has made his fortune which generally ruins others. Indeed the whole business of his life has been a continued series of the greatest vigilance over his own interest, and all the friendships he ever makes are to himself. The same industry has made him perfect master of the knowledge of his immense collection, begun by Mr Charltons gift, carryd on by his own riches and pains and interest, and may be said to be the greatest that ever was a private mans possession, his estate now being excessively great, dos but double his diligence for getting more, tho' he has no male heirs to leave it to and his daughters are very richly marryd. He has no faculty for speaking, either fluently or eloquently, especially before any number of people, and he do's it with great timidity. His most commendable quality is his love for natural learning and the pains he takes to promote it.

The world is in debt to men such as him, founders of the great museums. Without their inspired acquisitiveness, many of the great jewels in history would by now have been squandered, altered, or lost without trace.

Value

Attitudes to jewels developed from a simple love of anything shiny and colourful. Often this also meant a pretty, carved lucky stone as with the Sumerians 5,000 years ago whose tiny duck and animal pendant amulets supposedly had magical powers. Then came the quest for immortality. The Scythians and other central Asian tribes with their beautiful golden beasts, often containing clusters of small animals within the main composition, thought of their jewels as life savers: the more living spirits they carried in model form, the more effectively the jewel sustained life. For the Egyptians and many others, jewels were to smooth the passage into the next life after death, to give the king or chief a good start there. In the Middle Ages one can watch the flowering of the jewel from a clasp to hold the dress together, into a decorative ornament, often still with a saint's relic or a sculptured scene to bring some blessing to the bearer. And then we reach the time of diaries and letters, and can trace the transition between showing off for its own sake and, in recent times, the idea of jewels as deception: paste will do as well as diamonds if nobody can see the difference.

The relationship between seals (possibly the oldest form of jewelry), jewels (which were, of course, normal from very early times) and coins is interesting. The seal in Mesopotamia was used as a lock guaranteeing that clay fastenings on jars and boxes and openings were intact, just as an important wine bottle today will have on its cork the château mark unbroken in sealing wax. Then it was used apparently partly as a lock to keep secrets—it held the face of two clay tablets together, so that the writing could not be seen until the seal was broken. Very often it was just a signature, rolled across the bottom of a list or order to make it authentic and personal. For the Greeks, although seals themselves are not rare, surviving tablets are: perhaps the seals were used as signatures on imported Egyptian paper, more than as dockets or *bullae* on tablets.

Both in Mesopotamia and in Greece, seals tended to bear signs of grandness, implying that the owner was either himself superhuman, or was close to a god who is shown on the seal: for instance, a beautiful circular seal impression on clay, or a docket, perhaps attached to bales of cloth from which the seventh-century BC King Shalmaneser III levied a tax from his nobility at Nimrud, shows the king stabbing in the belly a lion standing rampant before him—hardly a likely human achievement. Assyrian cylinder seals of three thousand years ago often show a man-god, perhaps Gilgamesh, wrestling single-handed with great lions rampant and other beasts. From Mycenae of the thirteenth century BC there is a carved carnelian seal ring, showing a standing man with both arms outstretched. In one hand he grasps the neck of a lion that is standing on its hind legs; in the other, one hind leg of a lion that is balanced on its neck: nothing less than a divine man could have been so large and strong. So the value of seals was to indicate identity and to give security, surely a function similar to that of fabricated jewels, even if not to the earlier, more anonymous beads.

Coins from the seventh century BC may have partly displaced seals. One of the first coins is actually inscribed 'I am the seal of Phanes.' Seals as art became simply jewels; seals as a means of spreading royal or divine prestige, became coins; leaving seals themselves with only part of their original function, namely security, which they retained until the arrival of locks and keys and metal boxes.

The high money value of jewels has become the barrier between them and art. Mineral or geological quality can be scientifically analysed and therefore has a secure permanent value: once established it will always be constant. Artistic genius, on the other hand, seems different to each succeeding generation: art depends on the personal changing whims of fashion. Given the insecurity of life, it is hardly surprising that everyone latches on to stability wherever it

Stone seals were often drilled for wearing as pendants: one of the earliest cylinder seals is shown worn in a carving of c. 2450 BC from Ur. They were signatures, locks, identity cards and talismans, and usually of beautiful shape too. a) Persian cylinder seal in carnelian, with crowned king, perhaps c. 600BC; b) and c) Sassanian chalcedony seals with pilgrim and crowned king, c. AD 300; d) octagonal Assyrian seal in chalcedony, with worshipper, c. 600 BC; e) Parthian seal in jasper, with stars, c. 300 BC; f) probably Sumerian, 4th millennium BC; g) Sassanian chalcedony seal with bull, c. AD 300; h) Anatolian jasper stamp seal with horse, after 1700 BC; i) animal seal, Jemdet Nasr type, in grey stone from Uruk, c. 3000 BC; j) and k) neo-Babylonian, c. 600 BC, agate, with worshippers and with winged sphinx; l) man with staff, perhaps Commagene.

can be found, and where better than in the precious stone? Hence the modern opposition between the stone, which means impersonal miraculous constancy, and the design, which means the waywardness of human desire.

Since the 1929 slump diamonds and the finest stones have gone steadily upwards both in money value and in public esteem. The prices paid for magnificent rare stones have certainly increased much more sharply than those for elaborate art jewels of small mineral worth. The Saragossa Cathedral treasures were bought for about £880 ($2288) by London's Victoria and Albert Museum in 1870. That was one of the few recorded early sales of antique jewelry where the pieces survive intact, to be assessed today against their cost one hundred years ago. In 1935 the same museum bought just one outstanding Renaissance piece—the Canning jewel—for £10,000 ($26,000), whereas a similar pendant fetched only 5600 guineas ($15,288) at Christie's in 1961, and another, £40,000 ($104,000) at Sotheby's in 1971. But there is no very clear evidence here—the situation is confused by the human factor of art.

Because good stones, like postage stamps, ancient coins, or hall-marked silver spoons, can be diagnosed in a factual manner, they tend to dominate the jewelry market, and anything, like an original setting, that obscures the impact of the stone may also obscure its market appeal. Thus the most inspiring designs are usually not the most expensive: big stones lead to dull designs. One cannot claim, however, that precious stones merely represent money and that it is therefore bad taste to wear them. As Dr Johnson said, 'you would not value the finest head if carved upon a carrot'.

Intrinsic value has an obvious psychological lure; jewels are a 'billboard of prosperity, weapon of seduction', according to a recent article in *Art in America*: you cannot have a billboard without glitter and you cannot have seduction without elegance. Precious stones really are desirable, and add to the jewelry mystique. The sadness of much new jewelry, since the precious stone markets developed their present strength in the twentieth century, is that so few people will risk a union of the best materials with their constant value and the most elaborate craftsmanship which may be financially irrelevant. It was not always such a cautious approach.

Shylock in the *Merchant of Venice* is the ideal example of the lover of stones pure and simple. He liked their money value of course—we all do; but he adored Jessica, the owner, to whom he had given his great treasure, a turquoise, and he saw some of her in it. It had become more than mere money. The stone had acquired an overwhelming allegorical appeal for him. It was purity itself, above colour and race, above art and family. When he heard she had sold it in exchange for a mere frivolous monkey, he was horrified: 'Out upon her! Thou torturest me, Tubal. It was my turquoise; I had it of Leah [Shylock's wife] when I was a bachelor. I would not have given it for a wilderness of monkeys.' In *Dorian Grey*, collecting jewelry is even prescribed by Oscar Wilde as a psychiatric remedy: if you are in a fuss, because the world seems out of control, then the advice is, buy some jewels. They, more than anything, represent permanent stability.

Pliny the Elder, in his *Historia Naturalis* (Book XXXVII), investigates the mystical capacity of each stone, to which the ancients attached some importance. These superstitions lasted on into Christian times and still survive today, for instance in Africa and Iran, where the striped agate is used to spot pregnancy. The ancient investigation of the magical properties of stones developed into a sort of science like alchemy, and lapidaries were supposed not only to shape stones, but also to know their uses. The diamond, of course, could do almost anything from winning battles to keeping away ghosts. The sapphire was a symbol of good faith, keeping away poverty, blindness or snake bites; it features in the Bible (St John XXI, 19–20) and in Dante's *Purgatorio* (1–13); the philosopher Conrad von Megenberg rhapsodized in the fourteenth century about the sapphire's resemblance to heaven and the Madonna, and its capacity to revive hope. Perhaps the sapphire played a larger part than its brother, the ruby, in myth because it was much more common. The ruby helped in love, bringing peace and stopping nightmares. The emerald brought riches and fame and, put under the tongue, powers of prophecy; but it cracked in adultery. The amethyst helped wisdom and benevolence, and was a cure for drunkenness. Jasper preserved chastity and helped to stop the nose-bleed. And so on. Eventually stones were expected to work not only magic but medicine too. Lorenzo de' Medici, the great stone lover, had a prescription of powdered diamonds and pearls from his doctor Lazarus of Pavia, before his death in 1492.

Jewels were buried with the dead by most of the ancient civilizations, to provide necessary equipment for the next life. For the Chinese, jewels had a special power of communication: some of the best pieces rattle or jingle to show they are alive. Jade insects laid on appropriate parts of a dead body would ensure their proper functioning later on—a fish laid on an eye would enable the eye eventually to see as well as a fish; a jade cicada on the tongue would ensure the dead person's ability to chatter in heaven. The pi, or round disk, was a universal talisman.

Part of the thrill of stones is their beauty, part is their money value, part their historic associations. But rarity matters too. Human beings like whatever is rare. In the European Renaissance, for example, coconuts and nautilus shells were very strange and rare, so they were treasured, often being fitted with gold or silver mounts so that they could decorate the table. In some South Sea islands today, wood is very rare, so it is considered the best possible omen in life to be able to wear a wooden jewel. Similarly, a good dog-tooth, because it seldom grows perfectly, gives special comfort to the native who wears it as a pendant jewel; only that one tooth has the right overtones—all the other teeth are too common. In remote New Guinea the beautiful feathers of the bird of paradise serve as money.

This desire to covet and cosset whatever is rare has given birth in modern societies to the limited edition. Sculptors today number their bronze casts, and painters their lithographs and prints. In the same way some jewelers, like Bruno Martinazze of Turin, not only sign their jewels to give them a personal association, they also give to each replica its number, from perhaps one to six, so that each seems exclusive and therefore desirable. If the numbers were unlimited, we would feel no pressure to buy; we feel specially acquisitive for what we know is almost inaccessible. An extreme example of this strange human idiosyncrasy was the sale in Paris in 1971 of a not very special snuff box. It fetched the highest price ever

paid for a box—£78,000 ($202,800)—not because of any outstanding quality, but simply because it is the only signed piece of gold work by the famous eighteenth-century designer, Meissonier. It is unique, and therefore uniquely desirable.

Mysticism apart, the idea of value can be pursued through the price of materials. Silver has always been too common to excite any overtones in public reaction, beyond the simple mining, refining, purchasing and selling which may apply almost equally, for instance, to coal or potatoes. Platinum, conversely, is too rare—most people have never seen or heard of it and therefore do not want it. But gold provides some interesting statistics. Herodotus noted in the fifth century BC that gold cost thirteen times as much as silver; and it has always remained about there, an unexplained but happy chance of nature.

The value of metals, of course, depends partly on their scarcity: 'meteoric' iron—from meteors—may have mattered more to the Egyptians than gold because it was scarcer and came from heaven. The Persians were supposed by the ancients to be the first coin users, but it was in seventh-century BC Lydia that the idea emerged of an adjustable value between coins of different metals. The normal Asia Minor alloy was electrum —perhaps from the legendary river Pactolus—commoner in coins than in jewelry, of a purity from about 17 carat gold (with 8 carat silver) to about 10 carats, or less than half gold. Perhaps the imprecision of this alloy influenced the gold and silver coins too. Cyrus the Persian probably developed the Lydian system into a permanent relationship between gold and silver coins. The similar Attic currency idea was spread to Macedonia by Philip II for gold, and by Alexander the Great for silver. From Macedonia this scheme penetrated the whole western world, and still influences us today when we decide to buy a jewel of silver instead of gold, or of 9 or 10 carat 'gold', half way between the two.

One of the great mysteries is this almost constant relationship between the value of gold and silver despite all the changes in supply. In 1833 the average price of gold was about £4 ($10), in 1969 about £17 ($44), a more spectacular increase than silver, despite the fact that much of the world's gold

Beautiful money—early tokens of value were often used as jewels. From bottom to top: Silver bangle with dragon's head, too small and heavy to wear, Siamese, 14th century AD; Persian, c. 500 BC, bronze circular covenant ring, held in the hand to show friendship and grasped by two people as the original handshake; twisted iron bar, a kissi penny from West Africa, c. AD 1900; oval silver bar, an obang, the precursor of coinage, Japanese, 19th century AD; Sumerian cylinder seal, c. 4th millennium BC; West Nigerian manilla, c. AD 1900 when ten equalled about 5 pence or 13 cents; Indian gold and enamel upper arm ornament, Jaipur, 18th century AD (see p. 65); Chinese jade cicada pendant, perhaps Han Dynasty, c. 200 BC, often placed on tongues of the dead to help them chatter in heaven

has been pegged for the last thirty-seven years to the official bank price of $35 an ounce. As late as 1844 there were no declared additions to world official bank stocks, whereas by 1969, government currency reserves had mounted to about forty-five million ounces of gold. As George Bernard Shaw put in *The Intelligent Woman's Guide to Socialism and Capitalism*:

The most important thing about money is to maintain its stability, so that a pound will buy as much a year hence or ten years hence or fifty years hence as today, and no more. With paper money this stability has to be maintained by the Government. With a gold currency it tends to maintain itself even when the natural supply of gold is increased by discoveries of new deposits, because of the curious fact that the demand for gold in the world is practically infinite. You have to choose (as a voter) between trusting to the natural stability of gold and the natural stability of the honesty and intelligence of the members of the Government. And, with due respect to these gentlemen, I advise you, as long as the Capitalist system lasts, to vote for gold.

Nevertheless, gold is normally used every year for jewels, ornaments, coins and medallions more than it is for currency: gold still has its unique appeal. The most startling proof is the case of India, which banned the import of gold after 1947 to stop the drain on foreign currency. But Indian people prefer gold, usually in the form of jewels, to paper money, with such firmness that they will pay easily double the free price. Dubai, the tiny Persian Gulf island, has since the late 1950s become the world's leading gold importer: in 1970 legal imports were some 300 million dollars of gold, the equivalent of about one-fifth of the free world's whole production. But if government statistics show that Dubai exports and India imports no gold at all, so much the worse for statisticians. Human desire has created a very different picture.

Horace said 'money will be slave or master', Francis Bacon, 'money like muck, is not good except it be spread', Pepys, 'It is pretty to see what money will do', and Henry Ford, certainly the best advice, 'Money—use it or lose it'. Money, being no more than a commodity or means of communication, has never inspired the imagination of poets. Nobody writes hymns to sterling or the dollar, whereas many great rhapsodies include at least a mention of stones or gold.

Precious stones direct a less piercing light than gold onto the natural avarice of human nature because a stone, unlike metal, is of varied quality: with diamonds, for instance, one looks not only at the size, or carat weight, but at the colour, the clarity and absence of flaws, and the cut which may enhance the stone's exciting fire. So one cannot point to any steady change in the status of fine stones, because nobody knows how the quality may have changed over the years—it is sometimes claimed today that diamonds over the last thirty years have increased in price by fifteen per cent a year, but really this means nothing unless the type of diamond is defined. This, despite the efforts of dealers the world over, has so far proved impossible. A new development, taking diamonds closer to the stock market and further from the artist, is the establishment of diamond firms who, having sold a stone one year, supposedly guarantee to buy it back at a profit the next. The most expensive diamond ever sold in public was at the Sotheby Parke-Bernet gallery in New York, where Cartier paid $1,050,000 for a seventy carat stone, subsequently acquired by the actress Elizabeth Taylor who often wears it. One may surmise that precious stones, like gold, while useful in the context of money, will always have a deeper appeal than bank accounts or stocks and shares.

The real stone, as opposed to sham, still retains its powerful appeal today as is proved by a steady market value. In 1904 the French chemist Verneuil invented synthetic ruby and in 1909 synthetic sapphire, both of which were chemically and crystallographically the same as the natural stone. Prices for natural stones accordingly declined very suddenly, but it was soon discovered that the artificial product contained small circular channels of very fine bubbles, visible only under the microscope. Genuine stones quickly regained and held their old cost level. But artificial stones did not follow them, and are now sold extremely cheaply, for instance as watch bearings or as needles for record players.

The same thing seems to be happening in diamonds: the first man-made diamonds were announced by the General Electric Company in the USA in 1955; their first tiny man-made industrial diamonds were marketed three years later; in 1970 they achieved their first clear gem quality diamonds, some of them as big as one carat, at their Schenectady research centre. Man-made emeralds, pioneered in San Francisco at the Chatham Research Laboratories, gripped world markets without affecting the real emerald. Pierre Gilson, the French physicist, invented his process for 'growing' emeralds at Campagne-lez-Wardrecques in 1965. In the five years to 1970 his sales went from $1000 to $500,000; his stones may cost a tenth or a twentieth of the real thing. He claims the only way of telling the real from the artificial was under extreme heat, which wrecks the real, penetrating its impurities. John Donald, the eminent English artist-jeweler, thinks Gilson emeralds are a great new asset to the craft. Visually, they certainly are. Financially, nobody is so sure. Van Cleef and Arpels of Paris say they will never stock Gilson, another Paris jeweler calls Gilson emerald 'absolutely worthless . . . it is the same as glass'. Garrard in London sell natural and cultured pearls because they both come from the sea, but will not sell Gilson because, unlike the real emerald, it does not come from the earth.

The perfection in 1914 by Mikimoto of cultured pearl production started a similar expansion in the market, and gave similar evidence of this surprising public preference for the best rather than its practically indistinguishable substitute. In 1921 cultured pearls became common, and the price of natural pearls dropped; but tests to differentiate between the two were evolved, notably the ability to see, through the hole bored in the pearl for stringing, whether or not there was at the centre a mother of pearl fragment. It is the insertion of this small chip which irritates the oyster and produces a cultured pearl, and it is its presence, not too easy to detect without a special optical device, which makes the cultured pearl price about one-sixth that of the natural pearl and which leaves the natural pearl with unshaken prestige as an organic 'gemstone'. New Japanese inventions are diminishing still further the gulf between cultured and natural, but so long as a tiny difference can be perceived by experts, the buying public will continue to think it important to pay for it.

In *Heaven and Hell* Aldous Huxley refers to the 'vision-inducing' art of the goldsmith and jeweler. Polished metals and precious stones are 'intrinsically transporting . . .':

When to this natural magic of glinting metal and self-luminous stone is added the other magic of noble forms and colours artfully blended, we find ourselves in the presence of a genuine talisman. The products of the goldsmiths' art are intrinsically numinous. They have their place at the heart of every Mystery, in every holy of holies. . . . For Ezekiel, a gem was a stone of fire. Conversely, a flame is a living gem, endowed with all the transporting power that belongs to the precious stone, and, to a lesser degree, to polished metal.

It is impossible to assess jewels simply in terms of carat weight, of cost price, of craftsman's skill or of creator's genius. They all contribute; and as long as man's sense of wonder persists, so long will jewelry continue to attract a sort of supercharged attention.

Attitudes of some of the makers of history vary. Tamberlaine the Great hardly mentions jewelry in his memoirs but he seems to have been fond of rubies, as he wore two armlets on one arm which were set with the stones. He divided his ornaments, on critical occasions, among his followers. For him, jewels had no value except to purchase good will. He was in a tiny minority among the world's great rulers. For nearly all of them, jewels were both natural and necessary: power without the show of power was useless, and show without jewels was impossible. Even common people sought to own them. Just as in Nazi Germany, guns were preferred to butter so in seventeenth-century India, jewels came before food: Bernier, the French traveller, wrote that a private soldier would not refuse to give jewels 'to his wife and children, though the family should die of hunger, which is a common occurrence'.

But precious jewels have never been abundant. Up to the end of the Middle Ages stones were simply rubbed smooth, usually being left more or less in their original rounded or angled shape. Even in the sixteenth century, when stone cutting and faceting started, precious stones themselves were still extremely rare: Vasari thought it worthwhile recording that 'Cellini mounted with rare talent a diamond, cut to a point, and surrounded by several young children carved in gold'. It was not till three hundred years ago that the stone became dominant. With the consequent high financial interest came, in the eighteenth century, advertising, retail shops, and auction sales, all of which nourished people's interest in the money, rather than the art aspect of jewels.

John Gay expresses this new automatic identification of gold with money, rather than with mystical appeal, in his *Beggar's Opera* of 1728:

A Maid is like the golden ore,
    Which hath guineas intrinsical in't,
Whose worth is never known before
    It is try'd and imprest in the mint.

James Christie, the world's first art auctioneer, ex-midshipman and expert showman, is caricatured in 1794 on the rostrum saying:

Let me entreat you, ladies and gentlemen, permit me to put this inestimable piece of elegance under your protection. Only observe, the inexhaustible munificence of your superlatively candid generosity must harmonize with the refulgent brilliancy of this little jewel.

The new art of the advertising blurb was born—no longer would good quality and value speak adequately for themselves. In their introduction to the 1867 catalogue for the Esterhazy jewel sale, Christie's overcame their natural modesty so far as to note,

In submitting the following extraordinary Collection of Jewels, it has been deemed quite unnecessary to dilate upon the rare quality which pervades the whole, or upon the almost complete absence of Stones of any but the finest water and shape.

A Christie's 1970 jewelry sale catalogue at Geneva has the same tone:

A superb antique necklace from the casket of an English noble family. A complete diamond parure by Cartier from the collection of a Princely House. The Royal Sapphire of Burma from the collection of the late Nizam of Hyderabad. The diamond jewels of the late Begum of B. A superb sapphire necklace from the collection of the Baronne von Kories of Paris.

Salesmanship is a necessary art, and jewels at auctions are still identified by the stones and owners more than by the artists' name or quality.

Good examples of this simple love of stones are in the diaries of Sir Henry Channon, the American-born British Member of Parliament who knew everybody. He wrote of Mrs Simpson 'literally smothered in rubies' and 'dripping with emeralds—her collection of jewels is the talk of London'. In 1942 he wrote of 'the King and Queen waiting to receive us ... she, though unfortunately very, very plump, looked magnificent in a white satin semi-crinoline number with the Garter and splendid rubies ... Mrs

Greville's I suppose. . . . No one yet knows what will happen to the world-famous Greville jewels.' The war ended in 1945, his diaries stop in 1958, but Channon hardly mentioned jewels during this new age of austerity. The pre-war snob society was dead. The last time he seems to have noticed jewels was in 1953, and it took a full-blown coronation ceremony in Westminster Abbey to get the old treasures out of store.

Matthew Boulton's friend Kerr had already in 1814 foreseen one reason for the decline of very precious jewels: 'The more a work of taste is multiplied, so that many may possess it, the more its imaginary value is diminished.' Aldous Huxley summarized the idea very clearly: 'Familiarity breeds indifference.

Proust defines how appearance around 1900 was beginning to matter more than honest, intrinsic value: describing the duchess's gown he could not be sure if its spangled ornaments were real or false—they were 'either little sticks and beads of metal, or possibly brilliants'.

In America A. T. Stewart, wholesale merchant and owner of New York's first department store, was a classic *nouveau riche* who thought he could climb the social ladder by buying works of art and, in particular, jewels for his wife. As a widow, she was reputed to be the richest woman in America. 'Vain and friendless ... ailing in body and abandoned to the caprices of dotage', she wandered round her apartment wearing a brown wig and laden with jewels. In 1887, when she died, came the big surprise: her whole collection including the jewels, fetched only $565,568 at auction; certainly there was more show than value here.

The vogue was already beginning for worthless costume jewels, even for borrowing other people's jewels: in 1970, gems worth £200,000 were stolen from the Vicomtesse Jacqueline de Ribes at Claridges Hotel, London, but they belonged to her jeweler, not to her. Monsieur Gérard, whose salon is in the Avenue Montaigne, Paris, said, 'We neither lend nor hire jewelry to our clients—that is simply unknown here—but when I see that a certain jewel pleases a good client I say, wear it two or three times and see if it does something for you!' It was on this basis that the Vicomtesse took a selection of Gérard jewels to London to attend a party.

The American sociologist Thorstein Veblen invented the phrase 'con-

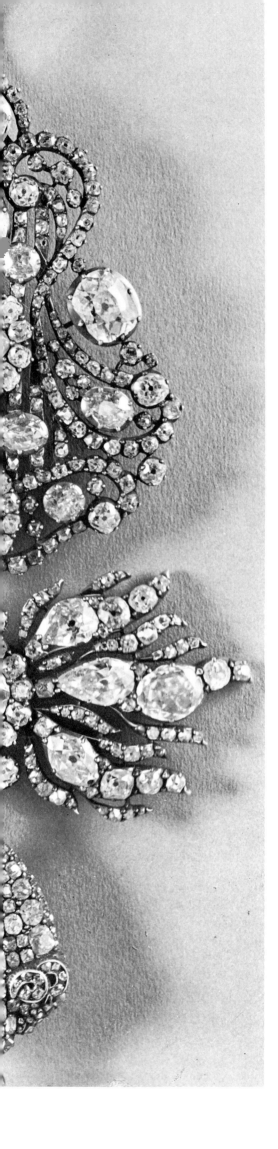

Exclusive societies were often an excuse for great indulgence by their members; this order of the Golden Fleece, with very large white and pink diamonds set in silver gilt, was made for the Bavarian Elector Max Joseph III in 1765 by the Munich court jeweler, Johann Staff. 6.6 × 3.6 inches. Residenz Museum, Munich

spicuous consumption' in his *Theory of the Leisure Class* as long ago as 1899. He defined it as one of the ills of our time, though, in fact, without this planned obsolescence, much of our modern industry would grind to a halt: if things were made to last for ever, there would be no demand for replacements. As permanence is absolutely basic to fine jewels, one may wonder how long their glorious dignity will survive our modern lust for the temporary, encouraged as it is by all the onslaughts of modern advertising.

There have always been puritans: one of the first was St Chrysostom, who reasonably said 'how much better to feed the hungry than to bore through the lobes of thy ears and to hang from them the food of countless poor for no purpose!' Another holy man who found beautiful, expensive gold immoral was St Bernard. In the twelfth century he wrote a famous letter to the Cluniac monasteries criticizing their riches:

I, as a poor monk, ask of my brother monks 'Tell me, ye poor (if, indeed, ye be poor) what doeth this gold in your sanctuary?' The costly polishings and curious carvings distract the worshipper's attention from higher things.

Abbot Suger, St Bernard's contemporary, chief minister of France, and perhaps the inventor of Gothic architecture at St Denis Abbey, took the commoner opposite view: he saw clearly that only the best and most beautiful work with the finest gold and stones was worthy of God. Holiness would be generated by beauty.

J. R. Ackerley beautifully describes the strange maharaja in the kingdom of Oudh, for whom he worked fifty years ago, in *Hindoo Holiday*:

[his guest] begged to be allowed to see his finery and jewels, and he at once sent Hashim off in the car to fetch some of his wardrobe from the Palace. They were certainly lovely things: necklaces and brooches of precious stones; beautifully skirted coats of rich brocade, and turbans to match them jewelled and plumed. The jewellery was all Indian work—but the robes, he said, were made in Paris. Mrs Drood went into raptures over them, and her husband too expressed the greatest admiration. When they had finished examining and ejaculating, His Highness, who had been looking on in silence, waved the things away with a slight movement of his hand.

'I do not like them,' he said, 'I like people.'

The power of jewels is well testified

throughout history: from Trollope's *The Eustace Diamonds*, to A. E. W. Mason's *The Prisoner and the Opal*, from Rudyard Kipling's river of gold in *Puck of Pook's Hill*, and the cure of a pearl in *Kim*, and Balzac's pawned necklace in *Le Père Goriot*, to Shakespeare's caskets of gold, silver and lead in *The Merchant of Venice*, we can enjoy them everywhere.

Whether they are art or craft can never be decided. Most jewelry craftsmen would like to be artists as well: but it is a tricky road from craft to art, and there are not many signposts on it. The difference between craftsmen and artists is, in theory, obvious: the craftsman gets paid by the hour, his product is evaluated by its weight and by the quality of its stones and minerals, he is happy making other people's designs; he usually gets no personal credit in public for his work because somebody else's name—often that of a retailer—is imposed upon it; and he usually has no pretensions about expressing himself—he just enjoys working skilfully with his hands. An artist, on the other hand, always wants his name fixed to his product, because everything he makes is part of his own personality; if he is good, he simply cannot help being original—just as each human being among the five thousand million or so alive today has a different face, so each real artist finds it natural to design in a personal manner. He expects to be paid for his inspiration—the materials of painting and sculpture (the main product of artists) have no intrinsic value, so inspiration is all there is. And he usually dislikes repeating himself, so his livelihood is automatically insecure—he cannot build up a steady demand for his product, because his product is continually changing and developing.

In gold, silver and jewels, however, the value of the materials is often so high, and so easy to ascertain, that it dominates the buying and selling price; the intrinsic value usually commands more attention than the art behind it. Thus, few artists in metalwork have ever gained proper financial recognition for their genius. All over Europe, from the sixteenth to the nineteenth century, few jewelers achieved much prominence. Perhaps Dinglinger in Dresden did, some of the mid-eighteenth-century box makers in Paris and London, Fabergé in Russia, and Cellini, of course: not many names compared with architecture, painting or music. Little is known about the private lives of jewelers during these centuries; perhaps they were content to remain obscure. They hardly featured even in the history of their London guild, the Worshipful Company of Goldsmiths; not even famous painter-jewelers like Holbein and Hilliard in Tudor times, or the Regency financier-jeweler Philip Rundell who left over £1,000,000 ($2,600,000) when he died.

A second depressing observation is the obstinate question asked by every purchaser today: 'What is it worth?' This probably hardly occurred to the kings and princes who were yesterday's patrons, because they never imagined they would have to sell what they commissioned. (Of course some of them were wrong—there were famous and humiliating sales of those who had suddenly fallen from greatness like Charles I of England in the seventeenth century or the Duc de Choiseul of France in the eighteenth). Price consciousness was not an outstanding feature of court life; yet there is no record even then of many goldsmiths obtaining special payment for their inspiration. Indeed, much antique table plate has its weight carved underneath, presumably to reassure the buyer as to the melt value.

Today there are, alas, few good patrons: most goldsmiths' work is not commissioned specially, as in the past, but sold ready-made, and the majority of consumers are investment-minded. But there are probably more jewelers now than ever before who think of themselves as artists, and who find their best work is too exotic for most shops. Some fine shops are indeed already changing into something more like galleries, especially to accommodate this new and international upsurge of creators in metal; perhaps our retail outlets will eventually divide into two groups: galleries for handwork, and shops for mass-production.

It is of course too soon to say whether this powerful movement towards art, shared by dozens of craftsmen all over Europe, will succeed; they want to get into art galleries and away from the bullion broker. If they achieve their ambition, goldsmithing will be back where it was in the Middle Ages, the aristocrat among the arts. The silly barrier between fine and applied art would vanish and goldsmiths would lose the present stigma of being humble craftsmen, enjoying once more the same public estimation as musicians, painters and sculptors.

Very rich people will always exist, and they will always buy very expensive jewels: but it is the artist alone who can provide the ethical justification. Monetary price may fluctuate with fashion. Only the value of true art stands the test of time.

Gold ceremonial axe for votive use, c. 2000 BC. From the Temple of the Obelisks at Byblos, one of the world's oldest cities, from which the Bible was named. Jewels and precious metals have always been, and no doubt always will be used to carry as well as to wear as symbols of power and value. National Museum, Beirut

Bibliography

Aldred, Cyril, *Jewels of the Pharaohs*, London, 1971

Artamonov, M. I., *Treasures from Scythian Tombs*, London, 1969

Aschengreen, Christina Piacenti, *Il Museo degli Argenti a Firenze*, Milan, 1968

Barsali, Isa Belli, *Mediaeval Goldsmiths' Work*, translated by M. Croslord, London, 1969

Barsali, Isa Belli, *European Enamels*, translated by R. Rudorff, London, 1969

Benda, Klement, *Ornament and Jewellery*, Prague, 1967

Bhusan, Jamila Brij, *Indian Jewellery, Ornaments and Decorative Designs*, London, 1964

Blakemore, Kenneth, *The Book of Gold*, London, 1971

Bott, Gerhard, *Jugendstil: Kunsthandwerk um 1900*, Darmstadt, 1965

Bott, Gerhard, & Reiling, Reinhold, *Schmuck*, Pforzheim, 1971

Bruton, Eric, *Diamonds*, London, 1971

Coarelli, Filippo, *Greek and Roman Jewellery*, London, 1970

de Barradas, J. P., *Orfebreria Prehispanica de Colombia*, Bogota, 1966

Desroches-Noblecourt, Christiane, *Tutankhamen*, London, 1963

Dongerkery, Kamala, *Jewelry and Personal Adornment in India*, Harrow, 1971

Duzhenko, Y., & Smirnova, E., *Treasures of the USSR Diamond Fund*, Moscow, 1969

Evans, Joan, *History of Jewellery 1100–1870*, 2nd edition, London, 1970

Gans, M. H., *Juwelen en Mensen*, Amsterdam, 1961

Godard, André, *Le Trésor de Ziwiye*, Haarlem, 1950

Gregorietti, Guido, *Jewellery through the Ages*, London, 1970

Handley, Thomas Holbein, 'Indian Jewellery' from *Journal of Indian Art 1906–9*, London, 1909

Higgins, R. A., *Greek and Roman Jewellery*, London, 1961

Hoffmann, Herbert, & Davidson, Patricia, *Greek Gold*, Boston, 1965

Holzhausen, Walter, *Goldschmiedekunst in Dresden*, Tübingen, 1966

Hughes, Graham, *Jewelry*, London, 1966

Hughes, Graham, *Modern Jewelry*, London, 1968

Jacobsthal, Paul, *Greek Pins*, London, 1956

Joffroy, René, *Trésor de Vix*, Paris, 1954

Kris, E., *Meister der Steinschneidekunst in der italienischen Renaissance*, Vienna, 1929

Lanllier, Jean, & Pini, Marie Anne, *Cinq Siècles de Joaillerie en Occident*, Fribourg, 1971

Lasko, Peter, *Ars Sacra*, London, 1972

Lewis, M. D. S., *Antique Paste Jewellery*, London, 1970

Mallowan, M. E. L., *Nimrud and Its Remains*, London, 1966

Marinatos, Spyridon, *Crete and Mycenae*, London, 1960

Maxwell-Hyslop, K. R., *Western Asiatic Jewellery, c. 3000–612 BC*, London, 1971

Oved, Sah, *The Book of Necklaces*, London, 1953

Pfeiler, Bärbel, *Römischer Goldschmuck*, Mainz am Rhein, 1970

Plass, Margaret Webster, *African Miniatures, Goldweights of Ashanti*, London, 1967

Richter, G. M. A., *Engraved Gems of the Greeks, Etruscans and Romans*, Part I, London, 1968

Rudenko, Sergei I., *Frozen Tombs of Siberia*, translated by M. W. Thompson, London, 1970

Rybakov, B. A., *Treasures in the Kremlin*, London, 1964

Steingräber, Erich, *Antique Jewellery: its History in Europe from 800–1900*, London, 1957

Steingräber, Erich, editor, *Royal Treasures of Europe*, London, 1968

Strong, Roy, and Oman, Julia Trevelyan, *Elizabeth R*, London, 1971

Sutherland, C. H. V., *Gold*, 2nd edition, London, 1969

Twining, E. F., *History of the Crown Jewels of Europe*, London, 1960

Untracht, Oppi, *Metal Techniques for Craftsmen*, London, 1968

Vilímková, Milada, *Egyptian Jewellery*, London, 1969

Wessel, Klaus, *Byzantine Enamels*, Dublin, 1965

Wilkinson, Alix, *Ancient Egyptian Jewellery*, London, 1971

Willsberger, Johann, *Gilbert Albert, Jacques & Pierre Chaumet, Alexandre Grassy, Andrew Grima, René Kern, Harry Winston*, Munich, 1971

Wiseman, D. J., *Cylinder Seals of Western Asia*, London, 1960

Catalogues
Die Burgunderbeute und Werke Burgundischer Hofkunst, Bernisches Historisches Museum, 1969

Byzantine Art, Athens, 1964, (from the ninth exhibition of the Council of Europe at Zappeion Hall)

Karl der Grosse, Aachen, 1965

Les Années "25" Art Déco, Paris (Musée des Arts Décoratifs), 1966

Painted Enamels of the Renaissance in the Walters Art Gallery, Baltimore, Philippe Verdier, London, 1967

Ringe aus vier Jahrtausenden, Fritz Falk, Pforzheim, 1971

Toutankhamon et son temps, 2nd edition, Paris, 1967

Treasures from Romania, London (British Museum), 1971

Tutankhamun Treasures, Exhibition catalogue sponsored by the American Association of Museums and the Smithsonian Institution for sixteen American museums, 1961–3

Photographic Credits

Asterisks mark colour illustrations.

10 The Lady of Elche. *Photo: Archaeological Museum, Madrid*

12 Safety pins or fibulae. Private collection. *Photo: Graham Hughes*

14 Cambodian stone head. Private collection. *Photo: Graham Hughes*

15 Head from Assyrian frieze. British Museum, London. *Photo: Werner Forman*

*17 Beads. Private collection. *Photo: Graham Hughes*

*18 Egyptian pendant jewel. Louvre, Paris. *Photo: Roger Wood*

20–1 Egyptian crowned heads. Cairo Museum. *Photos: Roger Wood*

21 Figures from Minoan fresco. *Photo: Heraklion Museum, Crete*

22 Minoan bee pendant. Heraklion Museum, Crete. *Photo: Roger Wood*

23 Archer's ring. Private collection. *Photo: James Mortimer*

24 Persian dress pins. Private collection. *Photo: Graham Hughes*

25 Etruscan gold fibula. *Photo: Archaeological Museum, Florence*

26 Head of Athene. Private collection. *Photo: Stefan Buzas*

*27 Bronze snake head bracelets. Private collection. *Photo: Graham Hughes*

*28–9 Gold plaques from pectoral ornament. British Museum, London. *Photo: Michael Holford*

*30 Knot of Heracles from diadem. *Photo: Benaki Museum, Athens*

31 Gold diadem. *Photo: Benaki Museum, Athens*

32 Greek gold earrings with cupids. *Photo: Benaki Museum, Athens*

32–3 Hellenistic diadem. *Photo: British Museum, London*

33 Gold earrings with heads. *Photo: National Museum, Taranto*

34 Figure from fresco at Pompeii. *Photo: Graham Hughes*

34 The Grande Camée de la Sainte Chapelle. Cabinet des Médailles. *Photo: Bibliothèque Nationale, Paris*

35 Sections from Roman gold bracelets. Cameo Corner. *Photo: Graham Hughes*

35 Panther of gold and stones. Hermitage Museum, Leningrad. *Photo: Werner Forman*

36 Mosaic portrait of Empress Theodora. Church of San Vitale, Ravenna. *Photo: Graham Hughes*

37 Mosaic portrait of Emperor Justinian. Church of San Vitale, Ravenna. *Photo: Graham Hughes*

37 Byzantine ring. *Photo: National Museum of Antiquities, Bucharest*

*39 Roman earrings. Private collection. *Photos: Graham Hughes*

*40 TOP Roman ring of gold and jasper. Private collection. *Photo: James Mortimer*

*40 BOTTOM Roman ring of cameo, onyx and gold. *Photo: National Museum of Antiquities, Bucharest*

41 Necklace using Tippoo Sultan's rubies. Private collection. *Photo: Graham Hughes*

42–3 Group of portraits of Indian princes. Private collection. *Photos: James Mortimer*

*45 Byzantine necklace with coin. British Museum, London. *Photo: Michael Holford*

*46 Byzantine pendant cross. Private collection. *Photo: Graham Hughes*

48 Indian necklace. Private collection. *Photo: Adrian Flowers*

49 Ashanti dress ornaments. *Photo: British Museum, London*

*51 Peruvian funeral mask. Mujica Gallo Museum, Lima. *Photo: Michael Holford*

*52–3 Celtic gold ornament. *Photo: National Museum of Ireland, Dublin*

*54 Gold lunulae. *Photo: National Museum of Ireland, Dublin*

56–7 Gold eagle or condor pendant. Private collection. *Photo: Adrian Flowers*

58 Ceremonial knife. *Photo: John Wise Collection, New York*

*59 Sections of four Indian necklaces. Private collection. *Photo: Graham Hughes*

*60 TOP Carved jade hairpin. Salar Jung Museum, Hyderabad, India. *Photo: Graham Hughes*

*60 BOTTOM Gold and enamel Moghul bracelet. Private collection. *Photo: Graham Hughes*

62 Viking pendants and neck ring. National Museum of Antiquities, Stockholm. *Photo: Pål-Nils Nilsson/Tio*

63 Viking snake head rings or bracelets. National Museum of Antiquities, Stockholm. *Photo: ATA*

*65 Back of a Jaipur arm jewel. Private collection. *Photo: Graham Hughes*

*66 African gold jewels. Private collection. *Photo: Werner Forman*

68 Bird brooch of gold and garnets. *Photo: German National Museum, Nuremberg*

69 Lothair's crystal. *Photo: British Museum, London*

70–1 Pair of gold fibulae. *Photo: National Museum, Taranto*

71 Alemannic safety pin. *Photo: Historical Museum, Berne*

71 Merovingian fibula. Cluny Museum, Paris. *Photo: Musées Nationaux*

71 Visigothic belt buckle. *Photo: Archaeological Museum, Madrid*

71 French ring brooch or fermail. Cluny Museum, Paris. *Photo: Musées Nationaux*

71 French gold brooch. Cluny Museum, Paris. *Photo: Musées Nationaux*

72 Reliquary jewel. Private collection. *Photo: Graham Hughes*

73 Fragment of Burgundian chain. *Photo: Museum of Fine Arts, Vienna*

74 Reliquary containing scalp of Charlemagne. Aachen Cathedral Treasure. *Photo: R. Baurmann*

75 Silver gift reliquary. *Photo: British Museum, London*

76 Detail from painting by Piero della Francesca. Brera Gallery, Milan. *Photo: Phaidon Press*

77 German mermaid pendant. *Photo: British Museum, London*

79 Painting of noblewoman at her jewel casket. *Photo: Dijon Museum*

80–1 Ecclesiastical gold jewel. Caceres Convent. *Photo: Adrian Flowers*

81 Burgundian portrait medallion. *Photo: Residenz Museum, Munich*

82 Renaissance ring. Private collection. *Photo: Adrian Flowers*

82 Back of mirror with Limoges enamel. *Photo: Walters Art Gallery, Baltimore*

*83 Head of very large bird brooch. *Photo: National Museum of Antiquities, Bucharest*

*84 Detail of stylized bird brooch. National Museum of Antiquities, Bucharest. *Photo: British Museum, London*

86–7 FAR LEFT AND RIGHT Silver gilt sword hilts. *Photo: Residenz Museum, Munich*

86–7 CENTRE Three walking-stick handles. Grünes Gewölbe, Dresden. *Photo: Graham Hughes*

88 Detail from table jewel. Grünes Gewölbe, Dresden. *Photo: Joachim Menzhausen*

89 Two shoe buckles. Private collection. *Photo: James Mortimer*

91 Pendant decorated with flowers and cherubs' heads. *Photo: Museum of Fine Arts, Vienna*

*93 Hat badge of gold and enamels. Private collection. *Photo: James Mortimer*

*94–5 Renaissance gold pendant. Private collection. *Photos: James Mortimer*

*96 German pendant with ram. Private collection. *Photo: James Mortimer*

97 Chatelaine of pinchbeck. Private collection. *Photo: Adrian Flowers*

98 English cameo necklace. Private collection. *Photo: Adrian Flowers*

98 Group of mourning rings. Jewelry Museum, Pforzheim. *Photo: James Mortimer*

99 Berlin iron-work bracelet. *Photo: Austrian Museum of Applied Art, Vienna*

99 Gold pocket watch. Private collection. *Photo: Graham Hughes*

100 Detail of gold and garnet necklace. Private collection. *Photo: Graham Hughes*

100–1 Bohemian hair ornament in black jet. *Photo: Jablonec Museum*

*105 Brooch showing Noah's Ark. Private collection. *Photo: James Mortimer*

*106 Pendant jewel with crown and monogram. Private collection. *Photo: Graham Hughes*

108 Choker in gold, glass and diamonds. Gulbenkian Museum, Lisbon. *Photo: James Mortimer*

109 Art nouveau pendant. *Photo: German National Museum, Nuremberg*

*111 Rococo necklace of gold and rubies. Private collection. *Photo: James Mortimer*

*112 Group of machine-made buckles. Private collection. *Photo: James Mortimer*

114 Dragonfly corsage ornament. Gulbenkian Museum, Lisbon. *Photo: James Mortimer*

115 Cockerel's head comb. Gulbenkian Museum, Lisbon. *Photo: James Mortimer*

*117 Art nouveau hairpin, brooches and necklace. Private collection. *Photo: Graham Hughes*

*118 Four silver buckles. Jensen Silversmithy Collection, Copenhagen. *Photo: Graham Hughes*

*119 Four hair combs of tortoiseshell and silver. Jensen Silversmithy Collection, Copenhagen. *Photo: Graham Hughes*

*120 Hatpin with sunflower and wasps. Kunstindustrimuseet, Copenhagen. *Photo: Ole Woldbye*

121 Detail of the cross of nails from the coronet. Crown Jewels, Tower of London. *Photo: Graham Hughes*

122 Detail of the orb from the coronet. Crown Jewels, Tower of London. *Photo: Graham Hughes*

123 Coronet of the Prince of Wales. Crown Jewels, Tower of London. *Photo: Derek Scarborough*

123 Traditional Japanese combs and hairpins. Private collection. *Photo: Graham Hughes*

124 Modern Japanese brooch. Private collection. *Photo: De Beers*

*125 TOP Four finger rings. Goldsmiths' Hall, London. *Photo: James Mortimer*

*125 BOTTOM Flower-shaped gold brooch. Private collection. *Photo: Graham Hughes*

*126 Gold necklace and pendant. Private collection. *Photo: Hermann Jünger*

128 Necklace of gold wire. Private collection. *Photo: Suki Hiramatsu*

*131 Gold and diamond brassière. Spritzer and Fuhrmann, Curaçao. *Photo: Graham Hughes*

*132 TOP Gold and emerald ring. Private collection. *Photo: Graham Hughes*

Index

Numbers printed in *italics* indicate illustrations